Iain Finlayson

is the author of *The Moth and the Candle: a Life of James Boswell*, *Writers in Romney Marsh*, and *The Scots*. He is co-editor of *The Chambers' Dictionary of Scottish Quotations* and is now at work on a biography of Robert Louis Stevenson.

By the same author

THE MOTH AND THE CANDLE: A LIFE OF JAMES BOSWELL
WRITERS IN ROMNEY MARSH
THE SCOTS
CHAMBERS' DICTIONARY OF QUOTATIONS *(co-editor)*

IAIN FINLAYSON

Tangier

City of the Dream

Flamingo
An Imprint of HarperCollins*Publishers*

Flamingo
An Imprint of HarperCollins*Publishers*,
77–85 Fulham Palace Road,
Hammersmith, London W6 8JB

Published by Flamingo 1993
9 8 7 6 5 4 3 2

First published in Great Britain by
HarperCollins*Publishers* 1992

Copyright © Iain Finlayson 1992

Iain Finlayson asserts the moral right to
be identified as the author of this work

ISBN 0 00 654519 X

Set in Baskerville

Printed in Great Britain by
Loader Jackson Printers, Arlesey, Bedfordshire

This book is for my mother,
Mary Harris Finlayson

Acknowledgements

I am very much indebted to many people who have borne patiently with my demands and taken great trouble to satisfy them during the periods of researching and writing this book. First of all, I very sincerely thank Tessa Wheeler who loaned me her house on the mountain, Dar Sinclair, for several months; and Daniel Laurain who subsequently housed me in Tangier and gave me his generous friendship.

Among those in Tangier who were particularly helpful and hospitable, I gladly take this opportunity to thank Bachir el Attar, Georges Bousquet, Paul Bowles, Jean-Claude Dupuis, Isabelle Gérofi, Robert Gérofi, Yvonne Gérofi, Mark Gilbey, the Hon. David Herbert, Gavin Lambert, Annie Lambton, Marguerite McBey, Mohammed Mrabet, Rachel Muyal of the Librairie des Colonnes, Boubker and Nour Temli, Barbara Temsamany, Patrick Thursfield, Richard Timewell, Peter Wildeblood and Gavin Young.

Among those I harassed beyond Tangier, who courteously and helpfully gave me their time, confidences and materials, I owe a debt of gratitude to Allen Ginsberg, Tracey Beresford of Peter Owen Ltd., Rosie Boycott, Meredith Etherington-Smith, Oliver and Jenny Harris, David Leitch, Chris Mitchell, Phillip Ramey, Ned Rorem, Virgil Thomson and Vicki Woods.

For steady personal support, friendship and, too often in too many cases, financial assistance, it is difficult to thank adequately Dorothy Adibi, May and Beth Finlayson, Stuart Proffitt, Philip Gwyn Jones, and of course my agent Deborah Rogers and her staff.

Sarah Anderson, formerly of The Travel Bookshop, found necessary books for me and for a while subsidized them. Gill Charlton, formerly of the *London Daily News* and Miles Chapman, formerly of *Vanity Fair* kindly commissioned articles about Tangier and thus helped with research expenses. The manager of the El Minzah Hotel was good enough, in January 1990, to give some very welcome assistance.

I am very grateful to Aberdeen City Arts Department, in particular Jennifer Melville and Catherine Williams, for materials about James McBey; to the University of Reading and the Keeper of Archives and Manuscripts, Michael Bott, for materials about Richard Hughes; to Hugo Vickers and St John's College, Cambridge, particularly Malcolm Pratt and Jean Curtis, for materials about Cecil Beaton; and to Lord Bute who, through the efforts of his assistant Hanne Mason and his librarian Alexander Hunter, kindly provided some materials relevant to the fourth Marquess of Bute's interests in Tangier. I would also like to credit the following for giving generous permission to reproduce extracts as indicated: Peter Owen Publishers (Paul Bowles, Herbert, Choukri, Mrabet); David Higham Associates (Richard Hughes' letters); City of Aberdeen Art Gallery and Museums Collections (James McBey's memoirs); Robert Hale Ltd and Rom Landau; North Point Press and Ned Rorem; Allen Ginsberg; Random House Inc. (Capote); The Literary Executors of the late Sir Cecil Beaton; and the William Morris Agency (Bowles). Where acknowledgement is not specified, every reasonable effort has been made to trace copyright owners before publication.

Finally, I must acknowledge that the idea for a book about Tangier derived from a discussion over lunch several years ago with Emma Hogan and Jonathan Scott. My own book is very different in emphasis and construction from that envisaged by Jonathan Scott and which I hope he may yet write.

CONTENTS

ILLUSTRATIONS

If you see her, say hello. She might be in Tangier.

'If You See Her, Say Hello',
Bob Dylan, from *Blood on the Tracks*

FOREWORD

They say, weathered old colonials, 'Morocco is not Africa.' A faraway look in their eyes settles irritably on the Rif Mountains which rise beyond Tangier. They say, experienced travellers, 'Tangier is not Morocco.' Their minds are on sandfast Marrakesh, perhaps, or Fez, most sinister and disorientating of the Imperial cities of the south. They say, elderly Tangerinos, 'Tangier is not what it was.' Wistfully, they regret the passing of its reputation as a glamorous focus for international society. Taps have sounded for Lily at the Parade Bar; the Art Deco doors of Madame Porte's Salon de Thé have closed on the last major martini; the last lush long ago tottered out of the hole in the wall that was once Dean's Bar; the odorous Carmella – a reputed Spanish gypsy known as 'Miss Pits' – has murdered her last song in the last dawn to rise over the smoke and sawdust of the waterfront Bar la Mar Chica.

The consuls have taken their *congé*, having stuck the last wild pig in the Diplomatic Forest; the last chukka has been played on the polo field at Brooks Park; the last tango has been hot-trotted at Emsallah Gardens. The city, now mawkish and moribund, arid as a stuccoed sepulchre, suffocates in a thinner air and subsides with an attitude of deflated exuberance. It feeds lethargically on the crumbs of tourism and a few desiccated pickings from the rich feast of entrepreneurial opportunities, some of them legal, few of them ethical, that nourished the sleek and avaricious city until 1961 when the King, Mohammed V, abolished the last privileges of Tangier as an International Zone ruled by the governments of Europe and the United States.

Yet still the legend persists. Curling, yellowed clippings from the world's more sensational newspapers detailing a lurid history of Tangier vice, crime and scandal, most of it inflated far beyond the petty, banal reality, continue to colour the popular imagination.

The insistent image is of a never-never land of international intrigue, shady financial dealings and esoteric sex for sale or rent. Seedy, salacious, decadent, degenerate – Tangier is inevitably identified with 'Interzone', William Burroughs' fevered, fictional, drug-inspired evocation of the boomtown years of Sodom-on-Sea.

Burroughs' novels, particularly *The Naked Lunch*, cooked the raw material of Tangier over the heat of his imagination, like coke in a spoon, and shot it into the bloodstream of visionary literature, hooking a generation of sensation-seekers who sought out the frontier town of Tangier for themselves in the 1960s and 1970s. But they were too late and too naive. By the 1950s and early 1960s, the city was wearily familiar to sophisticated travellers who mostly characterized it as a bordel. In the mid-to-late 1940s, wrote the British journalist Michael Davidson, 'almost any thirst could be assuaged; boys or pubescent girls of half-a-dozen races were two-a-penny, guilty manipulators of foreign currencies and the procurers of illegal commodities lurked at every café table; and the sombrely sinful streets behind the Petit Socco were full of caravanserai with evocative names like Hotel Satan or Pension Delirium.' Of Tangier in this period, Paul Bowles wrote in *Let It Come Down*: 'It was one of the charms of the International Zone that you could get anything you wanted if you paid for it. Do anything, too, for that matter – there were no incorruptibles. It was only a question of price.'

Money mattered in Tangier, where nothing but money was valued as the only dependable resource in a multi-national society whose ethical values moved in line with political and personal expediency as inevitably as the foreign currency exchange rates moved in line with political and market forces. Simple survival in Tangier required more than usual tenacity of purpose and quickness of wit. The city had never tolerated broken men: scenting the blood of a man at bay, it never hesitated to move in for a kill. The predator ruthlessly, remorselessly paralysed its prey: the strongest might resist only for a while.

For a hundred years, Tangier had fallen under the *de facto* rule of European and American consuls, and was regarded by most pious Moroccans as a place apart, a plague zone infested and infected by infidels. It was to Tangier that the French exiled the Moroccan Sultan, Moulai Hafid, in 1912 after having effectively bought his abdication and his consent to the establishment of a

French Protectorate. In Tangier, according to the report of *The Times* journalist Walter Harris, 'Moulai Hafid was completely content. He realized that at last, after the sombre pomp of the palace at Fez, he had settled down to modern life and refinement, and had attained "taste".' Moulai Hafid 'sat down, happy, to enjoy civilization'.

By no means crushed or pained by conscience, the former Sultan began to negotiate the terms of his abdication settlement with the French. Neutralized in Tangier, Moulai Hafid was an expensive act to maintain, a pretentious and petulant prisoner who enjoyed rattling the bars of his cage and the nerves of his keeper. He lasted, in the event, only two years in Tangier. In a satirical little squib, quoted in translation by Harris in *Morocco That Was*, the ex-Sultan expressed his true opinion of the city:

> In the last day the people of Tangier came to the judgement-seat of God; and the Supreme Judge said, 'Surely you are the least and worst of all people. Under what circumstances did you live?' And they replied, 'We have sinned; we have sinned; but our Government was international: we were ruled by the representatives of Europe.' And the Supreme Judge said, 'Surely you have been sufficiently punished: enter into Paradise.'

In 1914, Moulai Hafid left Tangier for Spain where, suspected of some intrigue to foment unrest in Morocco, his pension was cancelled by the French who were surely thankful for an excuse to be rid of a considerable nuisance. He was not much regretted: he had been barbarously cruel as Sultan, an irritating and superfluous distraction in Tangier, and had certainly survived long beyond anything but a caricature of his old self. There was a new colonial order in Morocco, and a new international order was soon to be officially confirmed in Tangier. The old feudal fiefdom of the Sherifian Empire was coming to an end, an end that rendered its former absolute ruler an anachronism, an ogre who had become a slippered buffoon. The 'civilization' of Tangier to which Moulai Hafid had aspired with a bewildered naivety, the 'modern style' to which he clumsily attempted to adapt, was inimical to his particular brand of subtlety, and unresponsive to the princely craft he had developed to control his court and country. The modern world required new political and social skills. Tangier effectively rendered the redundant Sultan, for all his elaborate former majesty, his careless despotism and his casual cruelties, somewhat absurd.

Like the ailing Sultan, Tangier became almost entirely degenerate but still liable to random, fretful activity and noises not quite in time with the mechanisms that animated it. It is like the missorted collection of an antiquary whose indiscriminate taste has created an eclectic, eccentric and largely bewildering combination of intriguing objects, jumbled together beyond any hope of rational cataloguing, that will render them in any way relative to one another.

The city is not, to put it mildly, homogeneous. It is a characteristic of life in Tangier that things, and particularly groups of people, seem discrete. There exists – and has always existed – a variety of complex social divisions and subdivisions that accord with a general instinctive perception of class, national, racial, religious, political and sexual discriminations, and – perhaps surprisingly – degrees of moral standing. These social distinctions, if they do not have the force of law, are at least sanctioned by immemorial usage and, of course, constantly modified by the shifting and unpredictable canons of contemporary political, social and personal convenience. The social borders of this frontier town are as fluid as the boundaries of any Balkan or Middle-Eastern country.

They are at least partly topographical. The separation between the old and the new parts of the city was, until the middle-to-late 1950s, very distinct. The European inhabitants of the modern city and the *haute bourgeoisie* of its bosky suburbs were regarded with a certain awe by the native population of Tanjawis who considered resident foreigners as being not perhaps better than themselves but as remote and incomprehensible figures in a dream landscape that they had constructed for their ineffable purposes. Joseph Kessel's novel, *Au Grand Socco*, published in Paris in 1952, is a series of tales narrated by a little Tangier hunchback, Bachir, who – in the traditional oral form of Moroccan storytelling – interprets the foreigners for the benefit of an audience crowding around him in the Grand Socco, the great tree-shaded marketplace. They learn, to their wonderment, about the strange, remote lives led by the European residents of the Mountain. Bachir's first task is to explain the extraordinary reserve of the foreigners, their isolation from the life not only of the native city but from each other:

'You all know the place, my friends: a league from the town, called the Mountain by the foreigners. You could see it from here, by climbing on a high roof, these hills lush with trees and flowers, so fresh, even on the hottest days. But, really, those among us who have gone up there, what do they know of the Mountain? They have only seen the roads, along which go the cars of the rich and the donkeys of the poor; the long walls, the iron gates. Nothing more. For the Mountain, however vast it may be, is wholly parcelled out in closed up properties, well guarded, and none may enter in without permission of the masters. And they are all foreigners, come from all countries.

'But these foreigners, my friends, bear little resemblance to the others, so many and so excited, you meet every day here in the Grand Socco or following a guide through the old town. Oh, no! The masters of the Mountain have nothing at all to do with these tourists who, all the year long, throng the hotels and the streets of Tangier. And no more are they to be compared with the foreigners who live in the apartments and houses of the new town. Those ones keep themselves busy, indeed, being money-changers, or merchant traders, or estate agents, or yet again they may be ship owners, doctors, civil servants, or smugglers. They all have some work to do, some business interest. But those of the Mountain, those ones, they do nothing, really nothing, absolutely nothing. They, having settled themselves in the prettiest spot on earth, the happiest plot in the world, live at their ease and for their pleasure on the benefits of a great and old-established fortune.

'On account of that, they are looked up to, greatly honoured.

'The owners of the Mountain, so far as social position is concerned, are of the first rank in foreign society. And among them, the English hold the premier place. And why should that be, my friends? Because they know best how to shut themselves away in their estates, to do without the others and despise them. So then, of course, the others search them out . . .' The same feeling arose, after these words, in the crowd of wretches that pressed around Bachir. Picturing in their minds such opulence and power, the humblest faces acquired an expression of profound pleasure.

There was virtually no malice and very little envy at that time among the native population of Tangier which was perfectly accustomed to the concept, which they accepted somewhat fatalistically, of the rich man in his castellated villa and the poor man at his gate. To expatriates in the years immediately after World War II, Tangier seemed like a lotus-land. Even for those with only a little money, personal and domestic servants cost very little; were, indeed a drug on the market in comparison with Europe, and particularly Britain, where servants had become not only scarce and expensive but decidedly uppity and less respectful of class distinction. In Tangier, the alliance of servant and master gave mutual pleasure at very little expense. Both experienced a delightful sense of wonder, of theatre, of fiction come to improbable life and close at hand. But the history of Tangier is not an anachronistic idyll. When the magic had worn a little thin, mutual incomprehension too often and too readily turned to distaste among the many social and ethnic groups that constituted the shifting population of the city.

The new town, which dates in origin only from 1910, floated airily on a plateau above the old, like a wedding cake, stuccoed white, artificial and *mondaine*. The streets, in their regular angularity, might have been inspired by Haussmann, radiating in a geometrical pattern from the Place de France like the beams of a star. Here the air was fresher, less humid, less noisome. Refreshing breezes bowled along behind the new motor cars – Fords, Cadillacs, Renaults – and bicycles that cruised along the boulevard or the avenue d'Espagne that ran straight, like a tangent glancing off the semicircle of the bay. Palms, white sand and the blue of the Strait melting into the hazy purple coast of Spain hinted at the elegance of the French Riviera. The cosmopolitan tone of the town was gracefully complemented by the names given to its streets – boulevard Pasteur, avenue Mendès-Portillo, rue Velasquez, rue d'Angleterre, rue du Portugal, rue de Russie, rue de Mexique, rue de Belgique, avenue des Nations.

Foreign individuals or groups of tourists had no hesitation in wandering the picturesque streets and quaint little soccos of the Medina and Casbah, but few natives dared, or cared, to venture up to stroll casually along the new sidewalks, browse through the shops full of European goods, dine in the French restaurants along the boulevard, or sip tea at the chrome cafés and cocktail bars. The dividing line might be a matter, merely, of crossing a street: on one side, djellabah-clad Tanjawi men and veiled women in traditional dress, on the other the Consuls and *grands monsieurs* in their natty white suits and jaunty Panamas, flicking fastidiously at the garbage with their canes, and women with porcelain complexions protected from the sun by wide-brimmed Parisian hats, leading little dogs on a leash. The frontiers were clearly demarcated, superficially by fashion and wealth, by power and privilege. The Mountain, literally, would not come to the Mohammedan: the Mohammedan was expected, even required, to make himself available to the Mountain.

The Europeanization, and the Americanization, of Tangier was unsatisfactory, intrusive and inevitably degrading to *aficionados* of pre-War Tangier. Paul Bowles, writing in the July 1954 issue of *London Magazine* regretted

> that period of frenzied activity that started shortly before the War of 1939 and continued until the riots of 1952. Even in the Casbah there is scarcely an alley that has not undergone a change: the Muslims of Tangier, no less than anyone else, have a passion for building and remodelling. It was not so long ago when the Place de France was at the edge of town, and you could stand there at noon and hear the cicadas screaming from the eucalyptus trees. The Zoco de Fuera was, among other things, a grove of trees that provided shade for the performances of cobras, acrobats and dusty little apes from the mountains. To go to Sidi Amar, instead of a municipal bus, you took a carriage with a torn beige canopy, drawn by two horses laden with jingling bells. Instead of the rasp of radios and the noise of traffic you heard the shrill sound of rhaitas being played, and there were torchlight processions in the Medina where the bride was carried to her new abode doubled up in an *almería* on the back of a donkey. Now she goes in a taxi like any Christian or Jew.

Bowles, here as in his novels, characterizes the foreign inhabitants of Tangier as soulless parasites, prepared to decamp at an instant's notice once the city's potential for their enrichment was compromised by the activities of the native population airing and asserting their proper grievances and rights against foreign occupation and exploitation. In any case, most expatriates engaged in business were transients, opportunistic traders or speculators, intent only on one thing – personal gain – and oblivious to anything else. If Tangier was a dull town for the artist and intellectual – few stayed for any length of time – Bowles doubted that many of the expatriates noticed the absence of cultural life 'since most of them were not conscious of the presence of any such thing in the places from which they came'. They would have been boors and philistines wherever they happened to be. The expatriate Tangier banker, entrepreneur, *négociant* or *contrebandier* could just as well sit 'on the terrasse of one of the cafés on the Place de France until half past eight, join the vast parade of Spaniards taking their nightly *paseo* along the Boulevard Pasteur until nine or so, have dinner and go to a cinema at half past ten, quite as if he were back in Marseilles or Madrid or Rome, instead of a quarter of a mile from the dim fondouks of the Souk ez Zra, where the Berbers from the mountains lie wrapped in their djellabas among the donkeys.'

This is an extreme view, perhaps: Bowles himself admits that it would have been difficult for a foreigner to penetrate deeply into the native way of life. The huddled Berbers sound asleep in the chiaroscuro of shadows and moonlight that rendered the fondouks mysterious by night might inspire a romantic melancholia in even the most sternly materialistic voyeur, but the world of the Berber, from peasant to prince, would remain fundamentally inscrutable. The foreigner had gone too far in sophisticated adult cynicism and Western civilization fully to comprehend the nature of the Moroccans. It took an act of imagination even to begin to connect. The interested observer, remarked Bowles, required 'a strong streak of infantilism' in his nature to come even partly to terms with the fascination of Tangier which partially consisted in 'an element of make-believe in the native life as seen from without (which is the only viewpoint from which we can ever see it, no matter how many years we may remain)'.

The native city, its history, traditions and social complexities would remain forever inaccessible, only partly comprehensible even to a receptive mind and eye which could perceive Tangier as 'a toy cosmos whose costumed inhabitants are playing an eternal game of buying and selling. The Casbah and Medina below are a great pile of child's building blocks strewn carelessly over the side hill;

when you huddle or recline inside the miniature rooms of the homes you are immediately back in early childhood, playing house, an illusion which is not dispelled by the tiny tables and tea glasses, the gaudy cushions and the lack of other furniture.' The idea evoked here by Bowles is not so much an *Arabian Nights* fantasy or a fairy story – it is an Alice in Wonderland set of images which evoke 'the forgotten but suddenly familiar sensation of being far *inside*.'

Any view from an eminence, as from the plateau of the new town of Tangier to the teeming old town at one's feet, is bound to contain some element of *de haut en bas*. The romantic Bowles inevitably perceives an innocence, or at least a naivety, in a scene that is powerfully evocative of childhood and childish things. A faint nostalgia is aroused in the knowledgeable *paterfamilias* figure as he watches the children play house or gravely barter their belongings among themselves. It is the lost, irrecoverable world of *Le Grand Meaulnes*. Within two years, the paternalistic, affectionately indulgent tone had gone from Bowles' journalism. In *The Nation* of 30 June 1956, in the year of Moroccan independence, the international city of Tangier trembles for its future. Europeans no longer confidently cruise the Casbah or the Medina:

Where are they? Safe in their houses, or sitting in the fluorescent glare of the French and Italian cafés of the Boulevard Pasteur. They know better than to wander down into the part of town where they are not wanted; besides, everyone is whispering that members of the Army of Liberation have arrived in Tangier, and that is certain to mean trouble. But the weeks succeed each other, and nothing happens. Is it possible that Tangier is going to stay like this – sober and joyless, the brothels boarded up, the *camareros* of the cafés piling their chairs and pulling down their blinds at twelve-thirty or one, and after that the streets so quiet that one can hear the crickets singing and the roosters crowing from the rooftops?

The dreamers had woken from their sleep in the cool dim of the fondouks and wiped the glamour from their eyes. The paper city, the dreamscapes of consular colonialism, the illusory charade of foreign authority had been revealed as no more than a fiction that had reached its conclusion like any tale spun by a storyteller in the

Socco. The expatriates of Tangier were startled and alarmed by the shift in reality which revealed them to themselves as bit part actors in a drama that had played itself out, their actuality evanescent.

'Walk down into the Zoco Chico any night,' reported Bowles.

In the little square lined with cafés you can see that in fact, if not officially, the integration of Tangier with the rest of Morocco has already taken place. Instead of the customary assortment of European tourists and residents, elderly Muslims in djellabas and native Jews from the nearby streets of the Medina, you are likely to see sitting at the tables no one but young Muslims in European dress – mostly blue jeans. From time to time a noisy cortege passes from a side street through the open space and disappears into the darkness of another alley: two or three policemen leading a protesting Muslim in torn clothing. He has been caught drinking wine or beer and is on his way to the commissariat. Tomorrow he will be given a sentence of six months in jail and a fine of 500 pesetas. If it is a woman, she will receive the same sentence plus an additional penalty: her hair and eyebrows will be shaved. It is a good law because it was made in Rabat by Muslims: there is no need to consider it further.

The sense of menace in this passage is acute: particularly the reference to young toughs in blue jeans – the implication being that youthful idealism had driven out the traditional circumspection and cautious wisdom of the elderly. Independence and the restoration of the Sultan was one thing: denim culture and Coca-Colanization quite another. The dress and the drinks might be Western, but the religious and cultural ethos was likely to be Islamic. This could only lead to tension. For a while, the moral winding sheet had been unwrapped from Tangier, but the shroud of Islam was again slowly dropping in suffocating folds over the city. Tanjawis, like all Moroccans, were 'just beginning to awaken to the fact that the difference between their world and the world outside is not one in kind, but in time . . . Not knowing where we [Westerners] are trying to go or why we want to go there, being merely determined to go along with us, they imagine that they can do so merely by ignoring the historical distance that separates our two cultures.'

America – symbolized by blue jeans, Coca-Cola and, occasionally, hard liquor – was perceived by Tanjawis in the mid-1950s as
being, on the one hand, all powerful in the world and, on the other,
indifferent to the ills of Morocco. 'She could change everything if
she chose, but she does nothing because she does not love the
Muslims.' In all eventualities, America and the West would be to
blame in a no-win situation: if the West did not interfere to improve
conditions, it would be at fault. If it did officiously seek to alter
conditions in Morocco and Tangier, it would be perceived by
national and religious chauvinists as neo-colonialist.

Five months later, again in *The Nation*, in December 1956, Bowles
continued his polemical report of conditions in Morocco and Tangier: 'The process of Europeanization which in most other economically "backward" countries of Asia and Africa (however regrettably
from an aesthetic point of view) is a natural concomitant of awaken-
ing nationalism and of the emphasis placed on mechanization, in
Morocco is being hastened by a planned "deculturizing" campaign.
This project for the destruction of Moroccan culture has been under
way for the past three decades, but it is only now attaining its full
impetus, since the men who have been directing it in more or
less clandestine fashion have at last come to power.' He especially
regretted the decline in the traditional music of Morocco and, as a
result, the passing away of the ceremonies which it accompanied
and enriched. He believed that the argument generally advanced,
that 'these things are barbarous, that they are outward signs of
a feudal way of life which must be extinguished in the people's
consciousness as well as in objective fact', was specious: the true,
underlying aim was to eradicate the particular culture of the
Berbers and to assert the general Arabic culture which was being
diffused, principally from Egypt. Thereby, throughout a culturally
homogeneous North Africa, the aims of the Arab League might be
forwarded without inconvenient local hindrances in Morocco or,
indeed, elsewhere.

Bowles, and others of like mind, anticipated not only the degradation of Tangier as a redoubt of Berber culture, but also the
cultural degeneration of Morocco as a whole as the result not only
of Western but also, insidiously, Arab pressures. He did not necessarily despise or belittle the general Arabic culture, but he did
object when that culture was used to dilute or destroy unique

regional variations, in particular the Berber with which Bowles was most familiar, in which he discovered and wished to preserve not only unique profundities but great beauty and distinction. His fellow expatriates were otherwise preoccupied, too busy regretting the dismantling of the international administration of Tangier to bother overmuch about the precarious and delicate culture of the natives when their own immediate interests were so vitally imperilled. *Sauve qui peut.* The natives themselves were busy, throwing traditions overboard and tuning in delightedly to the radio which, as an instrument of cultural homogeneity, followed inevitably by television, attached them ineluctably not only to the rest of North Africa but Europe and America and the whole global village.

Most Tanjawis, genetically of Berber stock, regarded themselves primarily as Arabs by religion, language and history – there was very little soul-searching among them when it came to the question whether they identified themselves more with the interests of Islam and nationalism or the Christian, international government of their city. They had been naturally and characteristically polite to Americans and Europeans, but they had courteously kept their distance from those they regarded as unbelievers, as infidels. They generally held a dim view of anything Naserani. Christians, of whatever denomination – and Tanjawis made no fine distinctions – were inherently inferior to Muslims. They could never attain to Heaven, and it was no business of a good Muslim to befriend them. Natural curiosity impelled them to learn as much as possible about foreign ways, while at the same time zealously maintaining a strict secrecy about their own lives. They held foreign power and riches in some considerable respect, and it was not humiliating to trade with foreign Christians – the opportunity for profit was rarely considered dishonourable – but courteous commercial relations were one thing, informal personal friendships quite another.

Modern Tanjawis are perhaps, ironically – though they would not see the similarity – closer in character to American Midwesterners than either would care to admit. They are usually members of an extended nuclear family, married with several children; hospitable; God-fearing and regular mosque-goers; tight with a dirham; given to old saws and sayings; moralistic and fatalistic – believing in signs, portents and final justice. They are clannish, xenophobic and chauvinistic, suspicious of foreign manners and

customs though they may adopt them superficially. They are royal-
ist (as Midwesterners are loyal to the President and the flag) and
traditionalist at heart. The men and women are, superficially, gregarious – good old boys and gals, endlessly gabbing about their
particular spheres of interest. Mint tea is the root beer of Morocco,
the market stalls serving lamb kebabs the equivalent of the American cook-out. But the differences are more perceptible than the
resemblances, and the Western attitude, even now, to Moroccans,
as to most natives of underprivileged nations, is a mixture of sentimentality and unconscious cruelty.

Tanjawis, perhaps still smarting from the long memory of foreign
rule, and increasingly proud of their Muslim way of life, are touchy
on the subject of tourism. The submissive role of servitude irritates
them. Tourism is central to the economy of Tangier, but occasional
articles in the local press object to the representation of Moroccans
in tourist posters and brochures as a class of menials hovering in
respectful attendance with food and drink while Europeans and
Americans – white, exclusively – disport themselves by the swimming pools of luxury hotels. Moroccans are too rarely shown par-
taking as equals at the holiday feasts provided for tourists: they are
there as picturesque background, as purveyors of *tout confort* for the
privileged, lordly visitor.

Besides, the class of visitor nowadays is not what it was. The
expatriate colony, ruled for the better part of half a century by
the Hon. David Herbert, the King of the Mountain fastness, has
dwindled to a handful of elderly *flâneurs*, and the glad-handed traveller *de-luxe* is now no more than a memory, a faint echo of a Cole
Porter melody blowing in the *cherqi*, the constant bothersome wind
of Tangier. The millionaires have moved on and, in most cases,
literally died out. The definitive metaphor of the city, it may have
occurred to diners in the restaurant of the El Minzah Hotel on an
April night in 1987, presented itself as a scene from a movie about
the life of Barbara Hutton being filmed in the Andalusian-style
courtyard just beyond the plate-glass windows. A crowd of excitable extras, all in glittering period clothes of the late 1950s, was
partying in high style, riding camels round the patio, laughing
hilariously, tossing back the cocktails and hamming it up in best
Burbank style. Watching all this gaiety from the other side of the
glass was exactly like being at a duller party next door. 'But why

should anyone now be interested in Barbara Hutton?' inquired a jaded French expatriate. 'She was nothing but a fleeting fantasy figure in Tangier. She was no Maecenas: she threw away her money with no plan beyond a momentary whim. She was mythical; of no importance.' The separation between fantasy and actuality was as thin as a pane of glass: it was like watching ghosts.

Later, as if to affirm the sea change in the character of Tangier, a party of extras which had moved on to Scott's disco was challenged by a truculent group of Arab students from Casablanca who, less than impressed by the glamour of movie bit players, demanded to know what they were doing in Tangier. Had they taken the trouble to learn anything about the history of Morocco? Were they aware of the degradation of foreign aid? Had they bothered to learn the language? These were extreme demands. The extras were bewildered and, a little, intimidated by this aggressive questioning. They were in Morocco to make a movie about the glamour of Tangier: so what was the problem? It suits travel journalists and other interested parties to claim that the differences between natives of the city and visitors have narrowed. The market stalls sell jogging outfits and polo shirts, young women have largely lifted the veil, young men wear jeans and business suits. No problem. But the gap, subtly, remains: Tangier is still the port of entry where one leaves behind the certainties of Europe.

The confluence of cultures, aside from mutual business interests, occasionally requires bridges. The French Lycée Regnault, the American, Italian and Spanish schools, together with the French and Spanish Cultural Centres and libraries, particularly, helped to span the cultural and social frontiers between all nationalities in Tangier. The British contribution was less impressive – a British-owned newspaper and annual pantomime shows mounted more for the delight of the British performers than the pleasure of their

somewhat puzzled audience treated to an orgy of theatrical trans-
vestism, a purely British taste that translated badly and was liable
to mystified misinterpretation.

Possibly the most significant commercial venture, that united
natives, expatriates and casual visitors alike, was the Librairie des
Colonnes. In 1951 the French publishing house of Gallimard
acquired Tarpin, a paper shop on the boulevard Pasteur. Tarpin
already sold a very limited range of books, but Gallimard decided
to establish a proper bookshop, only the third in Morocco after
Cere in Rabat and Faraire, opened in Casablanca in 1949. To run
the bookshop, Gallimard recruited Yvonne and Isabelle Gérofi,
sisters-in-law, who had run a successful bookshop and art gallery
in Brussels. Yvonne's brother, Robert, who had married Isabelle,
was to become a successful Tangier architect, latterly acting as the
local consultant for Malcolm Forbes who engaged him to remodel
the Mendoubia, formerly the palace of the Governor of Tangier.

'Almost from the first', says Isabelle Gérofi, 'our bookshop was
cosmopolite. Besides a wide range of French language books, we
had a range of English and a little section of Spanish which was
essentially augmented by anti-Francoist books – there was no censorship in Tangier – published in France. Though the range of
books of local interest was limited, we persevered in our attempt
to establish a range of Islamic and Maghrebi books, the first in
Morocco, perhaps, as well as a range of art books and art reproductions. These balanced the necessity to sell potboiler novels and
scholarly books.' The range of materials attracted, naturally, a
range of customers who, perhaps for the first time, found themselves
elbow to elbow anywhere else but in a row of bar stools. In the
post-War years, Tangier 'gathered together a motley crew: political
refugees, smugglers attracted by the promise of fast, though illegal,
profits'. Mme Gérofi surveyed her customers with a shrewd and
speculative eye: 'there must have been some odd tricks played.
The town seemed to me to be a place of unlikely meetings between
some strange birds of passage. We catered for a wide variety of
readers.'

As a natural and convenient place of indiscriminate concourse
and promiscuous contact, Isabelle Gérofi rates the Librairie des
Colonnes as one of three major points of rendezvous in Tangier.
First and foremost, she distinguishes David Herbert's dinner table

as the acme of attraction for all nationalities, including – and this was a rarity – some upper-class and aristocratic Moroccans, who regularly encountered one another with varying degrees of mutual sympathy over the Pembroke family china, silverware and crested glasses. Equally important were Paul and Jane Bowles. Herbert first annexed the social luminaries, the Bowleses being first resort for literary lions and musicians. Inevitably there was a constant traffic between them: the literati were just as anxious to be presented at the court of the Hon. David Herbert as the socialites were keen to scrape acquaintance with the interesting Mr and Mrs Bowles.

The bookshop quickly established its own position as a sort of salon. Among the better-known of their customers the Gérofis counted the Bowleses, Tennessee Williams, William Burroughs, Truman Capote, the occasional Beat writer, the French novelist Paul Morand who owned a house on rue Shakespeare in the Marshan district, Rom Landau, friend and biographer of Mohammed V and an indefatigable apologist for Morocco, the sociologist Jean Duvignaud, Samuel Beckett on his occasional and mostly silent visits to Tangier, the British novelist Alan Sillitoe, the poet Ruth Fainlight who happened to be Mrs Sillitoe, Cecil Beaton, the Spanish painters Claudio Bravo and Juan Hernandez, Jean Genet who tended to use the shop as a bank to cash cheques against his account with his publishers, the native Tangier novelist Tahar ben Jelloun, and the writer Angel Vasquez who published several books written in an improbable hybrid language composed of Yiddish, Spanish and Arabic, which he called *tangerois*.

Morand was memorable, though not merely as one of the first customers to visit the newly established Librairie. He was accompanied by his wife, the Princess Soutzo. 'They were collaborators,' remarks Isabelle Gérofi tartly,

especially Mme Morand, very pro-German and anti-Semite. They came to the bookshop as a writer comes naturally to a bookshop. He was exquisitely courteous, but she was less polite. The first thing Mme Morand said to me, literally attacking, was, 'Why do you have nothing by Rebatet?' Rebatet had written some rubbish that nobody remembers any more. He was a man who had behaved himself horribly badly during the War, pro-German, anti-Semite. He had made himself odious, and I deliberately had not stocked anything by Rebatet. As I say, Mme Morand literally attacked me because I didn't keep books by Rebatet, and that struck me very forcibly because Paul Morand himself had been punished for his collaboration. One might have thought they'd prefer to be discreet.

It was hardly likely that Mme Morand could have expected to pick up collaborationist literature in Tangier in any case, quite aside from the commercial policy of the shop and the personal disinclination of its proprietor to stock such books. A significant number of German Jews, many of them grand families who settled in conditions of considerable comfort in Tangier, had fled to the city to escape Hitler's persecution. Perhaps unsettled by the experience and mindful of their position in a Muslim country, most of them fled again in the mid-1950s after Moroccan Independence, abandoning their great houses on the Marshan in favour of a more secure life in Geneva or South America. Tangier, again, had proved itself an insecure, temporary perch for exiles and nomads who discovered the city to be merely a limbo rather than refuge of last resort.

One of the benefits the Gérofis, recovering quickly from the bruising encounter with Mme Morand, most enjoyed about the Librairie was 'the diversity of meetings and the cordiality of the encounters'. Tangier was small enough, sufficiently compact, that the improbable became commonplace: 'In a big city you might know that Monsieur Tennessee Williams is there, that Monsieur André Gide may be visiting, that there are millionaires and notable people, writers, painters, actors, all co-existing in a large town, but with whom one would not normally be confronted. But there they were, day by day, in the Librairie – Jean Genet, Samuel Beckett, Alan Sillitoe.' Isabelle Gérofi enjoyed the visits made by the Sillitoes, who rented a house on the Mountain for several months at the beginning of their literary careers. That they, like so many others, did not stay in Tangier is a matter that pierces to the heart of Tangier's particular ethos.

Isabelle Gérofi has the answer to the characteristic and curious transience of creative artists who come, for whatever reason, to Tangier. Sillitoe, she says,

did not find the climate and atmosphere favourable for creation.
He did write here, but he felt he could not continue to be a writer,
or creator, in an atmosphere which was based, at heart, on a
certain nonchalance, a certain apathy. In the end, there is only
Paul Bowles who has truly continued to be creative: here he has
found his climate. This is exceptional. Many writers have told
me, like Sillitoe, that they were not capable of writing here. Their
reasons? A sort of want of vigour, a slackness, an indolence, a
lifelessness – *une espèce de mollesse* – in the air. No imperative. Here
one is never stimulated. You have to have, within yourself, certain
tendencies or certain reserves in order to resist this apathy.

Tangier, like a little star, shines white on the northernmost tip of
Africa. From a distance it sparkles in the lively air of the Strait.
The city, as Pierre Loti approached it on the packet boat from
Gibraltar in the last years of the nineteenth century, seemed to
smile. A white tooth, perhaps, gleaming in the dark head of Africa.
The snowy whiteness of the city walls, the high, crenellated Casbah,
the minarets tiled with old faïence, seemed a little strange, more
Muslim in aspect than the towns of Algeria. Setting foot in *Tanger
la Blanche*, Loti felt – as he later wrote in his travel book *Au Maroc*
– 'suddenly hurled back into former times'. And immediately, in a
striking piece of imagery, he recognized the whiteness of Tangier
for what it was in reality. 'Here, there is something which falls like
a white shroud, extinguishing the sounds of other people, arresting
all the modern disturbances of life: the old shroud of Islam . . .'

It is this image of the white winding sheet, blanched of colour,
respectfully wrapped around the stillness of death, that strikes
most powerfully. With the force of sudden revelation, it starkly
illuminates the character of the city for anyone who has spent
more than a few weeks in Tangier and come away not merely with

a feeling of vague dissatisfaction and disappointment but a perceptible sense of lassitude. Open to too many influences, surviving on the edge of two continents, neither wholly African nor entirely European, Tangier has endured a long, fatiguing process of corruption and decay. Its circumstances have for centuries been chaotic, undisciplined, unresolved and – above all – uncreative.

The city is exhausted. Its citizens are hectic in the recurrent, feverish activities that consume their energy to very little purpose. Tangier has always been sustained by various therapies, external life-support systems imposed by many authorities, like a terminal cancer case whose weakness derives from infections that lie deep in the history of the body. The sick room has attracted many visitors, few of them very respectful of the condition of the patient, and most of them carelessly inattentive to the danger of infection in the air. For all their gaiety, the atmosphere is dispiriting and they mostly drift away or themselves, in turn, become victims. Tangier is the anteroom of failure, the casualty ward of despair.

*The
International
City*

Clinging like a limpet to the massive head of Africa, lapped by two great seas, Tangier has forever been a focal point of international interest, legitimate or otherwise, and perceived as a refuge by men harassed elsewhere by law and morality. For centuries it has been a battlefield of conflicting political, religious, commercial and military advantage, of officialdom striving with outlawry, bureaucracy with banditry. In this little cockpit, the character of Tangier and the nature of its hybrid hegemonies have been created in a continuous drama that moves towards its denouement in the 1950s and 1960s, the hedonistic heyday of one of the world's most cosmopolitan and recondite cities.

Tangier's reputation had never been stainless. In the thirteenth century, Saint Francis had miserably condemned it as a city of sin. '*O Tingis! Tingis! O dementa Tingis, illusa civitas . . .*' Even then, Tangier was reputed as a city of madness and illusory vanities, liable to seduce the stoutest virtue and mislead the firmest foot measuring its steps through the alleys of depravity. Yet once, according to myth, it had been an earthly paradise – the Garden of the Hesperides is said to have been situated nearby. Here, too, Hercules defeated the giant Antaeus and fathered a child, Sophax, on the giant's widow, Tingé, in whose honour the son founded a city blessed with her name.

Legend also has it that Hercules, at the request of the North Africans, divided the mountains which joined Africa to Europe, tearing apart what are now the Rif Mountains from the Andalusian Cordillera. The two great buttresses known as the Pillars of Hercules stand as portals either side of the Straits of Gibraltar through which the long, muscular currents of the Atlantic flow into the Mediterranean. Historically, Tangier is one of the oldest settlements in North Africa, probably founded as a commercial colony

by the Phoenicians in about 1450 BC. Fourteen hundred years later
it became a trading port for the Carthaginians, and was subsequently allied, a century before the birth of Christ, to the Roman
Empire which, in 38 BC, recognized it as a free city and its inhabitants as *cives romanes*.

When Roman power declined, Tangier was abandoned to pred-
ators. It was occupied by Vandals in AD 429, fell under the control
of Byzantines in 533, and as a wealthy port it naturally attracted
the cupidity of the Arab invaders who overran and settled most of
Morocco in the late seventh and early eighth centuries. Throughout
these successive rapes, Tangier was recognized as a valuable commercial asset by its masters: it continued to function as a major
port and developed as an important naval base. Its fame spread in
proportion to the legend of its prosperity. Tangier's status, hyped
in somewhat Homeric terms by antique authors as 'a city with
walls of bronze and with magnificent palaces of gold and silver, the
royal house of the Kings of the West', was perhaps a little overstated
by interested parties who reverently recommended it as 'the mother
of the cities of the Maghreb, the most beautiful and the most
ancient'.

Discounting the blinding magnificence of flashing precious
metals, Tangier as a strategic commercial and military base was a
substantial prize. When, towards the end of the fourteenth century,
Moroccan pirates from Tangier and Salé began to terrorize shipping in the Strait and along the Atlantic coast, the Portuguese
seized on this menace as an excuse to attack first the port of Ceuta
in 1415 'as a reprisal for Moorish piracy', and Tangier in 1437.
They did not succeed in occupying Tangier until 1471, but thereafter held it for one hundred and ninety years as a Portuguese
colony which, in 1661, was ceded to England as part of the dowry
of Catherine of Braganza on her marriage to Charles II who inno-
cently and optimistically rejoiced in the city as 'a jewell of immense
value in the royal diadem'.

The Portuguese had given Tangier a distinctly European character. They had built new and beautiful houses for their settlers and
had furnished the city with Dominican and Franciscan chapels,
monasteries and a cathedral. This orderly and profitable outpost
was fatally disturbed by the irruption of the English who so
thoroughly succeeded in alienating the resident Portuguese that

most of them packed up and returned to Lisbon. The religious fraternities were stripped of their churches and the Jews of the city, generally suspected by the newcomers of being Moorish spies, were driven out.

More or less left to themselves, the English in Tangier were at first optimistic that they had acquired a base for further colonial adventures in North Africa, and Samuel Pepys for one looked forward to Tangier becoming 'the most considerable place the King of England hath in the world'. They were quickly disillusioned. They had reckoned without enemies on two fronts – Whitehall, the enemy within, could never settle on a fixed policy for the city and constantly complained of the expense to which it was put to maintain it. English indecision resulted in constant changes of Governor, none of whom lasted on average more than two years, and most of whom were more than usually incompetent. The tenacious and ambitious Sultan Moulay Ismail, who ruled Morocco from 1672, presented himself as the ill-wisher at the gate. In association with the Spanish, and calling on the resources of local Riffian tribesmen, he made determined efforts to dislodge the English foot from its North African hold by siege, guerrilla warfare and piratical harassment of supply ships from England. In the latter years of the English occupation, the city became virtually a prison.

For the first Governor, Earl Teviot, Tangier was very comfortable and pleasant, though intolerably dull: 'nothing to see but Moors and the four Elements'. The Elements were generally benign; but the Moors were temperamental and aggressive, though they could initially be placated with regular gifts of money and goods while the English set about fortifying their new possession. The most substantial, if temporary, English achievement in Tangier was the construction of a gigantic harbour Mole, an elaborate protective sea wall. Begun in January 1662, it finally measured 1436 feet long, with a mean width of 110 feet and a mean height from high to low water of 18 feet. In 1676, it was proudly described as being 'in its design the greatest and most noble undertaking in the World . . . now near 470 yards long and 30 yards broad, several pretty Houses upon it and many families; on the inner side 24 Arched Cellars and before them a curious Walk, with Pillars for the Mooring of Ships. Upon the Mole are a vast number of Great Guns, which are almost continually kept warm during fair weather, in giving and paying Salutes to ships which come in and out.' It cost a very great deal of money.

Money, indeed, was a constant problem. For two years, 1670–2, the Governor Sir Hugh Cholmondeley carried out work on the Mole on his own credit; pay for the troops was kept in arrears for as long as twenty-six months; there was plain embezzlement and frank fraud. The English compounded their problems and increased their expense by taking no lessons from the Portuguese, who had subsisted largely on the resources of the surrounding countryside and the sea – fish, eggs, poultry, game, vegetables and fruit were plentiful, cheap, nourishing and appropriate to the climate. The insular and suspicious English preferred to import their staple provisions from home – salt pork and barrels of other preserved foods, mostly unsuitable for the conditions of Tangier, liable to decay and certainly tedious as a constant diet.

In any case, Moulay Ismail forbade the local tribes to provision the city during the latter years of the English occupation, and fresh water had been a problem from the start. The Portuguese had thoughtfully left specific written details and plans of all the city's springs, wells and conduits – but the Commander of the Garrison, Lord Peterborough, had promptly lost the book. Water had therefore to be brought in from Fountain Fort, which stood exposed among the sand dunes on the beach. Official incompetence, in all departments, staggered belief. Fort after fort in the outlying districts fell to Moulay Ismail's Riffians who nagged constantly at the colony. Whitehall, out of patience and out of money, finally decided that Tangier was expendable: in 1680 the House of Commons impeached the management of Tangier and voted to squander no more funds on such a damnably expensive and difficult city. In 1683, Lord Dartmouth was sent with a fleet from England and secret instructions to abandon the colony after destroying the Mole and the principal buildings.

He was accompanied on the voyage by Samuel Pepys who, as a Secretary of the Admiralty, had been commissioned to consider claims against, and debts owed to, the Crown. Pepys went ashore for the first time on 17 September 1683 to take stock of the colony of some six or seven hundred civilians and about a thousand troops. He had reason to look with gratitude upon Tangier: much of his own fortune had derived from the million and a quarter pounds that had passed through his hands during his fifteen years as the city's treasurer in London. Nearly one hundred thousand pounds a year of the King's money had flowed into this remote little colony.

Riding unwillingly and apprehensively round the fields of the city, conscious that the ravening Moors lurked behind every bush and hillock, Pepys 'wondered all the way at the folly of the King's being at all this charge upon this town'. He made haste the next morning to visit a local bagnio where he was interested to learn from the crone in charge that the women of Tangier were such whores that mothers and daughters commonly called each other so. Far from lying with any of them that night, he made his bed uncomfortably on chairs, was charged the extortionate price of eight pence for a quart of milk for his supper, and was badly bitten by insects. He wholeheartedly endorsed the opinion of one of his correspondents who had written to him in London, miserably describing Tangier as a 'hell of brimstone and fire and Egypt's plagues. . . in a hellish torrid zone'.

There were other difficulties. The property holders of Tangier had been called to give an account of their tenures. First the Portuguese were to be summoned to appear before the Commissioners, resplendent and sweltering in the scarlet and ermine robes of authority. Other proprietors were to be next to testify, and finally consideration was to be given to English civilians and the garrison. This was also to be the order of evacuation when the time came finally to pull out of the colony. Nobody at first bothered to turn up, except the elders of the Portuguese Church excitably defending their property and displaying their title deeds, all in Spanish, which had to be laboriously translated.

The indifference of the proprietors depressed Pepys, who drafted another Proclamation and settled in, like a good and faithful civil servant, for a protracted investigation. From eight in the morning until lunchtime at one, from two thirty in the afternoon until eight in the evening, Pepys sat with his clerks 'without anything more observable than the slowness of the proprietors coming in with their titles and the infinite unreadiness in those that did to make them good'. Added to which, there was precious little to eat: not one provisions ship had arrived, and much of the foot brought by Dartmouth with the fleet was unfit for consumption – sixteen thousand pieces of rotting pork had to be condemned.

Pepys, by this time, was contemptuous of the ways of Tangier: 'never surely was any town governed in all matters both public and private as this place has been.' He attended church service to listen to a sermon devoted to a denunciation of the sins of the city. It was heartily deserved: 'nothing', he wrote, 'but vice in the whole place of all sorts, for swearing, cursing, drinking and whoring'. The Governor, Colonel Percy Kirke, had publicly boasted that one wench, Joyce, 'a mighty pretty creature', had spread the clap among some four hundred of his men and notably infected his own secretary. Kirke was as bad a hat as any Pepys had ever encountered. He set about cataloguing the Governor's excesses, the least of which was his refusal to pay a debt of fifteen hundred pounds to the townsmen of Tangier. 'God damn me, why did you trust me?' was all the answer that could be got from him in acknowledgement of the obligation.

Kirke had got his wife's sister with child so that she had to hurry to the anonymity of Spain to be brought to bed with his bastard. He had taught devout Moors phrases in English they could not understand but which were blasphemous in their religion. He maintained a private bagnio furnished with a madam to oversee his personal harem of whores. Lady Mary Kirke, the Governor's wife, repaid her husband's philandering by keeping a stable of gallants with whom she would 'play the jade by herself at home'. Kirke had certainly murdered one man, a sergeant, and deported a poor Jew and his miserable wife back to Spain to face death by burning at the hands of the Inquisition. His example was readily adopted by his men, to whom Kirke was an idol. He and his troops were a terror to the citizenry, beating up passers-by in the streets, raping almost at will, and finally falling down dead drunk after their lawless excesses.

Pepys, in his way a moralist who behaved sometimes not wisely but at least with a high degree of discretion and circumspection, was revolted by Kirke's overt barbarity. It outraged every decency. There was no justice in Kirke, no respect for the law – and it was this, perhaps, that most irritated Pepys. The Governor was no better, in his whimsical, tyrannical use of power, than the monstrous Moulay Ismail whose acts of apparent brutality against his own people were at least fathomable as deriving from a code very different to the tradition of fairness and justice Kirke might be expected to observe. To Pepys' mind, the Governor was primarily responsible for the loose speech and morals of Tangier: the infection resided in the bestial conduct of its primary authority. God Almighty, wrote Pepys to a friend, should lose no time in destroying the city, this latterday Sodom. Dartmouth had been instructed to do his best, but a helping hand would not come amiss: 'for with sorrow and indignation I speak,' wrote Pepys, 'it is a place of the world I would last send a young man to, but to Hell. Therefore, on God's account as well as the King's, I think it high time it were dissolved.'

By 18 October, Pepys had succeeded in his task of 'winding up a great many poor peoples' pretences, who have very little time to turn themselves in . . .' and at last he had leisure to inspect the environs of Tangier. He watched with interest the Moors mending their boats, chatted with Armenian traders, and rowed himself out into the bay, noting 'how blue the remote hills will look in the evening about the sun's going down, as I have sometimes seen them painted but never believed it natural.' Some experiments were meanwhile being made to accomplish Dartmouth's duty of destruction. Bombs were planted under the Mole arches, at first unsuccessfully but later with more exciting results. Pepys rushed from his dinner, on one occasion, to watch as a great mine cracked the Mole from side to side, showering rubble over the harbour and the ships in the bay. Later, he stood at a window with Dartmouth to observe the end of the Mole shoot up into the night sky, falling in fragments all around them. It was as good as a fireworks display.

On 27 October, the Mayor and chief citizens of Tangier took their official leave of Lord Dartmouth. They sailed the next day, at dawn, for England. By 5 November, all the townsmen had departed, leaving only the soldiers, the engineers and the fleet to continue the punishing work of demolishing the Mole. Pepys himself left for Spain on 6 December, and two months later, on 6 February 1684, Lord Dartmouth abandoned the ruins of Tangier to Moulay Ismail and the Berber tribesmen of the Rif.

Under the Governorship of two Riffian Berbers, Ali ben Abdallah and his son Ahmed ben Ali, who held power in Tangier from 1684 to 1743, the city was repopulated with Berbers from the Rif, largely rebuilt, and its influence was extended to Ceuta, a short distance to the north-west, and to Asilah and Tetuan in the south, so that

Tangier controlled the entire promontory facing the Strait of Gibraltar. Meanwhile, England had seized Gibraltar in 1704 and was confirmed in its possession in 1713 by the Treaty of Utrecht. From their vantage point across the Strait, the British took a particular interest in the future of Tangier which they had no wish to see acquired by a rival European power, least of all the French. Terms were struck between the Berbers of Tangier and the English in Gibraltar, whereby the English supplied guns, ammunition and other ordnance to the Berbers in return for uninterrupted supplies to feed and maintain the English fleet and garrison.

After 1743, Tangier fell completely under the authority of the Sultan of Morocco who appointed its Governors at whim. The city was of considerable interest to the French and Spanish, both of whom at various times and on various pretexts bombarded it. So eager was Britain to assume the position of protector of Moroccan independence against other European powers that a Foreign Office Despatch of 26 May 1845 to the British representative at Tangier specifically stated: 'Our permanent object must be to exert ourselves to the utmost in assisting to uphold the authority of the Sultan and to arrest every incident which might threaten it with fresh danger.' By this date, Tangier had become the diplomatic capital of Morocco and a focus for international interest in the country as a whole.

George Borrow arrived in Tangier from Gibraltar on 8 August 1839 to pursue further his mission to sell copies of the Bible. He was landed without ceremony on 'an immense number of large loose stones which run about five hundred yards into the bay', the rubble of the stupendous Mole which the Berbers had never attempted to repair. Time and tides had rendered them treacherous underfoot and dangerous at high water when the surf broke over them 'with great fury'. Safely within the walls of the city, Borrow's attention was instantly taken by a tall mosque, built of green bricks, beautifully variegated at intervals with bricks of a light red tinge, which reminded him of the Giralda of Seville, 'though with respect to size standing beside the giant witch of Seville, the Tangerine Djmah would show like a ten-year sapling in the vicinity of the cedar of Lebanon, whose trunk the tempests of five hundred years have worn.'

He peered curiously into the mosque and found the interior

pleasing: 'a quadrangular court paved with painted tiles and
exposed to the sky; on all sides were arched *piazzas*, and in the
middle was a fountain, at which several Moors were performing
their ablutions'. Here, Borrow considered, was indeed a house of
God, in externals at least, to shame the Papists: no idols, merely
'four walls, a fountain, and the eternal firmament above, which
mirrors His glory'. Satisfied with these observations, Borrow proceeded to the house of the British consul, 'built in the English style'.
The consul advised him to seek lodging with Joanna Correa, 'the
Mahonese widow', and Borrow set off to look for her house.

He entered a small square, standing about half way up the hill
on which Tangier was built. This was the market-place, the *soc*.

All around the square were small wooden booths, which very
much resembled large boxes turned on their sides, the lid being
supported above by a string. Before each of these boxes was a
species of counter, or rather one large counter ran in front of the
whole line, upon which were raisins, dates, and small barrels of
sugar, soap and butter, and various other articles. Within each
box, in front of the counter, and about three feet from the ground,
sat a human being, with a blanket on his shoulders, a dirty turban
on his head, and ragged trousers, which descended as far as the
knee, though in some instances, I believe, these were entirely
dispensed with. In its hand it held a stick, to the end of which
was affixed a bunch of palm leaves, which it waved incessantly
as a fan, for the purpose of scaring from its goods the million flies
which, engendered by the Barbary sun, endeavoured to settle
upon them. Behind it, and on either side, were piles of the same
kind of goods. *Shrit hinai, shrit hinai* [Buy here, buy here], was
continually proceeding from its mouth. Such are the grocers of
Tangier, such their shops.

The middle of the *soc* was bright with a lavish display of melons
heaped in pyramids, baskets of fruit, and scattered heaps of round
loaves of bread. Here Borrow noticed Berber women squatting on
the ground with their wares, 'the wildest-looking beings that the
imagination ever conceived, the head covered with an enormous
straw hat, at least two yards in circumference, the eaves of which,
flapping down, completely concealed the face, whilst the form was

swathed in a blanket, from which occasionally were thrust skinny arms and fingers. These were Moorish women, who were, I believe, in all instances, old and ugly . . . The whole *soc* was full of people, and there was an abundance of bustle, screaming and vociferation, and as the sun, though the hour was still early, was shining with the greatest brilliancy, I thought that I had scarcely ever witnessed a livelier scene.'

The house of Joanna Correa, the widow of a Genoese master of a felouk which had plied between Tangier and Gibraltar, stood at the corner of a little alley. It conformed in most particulars to the regular style of modest Moorish domestic architecture. The house was constructed around a small central courtyard, in this case 'not more than ten feet square. It was open at the top, and around it on three sides were apartments; on the fourth a small staircase, which communicated with the upper storey, half of which consisted of a terrace looking down into the court, over the low walls of which you enjoyed a prospect of the sea and a considerable part of the town. The rest of the storey was taken up by a long room, destined for myself, and which opened upon the terrace by a pair of folding doors. At either end of this apartment stood a bed, extending transversely from wall to wall, the canopy touching the ceiling. A table and two or three chairs completed the furniture.' Borrow spent some five or six weeks in Tangier, lodging in modest comfort with this enterprising woman who, with the responsibility of raising four children, not only rented out rooms to travellers but made bread 'which was in high esteem with the Moors', sold liquor in partnership with an elderly Genoese, and was on good terms with the British consul.

Exploring the city, Borrow could not miss the rue Siaghines, an important artery of Tangier. It still exists as a street of jewellers' shops and kiosks, but in the mid-nineteenth century it housed the most important premises of the most considerable merchants, some of them Algerians who had fled the Christians. In the bazaar, Borrow was breathlessly told by a guide: 'Silks from Fez you will find there; and if you wish for *sibat*, if you wish for slippers for your feet, you must seek them there, and there are also sold curious things from the towns of the Nazarenes. Those large houses on our left are habitations of Nazarene consuls; you have seen many such in your own land, therefore why should you stay to look at them?

Do you not admire the street of the Siarrin? Whatever enters or goes out of Tangier by the land passes through this street. Oh, the riches that pass through this street! Behold those camels, what a long train; twenty, thirty, a whole *cafila* descending the street.'

Much pleased and diverted by his excursions and explorations into the bustling heart of Tangier, Borrow dined with the British consul who was at pains to rid his glamourized guest of any delusions. The Consul firmly believed that 'no people in the world were more false and cruel' than the Moroccans. Their government, he alleged, 'was one of the vilest description, with which it was next to an impossibility for any foreign power to hold amicable relations, as it invariably acted with bad faith, and set at nought the most solemn treaties. That British property and interests were every day subjected to ruin and spoliation, and British subjects exposed to unheard-of vexations, without the slightest hope of redress being offered, save recourse was had to force, the only argument to which the Moors were accessible.'

The Moors, Borrow later learned, were equally suspicious of the Nazarenes – the Christian foreigners – who were themselves perfectly capable of dealing in ill faith and with an eye to their own profit. 'Between twelve and one,' he reported, 'the hour of prayer in the mosque, the gates of the town were closed, and no one permitted either to enter or go out. There is a tradition current amongst them, that on this day [Friday], and at this hour, their eternal enemies, the Nazarenes, will arrive to take possession of their country; on which account they hold themselves prepared against a surprisal.' The Moroccans were right to take even the most elementary precautions, though in the event the gates were to prove powerless against the *force majeure* of pieces of paper that were to confirm foreign possession more powerfully and permanently than powder and pistols.

Tangier, first observed by Borrow from the deck of the large Genoese trading boat that had brought him from Gibraltar, had 'showed like a white dove brooding on its nest'. On closer inspection, the dove took on some hawkish aspects: the city walls were 'frowning and battlemented', and 'two or three tiers of batteries, displaying heavy guns' commanded the harbour. The terraces of the town, so white they seemed cut from a rock of chalk, rose from the beach of white sand and the precipitous cliff 'like steps for giants'.

The language of the city was a babble of Arabic, Spanish, French, some Italian and English. The inhabitants were Arabs, Moors, Berbers, Jews and Nazarenes of all European countries. Evidently, the city was a familiar port of call for Mediterranean and Atlantic traders, and a settlement for a variety of nationalities. Borrow encountered one man in particular, a Mulatto who aspired to the hand of Joanna Correa and bragged mightily of his superior ancestry and traditions. The fact that he happened to be high on hashish perhaps inspired and inflated his ambitions and pride in his nobility. It was a performance Borrow took care to record as an example of the wondrous complexity of Tangier society.

Speaking mainly in Spanish, the tall, muscular, 'exceedingly and bitterly ugly' Mulatto proclaimed himself the most noble in Tangier, bar none.

> 'Who are the consuls? Who is the Pasha? They are Pashas and consuls now, but who were their fathers? I know not, nor do they. But do I not know who *my* fathers were? Were they not Moors of Garnata [Granada], and is it not on that account that I am the strongest man in Tangier? Yes, I am of the old Moors of Garnata, and my family has lived here, as is well known, since Garnata was lost to the Nazarenes, and now I am the only one of my family of the blood of the old Moors in all this land, and on that account I am of nobler blood than the sultan, for the sultan is not of the blood of the Moors of Garnata . . . Am I not Hammin Widdir, *el hombre más valido de Tanger?*'

Hammin Widdir's extravagant claim was doubtful to Borrow. He attempted to confirm it with an ancient of the city who gave it some credence on historical grounds: 'it is by no means impossible: many of the families of Granada settled down here when their town was taken by the Christians, but the greater part went to Tunis . . . there were hundreds of that name in Tunis, therefore why should not this Hammin, this drunken water-carrier, be a Moor of Granada also? He is ugly enough to be emperor of all the Moors.'

It was important in a town like Tangier to assert status since the principal animating spirit among its citizens appeared to be a mutual disrespect. A *haji* who had acquired saintliness by a visit to Mecca despised others less saintly; the Muslims despised the

Naserani; the Naserani were disgusted by the Moors; the Spanish hated everyone and were thoroughly disliked in return; the Jews were the whipping boys of everyone. A common water-carrier, however, might look at a consul and curl his lip. It was important, therefore, to assert control over this rivalry, suspicion and – no doubt – sedition. In 1860, the status of the lordly foreign consuls in Tangier was raised: they became, importantly, heads of legations.

The improvement in their position cut no ice with the Sultan and his Moroccan government at Fez. Negotiations with the autocratic Mohammed IV and his pompous court were conducted for the most part at second hand, through the Pasha [Governor] of Tangier. British influence and interest was strong, since Britain had intervened in 1859, after Spain's declaration of war against Morocco, to declare her readiness to safeguard Tangier by armed naval resistance if necessary. The Moroccan Sultan was no doubt charmed by this show of solidarity, but he was shrewd enough to take a wider view, sensibly perceiving that Moroccan independence depended on the mutual antagonisms of the major European powers. So long as they remained at one another's throats, Morocco was safe enough from the ambitions of any one European government to annex it as a colony. The prospect of European unanimity was dreadful to contemplate. Agreement was improbable,, but it might be as well to take out a firm insurance policy to reduce the risk to Morocco generally and to Tangier in particular.

In this mood of apprehension, Sultan Mohammed IV looked about for a powerful protector. It was not forgotten that Morocco had been the first country to recognize the independence of the United States. In 1871 he took the opportunity of a visit to Fez by the American consul, General Mathews, to appeal to the United States to act as arbiter in any dispute that might lead to the possibility of an armed struggle between Morocco and a European power. If necessary, the Sultan was even willing to put Morocco under an American protectorate. The offer was declined, though the State Department did take the trouble to say, in reply to the Sultan, that the United States 'would regret any attempt on the part of the Foreign Powers of a dismemberment of the Empire of Morocco and would consent to use its friendly offices to prevent such an act'. The Sultan considered Tangier particularly at risk, but in the end he appeared to concede that it should, for all practical purposes, be abandoned to occupation by the Nazarene representatives who could be safely confined there, at a distance of some seven hundred kilometres from Fez, and remote from the court which preferred to have as little to do as possible, culturally and politically, with Europeans. No Sultan had visited Tangier for decades.

The principal duty of the Pasha of Tangier, Sidi Mohammed Torres, was to frustrate any attempt by foreign legates, consuls, ministers, or other interested parties to penetrate without good reason the Fez court. As the Sultan's representative in Tangier, he was required to deal personally with complaints, most of which concerned the system of protection which had originated in the eighteenth century. Each consul and commercial house had been permitted to name a limited number of Moroccan subjects as agents. The advantage to Moroccans was that they thus fell under the protection of foreign law and could legally evade Moroccan taxes, the demands of Moroccan religious law and other onerous responsibilities. The practice soon became a racket. Foreign consuls and commercial magnates openly sold protection, to the extent that the Italian minister acquired more than a thousand protegés, only slightly exceeding the total amassed by the Spanish representative, who was no better and no worse than the Portuguese and Brazilian ministers.

The British minister in Tangier, Sir John Drummond Hay, extended his protection in the manner of a grand seigneur to whole villages, his entire troupe of camel drivers, and up to two hundred beaters employed to flush out wild boars on his frequent hunting trips into the countryside. The American consul who succeeded Felix Mathews in 1888 discovered that he had become the official protector of some eight hundred Moroccan agents. Unofficially the number was much greater and included an entire Moroccan village of some three hundred persons who, on the ground that they constituted an American colony, resolutely refused to pay taxes to the Sultan who was outraged by the numbers of wealthy Moroccans rushing to buy protection which, though expensive to the point, potentially, of ruin, was cheaper in the long run than meeting the extravagant demands made upon them by the government. Dismayed at the revenues lost through the flagrant abuse of protection, the Sultan demanded that the international powers represented at Tangier remedy the situation. The international community formed a cabal and consulted together, but appeared unwilling to renounce its privileges. It took them three years to come to terms and adopt the Convention of Madrid in 1880 which, despite the very specific nature of its regulations concerning the character and extent of protection, was widely disregarded.

Matters such as these naturally drew the consuls at Tangier together regularly to discuss their common interests and difficulties. Their longest-standing and most regular concern was the health and sanitation of the city. By 1840 their collective pressure had resulted in an agreement with the Sultan that they should be responsible for 'the honourable mission of maintaining the public health upon the coast of this Empire, to make all rules and to take all measures to reach this end'.

The principal worry was plague, brought back by pilgrims returning to Tangier from the holy sites of Islam. A Sanitary Council was established, each consul taking it in turn to act for three months as President. The Council became, eventually, a Health Commission which in turn evolved into an unofficial city council. As a form of international co-operation between the consuls it worked relatively well, but naturally became more interested in its own powers and the extension of those powers than the efficiency of its day to day operations. The practical effect on the public amenities of the city, to judge by some reports, was negligible. Henry Selous, posted as a diplomat to Tangier in 1910, was immediately assaulted in his nostrils 'by a stench so powerful and nauseating as almost to be possessed of beauty, so description-defying as to relegate to a position of "also-smelt" the main drain of Pisa in summer'. Agnes, Lady Grove, arrived on a visit to Tangier in 1902 and picked her fastidious way 'up through evil-smelling alleys – you cannot dignify them by the name of streets'. The Scottish writer and adventurer Robert Cunninghame Graham affably described Tangier in this period as a 'pleasant, evil-smelling, picturesque and old-world little town, where every European who could afford five-and-twenty dollars for a horse equipped himself with boots and spurs and rode about splashing the dirty water of the streets on the foot-passengers'. The genteel rode or were carried in sedan chairs, preceded by a guard running ahead shouting his head off in an attempt to force a passage.

The offshore view of Tangier was charming to Lady Grove who,

fresh from the civilized, Anglicized colony of Gibraltar, was warned
by the steamer Captain: 'Well, that's the best part of it. You'll
never like it so well again.' Stark, dazzling white against the deep,
pure blues of sky and sea, Tangier tumbled down a mild hillside,
apparently innocent and positively picturesque in sunlight. The
first shock was disembarkation by a flotilla of small boats, the only
craft capable of negotiating the shallows of the bay. The English
traveller and writer Lawrence Harris arrived in September 1908,
and was taken ashore in a 'clumsy barge-like lighter' whose deck
was pullulatingly alive with 'ragged rascals who fight and screech
for possession of my baggage and body'.

Ashore, 'the victors proudly shoulder my luggage and march me
to the Customs'. Here Harris encountered 'four venerable long-
bearded officials. Pious sons of Mahomet are these, who, while
counting their beads are not deterred from discussing other matters
between the muttered "A'llah il A'llahs" as they go through the
cycles of their rosary. Piles of merchandise, a few open boxes and
quantities of stuffs and materials scattered about on the dirty floor
await their attention. But why should a true believer hurry for an
infidel? For weeks, or even months, goods must wait at the Customs
till A'llah doth please to bring their minds to bear upon your
case. Wildly gesticulating merchants cannot disturb their serenity.'
Harris promptly showed them the colour of his money, noting that
'there is no regular tariff at the Customs in Morocco, and the duty
is assessed in proportion to the bribe previously administered.' This
was not strictly true, but a judicious bribe buys time, saves energy
and gives pleasure at very little expense, and Harris was keen to
get on his way.

Tangier, judged by the view from his hotel window, was entranc-
ing. Harris looked with satisfaction upon 'the broad expanse of
pure blue sky; on the distant horizon the coasts of Spain, a long
purple line; while the white sails of tiny boats sparkled in the
sun-kissed water rippling in the gentle breeze. Tangier stretches
away to the sea in an endless number of snow-white terraces. A
network of dark intersecting lines indicates the streets and by-ways.
Walls of mosques, covered with green tiles, sparkle in some places
like emeralds, and there, on the topmost summit of the hill, standing in spectral whiteness, the ramparts of the fortress cut a vigorous
outline against the blue sky.' Happily polishing the purple hue of

his prose, poetically primed for still more intense pleasures, Harris
proceeded from rhapsodic, remote contemplation of the white ramparts of the Casbah to inspect the market-square at close quarters.

There, enthusiasm rather than words failed him. The Grand
Socco had not changed in essentials since Borrow had observed it
some seventy years before. It remained a large expanse of flat
ground, muddy in the winter rains, baked hard in summer, just
beyond the main gate of the Medina. Here camel trains from the
south sank to rest, black tents were erected, crates containing all
manner of goods were scattered over the ground. Strolling among
the noisy groups of merchants, skirting the squatting covens of
Berber women, circling the hectic piles of fruit and vegetables,
muffling their noses against the ripe aroma of dates and the riper
stench of dung, were 'well-dressed men of all nationalities' idly
discussing the latest gossip of the city. Camels gurgled viciously,
asses brayed, countrymen jabbered, the Muezzin called from the
minaret and

> ragged Spanish boys rushed about with European newspapers,
> three days old. Camels squatted on the ground; small donkeys
> with loads much bigger than themselves pushed their way
> amongst the crowd in all directions; mules tethered to posts gave
> sly kicks whenever they saw a chance; here and there one noticed
> a European horseman on his way to business; yelling vendors of
> carpets and curios thrust their wares into one's face; loathsome
> beggars clutched my arm to whine and show me their repulsive
> deformities – and so I struggle up the hilly street, stumbling in
> the muddy ruts that a scorching sun was fast drying into an
> unwholesome dust.

Harris spat on the lot of them, with the fine disdain of a European
who understood, with perhaps some satisfaction, that he was the
object of Moroccan 'fanatical hatred to all Europeans or European
innovations'. Europeans were not loved in Tangier, and the feeling
was generally returned with interest.

'The brutal Arab', wrote Harris in his introduction to *With Mulai
Hafid at Fez*, published in England in 1909, carefully differentiating
between degrees of depravity, 'is opposed to the cunning Moor,
who is again terrorized by the violent Berber. They are all fleeced

by the oppressed Jew, and these, with a few renegades – the scum
of Europe, having a compound of all the vices – make up the
population of this benighted country.' English attitudes had not,
apparently, much altered since Borrow had been treated to a very
similar diatribe by the British consul in Tangier. Moroccan morals,
culture, system of government and traditions were not, certainly,
familiar or even pleasing to Europeans accustomed to their mon-
archical democracies. Harris, who later had an extended opportunity to observe court life at Fez, described immemorial Moroccan
practices, as 'entirely outside and beyond the purview of European
ideas and standards'.

Moroccans were, in a word, 'degenerate'. The 'enervating doc-
trine of preordained future' of the Mohammedan religion was 'fatal
to progress'. The government, in effect an autocracy, remote in the
south and fiercely discouraging intrusive visits from strangers, was
vigorously resistant to suggestions from well-meaning Europeans
for reform. Morocco appeared to Harris to be 'a land of corruption,
tyranny, and unscrupulous oppression'. The administration was 'a
sink of chicanery', resulting in national stagnation. The arts did
not flourish – Harris could find no literature worth the mention,
and he deplored the 'elementary and barbaric state' of music and
learning. Most ignoble of all, 'the Sultan of this degenerate race is
permitted impudently to impose conditions upon Great European
Powers and flout their representatives.'

These views, though intemperate, were not considered extreme
and would have been given a sympathetic hearing by the European
representatives at Tangier which, according to Cunninghame Graham, had become

> a miniature Constantinople, it had representatives of every Court
> in Europe, a consul-general from the United States, and ministers
> or consuls, who behaved like ministers, from many South Ameri-
> can Republics. Flags of the various nations fluttered from half a
> hundred houses in the town. Adventurers who styled themselves
> presidents of Patagonia, kings of Araucania, and other hypothetic
> states, hoisted the flags of their fantastic countries, and whilst
> their money lasted, if they were presentable, spoke 'diplomatic
> French', were not seen drunk in public, or committed any flagrant
> misdemeanour, were received as cordially in the tolerant society

of the place as if they had been representatives of real countries
to be found upon the map.

They were objects of wonder to the Moroccans, 'who looked on
them all with awe, mixed with amusement, and regarded them as
amiable madmen who, for some purpose of his own that he had
not disclosed, Allah had endowed with the command of fleets and
armies, and with mighty engines of destruction, so that it behoved
the faithful to walk warily in their dealings with them. Tangier was
then one of the dirtiest towns in the whole world, outside of China,
but perfectly safe to live in, for robberies were rare and crimes of
violence practically unknown, and though most Europeans
"packed", as cowpunchers used to say, a pistol, it was quite
unnecessary.' The city attracted adventurers, certainly: it had sheltered political refugees since Napoleonic times, and since 1900 it
had become a convenient place of exile for Spanish anarchists.

The foreign community at the turn of the century numbered
some ten thousand souls, mostly poverty-stricken Spaniards who
had no compunction about earning a living by smuggling, selling
liquor and – to the horror of pious Mohammedans – raising pigs.
'Here, there, everywhere,' commented the effervescent English
journalist and adventurer Walter Harris, 'can be seen Spaniards,
many of them drunk, all of them objectionable.' Tangier was a city
riven by class differences and fine social distinctions. Moroccans,
Spaniards, Jews, and other nationalities were all mutually suspicious, all more or less intolerant of one another's religion, morals,
traditions, customs, language, education, living conditions,
hygiene, manner of dress, and anything else that could usefully be
condemned as an affront to decency. This missorted citizenry lived
cheek by jowl without ever truly mixing. Disputes may not normally have come to blows, but the city thrived on gossip, slander
and stage whispers that kept the embers of mistrust and misanthropy hot and glowing.

The city of the consuls, a rarefied upper stratum of Tangier
society, no less infected with mutual antagonisms and malicious
gossip, nevertheless strove to maintain a fiction of politeness. Life
among the consuls was genteel, coolly and conventionally regulated
by a strict etiquette. The diplomatic corps had established its own
formal diversions: Lady Grove twittered delightedly when she

discovered that 'there are more tea parties than at any other place of its size I ever heard of. If you go to them all, it is possible to get yourself rather disliked; and if you do not go to any, you are certain to get more disliked.' She noted particularly the energetic sports pursued by the diplomatic community. 'Then there is pig-sticking, when you may stick fifteen pigs in one week, or go fifteen times pig-sticking and not stick one.' This popular activity – as simple as its name implies – was an inspiration of the British who brought it from India. It was developed in Tangier by the British minister, Sir John Drummond Hay, who augmented his hunting parties with callow subalterns imported from Gibraltar at weekends to make up numbers. They regularly stuck more of their own horses, and one another, than wild pigs.

'Add to this', said Lady Grove, 'golf, polo, gymkhanas, paper-chases, picnics, rounders . . . and there you have the social life of Tangier in a nutshell.' There were some, less satisfied than Lady Grove with tea parties and croquet, the simulacrum of a Sussex summer, who lamented the lack of theatres, concerts, dress shops and dressmakers. The intimate pleasure of talking about clothes was cruelly restricted since everyone was already familiar, to the point of boredom, with the entire wardrobes of everybody else. The American consul, however, had a phonograph which he delighted to play at full volume, drowning out conversation with a limited repertoire of recorded music. Life was comfortable, but tedious and artificial.

The upper circles of the foreign commercial, diplomatic and social community lived in one another's pockets, but international political tensions tended to thwart any true personal intimacies which were also dampened by professional and personal ambitions and rivalries. Mme Georges St-René Taillandier, a civilized and sophisticated Frenchwoman, the wife of the French minister in Tangier, noted that there was 'never the temptation to share a confidence, hardly to be humorous or joke. There was no backbiting for everything was repeated, no obvious preferences, never any of the subjects of conversation which create any real links of friendship among people who dine together twice weekly.' Manners were necessarily formal to avoid breaches of the peace, since there 'did not seem to be two people in the place who liked or trusted one another'. Every reception, every dinner, every tea party was a social minefield, negotiable only by diplomatic niceties which, scrupulously observed, might avoid overt unpleasantness.

Every occasion was calculated with advantage in mind: competition to maintain national prestige was intense. The Spanish minister, it was observed, acted as though he owned the place. The French and British ministers, each of whom properly suspected the other of having designs on Morocco, frankly hated the sight of each other. The German minister coolly regarded the frigid formalities with detached amusement, and the Italian representative held himself aloof from efforts to enlist his support until his own country's interest in Libya was recognized. 'Tangier', reported Lawrence Harris from the street, 'is a hotbed of social twaddle and the cesspool of European scum.'

Cunninghame Graham somewhat glossed over some serious threats to the peace of Tangier when he declared that violence was almost unknown. Two notable events had occurred in 1903 and 1904 intimidating enough to make the blood of the consuls run cold in their veins. To romantics, Moulai Ahmed ben Mohammed el Raisuli may appear to have been a sort of prototypical 'Red Shadow' direct from *The Desert Song*, a patriot who raised the tribesmen of the Rif against the corruptions and misrule of the Sultan, the government of Morocco, and the interference of the foreign powers in the country. He was born at Tetuan in about 1870 to upper-class parents who descended from the saintly Moulai Idris. Raisuli was given a sound religious and legal education, but turned to banditry, mostly cattle-rustling, at the head of a gang which venerated his extraordinary personal charisma and courage. Cattle-robbing turned inevitably to murder, a crime which Walter Harris asserted could not 'be classed with murder in England. Life is cheap, and the dead are soon forgotten.'

Harris was reluctantly fascinated by Raisuli who appeared to him to be 'a typical and ideal bandit', by nature cruel and by profession given unlimited scope to exhibit his cruelty. In appearance, Harris described him as 'tall, remarkably handsome, with the whitest of skins, a short dark beard and moustache, and black eyes, with profile Greek rather than Semitic, and eyebrows that formed a straight line across his forehead'. In manner, Raisuli 'was quiet, his voice soft and low, and his expression particularly sad. He smiled sometimes, but seldom, and ... I never heard him

laugh. With his followers he was cold and haughty, and they treated
him with all the respect due to his birth.' Harris, riding out to
observe an expedition despatched to storm Raisuli's stronghold at
Zinat, was captured by this scourge of the Rif who regularly kid-
napped for ransom and looted the trade caravans that set out from
Tangier on their journeys to the south.

Bundled into a small, dark room in Raisuli's house by Riffian
tribesmen who had brought him as a prize to their master, Harris
was disturbed to find himself keeping company with a savagely
mutilated corpse which, fortunately, was soon taken away for
burial. Raisuli's inclination was to kill Harris whose death would
be justified as an example and deterrent if any further attack was
made on Zinat and, usefully, cause more trouble and humiliation
for the Moroccan government. However, haste was not of the
essence, and Harris would be allowed to send a letter to the British
Legation and to remain in contact with the British authorities
at Tangier. The British minister, Sir Arthur Nicholson, was
thoroughly exasperated by his dealings with Raisuli on the one
hand and, on the other, with the Pasha of Tangier, Mohammed
Torres who, according to Nicholson's diary, 'behaved like an old
brute. Said that Harris was in the hands of the Lord. I said he was
not, but in the hands of a devil . . . I must say I *boil* to have to
humiliate myself and negotiate with these miserable brigands
within three hours of Gibraltar.'

Harris spent nine days at Zinat, during which he was never able
to wash, ate only intermittently, was covered with vermin and lived
in constant fear of execution. Raisuli and his Riffian tribesmen
heatedly disputed among themselves about the conditions for the
ransom of their prisoner, though their grandest expectations were
finally reduced to a demand for the liberation of a number of tribesmen confined in the prisons of Larache and Tangier. The number
first stipulated was twelve, but then increased to more than fifty.
The British Legation objected, whereupon Harris took matters into
his own hands.

He obtained the names of all the tribesmen whose release was
demanded and sent it to Tangier. Then he announced to his cap-
tors: 'You propose to kill me. Possibly you will do so, but you have
kindly given me a list of all your relations who are in the Moorish
prison – some fifty-six in all, I think. This list is now in Tangier.

You will have the satisfaction of killing me, but remember this – on fifty-six consecutive days one of your sons or brothers or nephews will be executed – one each morning; and more – their bodies will be burnt and the ashes scattered to the wind. You will see the smoke from here.' The tribesmen, who perhaps valued the transitory nature of life cheaply, were less inclined to risk an eternity of death. Believing firmly in corporeal resurrection, they were appalled at the very thought of cremation. Harris was released, much to his delight that the bluff had worked.

Raisuli took the lesson from this episode that the foreign consuls would exert the most tremendous pressure on the Moroccan government to concede his demands for the ransom of one of their own nationals. Harris had been a significant prize, but there were others. The next year, on the night of 18 May 1904, Raisuli's men broke into the Villa Aidonia to abduct Ion Perdicaris and his stepson, Cromwell Oliver Varley. Perdicaris, immensely rich, lived with his British wife, daughter-in-law and stepson in some splendour and was regarded as an adornment to the foreign community, bringing a breath of elegance and civilization to a frowsty, rather dilapidated city. He had been born in America to a Greek father and an American mother. Raisuli quickly issued his demands: a ransom of about seventy thousand dollars; certain villages to pay their taxes directly to Raisuli; the government to withdraw its authority from the territory 'held' by Raisuli; and the Pasha of Tangier to be dismissed, whereupon Raisuli would be appointed in his stead.

The diplomatic community was very much alarmed. Who would be next? One was not safe even at one's own dinner table. Arthur Nicholson cabled Whitehall for support and the American consul, Samuel Gummere, promptly contacted Washington. The result of their appeals was the appearance of six American cruisers and a British battleship off the coast. Raisuli was not much impressed: 'Since when have the sharks come out of the water to eat the mountain wolf?' He could live with gunboat diplomacy. President Roosevelt, in need of a cause to rally the Republican Party behind him, seized on the affair as a godsend: 'Perdicaris alive or Raisuli dead!' There was, however, one fundamental difficulty. Perdicaris, it turned out, had become a Greek citizen in order to protect some of his American property from confiscation by the

Confederate government. This inconvenient information was hushed up and did not emerge until nearly thirty years later.

Immense diplomatic pressure was exerted on the Moroccan government to capitulate to Raisuli's ransom demands and finally, after much quibbling, the Sultan conceded his terms. Perdicaris and Varley, who had been well treated, were released and the foreign armada sailed away. Perdicaris speedily sold up in Tangier and sensibly moved with his family to Tunbridge Wells. Raisuli, noted Walter Harris, 'found himself all-powerful – a hero in the eyes of the Moors, a menace in those of Europe'.

Raisuli's appointment as Pasha brought about a period of relative peace to Tangier and the surrounding country, but within a couple of years he became, according to Harris, 'a despot. He squeezed the people under him, and extorted money from the very poorest of the poor . . . He enforced his authority up to the very gates of the town, and his armed followers even entered and dragged out of prison men who were not in his jurisdiction. His representatives administered justice [!] in the market place, and beat people to death within a few yards of the French and German Legations.' The international community which had urged the government to cave in to Raisuli's blackmail began to suffer the consequences of the new Caid's rule that they had imposed upon themselves as a rod for their own backs. They were not spared the grim sight of public floggings, the screams of victims under the lash, the stench of the decomposing heads of Raisuli's enemies which he planted on spikes above the city gates. The Grand Socco came to resemble a charnel house.

Raisuli was at a loss to understand the complaints. 'I had brought peace and security to the country,' he remarked, 'but they feared a little blood spilt in the market place or a few heads stuck on the wall . . . Men complained that I was severe, but I was never unjust. It is sometimes wise to spend the lives of a few in order to buy the safety of many. The Arab has a short memory. He forgets his own troubles in a few days and other people's at once. You think if you imprison a man, it will stop others committing his crime. I tell you, the reason for a man's absence is never remembered, but the presence of his head on a gatepost is a constant reminder!'

Raisuli's matter-of-fact view was pretty commonly held among those who held or aspired to power in Morocco, but his reasoning did not inspire confidence in Europeans who put their faith in treaties which Raisuli scorned, in rules of moderate behaviour he found ineffective, and in a logic he found incomprehensible. The government, commented Harris, 'lived in terror of him, and let him know it, with the result that he ignored their orders and commands, and even the treaties with Europe'. The Sultan at Fez, Abd el Aziz, was incompetent, weak, given over to childish pleasures and profligate with money to the extent that he almost bankrupted the country which France eagerly moved to supply with substantial loans secured against tax receipts.

Raisuli's exploitation of the situation in Morocco was at once a cause and a symptom of a national political malaise which the European powers perceived as threatening the political stability of Europe. A weak and corrupt Morocco was a ripe fruit waiting to be plucked by a forceful power, most likely France or Spain which – without the safeguard of a treaty – might threaten the British position in Gibraltar as virtual guardian of the Straits. It was plain enough that Moroccan political reform to strengthen the country was desirable. Since there was no question that any lasting deal could be done with the Sultan, Europe consulted its own best interests and the result was the Entente Cordiale of 1904.

In exchange for recognition of British interests in Egypt, it was agreed that France, since it had a sizeable financial stake in Morocco, would take responsibility for keeping the peace there and assist in bringing about such administrative, economic and military reforms as should prove necessary. As a quid pro quo, it was neatly done, but did not wholly resolve the matter. Having disposed diplomatically of the British, the French entered into secret negotiations with Spain, the upshot of which was an agreement to partition Morocco between them. Tangier, the sore thumb that stuck out from this Franco-Spanish handshake, was the subject of a special proviso: the city would retain the special character it possessed as the residence of the diplomatic corps and its international grip on the city's municipal and sanitary institutions.

Germany was very much annoyed by this deal between France and Spain, considering herself sidelined and in no respect bound by the arrangements. Kaiser Wilhelm II, who had been on a Mediterranean pleasure cruise, was induced by his Chancellor, von

Bülow, to drop anchor at Tangier and make a statement on the German position regarding the Moroccan question. There was a general, triumphant feeling in Tangier and throughout Morocco, that the 'Sultan el Brouze' (King of Prussia) would come gloriously to the rescue of a Sultan Abd el Aziz beset and bewildered by the French and their intemperate demands. On 31 March 1905, Emperor Wilhelm appeared on the bridge of the German liner *Hamburg* in the Bay of Tangier. The weather was dreary, and he himself looked rather insignificant, a disappointing figure in civilian clothes and weeping moustaches, with his paralysed arm hanging limply by his side.

It took some hours for Wilhelm to decide to come ashore to greet the ranks of dignitaries, diplomats and guard of honour lined up in lashing rain and high winds. Only the Sultan's uncle, Abd el Malek, and a delegation from the government stoically held their ground while everyone else scurried off to shelter in the German Legation. Making his official appearance, most impressively dressed in military field uniform of silver helmet with chin strap, polished black boots, red gloves, revolver, sabre and a glittering chestful of decorations and gold, Wilhelm was rowed ashore and hoisted the last few yards through the shallows by two German soldiers. He spoke briefly in German to Abd el Malek, the Sultan's official representative, who did not understand a word, and was led to a white horse which he mounted for his triumphal progress through the narrow streets of Tangier. Crowds lined the route, cheering and waving at the Kaiser who looked as pale as his horse. 'It must have looked,' said Douglas Porch in *The Conquest of Morocco*, 'as if the cast of a Wagnerian opera had wandered by mistake onto a stage set for *Aida*.'

The procession terminated at the Grand Socco where Wilhelm mistook the pandemonium of the welcome from ululating women, Rif tribesmen shooting off their rifles, musicians pounding their drums, and the shrieks of the rabble for a fair-sized riot. The Kaiser's horse, became understandably unruly and its rider dismounted nervously to enter the German Legation where at last he caught up with the diplomats, uttered a few words about protecting the interests of German commerce, and speedily returned to the *Hamburg* which lost no time in sailing away. The event may have seemed, in retrospect, like *opera buffa*, but the *Coup de Tanger*, as it came to be known, had had a serious purpose and a significant meaning.

Kaiser Wilhelm II, in reply to the address of welcome by the Sultan's uncle, had made only a few perfunctory remarks which, dressed up the next day, became a famous declaration.

> It is to the Sultan in his position as an independent sovereign that I am paying my visit today. I hope that under the sovereignty of the Sultan a free Morocco will remain open to the peaceful rivalry of all nations, without monopoly or annexation, on the basis of absolute equality. My visit to Tangier has had as its object, to make it known that I am determined to do all that is in my power to safeguard efficaciously the interests of Germany in Morocco, since I consider the Sultan as an absolutely independent sovereign. It is with him that I wish to come to an understanding as to the proper means to safeguard these interests.

Morocco, thus encouraged by Germany, demanded an international conference be held in Tangier to consider what reforms Morocco should adopt. In the event, the conference was convened in Algeciras, Spain in January 1906 and principally succeeded in making the Moroccan question a matter of broad international interest. Rather than muddying the European waters, as it had hoped to do, Morocco realized that its policy of keeping the Europeans at loggerheads was at an end. The Conference recognized the anarchy existing in Morocco and agreed some measures for reform. The Nazarenes had apparently come together to settle their differences and were likely to take over Morocco entirely.

On 27 May 1906, the thirteen international governments signatory to the Madrid Convention* signed the General Act of the International Conference at Algeciras which, on 18 June, was reluctantly signed by Abd el Aziz. Walter Harris called it futile – 'futile, that is to say, in so far as it had any beneficial effect in Morocco ... three or four men were playing a great stake – representatives of England and France, and of Germany – and it was well played. The victory remained with the two former. The rest were puppets

* Germany, Austria-Hungary, Belgium, Denmark, Spain, the United States, France, Great Britain, Italy, Morocco, the Netherlands, Portugal, Norway, and Sweden. Russia sent delegates.

but didn't realize it.' Within two years, Abd el Aziz was deposed by his brother Moulai Hafid who was proclaimed Sultan and recognized by France, Spain, Britain and the other signatories to the Act of Algeciras. Abd el Aziz retired to Tangier, and the French continued to tighten their grip on Morocco by lending vast sums of money to Moulai Hafid who, on 30 March 1912, signed a Treaty of Protectorate granting France full rights to establish necessary reforms, occupy with its troops such territory as should be necessary to preserve order, to police the country and to direct its foreign affairs. Moulai Hafid, too, in due course, retired discreetly and comfortably on a pension to Tangier, itself recognized as a special case and permitted to keep its character as an international enclave.

The French Protectorate did not extend over the whole of Morocco. A large northern territory was granted by treaty to Spain. Tangier, it was agreed, constituted a 'special zone', its system of government still to be decided. There had already been talk of making Tangier a neutral zone. In 1887, Ion Perdicaris had suggested: 'Let Tangier be neutralized, let it be made a free port under joint guaranty of the Great Powers . . . and the Moorish question would then be shorn of its urgent and pressing danger to England's interests.' English interests, watched with a keen eye from Whitehall and Gibraltar, demanded that Tangier, if not neutralized, should at least be in the hands of a weak power that could not threaten the security of the Straits. A commission was appointed, and convened in Madrid in March 1913, to draft a plan for the internationalization of Tangier. France, Spain and Britain, the principal contenders for influence, fell to squabbling over small details for eight months before reaching an agreement which was promptly vitiated by the outbreak of war in Europe.

During World War I, consular rule in Tangier, normally a Box and Cox affair, degenerated into anarchy in all departments. The Treaty of Versailles abrogated all treaties and other arrangements between Germany and Morocco, and all German interests in the country, and in Tangier, were liquidated. In 1918, France and Spain contended for control of the city. Spain insisted that Tangier belonged geographically and therefore logically to the Spanish Zone. The French in Tangier petitioned Clemenceau to consider closely 'the political destiny of Tangier, whose importance is very great for France and the French position in Africa, the Mediterranean, Islam and the world'. They were of the firm opinion that 'Tangier and the whole of Spanish Morocco are an integral part of the Sherifian Empire, from which to separate it would be unjust.'

The Sherifian Empire, the historic fiefdom of the Moroccan Sultans, being virtually under French control, the implication could not be avoided that Tangier should also be a French colony. The French and Spanish vied with one another to establish the primacy of their influence on the city: the Spanish language was widespread, claimed the Spanish Ambassador in London, 'spoken by the high and low, Europeans, Moroccans, and Jews. Thought and feeling, life and sentiment there, are Spanish. The names of the streets, the money, the press, the theatre and the songs of the children are Spanish.' The French pointed to economic and social influences: a majority of the banks were French, including the State Bank of Morocco staffed by Frenchmen and whose president was French. Eighty per cent of the land, allegedly, was owned by the French. The education system was overwhelmingly French and the local health service was headed by the Pasteur Institute.

Britain viewed the confident North African imperialism of France with some suspicion. Tangier was commercially and strategically important as a port and a fortress, circumstances which Britain, itself an imperial power, understood very well. She could point to some legal claim of her own over the city, but was mostly satisfied to hold firm in Gibraltar and ensure weak government in Tangier. The important thing was to keep the Strait open and safe for shipping. The British were more inclined to favour Spain over France, if push came to shove, since Spain had shown herself more incompetent than France as regards administration in Morocco. On 29 June 1923, representatives of the governments of Britain, France and Spain met in London to consider the political position of Tangier.

The resulting Statute of Tangier, which dated formally and came into effect from 1 June 1925, was ratified by most of the signatories to the Act of Algeciras and placed Tangier under a regime of permanent neutrality. Amid the mass of detail, there were some broad principles: no military establishment of any kind could ever be installed there, and the international powers were assured of economic equality. No international treaty concluded by the Sultan would apply to Tangier without international consent, and all

Sherifian property in Tangier was to be handed over to an international administration. Within the International Zone, which
covered some hundred and fifty square kilometres including the
city, the port and outlying districts, Moorish francs and Spanish
pesetas would continue to be legal tender, and the official languages
were to be French, Spanish and Arabic.

Under these new arrangements, the Sultan's representative in
Tangier was the Mendoub, Mohammed Tazzi, whose responsibility it was to administer Sherifian law and collect taxes from the
native population of the International Zone. The government of
Tangier was constituted as a Committee of Control and an International Legislative Assembly. The Committee consisted of eight
European consuls whose duty was to ensure observance of the
provisions of the Statute of Tangier and to veto any legislation
that violated it. The Assembly consisted of twenty-six members,
including six Muslims and three Jews, who had complete legislative
authority over the native and foreign population of the Zone. In
many respects, these arrangements were a bureaucratic nightmare,
however logical the chain of command may have looked on paper.
The Statute had codified a constitution that most of the international powers found irksome in practice, chafing within its hair
shirt and complaining vigorously whenever it threatened to deny
them any privileges. The native population of Tangier resented
the Statute which effectively denied them control of what they
considered to be their own affairs and city. The French were obliged
to compromise constantly with the Spanish and the British; Spain
saw control of the city slipping further away from her than ever;
the Americans, who had considerable reservations about the
Statute, were cool; the Italians were outraged. The international
administration, suffering badly from teething troubles, more often
than not wrong-footed itself into confusion and conflict.

Internationalism at first appeared more like anarchy. Spain
almost immediately opened a propaganda war in an attempt to
reconstitute the International Zone as part of the Spanish Zone,
and formed an alliance with disaffected Italy. She seized on the
fact that Tangier allegedly served as the political headquarters of
a Riffian rebel called Abd el Krim who had raised the northern
tribesmen in an effective guerrilla war against the French and the
Spanish. The city's complex international postal facilities had been

used for his propaganda, and his people came and went between the International Zone and the Spanish Zone pretty much as they pleased. To Spain, which had lost heavily in terms of troops and military face at the hands of Abd el Krim, the reputation of Tangier was indefensible. Not that Tangier was under any immediate threat of occupation: Abd el Krim's view was that Tangier already provided him with every advantage – guns, ammunition, food, other supplies and a propaganda outlet. Why should he need to seize, by force of arms, what was already his?

In support of Spain, Mussolini decided to put on a show in Tangier. In the autumn of 1927, the opening of a new Italian school in the city presented itself as a convenient occasion to despatch the Prince of Udine, in command of a naval squadron of three warships, to make an impressive display in Tangier's harbour and pointedly demonstrate Italy's interest in the city. It didn't hurt Italian pretensions to influence that the spectacular visit coincided with some discussions regarding Tangier then being held in Paris. Great Britain gave her support to Italy, obliging France to reconsider her position, and a remarkable warmth speedily developed between Aristide Briand and Benito Mussolini. The Statute of Tangier was amended to the satisfaction of Britain, France, Spain and Italy, much to the dismay of the native population of Tangier who recognized that international control of their city had become more complete. Abd el Krim, far from dislodging the foreign consuls, had been defeated by a combined Franco-Spanish force in the spring of 1926 – but the Moroccans had given notice, unofficially perhaps, that nationalism was a potent force and that the inspiration of Abd el Krim and his Riffians should not be underestimated.

That the natives of Tangier had a grievance was – according to *The Times* of 1 June 1925 – indisputable.

The new régime throws an almost insupportable burden upon Tangier's impoverished shoulders. The Muslim population will be the principal sufferers, for financial stringency will prevent adequate relief or assistance. There will be no funds available, except by some unforeseen and providential turn of fortune's wheel, for the construction of hospitals, asylums, and the other needs of this patient and long-suffering community . . . A foreign régime has been introduced for purely selfish political reasons and the sacrifice that it is going to entail upon the already poverty-stricken people of the place seems to be a matter of pure indifference. That their plight will be worse than it is at present is impossible. That it will in any degree be better is most improbable. Had Tangier fallen under the protection of France or Spain, or any other one Power, its requirements would have become incumbent upon the protecting Power. Under what practically amounts to the protection of all Europe, no one is responsible.

This piece reads very much like the work of Walter Harris, correspondent for *The Times* in Morocco. His sympathies were mostly with the Moroccan people, whom, according to his tombstone in the grounds of the English church in Tangier, he loved.

Cosmopolitan Tangier, from the late 1920s until the outbreak of World War II, was considered convenient and safe to visit. It was still something of an adventure. The writer Richard Hughes, in 1929–30, acquired a house in the Tangier Casbah where his presence excited some interest and alarm. 'When I came to move in,' remarked Hughes, 'the neighbours complained that to have a Nazarene living in the street would send down the real-estate value of the whole street.' Hughes' immediate neighbour was a hereditary Muslim saint who suffered dreadfully from the indignity of living next door to a Christian, an infidel. Hughes, however, was circumspect and respectful. He carefully observed the Islamic code of manners, never gazing at anyone full in the face, never peering through open doors, and avoiding especially his roof in the evening when Moroccan women take to their own roofs to snuff the fresh air and gossip among themselves.

With a retired British Army colonel, Jack Sinclair, who had come to live in Tangier in 1924 and who was friendly with Walter Harris, Hughes made sorties into the social life of the city. He went pig-sticking, of course. 'Very exciting. The field consisted of about ten spears; and a tribe of beaters headed by a former Commander-in-Chief of the Moorish army. Casualties: one Spanish officer, fell off his horse in a thorn bush. Bag: one tortoise, found by me, and presented with much formality to the daughter of the former Governor of Zanzibar [Sinclair]. . . Five pig got away.' By 3 May, Hughes had 'gone native altogether' and pitched a couple of swagger tents in some cork woods a little way down the Atlantic coast.

'The establishment has accumulated the usual complement of extra Arabs and pariah dogs and a greyhound or two: I live in great luxury, with any number of carpets and quantities of shining brass and copper: desperate-looking gentlemen who live in straw huts bring me chickens, eggs and milk and butter, and truffles by the hundredweight: and I am so well defended by marshes that no motorcar can get near me.'

This partiality for roughing it, in whatever degree of luxury, mystified Tangier, which shuddered at the very thought. This was not a pleasure for which they had any taste. But Hughes was delighted when 'the wild boar come and grunt round the camp at night and snarl at the dogs . . . Jackals and nightingales sing all night: and by day the air is full of locusts. I have gradually taken to Arab clothes altogether: not by a sudden change, but simply by donning one convenient garment after another, till only today it came to me with a sudden shock that it is a long time since my legs knew the decent chafing of trousers.' Tangier and the surrounding area comprising the International Zone, for the enterprising traveller, was as exotic and wild as one wished it to be. The Sultan in 1890 had granted exclusive hunting rights to the diplomatic community over an area of snipe marshes, olive woods, brushwood coverts and palmetto-covered countryside bordered by the Atlantic. Close seasons had been established and local sport was well regulated.

The Tangier Tent Club, formed in 1892, organized meets every second Saturday during the hunting season which ran from November to April. A pig-sticking camp usually assembled for a week or ten days at the beginning of April: as well as pig-sticking with underhand spears capable of bringing down pigs as large as forty-two inches, boars were hunted with rifles. The snipe and duck hunting season ran from November to March, and quails arrived on their northward migration in April and May. There were partridges, hares and rabbits, more plentiful in the Spanish Zone which bordered the International Zone, but enough to give good sport in the close season from 1 February to 15 August. The Tent Club was still going strong in the 1930s, and was only disbanded after the War.

Golf and polo were played at the Country Club Diplomatique at Bouhana, a couple of miles out of town. A regular polo tournament in April featured teams from Gibraltar, the French Zone and the Spanish Zone. There was trout fishing near Tetuan, some thirty-five miles from Tangier. By the early 1930s, the population of Tangier was estimated to be in the region of fifty thousand, comprising some thirty thousand Moroccans, eight thousand Moorish Jews and twelve thousand Tangerinos of various nationalities. By 1934, the number of tourists visiting Tangier had risen to an annual total of forty-three thousand, two-thirds of them British, eleven per cent of them Germans, and ten per cent French. It was perfectly easy to get to Tangier which, when it was visited by the American writer Edith Wharton – who described the city in 1917 as 'cosmopolitan, frowsty, familiar' – had become a commonplace port of call on the tourist trail.

The most convenient route was by sea from Marseilles or London. A P. & O. liner left London on Fridays, the first-class fare in the mid-1920s being £16. Second class, £12. In 1928, the Bland Line instituted a regular car ferry from Gibraltar: the 1300-ton *Gibel Dersa II*, capable of carrying thirty-three cars which were secured by wire nets and swung on and off deck by cranes, called at Tangier on Fridays on one of its regular trips to Casablanca. Thomas Cook & Son maintained an office in Tangier, where conducted tours of particular interest to blameless botanists and enthusiastic entomologists could be booked, and arrangements made for glamorous-sounding trips by railway or coach throughout Morocco, a country that might have served Agatha Christie very well as background for one of her novels of mild international intrigue and murder. The likelihood of wild, unsettling adventure, however, was nicely balanced by middle-class faith in the name of Cook for reliable and undisturbed conduit through any potentially exotic crisis.

European control over passage between the zones was thoroughly bureaucratic. The independent traveller was advised that a knowledge of French was necessary for trips within the French Zone, Spanish for excursions into the Spanish Zone, and that within the International Zone some familiarity with French and Spanish would be helpful. A knowledge of Arabic was not considered necessary. Passports for everyone were indispensable, endorsed for travel in France and Spain. It was advisable to have 'Morocco' added to British passports for visits to the International Zone where travel documents were frequently checked. Passports were required at the border of the Spanish and International Zones; travellers by coach from Tangier to Fez could expect to have their passports inspected, at the expense of lengthy delays, four times during the trip; and at the French and Spanish Zone frontiers, passports were carefully and laboriously copied out on special forms by officials. Travel was tediously liable to regular official interruption, but not expensive in the mid-1930s: a return rail trip from Tangier to Marrakesh, for example, cost about 380 francs first class, 300 francs second class. Inexpensive hotel rooms cost as much as a good dinner – about 15 to 18 francs – and a breakfast was a mere 4 francs.

Roads had improved considerably since the turn of the century when there existed little more than caravan tracks. Now there were fine highways for military and civilian traffic. Roads implied motor cars which first appeared in Tangier in 1912 but made no real impact until the end of World War I. They were a great luxury, and the first to parade himself ostentatiously along the newly constructed Boulevard Pasteur was M. de Montravel, the Director of the Monopole de Tabacs, in a Delaunay-Bellville bearing the prestigious registration T1. Never to be outdone, the exiled Sultan Abd el Aziz acquired, for the tremendous sum of 1500 francs, an American Dodge whose registration, T2, he promptly removed and drove around importantly unencumbered by such vulgar plates. Motor taxis, largely replacing the fleet of horse-drawn carriages which could be hired from ranks in the Grand Socco and the rue Hasnona in the Marshan district of the city, were introduced by a Tangier merchant, M. Blanc, in 1924. Naturally, his fleet of Citroens was all white, becoming known as Taxis Blancs. They could be hired for twenty centimes and for a complete tour of the city at the advantageous price of thirty centimes.

The boulevard Pasteur, the principal and widest street of modern Tangier, dates only from 1910. In that year, there was nothing on the site but sand dunes until there arose a substantial building, in Hispano-Mauresque style, to house the office of the Moroccan Debt – *La Dette Marocaine*. The debt had been incurred in the years following 1904 by Sultan Abd el Aziz and increased by his brother Moulai Hafid who had established a bureaucracy to administer the debt, collect the tax revenues to service it, and generally deal with all matters relevant to his financial obligation to the French. Built by Desforges & Rousseau, one of the first public and private works contractors in Tangier, La Maison de la Dette became the focal point around which other office and apartment buildings were constructed along a route initially known as the boulevard de la Dette but tactfully renamed boulevard Pasteur in 1925.

Most of the building along the boulevard was constructed by the Toledano Brothers, of a notable Tangier family who had had the foresight to buy up most of the land around the Maison de la Dette. By the mid-1920s, the boulevard had become chic. Upper-class Tangier society shopped, took apartments, and drove along it. The old city, still teeming with people, became less important as the hub of the city. The modern town was taking shape according to the fashion for modern Western architecture and, up to a point, the demands of urban planning. By 1930, building along the boulevard was virtually complete. Within twenty years, an arid wasteland had been utterly transformed into a built-up modern *quartier* that extended from the Café de Paris on the Place de France to the crossroads at the rue Goya.

The Café de Paris, established in 1920, was run by Mme Léontine, the first woman known to have run a café in Tangier. It immediately became a fashionable resort for Tangier's *beau monde*. It still exists, a landmark meeting place opposite the building, built in miniature Buckingham Palace style, that serves as the French Consulate. For tourists and Tangerinos, for natives of the city and travellers passing through, it retains a powerful glamour that its competitors, plush and flash with comfortable banquettes and chrome, cannot aspire to rival, for all their mirrored magnificence. It is nowadays frankly dilapidated, but its prime site and familiarity transcends every aspect of its gloomy character. For purists, it had none of the authentic Tangier atmosphere of the Café Central in the Petit Socco, deep in the heart of the Medina, but for those of a nervous disposition who wished to dissociate themselves temporarily from the mobs in the Medina, or who simply found the clash and colour of the old city too tumultuous and exciting, the Café de Paris was a convenient, comfortable, safe rendezvous from which to watch the busy world go by on its various and inexplicable occasions.

There were serious foreign landowners, too, in Tangier. The

fourth Marquess of Bute had first visited Tangier as a young man in 1899, returned in 1902, and by 1929 had formed a real estate company, Rentistica, in association with a Jewish banker of the city, Aaron Abensur, and a Spanish lawyer, José Palmer. Bute acquired York Castle in the Casbah and other substantial properties including the Palmarium Casino, formerly the town house of Ion Perdicaris, which in 1930 he converted into the El Minzah Hotel. By the mid-1930s, it was estimated that Rentistica owned about twenty per cent of all the land and buildings in the International Zone. York Castle was of particular interest to Bute, who discovered drawings on the mortared walls – doubtless made by prisoners in the late seventeenth century. Romantically, it was reputed to possess secret passages connecting with a maze of ancient passages under the entire Casbah.

The tourist and property boom in Tangier between World Wars I and II inevitably excited the interests of the European powers which retained their communal grip on the International Zone. Despite the considerable sums of money that flowed in and out of Tangier, the financial burdens of the city were greater than its apparent economic resources. The International Zone was not self-supporting in terms of agriculture, and imports were very considerable. The books were always balanced, sometimes apparently only by a miracle, since the figures were always tight. Though the city income was inadequate to sustain more than a token attempt to provide public services and amenities, the foreign community significantly prospered. Tangerinos paid no income tax, there were no restrictions on the sale of gold, and it was possible to get pretty rich pretty quick.

When the Spanish Civil War broke out in 1936 it immediately caused a flutter of alarm in Tangier, geographically and culturally so close to Spain. In the spring of 1939, France and the Sultan of Morocco recognized the Franco regime which took over the Spanish consulate-general in Tangier. There was serious gossip that Franco intended to take over the International Zone, but a larger crisis was breaking in Europe and the rumours turned to the possibility of an occupation of the city by Mussolini. The international administration of Tangier was thrown into more confusion than usual by the outbreak of World War II: the Committee of Control was fundamentally split by political differences and rendered largely impotent. Tangier, under the provisions of its Statute, was required to remain neutral and unmilitarized.

Taking the likelihood of Italian intervention in Morocco as his cue, Franco marched troops of the Spanish Zone into Tangier on 14 June 1940, assuring the Committee of Control that he intended no hostility to the Allies and that his sole intention was to preserve the neutrality of the International Zone. No changes were to be made in the existing system of administration. Four months later, in October 1940, Franco's son-in-law, Serrano Suñer, was appointed Spanish minister of foreign affairs and instantly the situation radically altered. The high-minded reasons for occupation were forgotten, the promises rescinded. Suñer, a Nazi sympathizer, appointed Colonel Antonio Yuste, the head of the Tangier occupation forces, as Governor-General of Tangier. Yuste acted swiftly to dismantle the international administrative machinery, dismissed the Mendoub from office and permitted Germany to establish a consulate-general in the Mendoubia. In March 1941 the German flag replaced the Moroccan emblem over the palace.

Despite protests from France and Britain, the occupation was a *fait accompli*. The British were able to negotiate some concessions: the Zone would continue to be unfortified, they would be allowed to carry on regular publication of the British newspaper, the *Tangier Gazette*, and adequate compensation was to be paid to British personnel dismissed from the administration. British subjects were permitted free entry to and exit from Tangier. One immediate effect of the Spanish occupation was a shortage of foodstuffs. Necessary items such as flour, sugar and oil were rationed, greatly dismaying everyone in the city who traditionally drank mint tea sugared to the point of tooth rot and were devoted to sweet cakes.

A letter from Ada Kirby Green, a doyenne of the international community, to Lord Bute described some of the hardships, the anxieties and the maintenance of traditions among the British. The letter begins well, with stiff upper lip optimism: 'I myself think things here will turn out *not* so bad and that Tangier will boom after the war is over. The difficulty is to hang on until then, so many have sold their houses as big prices are offered by people of more or less dubious nationalities or those buying for third parties!! No doubt a desire for real estate which will be better than dirty paper after the war for them!! They also want to say what big interests they hold here. Ours were by far the largest always.'

There had been sad losses, to the detriment of British standing in Tangier: the English chemist, the dry cleaners, the general store and the grocery store. 'To send them a few consignments would have kept them going and been *good practical* propaganda,' complained Mrs Kirby Green. 'All now have gone into other hands, Italian, Spanish or Jewish.' This was as regrettable as the intense propaganda campaign waged by 'people of more or less dubious nationalities' in the city: 'they do spend vast sums on literature of all kinds and I do not think we are very good at that line. In any case there is so much of *all* kinds from every side, to my mind it has lost all value. The straight news of a *victory* is worth all of it which one gathers from the joyful greetings one gets on every side when we have one.'

Tangier, as a centre of international intrigue and gossip, was pretty well informed about the course of the war: 'we hear more than you do probably in this Tower of Babel. It needs a hair sieve though. And a lot of it is *paid* for of course. But we are getting good at sifting.' Socially, things continued much as usual, though food scarcities affected the form of entertaining. Mrs Kirby Green lent the lustre of her presence to a film show given, as she wrote to Lord Bute, by the Americans at the Hotel Villa de France. Suppers were provided in a downstairs room: 'They *began* at a moderate price but are reaching Minzah levels, I think.'

Food may have been the chief preoccupation, but there was no lack of liquor and no failure of vocal patriotism. Michael Davidson happened to be passing through the patio of the El Minzah Hotel when he noticed 'two tweed-clad English women, hefty and virile, with muscular grey hair. They were vigorously immersed in Scotch and, as I passed, one was saying in that loud English voice: "What are we *doing* for our country, you ask, Emmie dear? We are *drinking* for our country!" – and she lifted her whisky-tumbler in a splendid toast to old England. I never saw them again; probably they were quickly off to Britain to work magnificently in the W.V.S. or Civil Service – they were that kind.'

Domestic servants remained mostly loyal, but – like Betjeman's cook – a little unnerved. 'Many Moors have become quite useless, I fear, unsettled, but they would recover very quickly.' The letter to Lord Bute confirms that British nationals could enter and leave Tangier without difficulty: Mrs Kirby Green urged Bute to visit the city for 'a very *short* trip to look around. People go back and forth all the time and you have so many things to look up.' Among other significant interests in Tangier, Lord Bute also acquired the *Tangier Gazette* during the Spanish occupation.

Spain, anxious to make a good show in Tangier, made earnest efforts to relieve the shortages in the International Zone. From 1942 to 1944, Franco ensured annual supplies of more than five thousand tons of flour, in addition to significant quantities of olive oil, rice and beans, supplemented with regular imports of sugar, butter, beef and medical equipment. Nevertheless, sugar, gasoline oil and vegetables continued to be rationed and it was forbidden to drive cars at weekends. Prices rose steeply, but fell back in 1944. Mrs Kirby Green was right when she noted a brisk trade in property: Spanish interests were buying up as much real estate as possible in order to strengthen the Spanish position. The Spanish were not scrupulous about legal niceties in deciding ownership of property in Tangier, preferring to uphold and even grant financial support to claims against the British and French. They increased local taxes, heavily fined anyone making excessive use of the water supply and were generally arbitrary and often unlawful in many of their fiscal demands.

Tangier appeared to have become purely a Spanish city. Spanish troops made a point of parading, their officers in scarlet and gold at the head of cavalry detachments, contingents of Moroccan troops, regiments of the Foreign Legion and artillery. The Spanish language dominated the streets, cafés, offices and places of entertainment. The Moroccan franc still circulated, but official payments such as customs duties and taxes had to be paid in pesetas which, being in short supply, soared in value against the Moroccan currency. The cost of living rose artificially, pegged to the value of the peseta. The Spanish appeared to act in collusion with the Germans whose consulate-general was perceived as a headquarters for espionage. Contrary to assurances given, the circulation of the *Tangier Gazette* was interfered with, as was the administration of the British Post Office.

Tangier in the early 1940s, wrote Michael Davidson in his autobiography *The World, the Flesh and Myself*, 'was especially a mart for "intelligence" . . . Shabby little men with names like Pinto, Gonzales or Benmoussa haunted the foyers of belligerent consulates and furtively handed each other slips of paper in the Place de France or the Petit Socco; one at least, a Portuguese, would make his way every Friday from the British legation to the German, from the French to the Italian, collecting his wages from each.' With friends, Davidson would sit at dinner in the Hôtel de France, 'flanked by Enemies – Germans and Italians flaunting their musical-comedy uniforms. When one appeared among these parties of roistering foes, their voices would be raised in calculated but impersonal insult, or hushed into the whisper of artificial conspiracy . . . One seemed to swirl from one bar to another in an atmosphere of alcohol and hectic, though spurious, adventure; and the supporters of the two sides of the war aired the slogans of their countries like hearty cup-tie enthusiasts, or passed each other in the street with fastidious noses in the air.' Most Moroccans, on the contrary, says Davidson, 'urban Arab or pastoral Berber, were unmoved by the Nazarene conflict beyond the sea'.

Tangier was never bombed during the war: alarms were confined to occasional sightings of submarines off Cap Spartel and flashing warning lights from the Marshan cliffs. Known or reputed agents and officials of every nationality were dogged by local small fry – kids from the Socco market, car washers, shoeshine boys – who reported their every move to interested parties prepared to pay for enigmatic information. The American Office of Strategic Services thought it advisable to set up an espionage network in Morocco, in support of Free French sympathizers in Vichy-controlled French Morocco. They opted for Tangier as a base, importing a dozen OSS agents lightly disguised as vice-consuls, and busily set about establishing several secret radio stations, organizing an efficient information service, compiling a handbook for American troops who might soon invade the country, and – improbably – made a remarkable advance in the art of camouflage by inventing explosive camel turds to be strewn on the roads to inconvenience enemy traffic.

The German contingent in Tangier established their living quarters at the new and glamorous Hotel Rif which had opened for business in 1937. Among them, it was believed, were six professional assassins who had been ordered to dispose of all Allied agents in Tangier in the event of a German invasion. To counter this terrible threat, the American agents conscripted the hotel barman, a Cambridge-educated black African, who promised to poison the Germans' cocktails on a given signal. The Italians operated out of the Menebhi palace on the Marshan, and for rest and relaxation favoured the Restaurant Roma on the rue Mexique where fights regularly broke out between Fascists and anti-Fascists. The Americans lived at the El Minzah Hotel, and the Spanish lived everywhere. All mixed more or less indiscriminately at bars and restaurants throughout the city.

There were tensions, of course, throughout Tangier which, officially neutralized, irritated by enforced inactivity, found an outlet through the usual unrestricted gossip. Tangier society was quick to point the finger at sympathizers on either side of the political fence. The Allies, says David Woolman, a Tangier newspaper gossip columnist of the period, got up a blacklist of Tangerinos who co-operated with the Axis partners. 'Several hundred people found themselves thus stigmatized, among them Monsieur and Madame Porte whose bakery and teashop equalled any in Morocco. Apparently the Portes bought parcels of land and other property seized by the Germans from local French people, such dealings constituting the grossest treachery in the opinions of most Tangerinos. The Portes appeared on the blacklist twice, under "Monsieur" and again under "Madame". Fierce prejudice against the Portes remained among certain Tangerinos for a quarter century after the war.' Even today, there is still gossip about Fascist sympathizers who stayed on in Tangier and whose partialities during the war are not forgotten by elderly expatriates.

Recognizing the success of American and British military operations in North Africa in 1943 and 1944, Spain began to consider her position in regard to Tangier which, she suggested, should revert to its previous international character. By the time Germany surrendered in May 1945, Spain had already begun to withdraw troops from the city and by October 1945 had completely pulled out all military and police forces. In that month, the Mendoub returned to take up office again and the Committee of Control resumed the administration of Tangier. The Scottish artist James McBey, who had recently returned from New York with his American wife Marguerite to their house in Tangier, remarked on the post-war condition of the city in a letter of 22 July 1946. 'There is little outward change in Tangier since we saw it, exactly seven years ago. There is, though, a new hard core of refugees from Middle Europe who have cornered the gasoline, sugar, metal, cement, drinks, etc., so that most things are three times as expensive as they were in 1939. Gasoline oil and flour are rationed – a farce, as the black market is tolerated with good humour.'

A new wave of immigrant entrepreneurs was the yeast that encouraged the city to rise again, and natives adept at spotting a fast buck had not lost their beadiness of eye. 'Fortunes', wrote McBey, 'are being made every month because Tangier is the funnel through which Spain is being fed with everything which every nation pretends they will not sell her. "Export and Import" companies are being established weekly. Even I was approached and offered a good income for life if I would be a partner with a Jew and an Arab (without putting up a cent of capital.)'

The money market, too, was getting back into its stride. The currency question, to McBey who had started his working life as a young banker in Aberdeen, appeared comic.

The Spanish shops will accept only pesetas which fluctuate every quarter of an hour. At the present moment – 11 a.m. – they are 25.40 to the U.S. dollar. The French shops including the British Post Office, will accept only the French Moroccan franc, which, since we arrived two months ago, has risen from 310 to 220 to the US dollar. What or who causes the fluctuations here is a mystery as Tangier is a black market exchange. The sidewalks of what used to be the principal street are lined with money-changers, each with his little collapsible counter in front of him and a blackboard behind. On this is chalked what he is prepared to give, exactly like bookies at a racecourse. The £ sterling is way down about $3.40.

The McBeys found their house in the Old Mountain district of the city had survived, though pretty much a mess. Others had not been so lucky – their houses had been stolen away, stone by stone. The Spanish, somewhat neglectful of foreign-owned property, had planted a dead horse in the conduit which supplied the McBey's house with water, killing most of their precious and rare goldfish.

'The English had a bad time here during the Spanish occupation,' McBey learned, though the Spanish had been 'a bit wary of molesting the Americans'. There had been, according to McBey, only five US citizens outside of the Legation staff in 1939, but now there were anything between three to four hundred. They had opened two new US radio stations and it was rumoured 'that in the Diplomatic Forest, 9 miles south, an American city is being built of prefabricated houses. Real estate in the town is about the same price as Germantown, Pa., and buyers are hunting down every patch of land.'

The British and Americans, in the summer of 1945, were regarded as primarily responsible for deciding the future of the International Zone, and France was recognized as an interested party. At a conference in Paris in August, it was decided that until such time as plans for a new, more permanent multi-national organization could be prepared, the International Zone should be administered very much as before. Business, in effect, as usual. But there had been political developments in Morocco that the Paris conference largely disregarded. The Allied victory had stimulated the Moroccan desire for freedom, and some weight had been given to that cause in 1943 at the Casablanca Conference when Roosevelt had promised Sultan Mohammed V that he would do all in his power to support the Moroccans in their wish to be rid of the French Protectorate.

The French, whatever Roosevelt might have said about the matter, had no intention of giving up their Moroccan Protectorate, and many Moroccans felt bitterly betrayed when, as it appeared to them, the status quo ante was re-established at the end of the war. There were still three Zones – French, Spanish, International – still ruled to all intents and purposes by foreign powers ostensibly as protectors but in effect as colonialists. Nationalism was about to become a potent force that would vitally involve neutralized Tangier as a centre of operations for nationalist leaders prepared to fight for the independence of their country.

By 1947, Sultan Mohammed V had been persuaded that the arguments of the Independence Party, the Istiqlal, founded in 1944, were just. He insisted – against all French pressure – on paying a State visit to Tangier where, in April 1947, he made a historic speech in favour of Moroccan freedom and independence. Michael Davidson

> went to Tangier in the royal train (the only European on board it, I think), with the Sherifian flags draped about its engine's brow. A Triumph in imperial Rome must have looked like a village fête beside that imperial progress. The single-track railway was lined by delighted Moors. Beyond the Franco-Spanish border the train pulled up in open country, beside a huge imperial marquee where the Sultan was welcomed by grandees who lived under Spain and where he reclined for hours over a Moorish banquet. Tangier, crammed with tribesmen from mountain and plain, was as turbulently joyful as London on Victory night. The fantastic success of this royal desecration of the 'colonialist' temple surprised even its Istiqlal instigators.

The Sultan's speech, which significantly omitted a passage referring to solidarity with France and failed to recall the friendship that united the two countries, enraged France and delighted Morocco. Mohammed V explicitly endorsed the Arab League, linking Morocco with the larger Arab world, praised the democracies of Britain and America, emphasized the need for education and modern technology in Morocco, drew attention to the fact that Moroccan lives and resources had been given in the recent war, and indicated that his country now had legitimate grounds to seek its freedom. The State visit to Tangier was in itself important, quite aside from the views expressed in the speech: the presence of the Sultan in the city, in the International Zone, emphasized his spiritual leadership over the whole country, over all the Zones.

There had been civil disturbances for several years throughout Morocco, but Tangier had not yet been seriously affected by the independence movement until Istiqlal leaders, fleeing the French Zone, settled in the city and established a weekly newspaper fiercely critical of the colonial policy of France and openly espousing the nationalist cause. The French, leaning on the Committee of Control, managed to have the paper suppressed with some show of constitutional authority. Tangier became more or less the *de facto* focus for Istiqlal conspiracy, and officials of the movement were regarded with some suspicion by the authorities who had them watched, followed and occasionally arrested. The Sultan, increasingly resistant to the French, refused to condemn the Istiqlal. In April 1951, four groups of the Moroccan nationalist movement, including the Istiqlal, met in Tangier to unite in a Moroccan Nationalist Front. They agreed on the fundamental principle of complete independence in what came to be known as the Pact of Tangier.

If they thought at all about the effects of nationalism on their city, most Tangerinos tended to dismiss it as idle talk designed mostly to frustrate the more absorbing business of getting rich. From the end of the war, Tangier boomed as a honey pot for the sticky-fingered. Money, and the living, was easy. Foreign residents appreciated the benefits of expatriate life: there were no personal or corporate taxes and import duties were low – 12 per cent on most items, 7 per cent on gold and diamonds, 2¼ per cent on liquor, textiles and machinery. Banking laws were rudimentary, and it cost ridiculously little to form a Tangier Corporation. Public utilities – water, bus, telephone and electric companies – were privately owned, effectively monopolies, and most import licences also tended to be monopolistic in effect.

In *Let It Come Down*, Paul Bowles contrasted Tangier in this period with New York:

You must see how alike the two places are. The life revolves wholly about the making of money. Practically everyone is dishonest. In New York you have Wall Street, here you have the Bourse. Not like the bourses in other places, but the soul of the city, its *raison d'être*. In New York you have the slick financiers, here the money-changers. In New York you have your racketeers. Here you have your smugglers. And each man's waiting to suck the blood of the next ... The place is a model of corruption ... Tangier's a one-horse town that happens to have its own government. And you know damned well that all governments live on corruption. I don't care what sort – socialist, totalitarian, democratic – it's all the same. Naturally in a little place like this you come in contact with the government constantly. God knows, it's inevitable. And so you're always conscious of the corruption. It's that simple.

Under its international administration, Tangier was a free exchange market for every type of currency: profits on speculation and money changing were, in theory, unlimited. In practice, virtually any currency was acceptable even at street level – particularly pounds sterling, US dollars and Portuguese escudos, in addition to Spanish pesetas and, officially legal tender, the Moroccan franc. This fiscal freedom, amounting to virtual financial anarchy, naturally attracted a large number of banks and a significant amount of capital. The influx of wealthy refugees and expatriates of every kind with money to invest had rocketed land values. Capital was largely absorbed by a building boom – new office and apartment blocks mushroomed, altering the appearance not only of the modern town but substantially affecting the appearance and character of the old city. By 1955, the *New York Times* could report that 'Tangier, the boom city of yesteryear, is now a building contractor's nightmare.'

The hope was that Tangier would become a tourist paradise: the beaches of the city and the surrounding coasts were unparalleled; the climate was mild in winter and gloriously sunny in summer; access by ferry from Gibraltar, or by direct flight from the major capitals of Europe, was easy. In 1952, Tangier was visited by some hundred thousand travellers, about thirty thousand of whom arrived by air. The city was well furnished with modern comforts, sharply contrasting a modern, prosperous, bustling, even chic new town with the picturesque, exotic, enigmatic charms of the traditional Medina and Casbah. There was talk of establishing a Casino, so that the city might rival Monte Carlo as a resort for the rich and reckless and the optimistic poor. The curious tourist, hitting Tangier for the first time, found much to interest and please him. *Aficionados* of Tangier, already familiar with the pre-war city and nostalgic for its former glamour, tended to regret the – literally – concrete effects of progress.

From Rom Landau, a devoted apologist for Morocco, Tangier in the early 1950s was disappointing.

There were few potent reminders of Africa or of 'the mystery of the Orient' . . . There were more Europeans than Moors about the streets, and Moorish life and architecture formed but a half-hidden background to the far more glaring foreign features: ugly modern houses, oily Europeans, chiefly Spanish, and aggressively luxurious American taxis. Though Tangier lies actually on the Atlantic, it is just another Mediterranean town. But it is not Africa . . . Instead Tangier has become the El Dorado of financial sharks, profiteers, black marketeers, smugglers and of the *déracinés* from every country under the sun. There are aristocrats, professors, former courtiers, and landowners from Hungary, Austria, Poland, Spain, Russia and France . . . And they come to Tangier because it has no income tax, and offers infinite scope for unorthodox financial transactions.

With a barely repressed 'Pshaw', Landau remarked how,

Above the generous semicircle of a white-sanded beach, lined with a graceful avenue of palms, rises the town in a gangrenous conglomeration of flamboyant concrete semi-skyscrapers. Farther back lie the residential districts of Victorian villas, opulent and complacent behind the orange, lemon and oleander trees of their gardens and festooned with purple bougainvillea and pink geranium. The Tangier of bucolic diplomatic picnics, of cunning bandits capturing distinguished foreigners to obtain ransom, and of picturesque cavalcades into the green country beyond the town is but a memory . . . Judged on its own merits, it has many of the characteristic virtues of Mediterranean towns, and a strongly marked individuality. But you cannot expect that from the combination of escapism, financial jugglery and diplomatic cocktail-parties a soul can be born. Tangier appears completely soulless.

In the novelistic voice of a Moroccan character, Paul Bowles in *Let It Come Down* remarked that Europeans in Tangier 'were more prudent than passionate; their fears were stronger than their desires. Most of them *had* no real desire, apart from that to make money, which after all is merely a habit. Bur once they had the money they never seemed to use it for a specific object or purpose.' If Europeans in Morocco did not have a soul above petty material considerations, and had created Tangier to satisfy their soulless demands, the Moroccans themselves were affected by their inability or disinclination to participate fully in the modern world they had been permitted to glimpse. *Let It Come Down* gives voice again to its principal Moroccan character who, in contrast to the Europeans, 'knew exactly what he wanted, always, and so did his countrymen. Most of them only wanted three lambs to slaughter at Aid el Kebir and new clothing for the family at Mouloud and Aid es Seghir. It was not much, but it was definite, and they bent all their efforts to getting it. Still, he could not think of the mass of Moroccans without contempt. He had no patience with their ignorance and backwardness; if he damned the Europeans with one breath, he was bound to damn the Moroccans with the next.'

Tangier's population in 1952 amounted to some 160,000 to 180,000 souls, of whom more than 100,000 were Moroccans. Tourism and attending to the domestic needs of the resident foreign community provided the principal employment for Tanjawis. The multi-national administration of Tangier was inherently weak, fundamentally flawed by constant and recurring disputes between the various nations concerned. The increasing native population, and the conflicts in the Committee of Control enabled the Moroccan nationalists to flourish mostly unchecked. The postal system particularly, three distinct operations run by three different countries, facilitated censor-free communications between the nationalists in and beyond the International Zone.

In 1952, Sultan Mohammed V and his son, Crown Prince Hassan, were ignominiously deported to Madagascar by the French, resulting in a campaign by Moroccan terrorists who were in turn subjected to a counter-terrorist campaign by the French.

For the first time in more than forty years, there was rioting in Tangier. A large mob of Tanjawis gathered in the Medina and erupted into the Grand Socco, furiously demanding Moroccan independence and an end to the International Zone. The demonstration was at first confined by police to the native city, but nine people were reportedly killed and about eighty injured when police fired into the mob which set about looting, smashing up property, setting fire to cars and stoning any foreigners incautious enough to have been caught out on the streets. A Dutch teenager was beaten to death in the Socco. The riot gave a cue to Spain which, having tried to provoke trouble in various ways for the International Zone since the end of the war, now pointed to the unsettled condition of the city and demanded revision of the Statute of Tangier. The Anglo-French agreement of 1945, the Spanish claimed, was clearly no longer adequate, and Spanish intervention was necessary to protect substantial Spanish assets and interests in Tangier. In November 1952, a protocol was signed by the international powers represented on the Committee of Control amending the 1945 agreement. Spain was virtually restored to her pre-war status in Tangier.

The Tangier riot had shaken the confidence of businessmen and bankers in the city who were now seriously worried about the safety of their money. Investment flowing into the city noticeably dried up, and current investors fretfully considered their position. Money began to leak out to more secure havens. Anti-French demonstrations continued elsewhere in Morocco for the next few years, until it became clear that not even the more responsible nationalists could control popular feeling. In October 1955, Mohammed V was recalled from exile in Madagascar to Paris. The next month, on the twenty-eighth anniversary of his accession as Sultan, he returned to Morocco to constitute a government whose purpose would be 'to elaborate institutional reforms for the purpose of making Morocco a democratic state with a constitutional monarchy and to conduct negotiations with France destined to make Morocco acquire the status of an independent state united to France by permanent links of a freely consented and defined interdependence.'

On 29 October 1956, the Statute of Tangier was abrogated, followed by the abandonment of the last privileges derived from the Act of Algeciras and other pre-occupation treaties. Tangier, which had been rocked by riots in August, rejoiced with the rest of the country. Some further violence did break out on 30 October, but the popular demonstration on 18 November to mark the Feast of the Throne, the day on which the Sultan officially took over as chief of the new Moroccan government, was wholly peaceful and jubilant. The eye-witness account of David Woolman describes 'an endless parade through streets suddenly bowered with palm fronds and decked with large home-made banners carrying nationalistic slogans. Nobody seems to have organised this parade, and anyone who wanted to, singing the Istiqlal song, giving the new three-fingered salute (Allah, the Sultan, Morocco), and fervently kissing enormous portraits of Mohammed V, sauntered along behind bands ranging from the Fire Brigade's uniformed musicians to jellaba-clad tribesmen banging drums and cymbals and playing squealing flutes.'

Not everyone was delighted:

on the Boulevard a single distraught Frenchman climbed a tree and from its low branches cried out again and again, 'Vive la France! Vive la France!' until led away in tearful despair ... That night the authorities entertained the city with a brilliant fireworks display set off from the beach, and in the Socco Chico hawkers sold gullible Tanjawis white cards with a likeness of the Sultan outlined in black; if you looked at the Sultan for a few seconds and then looked up at the sky, you would see the Sultan outlined against the moon. Verily, His Majesty could go any place! Tangier's Coca-Cola plant got credit for giving the crowds one thousand cases of that very American beverage.

The international administration continued to function until late October 1956. The representatives of the powers governing the International Zone had met at Fedala, just outside Casablanca, to consider the future of Tangier. But there really had been very little to detain them: clearly, the city's future was as an integral part of Morocco. And so it was decided that the international regime should be abolished, the existing financial, monetary, economic and commercial conditions of Tangier to remain in force until the Sultan promulgated a Royal Charter establishing a new system which, it was envisaged, would not differ appreciably from the existing regime. Despite reassurances, there was some anxiety among Tangerinos that the good times, the high-living years for foreign residents with substantial assets in Tangier, might be ending – one of the more telling details being a new edict banning the sale of liquor within a certain distance from a mosque. There were a great many mosques, and a great many Spanish, Jewish and other foreign-owned bars. The mosques stayed open: the bars closed.

Mohammed V's Royal Charter, guaranteeing a free money market, the right of unrestricted imports and exports, and other useful privileges came into effect on 29 August 1957. There was a general revival of optimism among speculators and entrepreneurs, in the event short-lived since six months notice of abrogation of the Charter was given in October 1959 at the insistence, said some malcontents, of Casablanca merchants jealous of Tangier's special status. Others claimed that the government had been inspired by xenophobic and socialist motives, vexed that most of Tangier's wealth was concentrated in foreign hands. The government itself defended its action by saying that the country's unity depended on equal treatment for all its provinces, and that no one of them should be a privileged haven for foreign capitalists. The foreign capitalists promptly moved their money out of Tangier, almost literally overnight. Among other financial institutions, the oldest native bank in the city – Pariente's, which had been founded in 1805 – transferred to Geneva. The panic spread to more than two hundred and fifty companies which were quickly dissolved, and large numbers of the city's leading merchants stole away, abandoning the city to serious unemployment, widespread poverty and a lack of any immediate means to improve the situation, which became so bad that the Moroccan government was obliged to come to the aid of Tangier by undertaking a number of long-delayed municipal projects in order to absorb some of the unemployed. One motive for the abrogation of the Charter had been to stop the leakage of capital out of Tangier: but now there was none to leak. The free money market drain had been plugged after the bath water had run out. The government and its supporters were philosophical about the politics of the matter – abrogation of the Charter represented a victory for doctrinal politics over economic expediency. Tangier's new poverty was honourable if it meant wealth to a Morocco that intended to develop economically as a whole. On 19 April 1961 Tangier became fully integrated on terms of parity with the other provinces of the country into the Moroccan state.

Tangier felt like a poor relation stripped of her finery. The British Post Office had shut its outpost in the city in April 1957, and in February 1958 the Spanish Post Office also closed its doors. In 1958 there had been a crackdown on smugglers – the law prohibited boats of less than one hundred tons from loading tobacco and liquor in the port. The smuggling business was expected merely to move its operations to Gibraltar. A new currency, the dirham, with a value of one hundred Moroccan francs, was introduced. There had been a few alarming incidents, mostly rancorous confrontations between resident foreigners in Tangier and groups of natives who shouted insults. Foreigners were 'obscene', they had 'robbed Morocco', they 'must die'. The smart and expensive shops along the Boulevard had closed and were taken over by tacky souvenir sellers who hawked the local handicrafts and garments made in the city. Minor hand work was virtually all that was left to the citizens: there was precious little in the way of serious industry or commerce.

In these circumstances, tourism had dropped off – but tourism was likely to be the main source of income for many Tanjawis who, paradoxically, were more ready to resent an influx of foreigners than welcome them. Nationalism was still new and strongly supported: there was no desire for colonialism in another form, for further dependence on those perceived to have been oppressors. Independence provoked national pride, but that pride had to take something of a tumble when it was recognized that money could only be obtained and skills learned from outsiders. There had been some speculation in the foreign Press that Mohammed V would give Tangier to one of his sons as a Principality which might flourish as an international tourist playground along the lines of Monaco, but nothing came of that notion.

Still, there were signs that Tangier's potential as an amusing resort might be perking up. A *London Evening Standard* report of 23 April 1960 indicated that the British expatriates were keeping the flag flying:

Tangier, that rakish old girl who is having respectability forced upon her at last is not accepting this unhappy fate without a struggle . . . The British colony includes Mr and Mrs W. B. C. Weld-Forester, parents of Lady Bute, Mr David Herbert, Lord Pembroke's brother, author Rupert Croft-Cooke, and Lady Scott, mother of David Scott, Clerk of the House of Commons. She first went to Tangier during the Boer War. The colony may even increase. Diana, Lady Strathcona, flew there for Easter with Miss Fiona Campbell, Lord Stratheden's youngest daughter, to look at houses. Nor has the change of status deterred British tourists. Tangier was packed with them at Easter. Noel Coward spent four days here just before Easter.

The presence of the Woolworth heiress, Barbara Hutton, living a life of lavish luxury in her Casbah palace of Sidi Hosni, was a tourist lure, and there were many newspaper and magazine articles commenting excitedly on Tangier's change of status, making much of the city's sensational past. The emphasis, for nervous tourists, was on how respectable Tangier had become. Arthur Eperon, a travel writer, commented that 'Tangier – the smuggler's paradise, headquarters of modern-day pirates, home of international spivs – became as strictly law abiding as Southampton.' Lady Savernake, writing in the *Daily Telegraph* in February 1958, was at pains to assure the citizens of the Home Counties that the reception by officials at Tangier airport was friendly and uncomplicated, that there were luxurious, well-regulated hotels in the city from which to make darting, daring excursions into the winding streets of the Casbah, that the food was not terrifying, and that among high spots 'the most popular was the Whisky à Gogo with a "Hernando's Hideaway" atmosphere.' As a hot spot, it would not perhaps have been out of place in Croydon.

Kenneth Allsop, reporting in the *Daily Mail* of 13 June 1959, just missed Tennessee Williams who had been 'recently sipping mint tea' in the Petit Socco, 'the seething, clamorous "Little Market" ... But tomorrow he will be succeeded by a swelling stream of English and American writers who are diverting from the older strongholds of the arts along the French Riviera and in Spain to this almost-anything-goes North African playground ... The indigenous Tangier aroma, compounded of flowers, spices, hashish and Arab drains, is infiltrated by the pungent smell of typewriter ribbons from the overheated portables of best-selling London and New York novelists.' Allsop had visited the expatriate British writer Rupert Croft-Cooke in his villa, Alec Waugh 'who is following up his colossal success *Island In the Sun* with the story of life and living in a tropical oil camp' in his apartment at the Hotel Velazquez just off the Boulevard Pasteur, and 'in a suave bar named The Parade I encountered Gerald Brenan, whose last of many books on Spain was *South from Granada*, on his way through a hitch-hiking trip into Southern Morocco. In a tough waterfront flamenco tavern, the Mar Chica, I had a midnight appointment with Paul Bowles, the American author of *The Sheltering Sky*.'

Bustling about, Allsop met actresses, literary agents, socialites and a few more writers. 'Tangerines by adoption include Robin Maugham, Anita Ekberg, Francis Bacon, Lady Diana Cooper, Cecil Beaton, Lord May, Dawn Addams, Margaret Leighton, Errol Flynn, and a shifting, shifty population of contraband boat crews, confidence tricksters, Mayfair spivs and women with an international beat, men on the run and girls on the make. One's nightlife is an interesting mixture of Debrett's *Peerage* and the *Police Gazette*.'

In the summer of 1960, British newspapers reported that in June 'Detectives worked on a big "clean-up-the-city" drive – because the British are on their way.' Sixty-four girls had allegedly been swept into police patrol vans and driven to headquarters. 'They were ordered to leave the tourists alone – and warned that anyone caught swindling visitors would be jailed.' There was no mention of boys in the report: girls, it may be thought, were the least of any problem. Smuggling, too, according to the *Sunday Dispatch*, had suffered since Tangier had come under full Customs control in April 1960. The smugglers, it was said, had moved their operations to Gibraltar, and illegal imports into Tangier had dropped by eight hundred and fifty million American cigarettes.

In the *Daily Telegraph* of 23 September 1962, Hugo Charteris presented a generally gloomy report on conditions for the quarter of a million inhabitants of Tangier. He described it as 'a town with a long international tradition suffering from arrested development'. There had been an increase in the number of British residents since the integration of Tangier into the Moroccan state – 'this in spite of being required to fill in a return stating the number, sex and age of their camels, an intrusion which is regarded by some of them as the thin end of the wedge. Today almost every European resident of Tangier is either anxious or pretending not to be anxious about what will happen next. Will Tangier "die" altogether?' Charteris, exploring the question, decided that it might precariously survive.

On the whole, tourism seemed the most likely money-spinner that would absorb the energies of the estimated twenty thousand unemployed. 'Tangier will anyhow remain a centre of tourism *de demi luxe* but the all-in tour, which accounts for most of Spanish tourism, should soon be possible in Morocco.' Again, the safety of Tangier was emphasized – Tanjawis were described as 'honest and civilised', neither resentful nor envious of riches ostentatiously displayed. 'Was it foreigners who gave the place a bad name?' asked Charteris of one European barman – Dean, no doubt – who said: 'I've lived in Tangier for thirty years, and the longer I'm here the less good I've got to say about the place. People come here because they can practise any vice they like without feeling an atmosphere of hindrance or disapproval.' One resident suggested to Charteris that the abundance of good-looking young men and boys who 'turn up on the main beach as conscientiously as many Europeans attend their office' represented an economic benefit to Tangier as one of the city's strongest tourist and residential attractions. However, Charteris noted that a firmer line was being taken by the authorities in respect of the safety of juveniles and 'several foreign visitors have been "asked to leave"'.

His 'last memory of down-and-out Tangier was a curious one. My wife and I were sitting in the Rif Hotel when suddenly a poor cabaret was enlivened by one of the best exhibitions of jive I have ever seen. The young man looked French and the girl might have been half-French. I asked if they were on tour from Paris. "No", said the waiter. "That is the Moroccan Minister of Commerce." The following day I boarded the ship for Gibraltar. In the bar, a fellow traveller began telling me of a night club he had visited. "There was a wonderful jive dancer there," he said. "Do you know who it was? The Governor of Rabat."' Charteris drew no conclusions 'from the unemployment, the signs of chaos and the two dancing Ministers' – and it might take a novelist to render the combination significant – but 'Tangier will have to learn new wiles if it is to attract millions of holiday-makers.'

As a holiday resort, Tangier in the early-to-mid Sixties was somewhat neglected by the government which preferred, apparently, to upgrade facilities at the southern resorts of Agadir, Marrakesh and Alhucemas. New beach developments were also financed in the north, beyond Tangier, between Ceuta and Tetuan. The packaged holiday trip became more popular; formerly remote and virtually inaccessible places like the mountain and desert communities of Goulimine, Tafraout, Zagora, Tinerhir and far Erfoud, were opened up to inquisitive trippers, to the dismay of the rich, the artistic and the snobbish who deserted Morocco as it became more commonplace. Tangier particularly was perceived as having gone seriously down-market. The city had never been particularly Moroccan – centuries of colonization had seen to that – and now that its international glamour had wholly vanished it seemed to some, such as David Woolman, to be no more than 'a tough port with just enough left-overs – the beach, the Medina and Casbah – to catch at the throats of those, both Tanjawi and foreign, who love her, and to remind them of her former charisma'.

By the mid-Sixties, Tangier did conjure up some new wiles – or rather resurrect some ancient traditions – to milk a new breed of tourist. The rich and sophisticated had largely abandoned the city, but to take their place came a constant caravan of hippies who distressed Tanjawis less by their dress and kif-smoking habits than by the fact that they had no money to throw recklessly around. They holed up in small hotels and cheap rentals, ate native food, dressed in ethnic garments, and – to the outrage of serious professional street beggars – panhandled in the Petit Socco. Some set up as amateur pimps, hawking their girlfriends. Tanjawis cheerfully sold them kif, then just as cheerfully reported them to the police for a commission or reward. The police picked up the drug purchasers, seized their kif or hash, and promptly recycled it back into the local economy. It was all they were likely to get out of the youngsters, and they did a brisk trade.

Gavin Young, who first visited Morocco as an employee of Radio Maroc in 1957 before becoming a journalist for the *Observer*, returned to Tangier in 1988 when he found the inhabitants, at the behest of the authorities, in a frenzy of whitewashing walls and houses in anticipation of a visit to the city by King Hassan II. The King is coming! The King is coming! The promise or the rumour is constant – the King, it is said, is ill-disposed towards Tangier: a visit is ever-imminent and ever-postponed. After a while, the rumour becomes a fable of the city; one begins to wonder whether, in fact, the King exists at all. Like the tantalizing prospect of the Barbarians in the poem by Cavafy, the arrival will portend great changes for good or ill. The city, forever waiting for something or someone, awaits the Barbarians or the King. Passivity is a condition of its life.

Finally, the King came on Monday, 6 June 1988 – by royal train from Rabat. But he had arrived merely to embark on a yacht that would transport him to Algeria for a conference of Maghrebi leaders. His foot had no sooner touched the ground than it was aboard his ship waiting at the port which is conveniently close to the railway terminus. Nevertheless, for this significant occasion, detailed arrangements had been made. Access to the port area was seriously restricted, the entire beach was cleared of Tanjawis, Tangerinos and tourists, and residents of apartment blocks facing the beach were ordered by police to remove their shrubs and plants from their balconies lest a sniper conceal himself behind a convenient cactus or particularly large pot of geraniums. The King had survived several attempts on his life, and as a result his *baraka* – his charisma – was now so great that, careful security precautions aside, he was regarded as leading a charmed life. This was no small thing – the mere fact of his survival immeasurably increased his personal and royal power.

Tanjawis greeted their King enthusiastically, in anticipation – remarked Gavin Young – of reaping handsome rewards. 'They are hoping against hope that His Majesty has plans to inaugurate Morocco's Costa Brava and permit casinos, discos, duty-free shops and heaven knows what else up and down the Mediterranean coast of the once rebellious Rif.' If he intends any such thing, the King has so far kept quiet about it. Meanwhile, the restaurants appeared to Young to be inadequate: 'Tangier is no gourmet's paradise despite a delicious cuisine. For some reason, Moroccans – who eat superbly in their own houses – seem incapable to run really good restaurants.' The bars, too, are disappointing and too few: certainly there is nothing now like Dean's, of fond memory: 'I met Ian Fleming there, usually nursing a triple vodka and tonic and enjoying a break from dictating 5,000 words a day of *Diamonds Are Forever* in the Minzah. We used to stroll around the long, sickle-shaped beach of Tangier – now, I see, sadly built up – while he stowed seashells into a battered briefcase and eagerly pointed out potentially useful patches of greenery. ("Now there's a good place to read a book or make love to a girl, don't you think?").'

For those who have long memories of Tangier as an international enclave, the rest of the world must seem provincial. And yet Tangier itself had always been provincial, an enclosed, esoteric, incestuous society feeding off itself, largely heedless of international disturbances elsewhere. The seismic shocks of European war had been recorded in Tangier merely as tremors: foreign occupation, far from destroying the city, had largely preserved it less through the vice of officious interference than through the virtue of being almost wholly concerned with its own internal conflicts. A newer, Westernized city had been imposed upon the old, like sugar icing on a rich fruit cake. The substantial body of the cake had not been devoured, but merely decorated to give it a more toothsome appearance. The Moroccans themselves, going about their business, had taken advantage in their traditional manner of the opportunities presented by the weaknesses of their supposed oppressors and profited themselves as best they could, often decrying the abuses of the existing administration but properly wary of alternatives.

Tangier had been largely an artificial, legal construct: a thing of Acts and Agreements, Pacts and Protocols, Concords and Conventions, an international diplomatic fiction; a place with no meaning or reality beyond the ingenious invention of foreign lawyers and legislators. It had been a paper city, a place created and sustained by signatures and seals. To this extent, it was a natural place of exile since exile naturally denies unwelcome reality. Denial often becomes a conscious defiance in which absurdity becomes a commonplace. The lives of the exiles in Tangier pointed up the world as it exists as absurd: exile is perhaps a distorting mirror held up to reality. The international administration of Tangier in effect stopped time – as the court clock at Versailles was stopped at the hour the King died. The city became a place out of time, in which exiles could continue the habits, the routines, the conditions of life that had vanished elsewhere. After a while, return to the homeland became unthinkable.

Even today in Tangier it is not difficult to find British exiles who take *The Times*, sport signed photographs of royalty on their occasional tables, serve boiled potatoes at lunch and regard the Conservative Party in government as the saviour and only safe custodian of a country they cannot afford to live in and a society which would be prompt to condemn some of their practices. The English church in the city, St Andrew's, is well attended each year for the annual Remembrance Day service at which, a few years ago, the subject of the sermon was the moral choice to be made between dying honourably or clinging on to a degraded life. Rather a pointed theme, it might be thought. The preacher preferred, personally, death before dishonour – a choice dramatically made by a former incumbent of the parish who, allegedly too fond of young Moroccan boys, put his head in a gas oven and asphyxiated himself. The sermon dwelt on the sacrifices made by England and English soldiers on foreign fields of battle, and the service concluded to the music of hymns pounded out with gusto by an elderly lady pumping energetically on the pedals of her harmonium.

Within the space of a few minutes, she had worked her way through a repertoire that included *Land of Hope and Glory*, *Jerusalem*, *There'll Always Be an England*, and *Rule Britannia*. One Moroccan gentleman, a convert to Christianity, stood by the harmonium singing lustily all the words to the anthems, holding in his heart God alone knows what ineffable vision of that supposedly green and pleasant land.

Exile is principally about the loss of Eden, about rootless residence by the waters of Babylon. One is exiled not so much *to* somewhere as *from* a place: the condition of exile implies losing touch with the homeland to which it is impossible – too frightening – to return, and which acquires the glamour of a lost ideal. Tangier must, to a degree, have become a fictional place, an invention of those narcissists who, seeking a reflection of Eden, are swallowed up by waters of Babylon.

Like a *grande horizontale*, Tangier may appear to pander to most fantasies: no request may be too recondite for her to entertain and satisfy. Her gift, or curse, may be the knowledge that nothing is forbidden and that no taste is incapable of gratification – at a price: the price of one's soul, one's exile from Eden, one's final and irrevocable realization that one has become a victim and a prisoner, all the time believing oneself to have been a victor, free to take one's leave. Tangier is *La Belle Dame Sans Merci*, her lovers rendered bloodless by her demands. This is not so very fanciful: one of her own sons, the novelist Tahar ben Jelloun, has recognized his mother city as a *Maja Desnuda* resting by the sea in an eternal siesta. 'Tangier! Even swollen and stretched by all extremities, you continue to astonish me. I like to leave you for the joy of returning. I love to betray you, the better to compare you with other faces. I know now that a town is a story one never ceases to tell and which will remain ever unfinished, closed on a mystery and an enigma.'

Paul and
Jane Bowles
in Tangier

At two-thirty in the afternoon Paul Bowles is sitting propped up in a monastic single bed, wrapped in an orange-yellow bathrobe, his quiff of white hair brushed forward like a puff of cloud above his brow. He is eating half a melon: 'just finishing my lunch'. Two friends – Phillip Ramey, a young New York composer, and Rodrigo Rey Rosa, a handsome Guatemalan writer in his twenties – are somewhat in attendance at this *levée*. I suggest that he might be Tiberius in Capri, and remark that Norman Douglas, in *Siren Land*, had attempted to rehabilitate the reputation of Tiberius. Bowles, engaged mostly with digging into his melon, frankly grins. Suddenly, blue-eyed, he looks now like Tom Sawyer painted by Norman Rockwell. He gets up and slowly dresses. It is June 1988.

Tangier in 1988 appeared to Gavin Young, writing in the *Observer*, to be a 'a good-natured place' that had survived its purple patches, particularly those of its expatriate writers since the 1950s: 'the southern baroque of the Tennessee Williams–Truman Capote phase, the whoops-a-daisy *Naked Lunch* phase of William Burroughs, the priapic hurly-burly of Joe Orton'. Surviving them all is Paul Bowles, characterized by Young as the city's 'American writer-in-residence *par excellence*' who 'works in a little flat there, a neatly dressed, gentle, humorous man, almost a recluse'. Bowles born on 30 December 1910 in New York City, is at this date seventy-eight years old. He lives in the modern part of the city, a stone's throw from the former American Consulate building. The apartment is spartan, brown-toned, almost characterless. The windows are shaded by thick foliage that runs rampant across the face of the high-rise block. No pictures hang on the walls because, says Bowles, they won't stand the strain.

Through his novels, stories and translations, Bowles has virtually created our perception of Tangier. It is well nigh impossible to

walk along a street or wander the alleys of the Casbah and Medina
without feeling one is walking through a Bowles novel. His writing
haunts and informs his readers, the most devoted of whom must
feel a faint exasperation at the pervasiveness of his influence on
their own capacity to understand and come to terms with the city
for themselves. Tangier lives, largely, through Paul Bowles who
has rendered it not only in his own fiction but equally through his
translations of the stories, the modern folk tales, of young Tanjawis.
Tangier is to Bowles as Dublin is to Joyce, as pre-war Berlin is to
Isherwood, as Alexandria is to Durrell, as the Scottish Border
Country is to Scott. He has set the city in aspic.

He patiently demonstrates how to work his tape recorder, super-
vises the insertion and testing of a cassette, and begins to talk – to
reply warily to questions, at least – sitting on brown floor-cushions
ranged against a wall of bookcases. Towards the end of the tape,
an hour later, Mohammed ben Chaib el Hajjem – better known
under his pen-name as the novelist Mohammed Mrabet – enters
silently, with the stealth of a cat. He shakes hands wordlessly, and
settles on a low banquette where he fills his *sebsi* with kif and
lounges comfortably to smoke in what appears to be a contempla-
tive manner. He chooses, perhaps, not to talk – or is beyond words:
it is difficult to tell. Behind the silence is a constant alertness. He
is a good-looking, middle-aged man, more Spanish-looking than
Moroccan in his gipsy appearance. His presence is not inhibiting:
he is part of the worn furnishings, his right to be there tacitly
acknowledged, his place hallowed by usage and custom, by habit
and familiarity.

The custom, since Bowles has no telephone, is that visitors may
call at the apartment most afternoons from about four o'clock without previous notice. For a man said to be retiring, if not reclusive,
he receives a great many visitors who converse with him in Spanish,
French, Moroccan Arabic and English. This afternoon, a companionable silence is broken by the irruption of an American journalist, representing some Texas newspapers, who has called to
'confirm a couple of rumours'. She asks whether Bowles will mind
if she takes a few notes. He makes no objection, and she pulls a
hefty pad of lined foolscap from her bag. She had come tentatively
into the gloomy room, pushing aside the curtain that separates the
living room from the lobby, introducing herself with reference to a

mutual acquaintance, a young American photographer called Cherie. Cherie, she says, has summed up Mr Bowles in one word. 'Can you guess what that word can be?'

She tilts her head and adopts a provocative air, poised to burst out with this significant word. Bowles makes a token effort to locate an appropriate word, but the process of reductivism defeats him. 'Magical,' she says triumphantly. The word explodes like a confetti bomb in the dark little apartment. 'She said you were magical, Mr Bowles.' Bowles looks very faintly astonished. It is perhaps not the word that had occurred to him. 'The enchanter,' I say, compounding confusion. 'The mage of Morocco,' I add, to break the short silence. Bowles looks, if anything, even more nonplussed. At least, he has no comment to make and the word 'magical' drops quietly through a crack in the floor and drifts away towards the Rif mountains, dwelling-place of djinns and district of dream-inducing grass.

The first rumour requiring confirmation is quickly disposed of. 'Is it true that Gore Vidal owns a house in Casbah?' Her capacity to astonish or to be astonished is evidently a gift: it is instantly clear that she must mean York Castle, presently owned by a French interior designer, Yves Vidal. Vidal being a name regularly bruited about in the salons of Europe and America, it is understandable that it must imply 'Gore' as a necessary prefix. Bowles expresses some reserved amazement that Gore Vidal should possibly own – or wish to own – property in the Tangier Casbah. The second rumour is presented in the form of a tentative inquiry. 'You've been here, in Tangier, how long? Fifteen years?' Correction is gently made. 'I've been here – on and off – since 1931. Fifty-seven years.' She writes this down on her pad, and laughs a little nervously. 'Oh.' 'I lived on the Mountain,' remarks Bowles, a piece of information gratuitously offered and immediately misapprehended. 'Now, would that be the Rif or the Atlas Mountains?' 'No, no,' says Bowles. 'The little hill overlooking the city'. He remains carefully courteous.

Imminently expected, by now, is the arrival of an American Professor of English from New York. He visits Tangier regularly and takes his opportunities to visit Bowles, by whom he is evidently glamourized. Bowles remarks, somewhat wonderingly, 'he comes *several times*'. This is by no means to imply any dislike for the

professor, nor any strong objection to his visits; merely a confession
of incomprehension that he should, like some sphinx or oracle, be
considered to merit regular and detailed inspection and consul-
tation. The professor is already in the kitchen conferring with
Mrabet who has let him in. He is dressed wholly in cream and white,
and wears a white, buttoned bonnet on his head. He appears to
have a diary in his hand, and is inspecting it with an attitude of
concentration. Mrabet wears the weary air of a social secretary.
'The trouble with becoming a public monument,' says Bowles,
quoting his old friend Virgil Thomson, the composer, 'is that dogs
tend to come along and piss on you.'

If Bowles is bemused by the attentions paid to him, he is generally puzzled by most manifestations of the post-war Western world.
Especially bothersome is the insistence of some literary critics,
reviewers, and gossips who identify him as the 'cult author of the
Beat Generation', as though he gave literary birth to Burroughs,
Kerouac, Ginsberg, Gysin, Corso and the others. The latest such
description had occurred in the May 1987 edition of the French
magazine *Actuel*. He takes trouble to limit the implications. 'It's
wrong,' Bowles declares. 'I was never a Beat writer. To describe
me as a Beat writer is purely ignorant.' This minor outburst had
come at the end of a lunch I'd given for him. Preparing to leave,
Bowles had stopped to admire the late April sweetpeas in the
garden. His old friend David Herbert picked one to give to him,
saying 'I've stolen a flower for you.' I said, facetiously, 'now you'll
have to go and live with the Beast.' Mishearing, Bowles looked
startled. 'I'll have to go live with the *Beats*?' The idea evidently
appalled him.

Though Bowles is nostalgic for the Morocco he first knew in 1931
and in the years before Independence, and though he is resentful
of the 'corruption' of Tangier and the native population by Western

culture – which, far from having been assimilated, merely lies like oil on water – he expresses a resigned, if critical acceptance of present-day Morocco and Tangier. If this is a little like Margaret Fuller declaring 'I accept the Universe,' and Thomas Carlyle's comment, 'By God, she'd better,' it should be recognized that Moroccans themselves also distrust Tangier and Tanjawis, the natives of the city. For centuries, Tangier particularly has been regularly invaded and colonized by outsiders, so that it is regarded as irrevocably tainted with foreign manners and traditions. It has mostly languished, neglected by Sultans and their governments, as a territory apart from the rest of Morocco. By the late 1920s and early 1930s, Tangier was well known to artists, writers and European intellectuals as a convenient summer resort.

'You don't want to go to Villefranche,' said Gertrude Stein to Paul Frederick Bowles. 'Everybody's there.' Everybody particularly included Jean Cocteau who, she considered, did not like her. 'And St Jean-de-Luz is empty, with an awful climate,' she said with her next breath to Aaron Copland. Having dismissed their modest plans for the summer, she suggested another option. 'The place you should go is Tangier. Alice and I have spent three summers there, and it's fine. Freddy'll like it because the sun shines every day. At least, in the summer.' 'Freddy' Bowles didn't care. His single, most pressing wish was to be as far away as possible from New York. He had run away once, in 1929, and now here he was again, two years later and twenty years of age, 'at the center of all existence'.

Bowles had been a good-looking, blond adolescent in the spring of 1927 when he happened on a copy of *transition*, a Paris-based, Surrealist-inspired literary magazine, in a small bookshop on Sixth Avenue. 'I loved its concise format, the stange muted colours of the soft paper they used as covers, and the fact that each page had to be cut with a paper knife. Above all, each month when I bought the new issue, I had the illusion of being in Paris, for the feeling of the city I got from reading its pages coincided with my own feeling of what Paris must be like, where the people were desperate but sophisticated, cynical but fantastically loyal to ideas ... I knew that some day, with luck, I should go there and stand on the sacred spots.'

Few were more sacred than 27 rue de Fleurus, the residence of

Gertrude Stein. By the time Bowles rang her doorbell in 1931, he had published poetry in *transition* and struck up a correspondence with her. His person more than his presence startled her: 'I was sure from your letters that you were an elderly gentleman of at least seventy-five.' 'A highly eccentric elderly gentleman', chipped in Alice B. Toklas. They got on famously until, having asked to see some of Bowles' poetry, Miss Stein took the trouble to give her opinion: 'Well, the only trouble with all this is that it isn't poetry.'

She developed a greater interest in Bowles as a musician, consulting Aaron Copland, who had taught Bowles musical composition in New York, for a professional assessment of his talent. Copland, who had come to Paris to study with the composer Nadia Boulanger, and who had been introduced to Stein by Bowles, was impatient with his friend and pupil's inclination to go off and do things other than stick steadily to piano practice and the study of composition. He replied cautiously that he could imagine someone who spent more time at music than Bowles. 'That's what I thought,' said Stein. 'He's started his life of crime too soon.' And she and Copland would giggle together, and Copland would tell Bowles, 'If you don't work when you're twenty, nobody will love you when you're thirty.'

Bowles and Copland left Paris with no great expectations of Tangier. Bowles knew little beyond having been told 'there would be a house somewhere, a piano somehow, and sun every day. That seemed to me enough.' Their first sight of North Africa from the deck of the *Imeréthie II* was the coast and rugged line of the mountains of Algeria. 'Always, without formulating the concept,' Bowles later wrote in his autobiography, *Without Stopping*, 'I had based my sense of being in the world partly on an unreasoned conviction that certain areas of the earth's surface contained more magic than others,' magic being 'a secret connection between the world of nature and the consciousness of man, a hidden but direct passage which bypassed the mind'. Confessing himself a Romantic, he 'had always been vaguely certain that sometime during my life I should have come into a magic place which in disclosing its secrets would give me wisdom and ecstasy – perhaps even death'.

Bowles was instantly enchanted by Tangier which, looking for a house to rent, he explored for ten days or so:

If I said that Tangier struck me as a dream city, I should mean it in the strict sense. Its topography was rich in prototypal dream scenes: covered streets like corridors with doors opening into rooms on each side, hidden terraces high above the sea, streets consisting only of steps, dark impasses, small squares built on sloping terrain so that they looked like ballet sets designed in false perspective, with alleys leading off in several directions; as well as the classical dream equipment of tunnels, ramparts, ruins, dungeons, and cliffs. The climate was both violent and languorous. The August wind hissed in the palms and rocked the eucalyptus trees and rattled the canebrakes that bordered the streets.

Tangier was then a little city of about sixty thousand people, most of them excitable and noisy, constantly 'engaged in passionate arguments which continually seemed about to degenerate into physical violence'. Copland was less enchanted than Bowles: 'It's a madhouse, a madhouse.' 'It's a continuous performance, anyway,' said Bowles who knew instantly that he 'should never tire of watching Moroccans play their parts'. The Villa de France, the hotel recommended by Stein and Toklas, was full: a better, cheaper alternative was the El Minzah, open for its first summer season, costing them seventy-five francs a day, about three dollars, for full board. On the Mountain, the forested hill rising above the city, Bowles chanced upon a 'big, run-down, unfurnished and isolated' house that did not immediately impress Copland who, nevertheless, was persuaded to move in. He and Bowles began to buy necessary furniture and kitchen equipment, which was easy enough, if somewhat expensive; but their principal difficulty was the search for a piano.

They finally located an elderly black upright on the calle de Italia. It was hoisted on a donkey which made no significant objection to carrying it as far as the house, but balked when it saw the gate which it refused, even under extremities of pressure, to enter. The struggle to persuade it to pass through the objectionable *portière* resulted, naturally, in the piano crashing to the ground 'with an attractive but unreproducible sound'. The Moroccans hired to accompany the donkey were no kinder in their attempts to move the piano. By dint of much pushing, heaving and banging, they succeeded in establishing the instrument in a corner of the salon where it sulked, hopelessly out of tune – though little more so than it had been in the shop where Bowles and Copland had been promised the services of a piano tuner who, when he arrived several days later, was judged inadequate: 'The man had no idea of how to tune a piano and no sense of pitch.'

Admitting defeat, the tuner lapsed into silence. Perceiving this from the garden, hearing no sounds of atonal music, Bowles and Copland found him sitting with his head resting on his arms, and his arms folded on the keyboard He might have been depressed, asleep, or merely awaiting inspiration. There was a bottle of cognac on top of the piano. He was dead drunk. 'We awoke him; he seemed embarrassed, but jauntily ripped off some ragged arpeggios and barged into the "Pilgrims' Chorus" from *Tannhäuser*. The piano sounded, if possible, even more sour than before. Drastic action was essential. "The piano is tuned," said the man. "No," said Aaron. "You sit there, and we're going to tune it." And so for another two hours he loosened and tightened the strings while we cried "*Más alto!*" or "*Más bajo!*" until eventually the instrument sounded like any other piano in need of tuning – that is to say, one at least could tell what each note was supposed to be.'

Copland immediately got to work on his Short Symphony and Bowles progressed with his little Sonata for Oboe and Clarinet. Every morning after breakfast Copland gave Bowles a lesson in harmony and, for the rest of the day, a routine was established that enabled both to do some work. Copland, irritated by most aspects of Tangier that entranced Bowles, was in no mood to enjoy the constant sound of native drums on the Mountain. He considered them ominously threatening; he was vexed by Bowles' tendency to wander away on solitary little trips of personal exploration; and the piano sounded like hell. He admitted, in a letter to Gertrude Stein, that Tangier '*is* lovely to see' but he 'found the atmosphere not conducive to composing'. On 8 October, after he and Bowles had sold up the furniture and other domestic chattels they had bought, Copland left for Europe leaving Bowles contentedly behind in Morocco with an ecstatic vision of Fez in his head. 'Fez I shall make my home one day!' he wrote to a friend, Bruce Morrissette. To Stein, more specific in his perverse delight, he itemized flies and dust and rats among the notable attractions of Fez: 'It is quite dirty and *very* beautiful.' Copland, who had accompanied Bowles on a short trip to Fez, found it even more disturbing than Tangier and was confirmed in his distaste for Morocco.

Bowles, sticking to an insistence that he did not care to make choices, his preference for remaining uninvolved, and preserving a habit of hiding his intentions from everyone (to the extent, he admitted, that he was successful sometimes in hiding them even from himself), had adopted or arrived at a belief that he should 'strive for invisibility'. It was Bowles' concern not to judge, not to act to change, and not to interfere by intruding himself into the life going on around him. He was a spectator, merely, a presence which, if possible, should remain unobtrusive to the point, ideally, of complete self-effacement. This was difficult in Morocco. Apart from the fact that Moroccan eyes are particularly attentive to their circumstances and surroundings, missing nothing, Bowles stood out more than usually. 'Even with my practice of pretending not to exist, I could not do it in Morocco. A stranger as blond as I was all too evident.' This was a matter for profound regret. 'I wanted to see whatever was happening continue exactly as if I were not there.'

This desire and aim was, if not altered, at least put to considerable test by the arrival, a matter of days after Copland's departure, of a friend, Harry Dunham, from whom Bowles had borrowed the fare to Europe – Dunham had discovered the delightful art of photography and 'spent most of his time climbing into all kinds of places where he was not supposed to be, being screamed at by Moroccans and French alike, but snapping his pictures, several hundred of them each day'. In complete contrast to Bowles, he spectacularly and aggressively intruded his presence into Moroccan life, and, remarks Bowles, 'expected his presence to change everything and in the direction which interested him'. Severely, Bowles 'told him that was not an intelligent way to travel'.

At an age when most young men are defensively extrovert, particularly when faced with the puzzling contradictions of foreign manners and morals, Bowles – far from asserting the virtues of the familiar – was not only romantically infatuated with the esoteric and the exotic, but severe in the rectitude of that romanticism. His personal austerity, deriving in part from his New England heritage, provided him with a cool objectivity that balanced more natural enthusiasm for novel experiences. Dunham's boisterousness would, in any circumstances, have been a little distasteful – in Morocco, it was a crescendo of wrong notes that distorted and spoiled the subtler, unfamiliar music of the country that Bowles hoped to attune himself to hear and comprehend. Dunham was a piece of hot jazz who competed intolerably with the long ribbon of the muezzin's chant.

After travelling with Bowles to Casablanca and Marrakesh, Dunham decided to return to Europe. Bowles returned to Tangier where earlier, with Copland, he had met a Dutch painter, Kristians Tonny, who lived with a black woman from New York called Anita Thomson. Copland had been more interested in meeting this couple than Bowles, who 'foresaw a static evening with a square-headed Dutchman who would show us his canvases one by one, and I did not think it would be fun'. Bowles was, perhaps, too enamoured of the enchantments of his magic city to want to be reminded of Europe, New York and conventional Western art. In the event, Tonny was delightful and his drawings were 'quite wonderful: Moroccan landscapes out of Bosch, alive with hundreds of tiny figures wearing djellabas and haiks'. Tonny had caught the magical, grotesque element of Tangier to which Bowles had instinctively responded. Tonny was more taken with Copland, frankly remarking in a loud aside, 'The young man with you is slightly off his head, isn't he? I noticed it the other night right away. I heard shutters banging in the wind in there somewhere.' Bowles, far from offended, 'found this a sympathetic observation and liked him the better for having made it'.

Alone for the first time without Copland or Dunham, Bowles moved in with Tonny and Anita who were living in a little Moroccan house on the hill above the Dradeb, a teeming, working-class district of modern Tangier. Most of their friends were Moroccan. Young Moroccan males seemed irresistibly attracted to Anita who in turn had very little resistance to their attentions. She had moved originally to Tangier to join an old friend, Dean, who was barman at the El Minzah Hotel. Tonny, infatuated with Anita, had followed her. That at least, was the received version of the story. In fact, as Bowles understood matters, it had been Gertrude Stein who had contrived Anita's departure from Paris. Stein had adopted Tonny as a protégé, and had been concerned at the diverting effect Anita was having on his work. Neither Tonny nor Anita had much to say in favour of Gertrude Stein.

In Marrakesh, Harry Dunham had recruited a young Moroccan named Abdelkader as his valet and charged Bowles with the responsibility of ensuring the young man's passage to Paris. Abdelkader, equipped with all his travel documents in good order, arrived in Tangier and presented himself at the house. Immediately he took undisguised exception to the standards of Anita's housekeeping. With the fastidiousness of a censorious Cheltenham lady, Abdelkader would run a finger along the floor beside the wall and hold it close to Bowles' nose for inspection. Anita's careless, impromptu culinary principles, notably her decision on one occasion to pour a quart of gin into the sauce for a couscous, convinced Abdelkader that her intention was to poison the household. Such a tactic was not unknown in Moroccan families; women were liable to go to any exteme. There was friction, there was tension, there was frank discord between Anita and Abdelkader which only terminated when Bowles, as quickly as possible, embarked with his charge on the Algeciras ferry on the first leg of the journey back to Paris.

Bowles returned briefly to Tangier in 1932 and again, by way of an extended excursion into Tunisia and Algeria, in the early summer of 1933. He was not anxious to return to America: 'Each day lived through on this side of the Atlantic was one more day spent outside prison.' Relations with his parents had been strained and remote for a long time and family tensions had even, at one point, resulted in a physical attack by Bowles upon his father. Able now more or less to please himself, Bowles had discovered a milieu and a routine better suited to his ambitions than dependence on parents whose American middle-class standards and manner of life he distrusted as inimical to his personal development. Gertrude Stein had said he was self-indulgent, but Bowles had worked seriously at his music: 'with all the displacements I had been able to finish writing the Flute Sonata, Scènes d'Anabase, the piano Sonatina, and the cantata I had begun in Laghouat. This last was called Par le Détroit, a hermetic reference to my preoccupation in dreams with the strait of Gibraltar.' Accustomed by now to the city, he quickly found a house that suited his purpose – 'I had notes for a solo piano work, and I wanted to be able to play as loud and as long as I pleased; this meant that no one must be within hearing distance.' The house was on the Marshan, a northern district of the city. It fulfilled his requirements in every particular except that it had neither running water nor furniture. Bowles hired and installed a piano in the house, but slept in a Medina hotel. He set himself doggedly to work: 'If my insistence upon prolonging the wanderings was compulsive, no less so was the fanatical manner in which I forced myself to work regularly each day. The truth was that Aaron's little warning of two years before, "If you don't work when you're twenty, nobody's going to love you when you're thirty," although scarcely meant seriously, had remained with me and taken root.'

At this time, an old friend from New York, Charles-Henri Ford, who published some of Bowles' poetry in an avant-garde little magazine called *Blues*, arrived in Tangier to wait for his friend, Djuna Barnes, who had been visiting Peggy Guggenheim. Bowles installed Ford and Barnes in his unfurnished Marshan house on the understanding that they would vacate it each day by one-thirty when Bowles arrived to work. This arrangement was satisfactory except in one particular – Bowles had collected some objectionable skins with which to decorate his house: 'Before she would unpack, Djuna insisted on removing all seventeen jackal pelts from the walls where I had hung them; she also rolled up the python skin and put it away.'

After a few weeks of discomfort, Ford and Barnes moved to a house surrounded by an orchard a few hundred feet away, further up the lane, and lived Moroccan-style on the floor. Here, Djuna Barnes settled to type her manuscript, at first entitled *Bow Down* but later changed to *Nightwood* under which title it was finally published. She was remarkable not only as a writer and woman of character; her appearance was of the greatest possible interest to all who frequented the Petit Socco where she sat at the Café Central with Bowles and Ford, her face made up with blue, green and purple. 'She did not at all mind being stared at' and on occasions actively encouraged attention: 'a brief imitation of Sir Francis Rose she did one day galvanized the spectators in the café, as well as the passersby.'

Despite his reluctance to go back to the United States, Bowles in the early spring of 1933 discovered that he was about to run out of money. Whether constitutionally tight with a buck, or genuinely broke, he booked third-class passage on the *Juan Sebastian Elcano*,

bound from Cadiz for San Juan de Puerto Rico whence he boarded
a ship of the Ward Line and sailed for New York. In New York,
conditions were dispiriting. Though Copland had performed some
of Bowles' music and was impressed with it, 'Aaron of course has
a new pet so there is no snuggling there.' Copland had evidently
advised Bowles to return, writing 'there are just as many people
interested in what you have to offer in USA as there are in Europe.'
But Bowles was desolated by the prospect of returning to his
parents who, if glad to see him home, were no doubt equally
delighted to see him with his tail between his legs and dependent
upon them, once, again, in his defeated, enforced retreat from
Europe and Morocco.

Then, too, Bowles got into trouble with a group of New York
artists, including Alfred Stieglitz and Georgia O'Keeffe, who were
suspicious of, and irritated by, Americans who opted for expatriate
status. A group of musicians, calling themselves The Young
Composers Group, who included Copland, 'were interested in the
situation of the American composer' and tended to sideline and
isolate the likes of Bowles and Virgil Thomson who attempted to
preserve a European sensibility in their work. Bowles, refusing to
break with European values, wrote two songs based on texts by
Gertrude Stein and wrote to Cocteau for permission to compose a
song cycle, for voice and solo piano, based on six of his texts. The
completed work, entitled *Memnon*, took eighteen months to compose.

In the spring of 1934, an opportunity to travel to Morocco presented itself in the shape of one Colonel Charles Williams, an
elderly, choleric gentleman who was proposing to descend upon
the American Fondouk in Fez – a charitable organization devoted
to the protection and relief of suffering pack animals in Morocco.
The responsible functionary in Fez, Charles Brown, had incurred
the colonel's wrath and it was Williams' sole, unwavering aim to
reorganize the administration in Fez and dislodge Brown. Williams
required a secretary, and Bowles was hired to assist the colonel in
Fez. To pay his passage, Bowles in characteristic fashion turned
up a Wall Street stockbroker who required a guide to Spain, and
in the summer of 1934 they set out for Cadiz. Bowles did his duty
as a cicerone for a few weeks in Spain and then crossed to Tangier.
Colonel Williams was not a philosophic traveller: 'He was convinced that there was a permanent and ubiquitous conspiracy in

operation, whose purpose was to provide him with inferior accom-
modations, food and service. All Spaniards were idiots, all Moroccans thieves, and all French intolerably rude. He carried a cane
with him not because he needed it, but so that he could pound with
it as he gave orders.' They took the night train to Fez where Bowles
learned that the apoplectic, explosive colonel was exclusively
prejudiced against Brown because he met Moroccans socially and
invited them to his house;

'It was fatal, said the Colonel, to allow natives to suppose that
you considered them your equal; they were not accustomed to it,
and it could only make for misunderstanding and discord. It was
a well known fact that Brown had received Muslims at his house
and even seated them at table with Europeans. Under no circumstances could he be allowed to continue working at the American
Fondouk.' Brown was finally caught out in some trivial irregularity:
a minor lapse was magnified into a charge of gross negligence.
Brown, thoroughly browbeaten by Williams, was dismissed and
replaced by a retired British Army captain earmarked by Williams
for the job.

In mid-October 1934, about two months after leaving New York,
Bowles returned to the United States. With him, he took a collection of records he had acquired in Morocco – 'from Fez, choral
works of ancient origin, accompanied by strings and drum; from
the Atlas, (Sous) Chleuh songs and dances, from the desert, songs
with flute and chalumeau accompaniment, from Andalucia, saetas,
with drum and trumpets, songs by Marchena, with guitar, and
solos by Montoya, Sabicas and Maravilla. And some extra, from
Algeria and Egypt.' These were ultimately to form the basis of a
large and comprehensive collection of ethnic music, help to spark
and develop a continuing interest in North African music, and
provide an inspiration for some of his own compositions.

In New York, Bowles continued to write music, which included
a score to accompany a film by Harry Dunham. This film and
concert performance attracted some critical attention and Bowles
continued to compose music to accompany avant-garde films that
brought more personal fame than money. His reputation led to a
job, engineered by Virgil Thomson, writing the orchestral score for
Horse Eats Hat, a play directed by Orson Welles for the Federal
Theatre Project. The play and music being considered a success,

Bowles was promptly commisssioned to write the musical score for another Welles production, Marlowe's *Dr Faustus*. By the beginning of 1937, working on a score for a documentary film about Southern sharecroppers, Bowles was judged – by Virgil Thomson and other critics – to have hit the 'musical big-time'. But Bowles, for all his metropolitan success, was uneasy in America. Kristians Tonny and his wife arrived in New York from Paris. Immediately 'Tonny was full of complaints about the lack of civilization in the United States; surprisingly enough I often found myself taking issue with him, not so much in defense of the country as in disagreement with his reasons for disparaging it.'

In February 1937 he was introduced to 'an attractive red-haired girl with a pointed nose'. At their first meeting, 'she was not communicative' but a few days later at a Sunday afternoon gathering at e. e. cummings' in the Village, to which Bowles had taken the Tonnys, they met again. Bowles and the Tonnys were discussing a trip to Mexico and she decided she wanted to go with them. Instantly she telephoned her mother, who demanded to speak to Bowles: 'If my daughter's going to Mexico with you I think I should meet you first, don't you?' Bowles, and later the Tonnys, met Mrs Auer who – to Bowles' considerable puzzlement – agreed to let Jane, her twenty-year-old daughter, go with them to Mexico. Jane's caprice and her mother's indulgence appeared baffling to Bowles who, talking with Jane for the two weeks it took them to get as far as New Orleans by bus, exchanged all manner of confidences during 'many hours of conversation'. Jane, pestered by Tonny, asserted that 'she was a virgin and intended to remain in that category until she married'.

The notion of marriage may have seemed unlikely: Jane was very frank about the fact that she was lesbian, but on the bus to New Orleans she began to fall in love with Bowles, whose sexual temperament was at least ambivalent.

On his first visit to Paris, Bowles had been seduced first by a Hungarian girl called Hermina and then, cold bloodedly, by an uncle, Billy Hubert. Back in New York, he had taken up with an English girl with whom he was romantically infatuated. 'The only girl I have ever lost weight lying awake nights for,' he wrote, recollecting 'BAISERS INFINIS! Glory! Gorgeous! Preoccupation quotidienne.' This apostrophizing mode seems somewhat ingenuous, a youthful bellowing of calf love for a girl who pursued some peculiar preoccupations: ''Tis she who is intimate with drunks and subway guards, who masks as a boy and frequents men's toilets to read the inscriptions.' Bowles was thrilled 'Oh merveilleuse! Only! Only! Only!' This girl, referred to only as Peggy, is interesting in one effect she may have had on Bowles' later life – her character somewhat resembles the boyish, if not transvestite, character of the writer Isabelle Eberhardt whose Algerian journals Bowles was to translate some fifty years later.

Bowles' own sexual character was somewhat sourly commented on by his friends: 'Paul had a very low sex drive' said Thomson. 'It just wasn't important to him.' And Bruce Morrissette alleged, 'He was basically antisexual. Interested in people, yes, but not sexually.' They both regarded Bowles as 'never of an ordinary sexual temperament' and 'put off by the very idea of sex'. Bowles himself, in a letter, written at the age of seventeen admitted to a prudish and puritanical perversity: 'If I find I am doing a pleasing thing and that people like it, I switch; it must be bad what I am doing. I was long ago aware that whatever I put my hand to is made into some sort of a vice. There can never be any love, any affection, even any satiation "in my life". Whatever is to please me must be a vice.' Bowles at least equated sex with sin and the inevitability of punishment. Physical expression of his sexual nature was deemed to be, at best, a necessary – or unnecessary – evil.

He was, perhaps more in the abstract than physically, fascinated by homosexuality. He associated with homosexuals who admired his youthful, blond beauty, and in Paris he was persuaded to visit a Turkish bath where he 'fled in panic' from the overt attentions of a young Arab. Thomson, who himself possessed an appetite and capacity for having a good time, advised Bowles to 'go out and have sex with anybody, so long as he enjoyed it'. Bowles, taken aback by this incitement to libertinage, froze: it was not Bowles' business to have fun.

Nevertheless, to Morrissette, Bowles had written: 'Homosexuality is a thrilling subject to me, just as sanguinary killings are, and rapes, and tales of drug addicts. They are exciting because they are melodramatic. A struggle! And who would not give several years of his life could he but strangle someone with impunity?' The identification of sex with acts of violence and depravity, with blood and injury to the self as much as to others, bespeaks an effort to identify and objectify – put beyond the pale of serious consideration – deep passions that, for the sake of self-preservation, must be restrained in some manner – made abstract in order that they may not be physically expressed lest they utterly subvert and destroy conventional virtue. This is reminiscent of the description of Robert Louis Stevenson as a 'shameless bohemian haunted by duty' and of Stevenson's own feeling that, were it not for the constraints he firmly imposed upon himself, his potential for chaos and mayhem might be sufficient to destroy whole empires.

At the age of nineteen, Bowles had been 'astonished one night to discover that I had just thrown a meat knife at my father. I rushed out of the house, shattering the panes of glass in the front door, and began to run down the hill in the rain.' Thinking he had outgrown his childish fits of anger, he was just as appalled as his father, 'totally dissatisfied with my own behaviour because it had been as a result of weakness'. The terrible, awesome results of unleashing one's capacity for destruction are so incalculable that the potential must be disciplined and directed into creative rather than destructive channels. Loss of control was worrying – but Bowles could somehow stand outside it and recognize the relation between fact and fantasy. Both seemed equally unreal to him and, in that respect, nothing really mattered. There was little difference between the fall of an empire and the fall of a leaf. Both were insignificant and both, perhaps, inevitable. But loss of control was nevertheless dangerous: sex, involving some loss of personal control, could be perceived as threatening and therefore best avoided.

Marriage, as a form of conventionally approved bondage, may have appeared to Bowles to be a useful form of self-control, a means of evading worse temptations and dangers. It would at once be a means to astonish everyone who would be surprised by such a move, and a method of pinning down fantasy in reality.

On 21 February 1938, a day short of Jane Auer's twenty-first birthday, they were married in New York in a small Dutch

Reformed church. That Jane was Jewish seems to have been no impediment to this. The reasons for the marriage were simultaneously fantastical and practical. Bowles has written: 'Jane and I used to spin fancies about how amusing it would be to get married and horrify everyone, above all, our respective families. From fantasy to actuality is often a much shorter distance than one imagines; suddenly we were seriously discussing the possibility.' Jane would inherit a little money on her marriage and – as she confessed to the composer David Diamond – 'honey, I'm so lonely.'

Far from being horrified, Mrs Auer was delighted – she conceived the marriage as not only Jane's salvation from lesbianism, but also as the removal of a barrier to her own remarriage. Bowles, like his own parents, may have regarded marriage as the done and proper thing – however much it may have been regarded by others as merely a marriage of convenience. There was no doubt, however, that Bowles and his wife were genuinely attached to one another: they took pleasure in each other's company, complemented one another in their differences of character, and each stimulated the other's wit. As regards sexual relations, Virgil Thomson and other close friends doubted they were ever sexually intimate, although Jane Bowles' biographer, Millicent Dillon, disagrees: she maintains that sexual relations did occur early in the marriage but were discontinued, after two and a half years, as Bowles himself confirms.

For the next decade, Bowles worked at composing music largely for the theatre: 'It is true that I "produced" during those years, but in such a way that I always seemed to find myself doing what someone else wanted done. I furnished music which would embellish or interpret the ideas of others; this is taken for granted, of course, in the writing of functional music.' He wrote a couple of pieces of his own music, but almost immediately afterward 'accepted more theatrical commissions and consequently never attained the state of freedom I sought'.

Jane, too, worked: she wrote her most famous work, her only fully accomplished novel, *Two Serious Ladies*, and her one play, *In the Summer House*. Bowles, too, had begun to write: though music still dominated his professional career. By 1943 he had begun to write music criticism, and in 1945 a short story, *The Scorpion*, was published in *View*. He had already translated Sartre's *Huis Clos* for a production staged by John Huston – giving the play its irrevocable

English title *No Exit* – and later translated Giraudoux's play *La Folle de Chaillot*. *The Scorpion* was followed by *By The Water* and *A Distant Episode*. By now, his commitment to music commissioned for the theatre was irksome: 'To my way of thinking I was only marking time . . . I was made aware of a slowly increasing desire to step outside the dance in which inadvertently I had become involved.' At this point, in the spring of 1947, Bowles had a dream.

This dream was distinctive because although short and with no anecdotal content beyond that of a changing succession of streets, after I awoke, it had left its essence with me in a state of enameled precision: a residue of ineffable sweetness and calm. In the late afternoon sunlight I walked slowly through complex and tunneled streets. As I reviewed it, lying there, sorry to have left the place behind, I realized with a jolt that the magic city really existed. It was Tangier. My heart accelerated, and memories of other courtyards and stairways flooded in, still fresh from sixteen years before. For the Tangier in which I had wandered had been the Tangier of 1931. The town was still present the following morning, fresh and invigorating to recall, and vivid memory of it persisted day after day, along with the inexplicable sensation of serene happiness which, being of the dream's very essence, inevitably accompanied it. It did not take me long to come to the conclusion that Tangier must be the place I wanted to be more than anywhere else. I began to consider the possibility of spending the summer there.

As if to confirm fantasy as reality, Doubleday offered Bowles a contract and an advance for a novel. 'Once I had signed the contract I began to make plans for my trip to Tangier. North Africa had long since acquired a legendary aura for me; the fact that I now had decided to go back there made the place more actual and revived hundreds of small forgotten scenes which welled up into my consciousness of their own accord.' The novel presented itself to Bowles on a Fifth Avenue bus. Between Tenth Street and Madison Square, 'I knew what would be in the novel and what I would call it . . . The book was going to take place in the Sahara, where there was only the sky, and so it would be *The Sheltering Sky* . . . in essence the tale would be similar to *A Distant Episode*, the short story I had just published in *Partisan Review*, and it would write itself, I felt certain, once I had established the characters and spilled them out onto the North African scene. By the time I got up into midtown I had made all the most important decisions about the novel.'

Bowles booked a passage for Casablanca on the SS *Ferncape*. He would be travelling with a friend, the writer Gordon Sager, who called for Bowles on the day of departure. After lunch, Bowles collected his luggage together and looked around for his passport.

It had been lying on a bookcase shelf earlier that morning. Now it was nowhere to be seen. We searched feverishly, the car was due to arrive in a half hour. Gordon was for going through all my valises; he thought it likely that at some point I had unthinkingly slipped it inside one of them. We continued to look for it everywhere. Just before the car came, I unearthed it, buried beneath a neat pile of Jane's underwear in the back of a bureau drawer. It was a mystery: Jane earnestly claimed to know nothing about it. Yet no one else had come into the apartment. We looked at her accusingly. She laughed. 'You *know* I don't want you to go,' she said. 'So I must have.'

Writing later to Bowles, Jane attempted to explain: 'as for packing your passport away – I thought it was mine – I looked to see whose picture was in it – and I dimly remember my own face and not yours. As Libby said when I told her, "How psychosomatic can you get."'

Libby Holman, the original 'torch singer' and major musical revue star, had become friendly with Jane in 1945, two years after publication of *Two Serious Ladies* which she had much admired. Jane was never sexually intimate with Holman, establishing rather a close friendship that was to last the rest of her life. Her waif-like indecision, desperate attempts to realize her own potential, and her profound vulnerability, were complemented by Holman's highly-coloured emotionalism, extrovert brio and appetite for life which enabled her to survive personal tragedies and dramas that would have knocked the stuffing out of a less intelligent and resourceful woman. A bright thread of Holman's practical assistance, care and concern for Jane's well-being was to run throughout their relationship. On Bowles' departure, Jane went to stay at the Holman estate, 'Treetops', in Connecticut where she dithered about being able to afford to make the trip to Tangier to join him. Money was tight, and another difficulty stood in her way: she was conducting an affair with an older woman, a Vermont matron called Helvetia Perkins, who stoutly refused to go to Africa with her. This affair was running down somewhat, and Bowles, who had established himself in a little house at the Hotel Farhar, opposite the house on the Mountain where he had stayed with Copland in 1931, was writing to urge her to join him.

Jane's indecisiveness was compounded by other concerns that she conjured up to detain her: she was working on a new novel, and she claimed to have developed a romantic interest in the Scots and the Irish: 'I think I shall simply never be interested in any one who is Latin or Arab or Semitic.' On hearing a report that Bowles wished to take her into the desert, she wrote: 'Of course, I'm sure that when I get there, if I do, all the part I would have liked will be over – like the wine and the nice hotels. I would like to stay in a hotel in Fez, I think rather than Tangier, and I still refuse to cross the Atlas in a bus.' She speculates about taking a cab instead.

These anxieties, superficially and humorously about personal comforts and habits of living, gave way to deeper concerns:

I wish to hell I could find some woman still so that I wouldn't always be alone at night. I'm sure Arab night life would interest me not in the slightest. As you know, I don't consider those races voluptuous or exciting in any way, as I have said – being a part of them almost . . . It is hard for me to think of going anywhere by myself, of course, I'm not even *going* to think about it yet. If my novel is not coming along at all by then, it would be more painful than pleasant to go over there and see your manuscript almost done or even half done. I don't think I could bear the sense of failure made so palpable, but I couldn't bear it either to have you in such a terrible state about yours as I am about mine. I really am very glad you are coming along with it and I don't believe any of the things you say about the value of it . . . None of this makes my life any simpler perhaps or maybe it will but that's beside the point. It will all work out, or it will never, I can't imagine.

One of her major concerns was for Bowles and his work – her acute sense of her husband's genius led her to minimize her own abilities by exalting and protecting his. She was consistently loyal to Bowles.

To Jane, Bowles had written 'that Morocco was still all that it had been and that she must come as soon as possible'. His novel was certainly moving ahead. For ten pesetas, Bowles had bought a big jar of *majoun* – a sort of paste made with cannabis – 'it was the cheapest kind and therefore tasted like very old and dusty fudge from which all flavour had long since departed. However, this in no way diminished its power.' Bowles climbed high on the mountain above his cottage to lie in the sun. He looked towards 'the distant line of the sierra in Spain' across the Strait and munched some *majoun*. The effect was sudden. Bowles, lying motionless, felt himself lifted towards the sun. He kept his eyes shut for a considerable time until he was indeed afraid to open them at all, such was the sensation of having risen too far above the rock. 'In another hour my mind was behaving in a fashion I should never have imagined possible. I wanted to get off the boulders, down the mountainside, and back home as fast as I could.'

Bowles had reached the point in his novel at which he had to describe the death by typhoid of his hero. In his cottage, surrounded by cypresses which rocked and roared in the wind, the nerve-racking *cherqi*, Bowles lay on his bed in the last of the twilight. 'For a long time I did not move. Among many things, I was trying to imagine the death of my protagonist. Later that night I noted a good many details, and the next day wrote out much of the scene. Very consciously I had always avoided writing about death because I saw it as a difficult subject to treat with anything approaching the proper style; it seemed reasonable, therefore, to hand the job over to the subconscious. It is certain that the *majoun* provided a solution totally unlike whatever I should have found without it.' Later, in Fez, Bowles made further inquiries about *majoun* and discovered a ready source of supply in a barbershop. 'I felt I had come upon a fantastic secret: to change worlds, I had only to spread a bit of jam on a biscuit and eat it.' He bought a quantity of this cannabis jam, sold in tins, and began a series of experiments to 'determine my own set of optimum conditions regarding the quantity to be ingested, the time of day for the dose, the accompanying diet, and the general physical and psychological ambiances most conducive to pleasure during the experience'.

This spirit of rational, near-scientific, certainly cool and very conscious investigation resulted in a formal, almost ritualized and exquisite routine:

Large quantities of hot tea were essential. Twilight was the best hour for taking the dose; the effect came on slowly after an hour and a half or even two hours had passed, preferably at the moment of sitting down to dinner. A clear soup followed by a small steak and salad seemed to interfere the least with the *majoun*'s swift circulation. It was imperative to be unmitigatedly content with all the facets of existence beforehand. The most minimal preoccupation, the merest speck of cloud on the emotional horizon, had a way of italicizing itself during the alteration of consciousness and assuming gigantic proportions, thus completely ruining the inner journey. It is a delicate operation, the taking of *majoun*. Since its success or failure can be measured only in purely subjective terms, it is also a supremely egotistical pastime. Above all, there must be no interruptions, no surprises; everthing must come about according to the timetable furnished by the substance itself.

Bowles spent a good deal of time exploring the city: 'Tangier was windblown and blue. I wandered for days in the upper Medina and Casbah until I knew every street and alley.' The houses in the old, Arab part of the city intrigued him. Blank-faced on the streets, they gave nothing away about the domestic life conducted behind their walls. He explored a few of the empty houses and began to consider owning one himself. They appeared to be ridiculously cheap: two thousand dollars for a large house with a covered courtyard; no more than two hundred and fifty dollars for a small two-room Spanish-style cottage with an orchard. Bowles chose a house costing five hundred dollars near the Place Amrah and wired a distant cousin, Oliver Smith, with whom he and Jane were friendly, asking him if he would care to contribute towards the purchase price. He did not consult Jane who, already in a rage with Bowles about having had to clear up the considerable personal belongings and clutter he had left in New York, was hurt and offended by the omission.

To Bowles, in October 1947, she wrote: 'I just *happened* to be in town when Oliver got your wire and I of course advised him to send the $500. I knew you were getting a kick out of the house and I cannot help but want your pleasure. I was hurt though that you had written to Oliver and Bob Faulkener about it and yet no word to me.' Oliver Smith had had some reservations about the house, and Jane contributed some objections of her own: she worried about being conspicuous in the Arab quarter and about the probability of the house being robbed. There appeared to be no bathroom in the house, a source of more concern to Oliver Smith than to Jane who regarded the cost of the house 'low enough in price to come under the heading of a "lark" because "lark" it is – which is all right – but surely it will end up costing more than not having a house'. On the whole, Jane would have preferred a house in the United States, something in a small town, where they could leave their belongings. On the question of her coming to Tangier, 'I am *bitter* that I have missed the hotel part of your sojourn (all for nothing too) and that I shall arrive in time for the mess. I know now that it was a mistake to stay here.'

Jane's indecisiveness and vacillation about whether or when to come to Tangier continued for another six months. She had launched on another affair, with a woman called Jody, a middle-aged New England woman. A clairvoyant had predicted to Bowles some fatality or injury on a trip and Jane took this more or less seriously; her mother was ill; there were dispositions to be made about the New York apartment; the prospect of the journey alarmed her; she was still struggling to finish her novel. She did not actually arrive in Gibraltar, accompanied by Jody, until 31 January 1948. They crossed to Tangier by ferry, but Bowles was not there to meet them. He had gone to Fez in December, where he had picked up some *majoun* at the barbershop, and thereafter headed out into the Sahara by way of Oujda, thence to Colomb Bechar in Algeria, and to Taghit. From Taghit, he had gone deep into the desert to Beni-Abbes and then to Timimoun. In the town of Adrar, he received a cable announcing Jane's arrival, and flew from Adrar to Algiers in a tiny plane, contriving to arrive in Tangier three days after Jane's arrival.

If Jane had acquired a new lover, Bowles had also developed at least a sympathetic and fond interest in a young Moroccan man, Ahmed Yacoubi, to whom he introduced Jane and Jody on a trip to Fez. Yacoubi's mother, a superb cook, had prepared a batch of *majoun* candy that Yacoubi brought round to the hotel one evening for the Bowleses who were staying at the Palais Jamaï. Bowles issued strict warnings to Jane, Jody, and a friend, Edwin Denby, who had accompanied them. Bowles insisted that they eat only a very little at first and wait for it to take effect before attempting to eat more. They sat around together, drinking copious quantities of tea, playing the phonograph, watching Yacoubi draw on hotel stationery, and getting a little high. At one point, Jane was heard to say, 'Ah, this stuff is nothing.' Bowles 'turned and saw her finishing off a further large piece of *majoun*. "It has no effect," she explained.' Bowles was angry. Jane was contemptuous.

The evening wore on. Jane got sleepy, and I began to be convinced that she was right. I went into my room and slept. The next morning she was in a highly emotional state. She had not yet been able to fall asleep, she claimed, and her night had been ten nights long and totally horrible. First she had begun to worry that something was happening to me; then as the drug came on more powerfully, she had become convinced that I was about to steal in and murder her. Finally she had noticed her hands and had not understood what they were. When she saw her fingers move, she became paralysed with terror. Illogically enough, from that day on, she remained an implacable enemy of all forms of cannabis. The fact that her experience had been due solely to an overdose seemed to her beside the point. 'Anything that can do awful things like that is dangerous,' she contended.

Bowles, accustomed to Morocco and Tangier, able to regulate his life with precision and work regularly at his novel, seemed to Jane to have overestimated her capacity to become acclimatized and acculturated. Even before arriving in Tangier, she had been worried about the slow, spasmodic progress she had been able to make in her own writing, and simultaneously envied her husband's apparent creative facility while resenting the struggle she experienced with her own work. She fretted about the possibility that Bowles would be disgusted with her uselessness, and attempted to compensate for this unease by becoming protective of both him and his work while in fact demanding his attention and care by becoming querulous. She was hurt that he had not been in Tangier to meet her when she first arrived, and only several months later – in his absence – did she feel able to remonstrate with him and air her sense of grievance in a long letter. Bowles had apparently been disappointed that Oliver Smith had failed to arrive on a particular day in May, and Jane had recognized Bowles' disquiet, contrasting it with what she supposed to have been his indifference towards Jane herself: 'I was particularly disturbed by the fact that you lingered on in Fez with Edwin instead of rushing to the Farhar [Hotel] to see me. I felt very jealous and left out; I sensed that you were really better off with Edwin and that there would be an unfortunate comparison made at some future date . . . I have never tried harder to be in your world – to see it the way you did which probably is why I was in such a foul temper the whole time.'

Continuing in this vein, Jane wrote: 'I wanted to be companionable and pleasant – a source of mild pleasure at meal times and otherwise calm and self-effacing. I am really and truly sorry that it turned out so differently. I don't quite know yet what happened but I do know I have never been so near to a crack-up before.' Jane was concerned that Bowles thought she had been shamming a heart condition in Fez – in fact she had been ill, a local doctor had diagnosed 'something organically wrong' with her heart, and, though the symptoms disappeared, she had been worried. Writing to Bowles, she commented: 'sometimes I feel that you saw the whole thing, I mean the state of my health, as nothing but a threat to your trip, which mattered to you more than anything.'

She was deeply concerned about her position in Morocco and as wife to Paul Bowles: 'I am not attached to you simply because I'm married to you, as you certainly must know.' There were financial difficulties, too, which placed strains upon the relationship: 'I get upset when you say you have enough money for one, but not for two etc. It's probably true, unless we live in a house – it's surely true when one is travelling.' In the few months since Jane's arrival they had done a good deal of travelling in Morocco, either together or separately. 'It is also true that I could have stayed behind in America indefinitely and have cost you nothing. But now that I am here I am damned if I'll ruin it by worrying about these things. I am extremely grateful to you for letting me stay and use the money. I don't believe I have it coming to me because I'm your wife. I just can't bear that idea and yet I'm not sure either that atavistically I don't probably consider myself – partly – entitled to this sojourn because I am your wife? In other words I feel both things at once. That you are completely free and someone who will help me when he can, out of affection, and yet also that you are a husband.'

Jane's many and various occasions for self-doubt, for loss of self-regard and failure to build on past experience and achievements was nowhere more evident that in her attempts to write. There was a certain element of competition with Bowles, but equally she regarded herself as quite distinct from him. To Millicent Dillon, Bowles gave an account of his wife's difficulty with the process of writing. For a start, she was so much in awe of his work that she despaired of her own success as a writer: or so she said to Bowles and others. Bowles considered this argument specious, though it sounded plausible to Jane. It diverted attention from the disabling effects of her very approach to the craft or art of writing.

'Her own method of work was at fault. The weight of the work was too heavy for her to pull. She didn't know how to get into training to pull such a heavy load all at once.' Jane chose to ignore her past achievements, which did not seem to her to be adequate, and so she was unable to carry her experience of accomplished work forward to inform and help her to deal with present or future work. 'It was as if each new work she began was from scratch.' Bowles says, 'I used to talk with Jane by the hour about writing.' Jane would say, 'I know you believe in me, but leave me alone.' Persisting, Bowles would attempt to advise her on the simplest matters.

I'd say to her, 'Just for the first page, say she comes in, sees this, does that.' And she'd say, 'No, no, no. That's your way, not my way. I've got to do it my way and my way is more difficult than yours.' No, it all had to be difficult from the first paragraph in order for her to have respect for it . . . she wasn't interested in making it easier. When she finished a thing, she wanted to be able to say she'd done it all herself. She had to make everything herself. She couldn't use the hammer and the nails that were there. She had to manufacture her own hammer and all the nails. She was a combination of enormous egotism and deep modesty at the same time. You could see that she thought no one was as good as she, but then she'd say, 'I'm not good at all.'

Jane's laboured method of literary composition appeared to derive from an inability to use any image in her text that she could not fully, consciously, comprehend. They had tried to establish a routine: after breakfast, Jane would set to work in her own room while Bowles worked in his. The door was left open to facilitate any necessary communication between them. Jane, at one point, 'had a terrible time with a bridge she was trying to build over a gorge. She would call out: "Bupple! What's a cantilever, exactly?" or "Can you say a bridge has buttresses?"' Bowles, immersed in that 'voluntary state of obsession' that he entered when writing, would answer with anything that came into his head. It would not be long before Jane shouted another earnest question. The bridge occupied her for three or four days until Bowles finally got up and came through to Jane's room to discuss the problem. '"Why do you have to *construct* the damned thing?" I demanded. "Why can't you just say it was there and let it go at that?" She shook her head. "If I don't know how it was built, I can't see it."' Bowles was incredulous. 'It had never struck me that such considerations could enter into the act of writing. Perhaps for the first time I had an inkling of what Jane meant when she remarked, as she often did, that writing was "so *hard*."' With Bowles' help, she completed her short story, *Camp Cataract*.

By 10 May, Bowles had finished *The Sheltering Sky*, which he despatched to his agent in New York, Helen Strauss, for delivery to Doubleday. In mid-July, he took passage on a ship for New York in response to a request from Tennessee Williams who had asked him to provide a score for *Summer and Smoke*, scheduled for autumn production. Bowles left Jane at the Hôtel Villa de France in Tangier, where she seemed content with the view from her window and proposed to do some work on her novel, *Out in the World*. She had taken trouble to begin learning Maghrebi Arabic, adopting the Tangier dialect which differed somewhat in vocabulary and pronunciation from the dialect of Fez which Bowles had acquired and preferred.

Bowles praises Jane's considerable powers of absorption: 'less than two months after she had arrived in Morocco, she was able to speak as well as I.' But Jane's own perception of her abilities were, in this regard as in most others, minimized by self-doubt and her tendency to measure herself harshly against her husband's seemingly effortless superiority. 'Because my vocabulary was larger and I was more fluent, she imagined that I was more proficient than she.' Proficiency in the Tangier dialect was essential to Jane, who loved the city. Bowles remarks on her taste for its 'hybrid, seedy quality', contrasting it with his own esoteric preference for the 'medieval formality of Fez, even in its state of decay'. Jane's devotion to Tangier was largely accountable to her rapid acquisition of Muslim friends whose houses she visited. 'She loved to be with Moroccans, principally, she claimed, because of their sense of humor. Like Jews, they spent their lives with their families, distrusting, ridiculing, and reviling one another, and yet managed to laugh together betweentimes.'

Bowles, though he assumed he would be in the United States only a couple of months, in fact did not return to Tangier until December 1948, some five months after his departure. In his absence, Jane – in addition to her declared intention to do some literary work – was largely preoccupied with two matters: settling legal negotiations about ownership of the little house Bowles and Oliver Smith had bought, and an increasing fascination with a peasant girl called Cherifa to whom Bowles had introduced her. Bowles himself had been mightily struck by Cherifa, reputed to be a descendant of the patron saint of Tangier. Bowles describes his first sight of her, seated in her accustomed place in the Grand Socco market: 'She was sitting in her hanootz, a booth not high enough even to crouch in, just high enough to clear the top of her hat if she sat on the ground. It was like a little box. Outside were mountains of wheat and barley and oats that she was selling. She was dressed as a country woman with a great big hat and a red-and-white striped blanket around her. At that time she was very extraordinary looking, with beautiful shining black hair that fell around her head. She had a laugh like a savage. She was like a public monument, one of those beings you took a visitor to see.'

Cherifa was about nineteen or twenty years old, illiterate, monolingual in the Tangier dialect of Maghrebi Arabic, and said to be a lesbian. Her appearance did not belie her character – she was a woman of powerful personality, ruthlessness, single-minded self-interest, and pride, immoderately contemptuous of every convention that would deny her personal gratification and independence. Jane immediately fell in love with this wild, black-haired woman who sat shamelessly unveiled selling grain in the market. Writing to Bowles, Jane declared: 'I continue loving Tangier – maybe because I have the feeling of being on the edge of something that I will some day enter . . . It is hard for me to separate the place from the romantic possibilities that I have found in it. I cannot separate the two for the first time in my life. Perhaps I shall be perpetually on the edge of this civilization of theirs. When I am in Cherifa's house I am still on the edge of it, and when I come out I can't believe I was really in it – seeing her afterwards, neither more nor less friendly, like those tunes that go on and on or seem to, is enough to make me convinced I was never there.'

Jane's difficulties with writing, insofar as they derived from her own character, were echoed in her attitude towards using the language she had acquired in Tangier: 'Now that I've mastered a few words it's become an ordeal for me to go into the market. I am frightfully shy and embarrassed by the whole thing – my pronunciation, my inability to understand them most of the time.' Nevertheless, her attempts to communicate in Tangier dialect mostly delighted the market peasants who were surprised to hear anyone but themselves even attempt to speak their language. In August 1948, a few weeks after Bowles' departure for New York, she wrote to him about her uncertain progress:

I wrote to you how exciting it was to feel on the edge of something. Well, it's beginning to make me very nervous. I don't see any way of getting further into it, since what I want is so particular (as

usual); and as for forgetting them altogether, it's too late. For me
Africa right now is the grain market and being an obsessive maybe
nothing will change that. I am still learning Arabic and I still
love Tangier but I cannot tell how long it will take me to admit
that I'm beaten. It is not any personal taste that I'm obliged to
fight but a whole social structure, so different from the one you
know – for certainly there are two distinct worlds here (the men's
world and the women's), as you've often said yourself.

Jane was not, like most expatriates, content to live among the
European and American community and conduct the sort of sterile
social life that mostly excluded all Moroccans save those of the
highest rank. To Bowles, she wrote: 'I know you don't like Tangier
much [Bowles preferred Fez, above all Moroccan cities] so perhaps
it's silly for me to think you can be pleased with my taking any
pleasure in it. Perhaps you are not at all pleased. But I think you
do approve of my having some Arab women friends and you do
see how boring it can be otherwise ... I am very happy – with
moments of depression because I always have them, but very few.
I am delighted I stayed. Tangier is wonderful in summer.' It is
worth quoting at some length Jane's letter to Bowles of August
1948 for the vivid picture she gives of her life during his absence that
year. Besides conjuring scene after scene with quick, impressionistic
strokes, the letter is alive with her wit, self-mockery, and her empathetic, earnest attempts to come to terms with the women and the
culture of Tangier that so bewitched her imagination and absorbed
her energies:

> I am off to Cherifa's hanootz. Our relationship is completely
> static: just as I think that at least it is going backwards (on
> the days when she sneaks behind a stall) I find that it is right
> back where it was the next day. Nothing seems to move. I
> have finally, by wasting hours and hours just hanging about
> mentioning the Aid Es Seghir [a Moroccan feast day] about
> every five seconds, managed to get myself invited for tonight.
> So I shall go soon to the grain market from where we will
> leave for M'sallah [a district of Tangier] together. I don't
> know whether I shall walk behind her or in front of her or
> parallel to her on the other side of the street. I made my

invitation secure by suggesting a chicken. I made wings of my
arms and flapped them – 'djdédda' – your phonetic spelling and
mine are different so don't correct the above in your mind.

Later: it would take far too many pages to explain how the Aid
Es Seghir came a day sooner than moon experts expected that it
would, and how I therefore went to Cherifa's the very night after
the carousing was over. Because in a normally arranged world
the whole appointment would have evaporated. On the feast day
they don't come to market at all, and on that day we had fixed
our rendezvous there which was in everyone's opinion the day
before the feast. I was to give her the chicken then so that it could
be plucked and put with the olives for the following day. It is all
so ridiculous – because others said it wouldn't come for five days.
Then I worried about the chicken rotting – well how can I ever
explain this?

But somehow in this peculiar world where nothing is arranged
there is a sudden miraculous junctioning, a moment of unraveling
when terribly complicated plans – at least what would be a complicated plan anywhere else – work out somehow as if in a dream,
where one has only to think of something for it actually to appear
(your novel). It would take years to believe in this, and not to
see it merely as an amusing mirage – I mean to believe that such
things *do* work out for the Arabs *when* they do, not because there
is a law of chance but because such a lack of concentration on
even the immediate future would allow all sorts of mysterious
rhythms to flower, which we are no longer in possession of. I
wonder. The Herrera soup coming down through the streets from
all the far sections of Tangier to the Arabs who remained in the
Socco after dark – always on time, always warm, and always
sufficient to serve the number of people gathered – just like
Cherifa's tiny blue tea pot with its endless supply of tea.

Well, in any case I wandered down there at 7.30 AM just thinking, Well, maybe she has thought of our appointment and come
to wait for me at some point. She wasn't there but the old yellow-
faced mountain dyke was, and alas I had to eat quantities of
perfectly terrible tortilla-like bread soaked in rancid oil, flies and
honey! Then I followed a parade thinking, 'Well it's such a funny
country, maybe I'll meet her this way.' The policeman said the
parade was going to M'sallah but of course it stopped a little

above the Villa de France, and the next policeman – also an Arab
– said they were *not* going to M'sallah but turning 'round and
going back down to the Mendoubia. By then I'd already waited
around for it an hour, while it just remained in the square behind
the Villa. I was planning to follow it to M'sallah. It was thus far
the hottest day in the year and the Tangier flies in August are
terrific. Funnily enough I don't mind very much because I am
having fun.

The men in the parade, some of those wonderful old men, were
really beautiful in pink chiffon over white, some in pointed red
fez and others in the usual square (?) ones. The horses were wildly
spirited even in the heat, and there were hundreds of women
gathered all on one side of the road in beautiful djellabas. I went
back to the market feeling that there was no chance of meeting
her, but somehow I went anyway. She *was* there – no glimmer of
surprise or pleasure in her eye when she saw me, in spite of the
arrangements having been completely bitched up because of the
Aid Es Seghir coming a day sooner. Probably because she'd forgotten there were any arrangements. I had to go through the
whole thing again about the chicken 'dar dialek gadi numshi
maak' etc. and she said I should meet her at 7.00 PM there in the
grain market.

At 10.30 we started for M'sallah with her cousin Mohammed
(who is a good musulman), as our escort. He always steps in
when she is on the outs with Boussif – which is now the case. I
shall tell you the rest of the story some other time. I miss you and
I wish that we could once be together some place where we could
both be having such foolish days and yet days that are so full of
magic too. It would be fun to come back and talk about them. I
can see that I would *hate* to have someone waiting here at the
hotel for me, with an eye on the watch and feeling very sad. How
eleven women wandered in and out of Cherifa's house and all
had tea out of the tiny pot in the morning is something I so wish
I could make you see in *color*. But I'm afraid I never can.

For Jane, Tangier as a place on the edge – which is, after all, the
place where things become interesting – was profoundly enigmatic.
She did not have any very pressing reasons to stay without Bowles;
rather, 'since I don't make decisions, ever, I am somehow here

because I didn't leave.' Her disadvantages so far as the Arab culture were concerned were clear – first, she did not yet have a completely fluent command of the language; secondly she was automatically considered to be a Christian in a Muslim country – and she would have been treated no better as a Jew; thirdly she was a woman and considered to be European on account of her white skin: 'any of the market women are ashamed to be seen with me in the streets.' These substantial impediments to her full acceptance greatly vexed Jane: 'I can't bear to be continually hurled *out* of the Arab world. The rest of Tangier doesn't interest me *enough*' – the result being that she was inclined, initially, to see very few people in the international expatriate community and to feel lonely. She had an unsatisfied greed for Tangier, however much she felt distanced, in some respects, from its full, impenetrable life. 'I can understand how if one could get all one wanted here and were admired, courted and feted, that one would *never never* leave. Even so, without all that . . . I have never felt so strongly about a place in my life, and it is just maddening not to be able to get *more* of it.'

Throwing herself precipitately into Tangier, even at the risk of being repulsed and denied the desired depths of intimacy by her Moroccan friends, was the means chosen by Jane to achieve substantiality. She would hurl herself over that edge that so alarmed her. Without some external confirmation of value and worth, without some cue and response from others, she felt too much exposed to the random nature of the world. To Bowles, she wrote: 'I wonder too if I would bother with all this if you didn't exist. I don't know. Surely I wouldn't have begun it – got the idea without you, I mean. It is the way I feel about my writing too. Would I bother if you didn't exist? It is awful not to know what one would do if one were utterly alone in the world. You would do just what you've always done and so would Helvetia but I don't exist independently.'

Aside from the pressing matter of ingratiating herself with Cherifa (who appeared, inscrutably, to be mad for a Moroccan named Boussif) and another Moroccan market woman called Tetum, Jane was also engrossed with difficulties that had arisen in connection with the Medina house that, it appeared, was likely to cost Bowles and Oliver Smith more money than had originally been thought – principally for the reason that they had paid about three hundred dollars more than the house was worth. Immediately fol-

lowing a lengthy letter to Bowles and Smith detailing – with excru-
ciating exactness – the problems and possible solutions, Jane wrote
promptly again in October 1948 to discuss the vexed matter of her
personal finances and the joint financial arrangement she had with
Bowles. Her agreed budget, in Bowles' absence, was one hundred
pesetas a day – about three dollars – amounting to roughly $223
for eleven weeks. Jane is scrupulous in her accounting, confessing
to the purchase of a skirt for nine dollars which has contributed to
her being eleven or twelve dollars over budget. Out of the $254 left
for her by Bowles, she has spent $234, leaving a balance in her
purse of $25 [*sic*]. The demands on Jane's budget are an interesting
indication of prices in Tangier in the late 1940s – her hotel room
at the Villa de France, with service and breakfast, amounted to
fifty-five pesetas a day, 'which leaves me 45 pesetas to live on.
When you figure in tips, laundry, drugs, stamps – you can see very
well that I can't be throwing money around. A decent meal costs
30 pesetas [about one dollar], as you know, minimum. Still one
can get an indecent one for 12, 22 or 18 pesetas, and I have eaten
at the Parade [Bar] *free* and a lot at a special rate. I am not
complaining but saying that 100 pesetas (unless one is in a house)
is less than I *thought* it was.'

Cherifa and Tetum have been expensive friends: Jane wonders,
perhaps not quite idly, if Tetum has not given her 'a gri-gri [a sort
of magic concoction] to eat – a gri-gri made for Europeans and
which prompts them to give away everything they own. Fortunately
I restrain myself.' Her letter to Bowles entreats him to wire one
hundred dollars as promptly as possible. The insecurity of being
'overdrawn and sitting in Africa without cent one' also prompted
her to appeal to Libby Holman, writing with elaborate directions
about how money should best be sent. Jane's social life among the
European expatriates at this time appears to have been confined
to the Parade Bar, where she and some others chipped in together
for 'very cheap big lunches . . . I live entirely on starch and vegetables and fish. I have forgotten what meat tastes like, and I don't
care, except that right now I don't have supper. I don't need it
really but it makes an awfully *long* day.'

Most of the day was taken up with Tetum and Cherifa at the
market, but at about

6.30 or 7.00 they leave the market, so I can either go to the
Parade or home to bed. At the Parade I have a special price
when I do drink, so don't worry about that. I am always so
terribly gloomy when Tetum ties up the grain sacks and says
goodbye. Often she and Cherifa leave the market together and
we part in front of the hotel. I watch them disappearing up
the road in the beautiful soft night and I just can't *yet* go to
my room. The Parade is a warm spot to go to thank God
otherwise I should be too lonely I think – I *know*. My breakfast
comes in at six and as usual any work that isn't done by twelve
isn't done at all. I am buckling down on the work but I
daresay something will upset it.

Jane's loneliness, her *horror vacui*, upset her. The wistfulness with
which she watched her friends disappear for the night into to their
secret lives enfolded her in dark misery. At that point, the city
perhaps disturbed her more than usually. It had a centre somewhere, if she could only attain to it. But her friends said goodbye
and left her alone, abandoned at the edge of discovery. She herself
had a centre, if she could only locate it and dwell therein. As it
was, she prowled around her own periphery. Cherifa, Tetum, and
the other women of Tangier might be the key to unlock secret
recesses. They lived intensely female lives, apparently and superficially ruled by the restraints imposed upon them by men, but
they remained powerful in their own personalities, possessed of
profound, magical and feminine arts that gave them the edge over
men. Cherifa, more than usually independent for a Moroccan
woman, tested the boundaries of traditional conventions that dictated a woman's role in Moroccan society: she possessed a strength
that Jane envied and desired.

Bowles, who seemed to be able to move without difficulty
through Tangier and the larger world, wrote infrequently and,
when he did write, somewhat tersely. Her abandonment seemed
complete. By November, she was seriously disturbed by his silence.
'Since the end of October I have been waiting in vain for a letter,
some indication of what you wanted to do and what you hoped I
would do. You say casually that you have neglected your correspondence because of your work but surely you could have found time
to scribble a line. I hate to think anyway that I am part of that

correspondence of yours and that you only write me when you pull out the list.'

Bowles returned to Tangier in December, accompanied by Tennessee Williams and his lover Frank Merlo. Jane went to Gibraltar to meet their ship when it docked, and Williams remembers his first sight of Jane Bowles who presented herself in her customary manner: 'small, piquant, darting between humor, anxiety, love and distraction. I had met nervous girls before, but her quicksilver animation, her continual cries, to me and herself: "Shall we do this or shall we do that? What shall we do?" showed such an extreme kind of excited indecision that I was sceptical of its reality – intrigued, certainly, but still somewhat incredulous . . . I soon came to see the reality of Jane. All that indecision was a true and dreadful concern that she might suggest a wrong move in a world that she had correctly surmised to be so inclined to turn wrongly.'

On better acqaintance, Williams recognized and admired 'her concern for others, for their comfort and their entertainment. The important little things, especially such as providing meals, acquainting you with the right doctors in foreign places, conducting you through markets, introducing you to the interesting people, and somehow, in the midst of confusion, finding the precisely right words to reassure you in your own confusion – these were her particular gifts – ways to get agreeably through day and evening.' Nevertheless, delighted though he was with Jane and with Bowles, Williams was not enchanted by Tangier: 'We arrived at just the beginning of the rainy season and for reasons of economy (the Bowles') we put up at a perfectly ghastly hotel called the El Far-Har (rhymes with horror) at the top of a very steep hill over the ocean. Spectacular view: every possible discomfort! The meals were about 25c each but were not worth it. I got ill there. A dreadful cold . . . and I developed a peculiar affliction – vibrations whenever I lowered my head, running up and down my whole body like an electric vibrator!' Williams and Merlo stayed two weeks in Tangier before making for Fez, with Bowles, in Williams' car, a new Buick Roadster.

Jane herself was preoccupied with her lover, Jody, who had arrived in Tangier. This visit temporarily diverted her from Cherifa and Tetum who, between them, had dispossessed Jane of her scarves, much of her money and her watch. She had promised

Cherifa a new djellabah and shoes, and Cherifa was earnestly and improbably negotiating for Jane to buy her a taxi. A new diversion had recently occurred to Cherifa: medical attention. 'I am now taking Cherifa to the doctor's twice a week. I shall have to stop however unless he is willing to make me a price. I think he will . . . I don't mind being liked for my money one bit. Being the richest woman in the world has certain disadvantages but I accept them. I feel that I have done everything, absolutely everything wrong, but perhaps something nice will happen anyway.' Tetum, wildly jealous of Cherifa's status as a regular visitor to a doctor, insisted on similar treatment: 'I asked her what was wrong, and as far as I could gather she merely wanted a *thorough checkup*. Last month they were burning crocodile dung and pig's bristles and now they all want x-rays. Cherifa was wild and said I couldn't take Tetum to the doctor because it would be a disgrace and that the doctor would be horrified if I came with a *second* Moorish woman. I have never understood why, but I am terrified of going against her orders and have therefore made an enemy of Tetum.'

For all Jane's attempts to ingratiate herself with Moroccan women, to delve deep into their lives and accommodate their whims in hopes that they would finally, fully accept her and – perhaps – initiate her into some understanding and participation in their mysterious lives, their close and impenetrable world of the female, she could not succeed in wholly effacing her own self. Her nationality, colour, language, religion and ineffable foreign character all weighed too heavily in the balance which would never swing in her favour, no matter how much money and efforts at empathy she added as a counterweight. Yet, her foreignness was her most powerful weapon: to Cherifa and Tetum she was as inscrutable as they to her, as fascinating in her strangeness. Few enough Tangerinos had made much attempt to enter into the lives of the native inhabitants of the city, and an opportunity to inspect the curious life of the Nazarenes at close quarters, to benefit from their odd, inexplicable magic, was not to be missed.

It was extraordinary to Cherifa and Tetum that anyone should wish to dissociate herself from her own people, but such foolishness was an opportunity for advantage. If Allah had chosen to put this woman in their path, He no doubt had his reason – and that reason, properly interpreted, could only be that He wished to enrich his

Muslim daughters at the expense of an infidel. Jane appeared to be a willing sacrifice. But it would do them no good to be seen to associate too closely with their victim: a decent distance must be preserved if they were not to lose face by being perceived to have gone over to the Nazarene camp. There was no question of sharing with Jane, however willing she might be to pay any fee for admission to the mysteries. A Moroccan could come forward to array herself in the benefits of Nazarene culture, but essentially her virtue as a good Muslim woman would remain untouched. But let a Christian woman into their lives, and she would necessarily defile them.

With Jody, Jane went to Marseille in February and returned alone to Tangier where almost immediately Bowles, returning from Fez, proposed a trip together into the Sahara. Following pretty much the same itinerary as Bowles' previous excursion into the desert, they spent about a month, in March 1949, travelling to Taghit where Jane wrote a short story, *A Stick of Green Candy*, which was to be her last piece of finished writing. On their return, she resumed her life with the market women. Tetum had finally achieved her ambition: an X-ray which, to Tetum's mind, amply compensated for the ten treatments Cherifa had enjoyed for her foot. 'It is all really about prestige,' Jane wrote in a letter to friends '– their life I mean – but I cannot tell them even that I know they are making an ass of me. I am always scared that they might find out I know.' Yet, for all this candid self-awareness, Jane could not cut short her voyage of discovery. If she knew she was nothing more that the dupe of Moroccan women, she could still hope that her perseverance would wear down their resistance, that finally they might prove to have a moral conscience that would oblige them to give something in return. They were hospitable enough, willing to tolerate her in the market and occasionally in their homes and domestic ceremonies, and Jane could not wholly believe that the final curtain would not soon be raised and that, through a full revelation, she would not finally become whole and assimilated into the central nub and mystery of Tangier.

For an exile, it is rarely enough simply to have left home: exile is often a quest for another actuality, a search for the true home in which one will finally find one's uncompromised nature and become integrated as a whole personality. Exile, at worst, is a life lived on the hard, unaccommodating crust of the earth, rootless and windblown. The company of other exiles is an arid reminder of loss and of inability to become assimilated into another culture. Neither Bowles nor Jane could tolerate the thin and dispossessed company of fellow exiles as a staple, insipid social diet. They hungered for the spiritual food that, mostly, Tangier denied them. Jane was, in a sense, starving to death. Neither Cherifa nor Tetum appeared willing to feed her. She it was who sustained them by her famished demands. It is difficult to rid oneself of the notion that Tantalus would have found Tangier a familiar hell.

In May, Bowles visited Paris to attend a performance of his *Concerto for Two Pianos and Orchestra* at the Salle Pleyel. Americans had begun to return to the city, among them Aaron Copland, Gore Vidal and Truman Capote. Bowles took an opportunity to resume his friendship with Copland, and Capote decided to spend the summer in Tangier. According to Bowles, Gore Vidal 'was pulling out all the stops in order to annoy' Capote and decided to get to Tangier before him 'and continue his game' of baiting Capote. Bowles went first to Tangier, followed by Vidal who arrived a few days later. ' "Come to the dock with me," he told me the afternoon Truman was to land. "Watch his face when he catches sight of me." As the ferry pulled in, Truman leaned out over the railing, grinning widely and waving a very long silk scarf. When he saw Gore standing beside me, he did a little comic-strip routine. His face fell like a soufflé placed in the ice compartment, and he disappeared entirely below the railing for several seconds. When he had assumed a standing position again, he was no longer grinning or waving. Gore stayed around Tangier only long enough to make Truman believe he was going to spend the whole summer, and then he quietly left.'

Capote, recognizing perhaps some fey, windblown quality in Jane, who fluttered through Tangier at a slight angle to its several

worlds, giving each a spin on its axis as she fingered them in her
quick, darting curiosity, was delighted by her. In an essay about
Tangier he calls her 'Jonny Winner' and describes her as

> A sweet funny girl ... She is very young, very American, and
> you would never believe, looking at her clouded, wistful face, that
> she is able to take care of herself: to tell the truth, I don't think
> she is ... Why Jonny Winner wants to spend the rest of her life
> in Tangier is of course her own business; obviously she is in love:
> 'But don't you love it, too? to wake up and know that you're here,
> and know that you can always be yourself, never be anyone that
> isn't you? And always to have flowers, and to look out your
> window and see the hills getting dark and the lights in the harbor?
> Don't you love it too?' On the other hand, she and the town are
> always at war; whenever you meet her she is undergoing a new
> *crise*: 'Have you heard? the most awful mess: some fool in the
> Casbah painted his house yellow, and now everybody's doing it
> – I'm just on my way to see if I can put a stop to the whole thing.'

Capote caught the Grand Socco market before it was entirely
turned into a bus station, taxi rank and car park. Jane had been
rushing about making her usual fuss, declaiming and despairing.
'The Grand Soko is the great Arab market square: Berbers, down
from the mountains with their goatskins and baskets, squat in
circles under the trees listening to storytellers, flute players, magi-
cians; cornucopia stalls spill over with flowers and fruit; hashish
fume and the minty scent of *thé Arabe* cling to the air; vivid spices
burn in the sun. All this is to be moved elsewhere, presumably to
make way for a park, and Jonny is wringing her hands: "Why
shouldn't I be upset? I feel as though Tangier were my house, and
how would you like it if somebody came into your house and started
moving the furniture around?"'

The summer of 1949 was, by the standards of the Tangier
expatriate community, the most brilliant social season since before
the War. Besides Truman Capote – a continuous party all by himself – two representatives of the fashionable *beau monde* in London
had arrived to take up residence in the Villa Mektoub. Cecil
Beaton, with his friend the Hon. David Herbert, moved into the
property on the Marshan owned by members of the Guinness

family, and proceeded to enjoy a vivacious round of lunches, dinners and parties quite in the style of the Twenties and Thirties. Tangier, according to Bowles, 'was not really to Truman's taste, but he stuck it out all summer at the Farhar with Jane and me because of Cecil's presence . . . The summer proved the apogee of postwar prosperity in the International Zone. Immediately afterwards the cracks in the façade began to appear, and they constantly grew wider, until the entire edifice collapsed in the riots of 1952.'

Dancing on the edge, Capote felt none of the political and social tensions: he observed only 'an international city with an excellent climate eight months of the year, roughly March to November'. He regarded Tangier as a lotus-land that snared the unwary: 'Tangier is a basin that holds you, a timeless place; the days slide by less noticed than foam in a waterfall; this, I imagine, is the way time passes in a monastery, unobtrusive and on slippered feet; for that matter, these two institutions, a monastery and Tangier, have another common denominator: self-containment. The average Arab, for example, thinks Europe and America are the same thing and in the same place, wherever that may be – in any event, he doesn't care; and frequently Europeans, hypnotized by the tinkling of an oud and the swarming drama around them, come to agree.'

Time, if it does not quite stand still in Tangier, at least appeared to Capote to move at a slower pace and he described, dreamily, an encampment of Moroccan peasants at Sidi Kacem, a beach just outside Tangier, after nightfall during Ramadan: 'According to the Arab calendar this is the year 1370; seeing a shadow through the silk of a tent, watching a family fry honeycakes on a flat twig fire, moving among the dancers and hearing the trill of a lonely flute on the beach, it was simple to believe that one was living in 1370 and that time would never move forward.'

Cecil Beaton left at the end of the summer, and David Herbert invited the Bowleses to move in and share the expenses of the Villa Mektoub with him. They stayed for six weeks, during which time Jane came down with measles and Bowles occupied himself with supervising the work of rebuilding his house in the Medina. *The Sheltering Sky*, published that autumn in London by John Lehmann, had received good critical notices. This was distinctly better than the reception his book had occasioned at the commissioning publishers in New York, Doubleday, who had refused the manuscript on the inscrutable ground that, whatever else Bowles may have produced, it was not a novel. 'They did not specify what I had given them, but they unhesitatingly rejected it.' Finally, the book was accepted in the United States by James Laughlin who published it in his New Directions list. Lehmann, keen to maintain interest in the book, encouraged Bowles to visit London, whereupon David Herbert invited the Bowleses to go with him to England and stay at Wilton, his family's seat in Wiltshire.

Bowles was received with enthusiasm in London literary circles, and sales of the book in Britain were good – though far outstripped, from mid-October 1949 to March 1950 by sales of up to forty thousand in the United States where it hit the *New York Times* best-seller list and remained there for ten weeks. By December, however, Bowles had embarked on a Polish freighter, the *General Walter*, bound from Antwerp for Colombo in Ceylon. He does not account for this apparently random decision in his autobiography – but he is not, in any event, scrupulously inclined to analyse reasons for his behaviour. At Wilton, browsing through some of David Herbert's scrapbooks, he had come across photographs of the charming, miniature island of Taprobane which lies just off-shore in the Bay of Weligama, at the southernmost tip of Ceylon.

Cut off from the mainland at high tide, it is no more than a hillock rising out of the water, lush with tropical vegetation and crowned with palms waving like the cockade of goose feathers on a Governor-General's helmet. On the crest of Taprobane is a house flanked by terraces shaded by great trees. Bowles determined to visit this little jewel of an island: he liked to travel, he now had the money to do so, and he was looking for some peaceful place where he could begin composing an opera commissioned by Libby Holman. He had decided to translate Lorca's *Yerma* and adapt it in the form of a libretto. It had occurred to him to go to the Sahara, but the incidence of pianos in the desert was uncertain, and no doubt there would be a better chance of finding a suitably tuned instrument in Ceylon. Jane had decided to winter in Paris with Jody, and perhaps Bowles did not wish to inhibit that relationship by his presence.

It may seem surprising to some that Bowles should choose suddenly and without apparent good reason to visit Ceylon, but what was there to stop him? There were reasons not to be in the States, there was a reason not to be in Paris, there was little reason to return alone to Tangier. It didn't really matter to Bowles where he went, and indeed, until almost the last minute, he had not been sure whether he wanted to go to Ceylon or Siam. It happened that the first booking he could get was for Ceylon, and so fate had decided the matter for him. Leaving himself open to chance was characteristic, perhaps exasperatingly to some of his friends but nothing extraordinary to himself.

The *General Walter*, after a rough passage to the coast of Portugal, approached the Straits of Gibraltar. The night the freighter sailed through, Bowles

> stood on deck staring longingly into the dark on the southern side of the ship. A rush of nostalgia for Tangier had seized me. I went inside and got into my berth. Then I began to write something which I hoped might prove the nucleus of a novel about Tangier. The first scene was on the cliffs opposite the point we were passing at that moment. Dyar stands at the edge of the cliff and looks out at the freighters going by in the strait. From that scene the book grew in both directions – backward as cause and forward as effect. By the time we had reached Suez I had made decisions about form and drawn diagrams clarifying motivations and was well into *Let It Come Down*.

Bowles stayed in Ceylon until late May 1950, leaving without – on this occasion – having visited Taprobane.

Jane, meantime, had fallen out with Jody and had fixed her ardent attentions on another American woman living in Paris. Oliver Smith had promised a provincial production of her play *In the Summer House* in Westport, and there was some talk – though nothing firm – about the prospect of transferring the play to Broadway. Jane began to busy herself revising the last act, and filling notebooks with notes and drafts for a new novel, *Out in the World*. Bowles arrived in Paris in early June to find Jane reluctant to return to Tangier: as usual, she had a sleeveful of excuses for delaying action, for dithering about making a decision that would involve some effort to disrupt her routines. After some discussion, they agreed to go to New York together, but were foiled by news from Libby Holman that she intended to visit Spain in July. Bowles, who had intended to work with her on his *Yerma* libretto in New York, opted to return to Tangier for the few weeks before she arrived in Malaga; Jane, in early July, travelled alone to New York to do what she could about the production prospects of her play.

In the event, Jane did not return to Paris until March 1951, staying on to comfort Libby Holman who, on 11 August, one day after leaving Tangier for Marseille, had received a message informing her that her son Christopher had disappeared on an expedition to climb Mt Whitney. A few days later, his body was discovered. Bowles remained in Tangier, working at *Let It Come Down*, writing occasional articles for *Holiday* and the *American Mercury*, and developing two friendships – one with the visionary artist, writer and poet Brion Gysin, the other with Ahmed Yacoubi, with whom he had become more intimate since their first meeting in 1947. Gysin, who had met Bowles in Paris and had been persuaded of the charms of Tangier, occupied the second floor of the several-storied house in the Medina which had finally been renovated. Bowles himself lived on the fourth floor, in a tower which he had built on top of the original structure. Their domestic arrangements were simple: 'Each of us could go in and out without coming near the other's quarters. As a cook we got the butler who had worked for David Herbert the year before. He had been employed by Barbara Hutton earlier and still went to her house occasionally; it was just around the corner. Sometimes as we were finishing lunch, he would come and stand in the doorway to the patio, holding a towel in his hand and tell us unlikely stories about her.'

Before leaving England for Ceylon at the beginning of December 1949, Bowles had given John Lehmann a collection of short stories, including *The Delicate Prey* and *Pages from Cold Point*. He sent another copy to Helen Strauss who placed them with Random House in New York. The full collection was published in the States, and in Britain without the two most significant stories. Reviews were excellent, and sales encouraging. Bowles, if not a rich man, continued his habits of frugality and was at least not in financial distress. He mentioned to Gysin that he longed to have his own car 'so that I could go where I pleased and leave when I felt like leaving'. Gysin could see no difficulty. 'Well, buy one. You can afford it.' This was very shocking to Bowles who had not seriously considered himself as the possible owner of a car. 'Nor had it occurred to me that money was something that could be spent. Automatically I had always hoarded it, spending as little as possible. Brion's suggestion was like the voice of Satan. I began to look at cars, and within two weeks I had bought a new Jaguar convertible.'

A new car led inexorably to the acquisition of a chauffeur, Mohammed Temsamany, who had worked for an American and was recommended by the English proprietrix of the Hôtel Villa Mimosa as efficient. She bullied Bowles into hiring him and providing the new chauffeur with a uniform. Thus suitably equipped, Bowles and Gysin set out first for Fez and Marrakesh, but then, more adventurously, 'for more recondite places, to which there were only trails'. In all, the trip took three or four months – deep into the south of Morocco, along hundreds of miles of rocky trails. The car radiator boiled during a two-day Sahara sandstorm, the car itself fell into quicksand, lumbered across rivers, and occasioned deep respect among the people of the south who were equally impressed by the lordly Temsamany in his sharp militaristic uniform. On return to Fez, Bowles heard from Jane who expressed a wish to leave Paris. With Temsamany and Ahmed Yacoubi, Bowles set out for the French–Spanish border to collect her. 'Jane was in fine form and seemed delighted to be out of Paris at last.' They spent a few days in San Sebastian before driving back in a leisurely manner to Tangier.

Remarking on these journeys, Bowles reflected later that 'We did not know it then, but we were living through the last two or three months of the old, easygoing, openly colonial life in Morocco.' The French had tired of the continual obstruction of their colonial policy by the Sultan, and were attempting to force him to abdicate voluntarily or provoke his deposition. One of their principal instruments was the Pasha of Marrakesh, Thami el Glaoui, a powerful French ally distrusted by Mohammed V who favoured the nationalist aspirations of the Istiqlal. In February 1951, with the connivance of the French, the Glaoui threw thousands of his troops against Fez and Rabat in an effort to depose the Sultan who was forced by a French ultimatum to condemn the Istiqlal. These violent political manoeuvrings provoked a certain anxiety among Moroccans and foreigners alike, and were to result in Mohammed V's exile to Madagascar and a subsequent terrorist war against the French.

Paul Bowles

ABOVE: The British expatriates' Tent Club
pigsticking in the Diplomatic Forest in the 1930s

BELOW: James McBey, 'El Soko 1912', etching

ABOVE:
Truman Capote and the
Bowleses sunbathing

RIGHT:
Left to right: Jane Bowles,
Joseph (Croft-Cooke's
'secretary'), Paul Lund, Carol
Lund, Rupert Croft-Cooke in
The Parade

TOP: Barbara Hutton and Lloyd Franklin

ABOVE: Hutton and David Herbert in
fancy dress

RIGHT: Jay Haselwood and Mrs Ada Green

In the autumn of 1951, Bowles left Gysin alone in the Medina house, nervously preferring the Hôtel Villa Mimosa on the Marshan. Within six weeks Bowles had bolted to Xauen to try to finish *Let It Come Down* in relative peace – it was now two years since he had started writing it, and only the final few chapters remained to be written. He made good progress in Xauen, interrupted briefly by the arrival, for a three-day visit, of Irving Thalberg Jr, who was fortunate enough to 'have happened to be present in a café during a Jilala ritual. A mountain Jilali came in, sat beside us, and soon went into a trance. As he danced, he slashed himself, covered his face with blood, and licked it from his arms and fingers. It was tremendously impressive, the more so for having been done without a word being spoken.' Jane would make the trip to Xauen for occasional weekends, and finally Bowles returned to Tangier to the Medina house where he finished his novel.

Bowles spent December of that year in Tetuan at the Dersa Hotel.

Ahmed Yacoubi was there painting, and Robert Rauschenberg was living just down the street. There was a night distinct from the others when Ahmed served a platter of very powerful *majoun* to Bob and a friend of his without explaining to them what the substance was. Finding it tasty, they spread large quantities of it on their crackers and cookies and washed it down with hot tea. Since they were both totally inexperienced in the use of cannabis, they had no way of understanding what was happening to them. They were in a very strange state when they left the Dersa. Later in the evening we went around to the Hotel Bilbao to see how they were. We climbed up the dark stairway and stood for a moment outside Rauschenberg's room. Through the door came the sound of groaning. We decided that since he was already embarked on an unhappy journey, our arrival could only make it worse, and so we went quietly down the stairs and out into the street.

For Thalberg and Rauschenberg, at least, association with Bowles was an unpredictable and somewhat risky business. Bowles understood, loved, and was coolly fascinated by the mystical, magical aspects of Morocco. Through Yacoubi, who had a fund of stories about native magic and supernatural beliefs, Bowles was able to explore further – just as his car had enabled him better to explore 'more recondite places to which there were only trails' – the esoteric traditions of the Moroccans among whom he had elected to live. Jane, in her own way, also continued to explore her feminine, well-nigh impenetrable Morocco through the lives of the market women of Tangier to whom she had become attached. Just as impenetrable to Jane was Yacoubi's charm and the fondess with which her husband regarded him. She felt exiled from their intimacy and, as such, more insecure and fretful about her own position with Bowles and in Tangier. Neither her work nor her attempts to ingratiate herself with Cherifa and Tetum seemed successful: the one was blocked, the other stymied. Yacoubi's painting had developed since Jane herself, in 1948, had encouraged him to use proper painting materials: his progress may have appeared in direct contrast to her own difficulties.

To a friend, Bowles wrote: 'Ahmed has been making a good many magnificent paintings . . . more complicated and sophisticated, but they have lost none of their madness and directness.' Jane, meanwhile, had extended her social activities among the expatriate community and had begun to frequent the Parade Bar much more regularly and had taken determinedly to drinking there and at parties. She obstinately refused to show her writing to Bowles, who was not encouraged even to talk about it to her – a complete reversal of their previous joint concern for her work. Bowles, diffident about being intrusive, did not insist: she would have heatedly refused if he had. Jane, depressed by her circumstances, feeling less and less in control of them and of her ability to deal constructively with her situation, identified Yacoubi as the disturbing factor, reinforcing her jealousy of him.

Yacoubi was a handsome, intelligent, quick-witted, talented twenty-year-old in 1951. He claimed to be a Sherif on both his father's and his mother's side – a descendant of the Prophet Muhammad. 'His paternal grandfather and his father,' noted Bowles in an introductory note to an exhibition of Yacoubi's paintings, 'exercised the profession of f'qih, which means that he healed by laying on of hands, by the manipulation of fire, by collecting herbs and brewing concoctions of them, and most important, by the writ-

ing of sacred formulas at propitious moments'. This was the profession for which Yacoubi himself had been educated. It was taken
for granted that Bowles and Yacoubi were sexually intimate – and
no moral opprobrium was invoked by Tangier society to whom
such a liaison appeared perfectly straightforward and matter-of-
fact. Christopher Sawyer-Lauçanno, however, states that both
Yacoubi and Bowles later denied any sexual association and he
comments that these denials were made in the particular circumstances of 1957 when Yacoubi was arrested on a charge of having
had sexual relations with a fifteen-year-old German boy.

It is difficult to know the truth of the matter. Yacoubi later
married and fathered children, but this in itself is not evidence that
he was not capable of forming a sexual liaison with Bowles to whom
he largely owed the initial success of his career. Bowles enjoyed
the company of men, a significant number of them homosexual,
and there can be little doubt that he himself felt homoerotic
impulses which he largely suppressed out of fastidiousness or fear.
Culturally, the Moroccan way of life intrigued him and he was
perfectly well aware that, among Riffians particularly, homosexual
relations were not stigmatized as unnatural or vicious. There could
be no question, if a sexual element were to enter into his relationship with Yacoubi, that the young man could in any sense be
corrupted by it. That was a peculiarly Western standard of judgement, quite alien to Moroccan ethics. Yacoubi himself, if an erotic
element were to enter into his friendship with Bowles, would have
accepted it as perfectly natural and accommodated himself to the
situation without feeling compromised.

More likely, however, given Bowles' characteristic remoteness
on the matter of sex, and the fact that Yacoubi stood somewhat *in
statu pupillari*, the matter did not trouble them unduly. If sexual
relations, in whatever form, occurred between them, they were
probably short-lived and both may have been relieved to have got
the matter out of the way. Sex, for Bowles, appears to have been
an embarrassment rather than a relief or a consummation of more
delicate feelings. His fondness for young men can perhaps be better
viewed as somewhat pedagogic and paternal, drawing out their
literary or artistic potential and assisting them to realize themselves
fully. In the process, the benefits to himself were substantial – a
more intimate understanding of Moroccan life and culture, insights

that could not readily be gained by other expatriates who did not
take the trouble to learn the language and listen to the oral tradition. What others thought of his largely innocent diversion did
not greatly trouble Bowles, for whom it was sufficient to know the
truth for himself without protesting his virtue which, in any event,
would probably have been received with some incredulity by others
less scrupulous. Tennessee Williams, for one, believed that Bowles
and Yacoubi were lovers, and that Yacoubi gained the upper hand
by refusing sexual favours: a scenario that probably suited Williams' imagination better than the actuality.

Towards the end of 1951, Jane decided to return to New York. She
still nursed ambitions for a Broadway production of *In the Summer
House* – which, indeed, would open in Ann Arbor, Michigan, in May
1953, before its major production on Broadway in late December of
that year, to close in February 1954. In the event, the play was not
to realize her hopes of recouping her financial and creative capital,
both seriously impoverished. In January 1952 she set sail on the
SS *Saturnia* from Gibraltar. She would not return for two years. In
February 1952, *Let It Come Down* was published in the United States
by Random House and in London by John Lehmann. Though it
did not achieve the immediate success of *The Sheltering Sky*, it sold
a respectable total of more than forty thousand copies in the first
year of publication. *The Sheltering Sky* and *The Delicate Prey* were
continuing to make solid sales in paperback – Signet Books by June
1951 had sold more than two hundred thousand of the former,
while in January 1952 the New American Library published a
paperback edition of over two hundred and forty thousand copies
of the latter.

Bowles, by this time, had bolted for the winter. While in Gibraltar to see Jane off on the *Saturnia*, he had seen 'a poster in the window of a shipping office advertising first-class passage to Bombay for eighty pounds'. It had not previously occurred to Bowles to go to India, but 'suddenly it seemed a good idea and an economical one – almost cheaper than to stay in Morocco'. He took Yacoubi with him. They were at this time inseparable, but Bowles, in his autobiography, is cool, almost heartless, in his reason for doing so. 'I would drop Ahmed Yacoubi, from the Medina of Fez, into the middle of India and see what happened.' This spirit of scientific, anthropological inquiry is typical of Bowles' dry, curt, deprecating humour, designed less to conceal than to skirt personal revelation. Bowles, determined on this trip to see the island of Taprobane, succeeded in reaching Ceylon and finally, after some adventures, reached his terrestrial paradise which he determined to buy – finally succeeding in doing so some weeks later in Madrid.

Now, in March 1953, Bowles was obliged to return to New York. Jane's play was about to be produced and Bowles had promised to write the score. From New York, Bowles and Yacoubi went to 'Treetops' to meet Jane who was staying with Libby Holman. The atmosphere there became stifling with tensions: Jane was still drinking copiously and her jealousy of Yacoubi had not abated. Libby Holman had arranged some shows of Yacoubi's work, and developed more than a connoisseur of painting's interest in the artist. She fell in love. She lavished affection and, significantly, money on the young man who – not unnaturally – responded by more or less abandoning Bowles. Bowles, hurt, left in May for Tangier. Yacoubi, rejoicing in his new shirts, suits, shoes and trappings, elected to stay at 'Treetops' with Holman and Jane. He didn't last more than a few weeks – by early June, Holman was telephoning Jane in New York to complain that Yacoubi had without doubt attempted to drown her seven-year-old son, Timmy, in the swimming pool. Finally, on Jane's recommendation, Yacoubi was shipped back to Morocco – first class – on the USS *Constitution*.

By mid-June, Yacoubi was back in Tangier and immediately went to see Bowles who, according to Temsamany who spoke of the matter to Millicent Dillon, forgave Yacoubi for his behaviour. 'But Jane, she never forgave Ahmed for what he did to Paul.' In extenuation of the episode, Bowles believed that Yacoubi's impressionable head had been turned by Holman's wealth: 'He thought if he were with this rich woman he'd have everything.' Bowles did not blame Yacoubi – rather, he believed his protestations of innocence, and indeed it may have been difficult for Yacoubi to adapt his innate Moroccan character to the behavioural mores of wealthy, upper-caste, artistic East Coast American society. Millicent Dillon characterizes Yacoubi as 'sharp and street-wise, even crafty, in the world he had come from. But he had been thrown into a completely strange world of great wealth and sophistication, where the limits of his own position and his own power were not made clear to him.' Bowles himself had wanted to see how Yacoubi, the boy from the Fez Medina, would react when thrown into India: he could scarcely have been surprised or injured by the results of throwing him into 'Treetops'.

He was not finished with Yacoubi's education, however, or with the attempt to promote his art. Bowles took Yacoubi with him to Rome to work, at the invitation of Tennessee Williams, on the adaptation into English of a Visconti screenplay, *Senso*. With Temsamany in the driver's seat, they took the Jaguar convertible to Barcelona where they met Williams who commented, in a letter to Donald Windham, on the relationship between Bowles and Yacoubi: 'He has two Arabs with him, his lover (stolen but now relinquished by Libby Holman) and a chauffeur . . . [Yacoubi] is torturing Paul by not sleeping with him. It seems that Libby [said] that such relations were very evil and the opinions of a lady with thirty million dollars cannot be taken lightly by a young Arab whose family live in one room [they did not]. Paul looks haggard and is almost too disturbed to do a good job on the film.'

On 25 September 1953, Bowles set sail from Italy to Istanbul, with Yacoubi, to research and write an article for *Holiday*. They returned to Naples in late October, and were driven by Temsamany to Rome to pick up Tennessee Williams, thence to Portofino to visit Truman Capote, and finally they drove back to Tangier where political trouble had broken out as a result of the deposition of the Sultan on 20 August. 'I was in a hurry to see what Morocco would be like now that the terrorists had started their campaign against the French; behind my curiosity lurked the fear that the country would cease to be inhabitable for foreigners under the new circumstances.' Bowles goes on to comment, in his autobiography: 'My fears seemed well grounded; there was now an element of distinct unfriendliness abroad in the streets of Tangier. I had the impression that everyone was waiting for a signal to be given, and that when it came all hell would break loose.'

Williams promptly left Tangier, followed by Bowles who sailed – without Yacoubi – for the United States to complete the score for the November openings of *In the Summer House* which were scheduled for Hartford, Washington, and Boston before the 29 December opening on Broadway. It had received some good notices, but there had been difficulties with the script, with the author, with the casting and the players. It had not only been difficult to produce, it was a difficult play altogether. It achieved something of a cult success among a small group of admirers, not enough to warrant more than a short six-week run. To a journalist from *Vogue*, Jane remarked: 'There's no point in writing a play for your five hundred goony friends. You have to reach more people.' With two friends, Natasha von Hoershelman and Katharine Hamill, Jane returned to Tangier. She opted to live in the Hotel Rembrandt, on the boulevard Pasteur, while Bowles lived with Yacoubi at the Massilia Hotel. The Medina house, Jane claimed, was 'too narrow' for habitation. Jane and Bowles met regularly – mostly for lunch. Arrangements for these appointments took half an hour on the telephone, daily, discussing the time and venue, Jane becoming ever more indecisive. Hamill and von Hoershelman, reminiscing to Millicent Dillon, remarked on Jane's dependence, her reliance upon Bowles and her need to see him – in marked contrast to her behaviour in the States. An article by the drama critic, Walter Kerr, in the *New York Herald Tribune*, referring to her remark in *Vogue*, had perhaps unnerved her rather more than she permitted anyone to know. Kerr had ironically praised what he took, for his own purposes, to be Jane's perspicacity: 'The hack may say what he means and say it flatly. The talented man may say what he means and say it richly. But the talented man who insists upon his right not to say it at all, to hug his meaning like a secret close to his breast, to serve his goony friends rather than the gaping audience, is better off out of the theater. All hail to Jane Bowles for her happy pronouncement.'

Bowles now fell ill: he had neglected to maintain his typhoid shots, and was suffering the symptoms of paratyphoid. For several weeks he was confined to bed, cared for by Jane who, with Yacoubi, had moved into the Medina house where they contrived to tolerate one another. In a letter of June 1954 to Hamill and von Hoershelman, Jane describes at very great length and in very great detail her life in Tangier at this time. She somewhat avoided the social life of the expatriate community, led by David Herbert: 'if one only turns up once every two weeks or so it's nice. Or occasionally one goes out twice in a row. They are all constantly at it . . . I scarcely ever go to the Parade.' Though, on at least one occasion, depressed by the reaction to the *Vogue* article, 'I did go to the Parade and did get very drunk.' Otherwise, her social life was committed to Cherifa and Tetum. Cherifa was now twenty-eight, and Tetum in her mid-forties. Hamill and von Hoershelman had met Cherifa: they described her as 'handsome'; she 'had a gold tooth. Like Janie she was unpredictable – except in one thing. She tried to get every nickel out of Janie that she could.'

They also encountered Tetum in the coal market: 'A woman about forty-five. She was furious because Jane had taken Cherifa to the doctor's. There was a great jealousy between Cherifa and Tetum. They weren't in love with Jane; it was clear that they just wanted to get as much as they could from her – although they would never get rich from Jane, because Jane didn't have any money. Jane didn't have any illusions about their feelings. She didn't care whether they liked her or not. She wanted to be in that life. But, yes, she did love Cherifa.' Hamill and von Hoershelman advised Jane to stick to Cherifa, who could now, regularly, be persuaded to visit Jane at the house in the Medina. 'In fact she spends two or three nights here a week in dungarees and Haymaker shirts. She asked for five thousand pesetas [about one hundred and fifteen dollars] so that she could fill her grain stall to the brim. I have given her, so far, fifteen hundred pesetas.'

Sex with Cherifa was the subject of endless, agonized speculation: Jane declared her inability to understand Cherifa's feelings, her inability to distinguish between lack of passion and clever manoeuvring, and her suspicion that Cherifa's fear was 'just plain fear of losing all her marketable value and that I won't care once I've had her'. Cherifa permitted kissing and other affectionate tokens, but still remained remote and unfathomable. Jane had applied to Bowles and Temsamany for advice. But, 'I can talk to Paul and he

is interested but not that interested because we are all women.'
The fact that both Bowles and Temsamany were men was not, in
this instance, helpful. Temsamany gave it as his opinion that 'if
you don't get them the first two times you never will.' Bowles said
that 'desire can come but only with habit. And never does it mean
what it means to us – rather less than holding hands supposedly.'

Jane fretted about her relationship with Cherifa in particular,
about world events generally, and about money specifically. She
determined to work to make some income and Bowles, manipulat-
ing Cherifa's innate greed and speculation about future benefits to
herself, contrived a situation whereby Cherifa constantly sent Jane
up into her little work room to make money. Jane was working on
another play, an enterprise black-dogged by an obstinate block that
may partly have stemmed from her own innate sense of insecurity
but which, in her own mind, was caused – or, at least, incalculably
strengthened – by what she perceived as the intensity of the
relationship between Bowles and Yacoubi. Bowles himself was
worried by the political situation. He had no wish to leave Morocco,
and certainly no desire to return to the United States. He was
uneasy, too, about Jane's relationship with Cherifa. It was plain
that Jane was bribing Cherifa with gifts to sleep over at the house
and Cherifa had begun to introduce Jane to women Bowles considered highly undesirable types – tough women, one of them
the wife of a notorious gangster, another the madam of a brothel.
Yacoubi, for his own reasons, was terrified of Cherifa who, he
claimed, would not think twice about poisoning him. His dislike
and distrust of her came to a head when Jane told Bowles that she
had found magical talismans – little packets containing antimony,
pubic hair, menstrual blood, fingernails and other powerful items
– under a pillow and a mattress. Jane did not seem particularly
perturbed, but Yacoubi took the discovery as proof that Cherifa
was a witch possessed of true, malevolent power.

Cherifa had denied putting the packets of *tseuheur* in the bed,
blaming jealous neighbours. Jane decided that Yacoubi's reactions
– refusing to eat food cooked by Cherifa, ritual washing and prayer
after seeing her, his demand (to which Bowles agreed) that Bowles
should not visit Jane in the house – were hysterical or at least
disproportionate to the threat he supposed was posed by Cherifa.
She was convinced that Yacoubi was using the incident to drive a

further wedge between herself and Bowles who tended to support Yacoubi in his fright. Jane, for her part, would not believe Yacoubi's allegations of witchcraft against Cherifa. Finally, Jane and Bowles agreed on a compromise. She insisted that she was not jealous of Yacoubi, but said plainly that she did not like to meet him walking in public with Bowles. And she did not like the idea of Yacoubi's name being associated with Bowles' on any occasion such as a party or an exhibition. Bowles agreed to indulge her in these matters.

Worried by the political situation, worried about Jane, Bowles was nevertheless working steadily at a new novel, writing from dawn to midday. The novel concerned the dissolution of the traditional pattern of life in the medieval-seeming city of Fez he had known and loved. In 1954, there were tanks around the immemorial walls and the city was a hotbed of hostility. In his own house in the Tangier Casbah, the political dramas were less apparent, though occasional disturbances were inevitable. To a friend, Bowles wrote: 'Everyone is in a foul temper, people are throwing stones at my house and screaming: Nazarene! (No one answers but the parrot, who gives wolf calls, laughs like a hysterical old maid, and then caws like a flock of crows.) It isn't even amusing for the Arabs, who want nothing more than to see great bloodshed, and spend their time moping around the house in hunger strikes and ripping pictures of Mendès-France out of the papers after which they either spit on them or, which is more likely, put them into their mouths and chew them up, grinding the saliva-soaked paper between their teeth until it's nothing but paste.'

In these circumstances, Bowles remembered that he owned the little island of Taprobane in Ceylon. He booked passages for himself, Jane (who was persuaded, with difficulty, to make the trip), Yacoubi and Temsamany, for Ceylon and they set sail, on the *Orsova*, in December 1954. Jane immediately regretted her decision to leave Tangier. It was hot; when she saw the island she groaned; she characterized the island and the octagonal house as 'a Poe story'; she was alarmed by the nightly invasion of bats with three-foot wingspans and large teeth; there was no electricity, and the wind made the illumination of their one oil lamp uncertain. Bowles immediately established his own own immutable routine: at six each morning he had tea, dressed himself in a sarong, walked round the island, watched the sun rise, and then set to work on his novel, *The Spider's House*, which he completed in mid-March and mailed to Random House.

Worried by snakes, about which she developed a phobia; unnerved by the lushness of the island's rampant vegetation; frankly terrified by the flying foxes; stunned by the humid heat; ignored (as she thought) by Bowles who over-estimated (here, as also, originally, in Tangier) her capacity to adapt to an unfamiliar and possibly inimical environment; well-nigh stupified by the regular daily ingestion of a fifth of gin on top of medication for high blood pressure, Jane was uncomfortable and depressed. The presence of Yacoubi – she had said 'he has holes for eyes', and could not speak his name without following up with a retching noise – was an added irritation. She was doing no work, and blamed herself – at least, in conversation with Bowles – for her malaise. She stuck Taprobane for two months before leaving, with Temsamany, for Morocco. Bowles and Yacoubi, after a tour of the Far East, returned to Tangier in June 1955.

If Taprobane had been like a bad dream ('I hit bottom, I think'), Tangier was a nightmare ('I hit bottom again in Tangier'). The house smelt of medicine and old, cold soup. The Casbah itself reeked of chemical sewage that had been dumped in the sea while attempts were being made to repair some broken sewers. To Jane these odours were 'like the madness I had been living in. A nightmare smell coming up from the port, and a special punishment for me, for my return.' Linked to these odours, symbolic of the stench of her life in her nostrils, was the wild, panicky terror of facing up to her writing. The block had not diminished and she was very afraid of confronting it: 'I don't know what I'll do if that nightmare closes in on me again.' She worried about its effect on Bowles: 'I am sorry too that you have to live through it. I won't go near you if it happens again. Actually I cannot allow it to happen again. But I must work.'

The need to work was partly prompted by another terror – she had received a tax demand. When able to think rationally and not give way to panic, she recognized that she might have enough money to cover the taxes: if not, she could sell a Fabergé gold bracelet or a valuable and valued painting. But she lacerated herself with regrets about having spent 'just a little too much in every direction' in New York and Tangier, including hotel rooms and gifts to Cherifa. 'I suppose I've been bad,' she wrote to Bowles, 'but not so bad. Please don't scold; I am miserable enough about the whole thing and would have pinched every penny as I am doing now, had I been less confident. Well, that is over the bridge and down the drain, like the money for Ceylon.' The enormity of her problems appalled her: she regarded the future as a holding operation, merely – it hardly seemed possible that life could continue its accustomed course. She appealed to Bowles for advice, though stopped short of begging for comfort or financial help. 'I have pulled every string possible in the sense of looking for a job. There is a terrible depression in Tangier. Hotels empty, the Massilia [a hotel] closing, and ten people waiting for every job. Most people think I am mad, and that I should write or live on you, or both. It is not easy to make friends take my plight seriously. Not easy at all, unless I were to say that I was starving to death, which would be shameful and untrue.'

Writing to Bowles, Jane claimed to have resolved some of her difficulties with Cherifa who, startlingly, had 'now expressed a desire to travel and to play tennis'. These ambitions, surely to be financed by Jane, were to be denied her: 'Now I do have an upper hand that I never had when I spent more money. What is it? I suppose one must close one's fist, and allow them just the right amount of money to make it worthwhile and not shameful in the eyes of the neighbors. I understand many more of the family problems than I did. It was difficult before to find one's way in the maze.' With a flash of her old humour, Jane remarked to Bowles: 'Will explain when I see you . . . I'm sure you can't wait. I remember the glazed look you always got when I mentioned her before.' Jane's confidence was faintly reasserting itself: having got Cherifa's demands under control, there remained only the demands of writing to be dealt with: 'If I could only work now I would feel quite peaceful.'

The problems of Tangier were occupying her mind somewhat: she was busily trying to preserve the Socco market, taking an interest in the appearance of her hair, frequenting the 1001 Nights which Gysin had established ('Brion's restaurant is the only thing that does business in town') and occasionally smoking kif, which noticeably altered the effects of liquor when, before supper, she sampled both. Though Jane made light of her relations with Cherifa, claiming to have taken a tighter grip on her money and resisted Cherifa's attempts to batten on her, Millicent Dillon quotes a friend of Jane's, Beatrix Pendar, who observed the reality of the situation, contrasting Jane's letter to Bowles with her actual conversation in the spring of 1954. Cherifa appeared to Beatrix Pendar as 'a woman with a lot of wit and virility ... substantial, hefty, square. Beside her Jane looked very young and fragile, though she too was strong and had an enormous amount of vitality – almost virility – in her make up.'

Confirming that Cherifa was without sympathy, single-mindedly intent on furnishing herself with gold teeth and money to support herself and her relatives, Pendar felt that 'even in fifty-four Jane was already beginning to feel Cherifa's possession. Jane would say to me about Cherifa, "I'll give her everything I have. I'll leave it to her when I die." I would say to her, "You'd better be careful." and she'd laugh ... she was intent on creating a world that was amusing and would amuse others. She didn't know how dangerous it was. The unconscious, the primal spirit, is very strong in a woman like Cherifa. I felt Jane had no spiritual imagination. She didn't realise the knife had two sides. Yet she must have known that she was living with a woman who had power over her food. She liked danger, I think.'

The Tangier to which Bowles and Yacoubi returned was a city in turmoil: shops and houses were being fortified; crowds of up to fifty thousand people thronged the streets clamouring for the restitution of Sultan Mohammed V. These demonstrations, and their public assertions of loyalty to the Sultan, had been expressly forbidden, but there was not much the Tangier police could do to limit or stop them. The shrapnel from tear gas bombs, thrown by the police, wounded some demonstrators, but there were no fatalities. The situation was difficult and, to most Europeans and Americans, somewhat daunting. They could still go about their normal business in the streets, but tensions were everwhere evident and the possibility of attack could not be discounted. Expatriates were understandably nervous, and many fled the country as a result of the hostilities that the worsening relations between France and Morocco had occasioned. To Virgil Thomson, Bowles wrote that, 'My feeling is that the usefulness of Morocco as a place to work has worn thin; it could hardly be otherwise when one is unable to keep oneself from being drawn into the daily life of everyone in the street, and from drawing everyone into one's own daily life.'

Bowles had first settled in Tangier as a retreat from the actuality of the larger world. As a little condominium ruled by foreign powers but still possessing a lively native character, it had seemed ideal: a sort of stage set in which nothing that happened could be considered quite actual, where the various characters and choruses had their lines and their bits of business, where the plot was largely predictable and the dramatic conventions were immutable. Bowles preferred to be an observer, a captive and captivated audience of one who kept his distance in the stalls and paid attention with all the detached equipment of the committed critic. Now, the stage and the production had been subverted by forces beyond the theatre, there were several competing directors who vied with one another to control the political outcome of the drama, and the critic, like it or not, could not avoid being drawn in as a factor in the dramatic process. Some of the audience and cast had rushed for the exits.

The summer of 1955 was notable for riots in Casablanca, the murder of a young Spaniard by a seething mob, and further deaths of some fifty-five Moroccans and eleven Europeans. Eighty-eight Europeans were reported as seriously wounded in the disturbances. Police fired on a mob in Fez, and the French feared all-out civil war in Morocco just two years after the deposition of the Sultan. On 20 August, massive rioting broke out at Khenifra, and that same day a colony of Europeans was brutally massacred by tribesmen of the Smah'la tribe at the town of Oued Zem. The crisis in Morocco was acute: the French, and Thami el Glaoui, were in despair – each felt betrayed by the other – and two months later, in October, the Sultan was flown back to Paris from Madagascar in a desperate effort by the French to restore order to Morocco.

Tangier, though remote from the most serious incidents, was nevertheless affected by the national unrest. Europeans walked warily, curbing their tongues and keeping a low profile. The house in the Medina was clearly impossible as a residence: to Bowles it seemed 'sensible to stay far away from hornets when they are in an irritable mood'. He rented a two-room cottage on the Old Mountain where he intended to go every day to work on *Yerma*, and took two apartments, for himself and Jane, on the top floor of a new apartment block in what was then an outlying area of the city. Somewhat remote from the troubles of the Nouvelle Ville, they enjoyed 'enormous terraces and splendid views over the city, the sea and the mountains'. Work on *Yerma* proved difficult and slow, but the summer was enlivened by acquaintance with the painter Francis Bacon and the writer William Burroughs – both of whom Bowles had come to admire and whose company stimulated him. Bacon struck Bowles as 'a man about to burst from internal pressures'. Though he admired Bacon's paintings, the techniques employed by Bacon – however articulately he was able to explain them – defeated Bowles who was 'unable to imagine for myself exactly what happened as he painted'. Much the same mystification applied to his understanding of Burroughs' literary techniques.

Bowles had two happy inspirations: he introduced Bacon to Yacoubi and Yacoubi visited Bacon's studio in the Casbah to watch him paint. 'He consented to this because Ahmed had been having great difficulty learning how to manage oils; for months he had been trying to invent a viable technique. Another problem was that there were no artist's materials to be had in Tangier. Francis went to London and brought back a good quantity of Winsor and Newton colours.' Then, Bowles introduced Burroughs to Brion Gysin 'because I thought they would get on well together. I was right: eventually they became inseparable.' Later that year, another visitor was Christopher Isherwood, who had known Bowles before the War. True to form and Moroccan hospitality, Yacoubi gave Isherwood some powerful *majoun* that seriously disoriented him on his return journey to the Hotel Minzah.

Christopher Wanklyn, a Canadian musicologist and writer, a friend of Bowles, visited Tangier at this time. He gave his account of Jane in the summer and autumn of 1955 to Millicent Dillon. He commented particularly on her obsessions – notably her inability to decide, in a restaurant, about what she wanted to eat, drawing out the process of selection until it ceased to be funny and became merely tiresome. Yet her caprices and single-minded attachments to people and things that others considered odd or whimsical or plain foolish were counterbalanced by her marvellous generosity, her intelligence and the manner in which 'she taught her friends the private language of her vision, though a good many people did not understand her'. Things and people that Wanklyn would not ordinarily have found amusing or interesting, were transmuted through Jane. 'Her life was invention as much as her work. There were no barriers between them. Perhaps that's why she couldn't finish anything. There was no relief for her in daily life.'

To casual observers, even to intimate friends, Jane's life appeared to be theatre in which they were roped in as performers in her creation. But Bowles was becoming less and less inclined to indulge her. Her refusal – or inability – to work, her constant vacillation, her insistent association with women of whom he disapproved and feared might cause her harm, finally resulted in an ultimatum that he could not see her unless she began to work and work seriously. She took this to mean that Bowles was only interested in her work, not in her: that he cared for her only as a writer, not as a person. The threat, aimed at provoking her back to work, was ineffective: she continued to dither, to agonize, to be fearful and fretful about the possiblity of achieving anything of worth. She dabbled a little, attempting to write, and she continued to see Bowles, though she returned to live in the house in the Medina.

In November 1955, matters with Cherifa came to a head. Cherifa made her ultimate play for complete dominance and insisted on a substantial sum of money. If Jane would not pay up, Cherifa would put an end to their relationship. Jane had no money to give and offered instead to make over the house to Cherifa. Bowles, though naturally reluctant, but wishing to please and pacify Jane, agreed to make the house over to her. Jane would then transfer ownership to Cherifa. The legal process took until March 1956 to complete, by which time Jane had left – in February – for New York to visit her mother and stepfather. She took time to visit Oliver Smith in California, and sailed for Tangier from New York in early June in time to meet Bowles' parents who had decided to make a visit to their son. Jane's companions on her return voyage included Tennessee Williams and Frank Merlo to whom she confided her antipathy to Yacoubi.

Mr and Mrs Bowles thoroughly enjoyed their stay in Tangier. Throughout the years, the relationship between Bowles and his parents had become more and more comfortable. He had corresponded regularly with them, they had delighted in his musical and literary success, and Bowles had perhaps set the seal on family amity by dedicating *The Delicate Prey* to his mother and *The Spider's House* to his father. He fussed a great deal about preparations for their visit, and did everything to make them feel at ease. Temsamany was particularly attentive to their comfort, and they took very well to Moroccan life, even to the extent of smoking kif, though they preferred whisky. They passed their time agreeably by the side of the swimming pool at the American Club, being driven around the countryside, exploring outlying towns such as Xauen, and they 'made a point of enjoying all the little, specifically Moroccan details of life which visitors ordinarily either overlook or criticize'. The visit did much to smooth over the animosities, egotisms, the hurts of his childhood when he had felt neglected and misunderstood. Bowles had established himself as a mature adult, with a life, temperament, beliefs and world peculiarly his own into which he could invite his parents and show them some of its delights. In their late seventies, Mr and Mrs Bowles were perfectly prepared to inspect that life and that world without apparent censure or disappointment.

Jane was living in the apartment Bowles had rented for her beside his own. Cherifa had moved in with her – whether as part of the agreement involving the transfer of ownership of the house to her, or of her own volition. She came ostensibly as a servant, probably to avoid being branded as a whore, but as a somewhat imperious servant who would not do any heavy housework. She would be a *châtelaine* – hiring and firing other servants and running the household on her own terms. She rented out her own newly acquired property at a handsome profit to a Moroccan family and was thus possessed of an independent income. According to Bowles, she would wake up in the morning, clap her hands, and have breakfast brought to her on a tray. Aicha, the tweenie, would spend the day running between Cherifa and the kitchen, commanded in a lordly manner by her dominant mistress. Jane took enormous pleasure in all this, establishing her household and indulging Cherifa. But the permanent installation of Cherifa in the apartment did not imply that the sexual element in her relationship with Jane was still active – according to David Herbert, in whom Jane confided, there had only been sexual intimacy between them in their first year or so together.

That summer, she was very social – she enjoyed the company of Tennessee Williams with whom she spent every afternoon on the beach; she cooked for her friends, drank with her friends; busied herself dispensing advice to friends; passed a petition round among her friends demanding that the new administration in Tangier should not root up the great trees planted by the French in the Grand Socco (she was unsuccessful); darted continually between her own apartment and that of Bowles; and sometimes she would try to write. But the domestic demands upon her, the continual interruptions of Cherifa and the servants, ruined her concentration and she would flee to a friend's house for some peace and quiet. There was no question that she could discipline herself as Bowles could do. He had set up a piano in his apartment and was conscientiously working on *Yerma*.

In November 1956, with Yacoubi, Bowles left for Ceylon. He had decided to sell Taprobane which had become expensive to maintain. Though giving as his reason the fact that Jane did not like it, he had become disillusioned with the island, and he preferred to get his money out of Ceylon. In the event, it took about a year to sell the island, and he was legally prevented from taking any of the proceeds out of the country. Finally, Bowles made nothing, and probably lost, on the deal. Jane had elected to stay put in Tangier. On 1 February 1957, she wrote to Bowles detailing her struggle with her writer's block. It was necessary to write in order to earn money which she desperately needed, but – as she wrote to Libby Holman – 'I could not really write very differently whether or not I needed the money because I do not know how to write a commercial line, nor could I write *Waiting for Godot* if I was sitting with a million dollars in my pocket.'

On 24 February, she wrote again to Bowles, dealing with another, no less insistent matter: 'I have just had my fortieth birthday the day before yesterday, and that is always, however long one has prepared for it, a shock. The day was not as bad as the day after it, or the following day, which was even worse. Something coming is not at all like something which has come. It makes trying to work that much more difficult (or could it possibly be more difficult?) because the full horror of having no serious work behind me at this age (or successful work, in any sense) is now like an official fact rather than something in my imagination, something to be feared, but not yet realized.' She adds a sentence implying that Bowles could have no understanding of her feeling, considering his own successful work stacked up behind him.

Bowles and Yacoubi returned from Ceylon in mid-May 1957, six weeks after Jane suffered a stroke. The first Bowles knew of Jane's condition was a telegram, signed by Gordon Sager, which was handed to him when he disembarked from his ship at Las Palmas, Gran Canaria. 'I did not know it, but the good years were over.' To Virgil Thomson Bowles wrote that Jane had suffered 'what has variously been described as a "syndrome confusionelle", a "spasme cérébrale", a "small bleed", a "microlesion" and a "gros accident cérébral". Whatever it was, it resulted in temporary amnesia and a permanent loss of one half of the visual field. The latter has naturally been a terrible shock.' She had also become somewhat aphasic. During Ramadan, Jane and Cherifa had been observing the ritual times of fasting which had caused some ill-feeling. Rising in the early hours of the morning to break their fast, Jane wanted the meal to be gay. Cherifa tended to be surly, and Jane had threatened to send her home. Cherifa, for her part, had threatened to go and not come back. On the afternoon of 4 April, an argument in the household about food had degenerated into minor violence: some food had been thrown out in a rage.

Jane, angered and perhaps alarmed – at any rate, disturbed – had gone to see Gordon Sager who offered her a glass of brandy to calm herself. She drank it, and several more. She then hurried back home, and ran up the eight flights of stairs to her apartment. There, she doused her face with water and soon after began to vomit. The vomiting continued for the rest of the night. At some point she said to Cherifa that she could not see, then she appeared to have difficulty speaking. Cherifa called Christopher Wanklyn, who was staying in Bowles' apartment. He remembers 'Jane lying down, with a slice of lemon tied with a cloth onto her forehead'. This must have been Cherifa's idea of first aid. With difficulty, Jane managed to say, 'what is worse than baisar?' (a kind of thick pea soup she particularly disliked). Wanklyn guessed that what she really meant was *majoun*, and surmised that she and Cherifa might have been eating some. 'Cherifa was able to say very little about what had happened. I thought she was probably ashamed of having given Jane the *majoun*. Cherifa hadn't been drinking because of Ramadan, so I thought that was why she had taken the *majoun* and Janie then must have shared it with her.' Jane had somewhat retreated from her original dislike of cannabis, to the extent of smoking a little with liquor, and it is likely that she may equally have revised her former antipathy to *majoun* as well.

Wanklyn called a French doctor, who diagnosed a minor stroke. Millicent Dillon, researching her biography of Jane Bowles, discovered among Jane's papers a slip of paper signed by a Dr R. Spriet, 'a diagnosis made apparently several days after the "attack": "Cerebral spasm with confusion and mental torpor for several days, but no sign of cerebral haemorrhage or of cerebral thrombosis."' There was a family history of vascular illness, and Jane's blood pressure had for years been controlled by medication. The combined effects of *majoun* (or kif), liquor, and Sparine, the drug Jane habitually used to reduce her blood pressure, may well have been sufficient to induce 'a transient episode of ischemia, a spasm in a blood vessel, which may lead to a stroke in someone predisposed to vascular illness'. This clinical, rational, objective scientific explanation was hardly glamorous enough for Tangier which quickly and dramatically came to credit Cherifa as the Borgia hand behind Jane's stroke.

Maurice Grosser, an artist who frequented Tangier and was friendly with Bowles and Jane, has described Tangier gossip as 'enormous and elaborate and fantastic'. Not knowing, perhaps, that Cherifa had already gained possession of the house in the Medina, rumour-mongers put it about that Jane had promised to leave it to Cherifa in her will. This was considered sufficient motive to substantiate allegations that Cherifa had casually poisoned Jane for material gain. Truman Capote reported that Jane had told him: 'All she thinks about is money. My money. What little there is. And the house. And how to get the house. She tries very seriously to poison me at least every six months. And don't imagine I'm being paranoid. It's quite true.' Allowing for the licence of literary creativity, this passage may have been born from a semi-serious conversation with Jane who, in her impish manner, may have amusingly embellished some minor episodes with Cherifa who had a reputation as an adept of magic which Yacoubi, for one, mightily believed, and Temsamany was inclined to credit: 'I swear Cherifa was giving her stuff to make her in love with her. There is a potion to give more love. Cherifa bought it from other people. I don't think Jane knew Cherifa was doing that. At the beginning Jane's love was a normal love, but later she was even more in love.' Gordon Sager comments, 'There's much talk in Morocco about poisons that attack the central nervous system. I think Cherifa may very well have engaged in magic, but I think that is probably as far as she went. Cherifa, while illiterate, was no fool. She knew Jane was not really well. I thought she was very good with Jane when she was ill.'

Bowles himself, says Christopher Sawyer-Lauçanno, 'claims now that he really has no idea whether it's true or not, [although] in the past, he did lean towards this theory.' Bowles, if he had been inclined to believe that magic or poison had truly precipitated Jane's stroke, may well have been influenced by Yacoubi who would certainly have believed Cherifa capable of any enormity. Two friends of Bowles and Jane, Edouard Roditi and the artist Buffie Johnson, believe that Jane's drinking was at least a significant contributory factor, and doubtless the principal cause. For most Tangerinos, however, it was difficult to separate their image of a dominating, powerful, wild, malevolent Cherifa, totally in control of Jane Bowles who was perceived as – in Capote's words – 'that genius imp, that laughing, hilarious, tortured elf', from the possibility – probability, more like – that her greed would turn to attempted murder. The totality of Cherifa's character, her perceived malevolence, spoke in favour of utter ruthlessness. It was, if anything, more difficult to believe that Jane might have been her own victim, succumbing at the the early age of forty to a distressing and insupportable combination of unwary dependence on drink and occasional indulgence in kif or *majoun*, debilitated by perpetual anxieties about her writer's block, her marriage, money, Cherifa, and her predisposition to vascular illness. She had spoken more than once about 'cracking-up', about the possibility of nervous breakdown – it could hardly be surprising that her psychological distress might have led, through the medium of erratic behaviour, to physical collapse.

Her financial problems, at least, were quickly remedied: Libby Holman sent a cheque for $500, with a pledge of regular monthly payments of $175. Katharine Hamill and Natasha von Hoershelman each promised a remittance of $25 a month and Virgil Thomson immediately sent Bowles $1000 which he had obtained from the American Institute of Arts and Letters which maintained a fund for the emergency relief of artists in distress. By 11 July, Bowles was preparing to take Jane to England to consult with a neurologist. By this time, gossip had spread far beyond Tangier and close friends. Bowles was vexed when, writing to a close friend, Peggy Glanville-Hicks, he described how 'letters began arriving from unlikely people asking me for details, because they had heard from Themistocles Hoetis who had heard from Gore Vidal who had heard from Truman Capote who had heard from Cecil Beaton who had heard from David Herbert that Jane had had a stroke and that I refused to allow her to have a doctor because I wanted her to die immediately. Too many gossip vultures hovering overhead.' Bowles surely had read Libby Holman's letter of 1 June to Jane, in which she spelt out the line of communication: 'Oliver [Smith] called Saturday night and had heard from Truman who had a letter from Cecil who had heard from David Herbert about your illness –'

On 21 July, Jane suffered two epileptiform fits which again affected her vision and very much frightened her. She was admitted to the Radcliffe Infirmary in Oxford on 6 August. There, Jane detailed her symptoms, her long-standing behavioural oddities, and her bouts of depression. Evidently, she was very frank: she spoke of her irrational fears of close places, the sea, and inchoate forces of nature. She admitted to an extreme inability to make up her mind about the simplest things. She confessed to compulsions that led her to court danger. Her symptoms of depression included terrible pressures within and on her head – as though there were steel bands around it – and bouts of weeping before and after her trip to Ceylon. She was terrified of being alone, and could not rid her mind of obsessive thoughts. Surgery was recommended, but Jane insisted on leaving the Infirmary and was transferred to St Mary's

Hospital in London where she was told that the brain lesion was not operable and that the damage to her vision was irreversible. Bowles recalls that one doctor said to Jane: 'You're not coping my dear Mrs Bowles. Go back to your pots and pans and try to cope.'

This advice, condescending at best, purely ignorant at worst, was demeaning and dismissive. To Virgil Thomson, Bowles wrote: 'the facet of her emotional reactions to the illness was left untouched, and that is at least fifty per cent of her present problem; that much should be apparent even to a neurologist.' He considered her suicidal: 'Jane has lost her nerve and is at the brink of a nervous breakdown. When things get to that point there is no end visible; a sort of spastic stubborness puts her into direct opposition to any therapy a doctor can offer.' Her dysphasia, her visual impairment and the consequent reduction of her capacity to talk, to read and to write would in any case have been serious impediments – to the mind of a writer they were devastating. In late August, Bowles and Jane took a ship back to Tangier. Jane had already developed alarming heart palpitations: on board, they led to another epileptiform seizure with resulting mental confusion, amnesia and complete hysteria. Bowles attempted to hospitalize her in Gibraltar, but Jane – after accepting and refusing the idea several times – finally resisted violently and they landed in Tangier.

On 5 September, Jane returned to the Radcliffe Infirmary in a state of extreme anxiety and depression. She was admitted to a psychiatric hospital in Northampton where Bowles went to visit her in late September. On 2 October, he wrote again to Virgil Thomson, who was ever anxious to have news of Jane's condition: 'Principally she seems profoundly unhappy and depressed.' Electric shock treatment had been suggested, but Jane was delaying a decision about such a radical recourse: 'She sees its effects on the other patients around here, and rejects it, without understanding that the others are manic-depressives, schizophrenics and alcoholics on whom it is often tried without much hope of being successful.' Bowles himself fell ill. He was exhausted and thus probably more than usually susceptible to the Asian 'flu virus that put him to bed for nine days with a high temperature. He got up and went out on the tenth day, only to become delirious the next day. He was admitted to hospital where he was obliged to stay for a month.

Jane had finally consented to a series of electric shock treatments, and was released from hospital on 11 November. She had
responded well to the treatment, backed up with psychotherapy,
occupational therapy and medication. Her vision had also improved, and in mid-November she returned with Bowles to Tangier
where she continued under the regular medical supervision of a
Paris-trained doctor for the few weeks they would spend there. The
good times had, indeed, come to an end. Yacoubi had accompanied
Bowles to London and travelled back with him and Jane to Tangier.
The day after their return, Yacoubi was arrested on a warrant that
had been issued in September. If Bowles had hoped for a quiet
period of rest and recuperation for himself and Jane, the particular
circumstances of Yacoubi's trouble and the wider political situation
from which it partly stemmed, were not favourable.

Yacoubi had been first arrested on 24 June, shortly after his
return with Bowles from Ceylon. The charge was, in effect, indecent
assault on a teenage German boy whose parents decided to make
a fuss about the matter and reported the alleged incident to the
police. Bowles had stood bail in the sum of two hundred thousand
francs (about $500) and Yacoubi had been released, only to be
rearrested in July and again in August. Yacoubi claimed that 'it
was all politics' – that the police and the new administration of
Tangier, which was no longer an International Zone, harboured
grave suspicions about his loyalty to the new government which,
under Sultan Mohammed V, was sternly nationalist. Yacoubi,
known to associate with expatriates, was perhaps considered pro-
French and less than wholeheartedly enthusiastic about Moroccan
independence. The charge against Yacoubi in September had been
altered to 'assault with intent to kill' and he was imprisoned for
several months, awaiting a trial which was constantly postponed.

Bowles and Jane visited him regularly in prison, bringing him
food. They hired lawyers to represent his interests. Bowles, though
concerned about Yacoubi, was equally concerned about the threat
to himself and Jane. The Moroccan police appeared to suspect the
expatriate community as a whole, doubting their political loyalty
to Morocco and, specifically, perhaps with a view to driving them
out, taking an unfavourable interest in their style of life which most
of the expatriates sensibly took to imply, specifically, their sex lives.
The sexual habits of most of the expatriates were well known: a

tradition had been established that Tangier was 'safe' for homosexuals. Local young men and boys were perfectly willing to exchange sexual services for modest payments in money or in kind, and such traffic had been taken very much for granted. No shame was imputed to either party in the transaction which was of mutual benefit and did not seriously infringe the sexual code of the Moroccans who largely accepted homosexuality as perfectly normal behaviour.

If, indeed, police interest in such activity which had suddenly been deemed 'immoral' was designed to frighten the expatriates, it succeeded. Some of them left the country, finally more alarmed by the prospect of imprisonment than they had been by the civil disturbances and prospect of bloody revolution. In January 1958, Bowles himself was questioned. Though his own natural inclination was to distrust authority in any form, he was capable of standing up at least to preliminary inquiries, but he seriously doubted Jane's capacity to withstand any form of police interrogation about her relationship with Cherifa. Sensibly, he decided to bolt. He locked up the apartments, leaving everything behind. He gave the Jaguar to Temsamany who sold it within six months and went to Germany to find work. Cherifa took off to stay with relatives in the mountains. In early February, Bowles took Jane to Madeira.

Temsamany had been called in four times by the police. He denied knowing anything about his employers' private lives. So far as he knew, Bowles and Yacoubi slept in separate rooms and Cherifa was Jane's servant. In late February, Bowles learned, in a letter from his Tangier lawyer, that he had fled only just in time: 'The only matter they [the police] are concerned with is the nature of your relations with Yacoubi, and for that reason they wish to interrogate you, with a view to implicating you.' In mid-May, Yacoubi's case finally came to trial and he was acquitted within a matter of minutes. Though matters had been settled in that particular instance, it did not yet seem advisable for Bowles to return. The moral air in Tangier was still poisonous to the foreign community and there were fears of further crackdowns. By mid-April Jane had flown to New York where she had been met by Tennessee Williams who took her to stay with Katharine Hamill and Natasha von Hoershelman who had offered to look after her. Bowles followed in June, taking ship to New York.

They did not return to Tangier until December, by which time the threat of police persecution and intimidation had abated. Jane required absolute reassurance on this point, so from Algeciras Bowles wired the American consul in Tangier who replied that they might return whenever they wished. In Tangier, Jane revived and appeared to most of her friends to have largely recovered. To Virgil Thomson, Bowles wrote: 'Jane immediately became another person entirely. She began to laugh and take pleasure in food, and become her old normal self, more so than she has been at any time since the stroke.' Physically and mentally she had improved, but she was still liable to epileptiform attacks. To Libby Holman, she wrote: 'The doctor does not want me to stay alone because of the danger that I might have a fit in the street or fall down and hit my head.' She had moved back into her apartment, with Cherifa and the maid, Aicha, and Bowles had hired a Spanish woman, Angèle, to act as her paid companion.

Jane still experienced difficulty with reading and writing: 'I don't always know which is the stroke and which is the writer's block ... I have trouble with names, numbers, and above all the ability to add and subtract. I know perfectly well the general outlines. Two hundred dollars is less than three hundred dollars, and ten plus ten equals twenty, but the complicated divisions and subtractions and additions –! ... So Angèle does that.' Her difficulty with words was more serious, though she believed that her aphasia was not likely to be permanent: 'I now know the meaning of all words. They register again on my brain, but I am slow because there is a tiny paralysed spot in each eye which I apparently have to circumvent when I'm reading. One side is very bad, worse than the other, but on the whole I'm getting more used to it.'

Bowles, while in New York, had completed *Yerma* for Libby Holman who took the lead in performances given in Denver and Ithaca, New York – twenty performances in all before it closed. He was summoned back to New York from Tangier to write the score for Tennessee Williams' *Sweet Bird of Youth*. During this time, in February 1959, he was awarded a grant from the Rockefeller Foundation to make a series of recordings of Moroccan folk music – *andaluz* music in particular, which he considered was 'most in danger of disappearing quickly'. He returned to Tangier in mid-May and set about preparations for a field trip through Morocco with a professional-quality Ampex tape recorder and two companions – Christopher Wanklyn, who had spent five years in Tangier and was fluent in Moroccan Arabic, and a Moroccan, Mohammed Larbi, who was an experienced Saharan guide.

In all, Bowles, Wanklyn and Larbi made 'four roughly circular itineraries of five weeks' duration each: south-western Morocco, northern Morocco, the Atlas and the pre-Sahara. Between trips we recuperated in Tangier.' In a country that, then, was almost wholly illiterate, Bowles considered that 'the most important single element in Morocco's folk culture is its music.' Illiteracy had, indeed, abetted the development of music: 'the entire history and mythology of the people is clothed in song. Instrumentalists and singers have come into being in lieu of chroniclers and poets, and even during the most recent chapter in the country's evolution – the war for independence and the setting up of the present pre-democratic regime – each phase of the struggle has been celebrated in countless songs.' In all, Bowles succeeded in recording more than two hundred and fifty selections from most of the country, excepting the south-east, of 'as diversified a body of music as one could find in any land west of India'. These recordings, the property of the Library of Congress, are largely unreleased except for a two-volume set of records issued in 1972.

Bowles undertook these excursions only after satisfying himself that Jane could safely be left to the care of her women. One of her constant preoccupations had always been the changing character of Tangier. Now that its status had altered, and was due to alter still further with the revocation of its status as a free port in 1961, she began to fret about future developments: to Lawrence Stewart, Ira Gershwin's literary secretary, and Leonore Gershwin, she confided her worst fears: 'The revolution is only five years away and what will I do when it comes? Where will I go? Paul won't be here.' She was still worried in case he should abandon her. Bowles had certainly talked about leaving. In his autobiography, he notes that

Jane and I spent most of the following year in Tangier, watching the city become progressively de-Europeanized. In spite of having come under Rabat's direct political control at the time of the sultan's return in 1956, Tangier had been allowed to retain its charter until April, 1960. This delay gave local Europeans time to bring their businesses to an end and leave the country without undue losses. When the charter expired, Tangier's finances would be subject to the same controls as in any other Moroccan town. There was a great deal of uninformed speculation and needless anxiety among the European residents as to their future. Most of us agreed that eventually we would be forced to leave; the arguments occurred over the amount of time we had left.

There were those, like Jane, who expected imminent revolution and fled; there were those who feared trial and imprisonment for their sexual proclivities and bolted; there were those who, considering that Tangier was no longer so profitable for business and banking, liquidated their assets and ran with their money, and there were those who, recognizing that the golden days of Tangier's attraction for international high society had ended, sold their properties and abandoned the city. To Lawrence Stewart, Jane remarked: 'We live on people passing through,' as though Tangier were a sort of canal lock being constantly filled and emptied. This attitude implied in Jane, and in many another expatriate, an inability to be satisfied with the everyday life of Tangier. 'People passing through' were a welcome distraction: though the new wave of visitors was not much to the taste of the established foreign community. A new era was developing, heralded by the arrival of Jack Kerouac, Allen Ginsberg, Gregory Corso and Alan Ansen who, representing and more or less personifying the vanguard of the 'Beat Generation', had come to visit their friend and mentor William Burroughs. Most of them were introduced to Bowles, whom they reverenced as a literary and personal inspiration, as the forerunner who, in every respect, had effectively worked the ground they proposed to cultivate. In the words of Norman Mailer, referring specifically to Bowles' story *Pages from Cold Point*, 'Paul Bowles opened the world of Hip. He let in the murder, the drugs, the incest, the death of the Square . . . '

The opening lines of *Pages from Cold Point* pretty accurately establish Bowles' attitude to living in the world as he finds it constituted. The vision is bleak. 'Our civilization is doomed to a short life: its component parts are too heterogeneous. I personally am content to see everything in the process of decay. The bigger the bomb, the quicker it will be done. Life is visually too hideous for one to make the attempt to preserve it. Let it go. Perhaps some day another form of life will come along. Either way, it is of no consequence. At the same time, I am still a part of life, and I am bound by this to protect myself to whatever extent I am able. And so I am here.' Here, in the context of the story, being apparently a distant Caribbean island where 'vegetation still has the upper hand, and man has to fight even to make his presence seen at all'. The story, written in 1947, on the MS *Ferncape* between New York and Casablanca, deals glancingly with adolescent homosexuality, a suggestion of incest between father and son (the natives find it difficult to believe they are related), and – in the words of Tennessee Williams – a preoccupation with the spiritual isolation of individual beings.

Bowles, wrote Williams in a review of *The Delicate Prey and Other Stories*, 'is apparently the only American writer whose work reflects the extreme spiritual dislocation (and a philosophic adjustment to it) of our immediate times . . . This does little to improve his stock with the the school of criticism which advocates a literature that is happily insensitive to any shock or abrasion, the sort that would sing "Hail, Hail, the Gang's All Here" while being extricated, still vocally alive, from the debris of a Long Island railroad disaster.' The key theme in Bowles' work, Williams considered, was 'the collapse of the civilized "Super Ego" into a state of almost mindless primitivism, totally dissociated from society except as an object of its unreasoning hostility'. It was perhaps inevitable that the 'Beat Generation' should have recognized his disengagement, his experiments with beatitude through the medium of mild hallucinatory drugs, and his escape from conventional, moralistic, middle-class ('square') values in his quest for actuality and a more profound encounter with more spontaneous and primitive traditions.

So far as Bowles was concerned, America as a whole was a railroad disaster from which he had instinctively escaped. Tangier was a window through which he could perceive another actuality without fully participating in it – total exposure would be destructive, but the observer could remain relatively intact while being moved and touched by the unfamiliar which was necessary to his fiction. To the *Paris Review*, Bowles remarked that 'The transportation of characters to such [exotic] settings often acts as a catalyst or a detonator, without which there'd be no action, so I shouldn't call the settings secondary. Probably if I hadn't had contact with what you call "exotic" places, it wouldn't have occurred to me to write at all.' Morocco, a traditionally violent country, offered no fixed certainties. Tangier, a cosmopolitan city of many races, creeds and castes, offered no fixed centre of religious or moral law. It was, to that extent, anarchic and potentially disturbing, a key or parallel for the destruction of character. Bowles, remote and coolly objective, could turn his situation to literary and personal advantage. Jane, less resilient and less able to assimilate contradictory forces, wilted and declined.

At the beginning of the Sixties, Tangier was radically affected by the implications of political integration with the rest of Morocco. For one thing, it became markedly less cheap. 'We are losing our charter in Tangier,' wrote Bowles to his parents, '. . . which will mean that money can no longer move in and out of Tangier; once it enters it will be frozen, and the rate will be fixed in Rabat. I suppose it means inevitably that prices will soar sky high, but we'll have to wait and see just *how* high before we make any decision.' Most of the departing foreigners tended to be French or Spanish – the Americans and British mostly stayed put. Prices did indeed jump alarmingly, there was a run on consumer goods, many shops and businesses closed. Jane occupied herself principally with house-keeping – the minutiae of domestic life wholly absorbed her: at least the question of personal appearance, her clothes, her daily routine became obsessive.

She refused to accompany Bowles, or any of her friends, on trips to other Moroccan cities: she worried about being left alone, even for a moment, insisted on being constantly within reach of her Tangier doctor – who perpetually expected Jane to have another convulsion – and she was all too conscious not only of the limits of her vision but, also, of difficulties with her left hand. In late December 1961, Jane had been awarded three thousand dollars by the Ingram Merrill Foundation to write a play. She made a start, setting the drama in Camp Cataract, the location of the story she most highly regarded as her best work. But a brief love affair with an English woman writer, the daughter of a countess, became the displacement activity which precluded sustained literary work. Her health was not good: she had two hernia operations, in September 1960 and July 1962. In January 1962 she had suffered a painful and debilitating attack of shingles.

Bowles was somewhat at a loss. Jane's state of health was a constant pressure: 'Our combined worlds orbited around the subject of her poor health. Each week she seemed to have a new symptom to add to the old ones; the horizon of her illness was slowly widening. It took me a long time to realize that my life had undergone a tremendous change. The act of living had been enjoyable; at some point when I was not paying attention, it had turned into a different sort of experience, to whose grimness I had grown so accustomed that I now took it for granted.' Occupied with recording Moroccan music, writing stories on Moroccan themes and, largely, from a Moroccan viewpoint, Bowles was ripe to channel his energies into an enterprise that would enmesh him still more closely with the life of Morocco. He had already translated some stories told to him by Yacoubi: now, possessing a sophisticated tape recorder, he met a young Moroccan, Hamed Charhadi, later better known as a writer under his *nom de plume* Larbi Layachi, who worked as a watchman at a café at Merkala Beach. In the spring of 1962, Layachi began to tell Bowles his story, speaking into the tape recorder. Says Bowles, 'Immediately I knew that whatever the story might turn out to be, his manner of telling it left nothing to be desired. It was as if he had memorized the entire text and rehearsed the speaking of it for weeks.'

Bowles carefully, scrupulously, translated this oral material, adding, deleting and altering nothing. He sent a few extracts to *Evergreen Review*, which had published some of his translations of Yacoubi's stories, and Grove Press asked to publish the completed work. In September 1962, Bowles and Jane went to New York, Bowles to write the score for Tennessee Williams' play, *The Milk Train Doesn't Stop Here Any More*, Jane to visit her mother who came from Florida to New York to meet her. Jane began drinking heavily in New York, and was persuaded to return to Tangier on 13

November. Bowles was anxious that she should work on her play. Jane was now comfortably off, having inherited thirty-five thousand dollars from an aunt. To the casual observer, she appeared to be an engaging, somewhat eccentric character. She seemed witty, social, absorbed by the daily lives of her intimates, and well placed to resume her career as a playwright. Bowles himself appeared to be comfortable in his life and work – his success as a musician, as a writer, as a perceptive journalist and musicologist, and as a translator who was at ease with, and empathetic to, Moroccans and their traditional culture, all spoke in favour of a life conducted seriously and resolutely towards achieving well-defined and satisfying ends. Bowles found solace and satisfaction in his work, and hoped that Jane could discover her own salvation through disciplined literary activity resulting in the satisfaction of an accomplished play.

But Jane, characteristically, was again thoroughly blocked. Bowles returned to Tangier in January 1963. He had written to her in December: 'I was sorry to hear that as you put it, everything has got to be a mess in Tangier and therefore you haven't worked. That was the very thing we were making great resolves about while you were still here – that you wouldn't *allow* the mess-tendency to take over, because that has always been the pattern, and that has been exactly what has always got in your way. Of course everthing's a mess, but *please* forget the mess now and then each day, because otherwise you won't ever work. The mess is just the decor in which we live, but we can't let decor take over really.'

Two matters diverted Jane's attention in 1963 and 1964: first, she fell in love with the Princess Martha Ruspoli de Chambrun who had lived in Tangier since 1949. She was a sophisticated, intelligent, dramatic woman, some ten years older than Jane, and Tangier society was divided in its attitude towards her. Some regarded her as a distinguished ornament to the expatriate community, others as a *poseuse* and terminal bore. Whether her impact was negative or positive, she was a considerable force who intrigued Jane and, contrary to the pattern of Jane's life, instigated the affair with her. Cherifa appeared initially to accept the liaison without apparent jealousy: she was, perhaps, confident of her entrenched position in Jane's life, her household, and her affections. Jane would not lightly abandon Cherifa in whom she had invested so much and whose security largely depended on her loyalty. Then, too, early in 1964, a revival of *In the*

Summer House bombed off-Broadway after a short run. This, at the point when Jane was committed to writing a new play, was a decisive blow to her confidence, which, in any event, was shaky. She recalled the extent to which Bowles had helped her with *Two Serious Ladies*, how his interest in her writing had stimulated him to begin writing seriously on his own account and to persevere with literature in tandem with music. She determined, to judge by remarks made to friends, that his career took precedence over her own and that her job now was to protect his interests.

In the summer of 1964, Bowles rented a house 'at the edge of a cliff overlooking the sea, 400 feet above the waves'. The property was surrounded by twenty-five acres of forested land where he would stroll, notebook in hand, writing on the hoof, preparing his novel *Up Above the World*. It was a busy summer – visitors included Tennessee Williams who, despite his professions of distaste for Tangier, regularly returned – though, on this occasion, 'he was feeling so low that not even Tangier could touch him': his lover, Frank Merlo, had recently died. Susan Sontag 'put in a brief appearance'. Larbi Layachi, working as Bowles' houseboy, was increasingly, and correctly, worried about official reaction to his book, *A Life Full of Holes*, which was soon to be published in a French edition by Gallimard. So worried was he, that Bowles obtained a visa for him for the United States and he left Morocco that year with William Burroughs. Jane's mother and stepfather visited Tangier, and she had signed a contract for British publication of *Two Serious Ladies*. But, despite these distractions, Bowles finished *Up Above the World* by mid-November when he moved back down from the Mountain into the city.

If Bowles appears to have lived in a constant state of movement, apparently based in Tangier but rarely settling for any length of time in any one place, his restlessness may be attributable to a belief, expressed to the *Paris Review*, that 'Moving around a lot is a good way of postponing the day of reckoning. I'm happiest when I'm moving. When you've cut yourself off from the life you've been living and you haven't yet established another life, you're free. That's a very pleasant sensation, I've always thought. If you don't know where you're going, you're even freer.' His itch for freedom, or the illusion of freedom that movement provided, contrasted with occasional yearnings to establish roots, to own a place in the world.

Taprobane had seemed likely to provide a focus, but the difficulty for Bowles was that 'I've never thought anything belonged to me ... I· thought that when I had my two feet planted on it I'd be able to say: "This island is mine." I couldn't; it was meaninglesss. I felt nothing at all, so I sold it.' Bowles' apparent careless ability to indulge his whims perhaps largely derive from his rootlessness in a world and a city from which he remains detached, an exile continually establishing desperate encampments which can never truly be home. Home can never be a physical location – it becomes a state of mind, reinforcing spiritual isolation and introspection. Believing nothing belonged to him, Bowles could never believe that he belonged to anything or anywhere in particular.

He did, however, prudently preserve his own and Jane's work, guy ropes in a windy world. The British edition of *Two Serious Ladies* had been well received on publication. It had been translated into five languages, and now Bowles unearthed copies of Jane's stories, which he had carefully stowed away, to satisfy demand for a further book. The result was a collection of short stories entitled *Plain Pleasures*. Bowles' own novel was accepted for publication by Simon & Schuster, and he turned his mind to future prospects. 'Daily life in Tangier then, while it did not provide the solitude and unlimited leisure needed for fiction writing, left me enough work periods of short duration so that I could busy myself with translating. I had been working during the winter [of 1964–5] on an English version of a book-length story which I had taped in Maghrebi Arabic, this one an invention by Mohammed Mrabet.'

This book was *Love With a Few Hairs*. It initiated a continuous, lasting, creative partnership between Bowles and the finest of his collaborators. Bowles recognized Mrabet as a natural storyteller in the Moroccan oral tradition. To the *Paris Review*, Bowles remarked: 'When I met Mrabet I knew that there was an enormous amount of material there, and fortunately he wasn't averse to exploiting it ... From his early childhood he preferred to sit with elderly men, because of the stories they told. He's impregnated with the oral tradition of his region. In a story of his it's hard to find the border-line between unconscious memory and sheer invention.'

Bowles adverts to the current and common Moroccan attitude to their limited national literature:

What they seemed to resent most of all is not that the texts were taped, but that they were taped in the language of the country which, by comnon consent, no one ever uses for literary purposes. One must use either Classical Arabic or French. Maghrebi is only for conversational purposes. Then they object to the subject matter. For them contemporary prose must be political in one way or another. They don't conceive of literature as such, only as ammunition to implement their theories about economics and government. Most Moroccan intellectuals are confirmed Marxists, naturally. The same pattern as in other third world countries. I can see clearly why they'd execrate the very concept of such a phenomenon as Mrabet. His books could as easily have been written under the colonial regime as during independence, and this strikes the local critics as tantamount to intellectual treason.

Bowles considers that he found Mrabet, or Mrabet found him, only just in time. The oral tradition of storytelling is markedly in decline. There are no more storytellers in the cafés, sucking on a *sebsi* and holding court with an audience of avid listeners. 'Now practically every café has television. The seats are arranged differently and no one tells any stories. They can't because the television is going. No one thinks of stories. If the eye is going to be occupied by a flickering image, the brain doesn't feel a lack. It's a great cultural loss. It's done away with both the oral tradition of storytelling and whatever café music there was.' Now, says Bowles, the café customers are 'completely passive. There used to be musicians playing, and often the clients, the customers themselves, clapped their hands along with the rhythm of the music, sometimes even sang, they were all together. They enjoyed themselves. I don't know whether they enjoy themselves with television or not. When they talked, they'd be talking about prices – nothing very exciting – sometimes about prostitutes that they knew – but often there were stories, stories became entertainment. People listened. Generally, it was older men telling the stories, for whom everyone had respect. That was a much better education for Moroccan youth than television could be.'

Mrabet and Yacoubi disliked one another. Their mutual animosity placed Bowles in a dilemma: it seemed likely that he would have to choose between them. In the event, relations with Yacoubi became naturally less intense in the early years of the 1960s when he married, became a father and more absorbed by family responsibilities. The ties with Bowles necessarily loosened, although they remained friends. Mrabet's star was in the ascendant: his genius for storytelling perhaps was closer to Bowles' interest than Yacoubi's ability as a painter. Then, too, Jane liked Mrabet – in direct contrast to her distaste for Yacoubi. Mrabet lost no opportunites to bad-mouth Yacoubi, and in particular he would relish an occasion in 1965 when, working as a barman at the Tanger Inn, he says he intercepted Yacoubi and his family in the last moment of an attempted moonlight flit from the hotel and presented him with a bill which he was obliged to pay. Mrabet also cordially disliked Cherifa, regarding her as a leech upon Jane who continued to treat her with a glad-handed generosity that shocked him – Mrabet had a thorough respect for the value of money – and alarmed Bowles who had learned to tread warily around Cherifa: she was perfectly capable of attacking him physically and had, indeed, on one occasion, attempted to put out his eyes with her fingers.

Cherifa, from initial tolerance of Jane's affair with Martha Ruspoli, had proceeded to furious opposition to the liaison. She was frankly antagonistic towards Martha whose title she disparaged, contrasting it unfavourably with her own claims to social and moral standing. 'I'm better than she is. I'm a saint. And I have my papers to prove I'm a virgin.' Her claim to be in good standing as a descendant of a saint compounded with the moral virtue of never having been penetrated by a man, so far as Cherifa was concerned, concluded the matter of her status more than satisfactorily. She was determined to retain the upper hand in all respects. Jane was being relentlessly social in the summer of '65: lunches, dinners, cocktail parties. The trivial, convivial round, in which she wittily glittered, perhaps contributed to autumnal bouts of depression; the death of an old friend in Tangier, Cherifa's violent antipathy to Martha Ruspoli and difficulties in the relationship with both of them, intemperate resort to the bottle which sorted badly with her regular medications, and continuing concern about her state of health, all resulted in long periods of depression during which she kept to her room, loss of interest in maintaining a regular and reasonable diet, and a tendency to wake in the middle of the night when she would prowl around wringing her hands in anguish. She would take her medicines – for high blood pressure, anticonvulsants, for anxiety and for insomnia – quite indiscriminately and mix them with liquor which had been strictly forbidden to her by her doctor.

The British critical success of her books did nothing to break her block: in the mid-1960s, Jane herself remarked: 'From the first day, Morocco seemed more dreamlike than real. I felt cut off from what I knew. In the twenty years that I have lived here I have written only two short stories, and nothing else. It's good for Paul, but not for me.' Whether or not her relative isolation in Morocco did indeed contribute, as a major factor, towards her inability to write is problematic: she was pleased to be Mrs Bowles, took evident delight in Bowles' pleasure, and – in conventional terms – took seriously, at some level of her being, the responsibility to submit to her husband's preference about where to live, to choose the place which, to all intents and purposes, served his best interests – whatever those might happen to be. Tangier was Bowles' choice; writing and music his chosen professions.

But Paul and Jane Bowles, on Bowles' own disingenuous admission, did not have a conventional marriage: Jane was not merely 'the little woman' who abided decorously and modestly by her husband's decisions. Said Bowles to the *Paris Review*: 'We played everything by ear. Each one did what he [sic] pleased – went out, came back – although I must say that I tried to get her in early. She liked going out much more than I did, and I never stopped her. She had a perfect right to go to any party she wanted. Sometimes we had recriminations when she drank too much, but the idea of sitting down and discussing what constitutes a conventional or an unconventional marriage would have been unthinkable.' Their life together had, in Bowles' judgement, been enjoyable. 'We were always busy helping each other. And we had lots of friends. Many, many friends.' Their life, by and large, had been all that they had wanted it to be. Jane loved Tangier, forever seeking to penetrate its beating heart which, for her own salvation, she hoped would finally return her love and make her whole.

Still, Jane drank, was creatively blocked, and – to some – seemed to have despoiled, if not squandered, her life and literary genius. It is not much to the point to judge whether she would, as Edouard Roditi complains, have been more productive in another environment more suited – according to the critical mind – to her natural inclinations. Roditi speculates that Bowles may, unwittingly, have been at fault by 'dragging Jane away from her own familiar world on a wild-goose chase to Central America, Ceylon and Morocco, in his romantically outdated quest for the Eldorado of a doomed exoticism.' He claims that the 'natural setting of Jane's finest writing had indeed been middle-class American suburbia, whether on the East Coast of the United States or in Southern California'. One might equally say that a Rimbaud, or a Jane Bowles, would have in any circumstances have remained a Rimbaud or a Jane Bowles – that her own character, naturally indecisive and responsive to the wishes and strength of mind of others, dictated her role in life and its consequences. It is vain to wish that she could have been more disciplined, that she should have steered clear of neurotic involvement with stronger women, that she should have recognized and remained true to what critics may consider the root inspirations for her work. It is equally vain to insist that, had Bowles not maintained his attitude of passivity towards her, had he not indulged his tendency towards 'benign neglect' in all matters and in respect of most people, that Jane would somehow have flourished as a writer and as an integrated human being. In fact, he did not neglect Jane – he pushed her to the point, almost, of bullying her into disciplined work. It was Bowles who preserved her manuscripts and prepared them for publication. It was Bowles who remonstrated against her drinking and her choice of Moroccan women friends. It was Bowles who cared for her, with tenderness and respect, throughout her long illness. Though it was Bowles, too, who perhaps overestimated her fortitude, her ability to adapt to unfamiliar environments, who recognized his own needs and was not prepared to forfeit his own life and art for the sake of others. It may be that Jane was a voluntary or involuntary sacrifice – that she, rather than Bowles himself, was cast – or elected to play – the role of victim.

Bowles, as a consequence of the amorality that is perceived by critics to inform his writing, is generally assumed to be amoral in his personal life. To the extent that he is seen to be detached, largely to abstain from active involvement with the world and its habitual concerns, an observer merely of its vices and virtues, and passive in his attitude to its perversities, he may be considered at least non-judgemental, a perfectly respectable position that implies puzzlement, perhaps, rather than a wilful refusal to adopt a conventional moral stance. It may be more likely that any determined attempts to make sense of the self-evidently non-sensical, to impose an arbitrary order on manifest chaos, did not seem to Bowles worth the intellectual effort, particularly in a country and a city that defies the orthodox Western mind. To the *Paris Review*, Bowles maintained that any feelings of cultural estrangement or superiority by foreigners in Morocco – or, by implication, in any society radically different from their own – are not useful. 'Of course I feel apart, at one remove from the people here. But since they expect that in any case, there's no difficulty. The difficulties are in the United States, where there's no convention for maintaining apartness. The foreigners who try to "be Moroccan" never succeed, and manage to look ridiculous while they're trying. It seems likely that it's this very quality of impenetrability in the Moroccans that makes the country fascinating to outsiders.'

On the question of a foreigner in Morocco being a natural victim, Bowles remarks, matter-of-factly: 'Well, he *is* a victim. The Moroccans wouldn't use the word. And their attitude toward it is very much the same as ours is toward infection. The possibility is always there, and one must take precautions.' To the interviewer from the *Paris Review*, Bowles stressed the essential isolation of the individual: 'Everyone is isolated from everyone else. The concept of society is like a cushion to protect us from the knowledge of that isolation. A fiction that serves as an anaesthetic.' His involvement with Jane may be considered in this light. He acted to help her when she had decided what to do for herself. His aim was to show her how to act independently and to be supportive towards that end. Belatedly, he recognized that she was not as strong as he expected her to be, or indeed as she claimed to be: 'I think she overestimated her physical strength. She was always saying "I'm as strong as an ox," or "I'm made of iron." That sort of thing.' Bowles tended to believe these assertions which she, in turn, may have made in order to reassure him and in order not to lose face with him or – as she fancied – be despised. Bowles, for his part, occasionally deferred or abandoned his own plans to suit her, made considerable efforts to help her into print, attempted to discipline her in respect of her working habits, and at least tolerated her sexual preferences and her steadfast loyalty to Cherifa. Of course, as a *quid pro quo*, Bowles may have felt entitled to expect a considerable degree of latitude from Jane as regards his own affairs and imperatives.

Two deaths, at Christmas 1965 – first, Helvetia Perkins, then Jay Haselwood, proprietor of the Parade Bar and a close friend – seriously disturbed Jane, who became even more depressed. In the spring of 1966, *Up Above the World* was published, and Universal Studios bought the film rights for twenty-five thousand dollars. There was some encouraging news, too, for her: Farrar, Straus and Giroux wanted to publish her novel, *Two Serious Ladies*, her play, *In the Summer House*, and her short stories, *Plain Pleasures*, in one volume entitled *The Collected Works of Jane Bowles*. In June, Bowles' mother died. His father, an invalid, died shortly afterwards in July. Bowles had contracted to write a book about Bangkok, and decided to travel to the United States before setting out for the Far East. Jane was in no state to be left on her own, so she accompanied him to New York which they reached in the third week of July. On 28 July, Bowles set sail for Bangkok, returning to Tangier in late February 1967. Jane had preceded him by several months during which time, according to Gordon Sager, she was prey to terrors about money. She needed constant reassurance about the state of her bank account, frequently asking to be taken to the bank or that letters should be written urgently requesting transfer of funds from New York. Carla Grissman, a teacher at the American School in Tangier, who volunteered to help Jane with her writing, has described how Jane would 'sit on her bed picking at her wig. She kept her money in a suitcase with a combination lock. She'd keep trying to get the combination right, but it was not easy for her.'

To Bowles, in September 1966, Jane wrote: 'I'm very frightened being here by myself and never realized how complicated it would be for me. Gordon [Sager] is trying to help me, although he gets very fed up since I don't understand very much, indeed anything, about how to handle the money.' To a friend, in November, she wrote anguishedly: 'My life is one of great pain and torment now and I don't see my way out of this trap.' To Libby Holman, in February 1967, she wrote one line: 'I have been for six months in a nervous depression – I will be well soon.'

Dr Roux, Jane's doctor, alerted Bowles to Jane's condition in a letter of 9 January:

She continues to be in a state of depression with obsessive ideas (in particular the fear of not having enough money). In December she had a violent epileptic seizure (doubtless as a result of having taken too many whiskies . . .). It has been three years since the last fit. Impossible to make her follow a regular medical treatment. Dr Montsarrat and I have therefore given up trying, and Mrs B. stays quietly at home with Cherifa and Aicha. She goes out very seldom, does not read, writes to no one, and spends all day ruminating. She never telephones me anymore. I am obliged to call her and to force her, from time to time, to come and see me. Perhaps your return will give her the necessary impetus to come out of her depressive state, but I am not certain.

Bowles, disturbed by this report and what he knew about Cherifa, who was liable to take over with her potions and send Jane into a tailspin, was obliged to hospitalize Jane. To Virgil Thomson, he wrote on 27 April: 'Jane is in Malaga in hospital. I took her over two weeks ago . . . She could be lucid only if one managed, for a minute or two, to get her mind away from her "illness". Behind it all she seemed to be quite clear about her state, and could discuss it rationally now and then in moments of stress. Fundamentally the trouble was that she did not seem to care one way or the other. It was all happening in someone else about whom she didn't give a damn, and so she shrugged her shoulders. I'm hoping the hospital can get her interested in something, even if only in getting out.' Despite Jane's strenuous objections, Bowles consented on her behalf to electric shock therapy which apparently did some good. In July, she was able to return to Tangier where she became almost hyperactive, unable to sit still for more than a moment.

During her absence in Malaga, Bowles had fired Cherifa, his tolerance at an end. Cherifa began to abuse him vociferously to anyone who would listen, accusing him of having lost interest in Jane and bundled her out of his way. There were some in Tangier who were ready to listen attentively to these criticisms. Cherifa, according to Bowles, as detailed in an account he gave to *Rolling Stone* in 1974, was scarcely blameless. Bowles had been alerted by Mohammed Mrabet to remove a philodendron plant from Jane's apartment. 'The maid [Cherifa] was a horror. We used to find packets of magic around the house. In fact, in my big plant, in the roots, she hid a magic packet. She wanted to control the household through the plant. The plant was her proxy, or stooge, and she could give it orders before she left and see that they were carried out during the night. She really believed these things.'

Having rooted up the *tseuheur*, Bowles himself – no Moroccan would touch it – flushed the talisman down the toilet. The *tseuheur* had been the last straw. All Bowles' latent hostility towards Cherifa boiled up and he discharged her, reckoning that she had been responsible for any number of poisoning attempts not only on Jane but successfully on a parrot in 1966. Jane at first appeared to accept Bowles' decision about Cherifa, but in the autumn she reinstated her against all Bowles' wishes and instincts. Late in December, Jane suddenly moved out of her apartment, with Cherifa, and went to stay at the Atlas Hotel in the middle of town. Here, she sat in the bar of the hotel, or in the nearby Parade Bar, giving away her money. Her glad-handedness was indiscriminate: she gave to Cherifa, to the crowds of hippies who clustered around her, to a man who ran a grocery store and relentlessly kept selling her refrigerators. When her cash ran out, she resorted to writing cheques. She gave away her clothes. She gave away her jewellery.

All this, in complete contrast to her previous concern about having no money, was aggravated by her drinking. In all, she made a thorough nuisance of herself. Lily Wickman, who then ran the Parade Bar after the death of Jay Haselwood, gave a vivid account of Jane's behaviour to Millicent Dillon:

She drove me and the customers crazy, walking up and down, wringing her hands. The customers were complaining. She made them nervous. 'If you move again,' I said to her, 'I'll kick you out.' She went away and came back with a paper bag. She sat at the bar and started taking things out of the bag: a bottle of milk, a powder puff, other things. She took them out and put them on the counter. 'Now I'm not moving. Right?' she said ... When she was here, she kept repeating and repeating what she was saying. Then she'd take her wig off and put it on. She was, in fact, very gay when she was here. She was doing silly tricks with her wig. She knew a lot of people here. She would go into the kitchen and talk to the cooks and laugh. One day she came without clothes.

Lily Wickman finally called Bowles who, she says, assured her that 'it will be all right' and asked her to 'have a little bit of patience'. People who had once enjoyed her company began to avoid her in bars and in the streets.

By mid-January, besides an incalculable sum in cash, Jane had given away almost three thousand dollars in cheques. Bowles managed to stop her writing any more, persuaded her to come back to her apartment, and sternly forbade the servants to give her liquor under any pretext. To get a drink, Jane took herself off to the American Consulate where she lay down at the feet of the Consul-General. He said he had nothing to give her, and she refused to get up. In desperation, he offered to drive her to Guitta's Bar, an offer she pleasantly accepted. Guitta's Bar became her habitual resort, so that Bowles knew where to find her and would come to pick her up and take her home. He had taken responsibility for honouring her cheques and repaying people from whom she had borrowed. This was not merely a matter of honour – the Moroccan government had moved in, claiming that it was Bowles' responsibility, since the account on which Jane had drawn had been a joint one.

This manic-depressive episode resulted in Jane being hospitalized once more in Malaga. In September, with Jane stable but showing no improvement in her condition, Bowles left Tangier to teach a creative writing course at San Fernando in California. He returned in February 1969, five months later. Jane begged him to take her with him away from the dispiriting clinic to Tangier, and he did so, against the wishes of Dr Roux. Before taking her up to her apartment, Bowles got out of the car and went upstairs to evict Cherifa. She left, muttering darkly, but though Jane appeared relieved that Bowles had got rid of her, she fell immediately into a deep depression. She had often spoken of suicide, but now she made an attempt to throw herself from a window in her apartment. The defenestration was foiled by the fact that she could not climb up on the sill – her condition had so deteriorated that she had the greatest difficulty moving unaided: her women servants had to help her out of bed and to walk. Mostly, Jane spent her time lying on the floor of the living room in Bowles' apartment, curled up, looking at him in silence.

In a letter to Lawrence Stewart, in May, Bowles wrote: 'Jane is not improving; one would say she is determined not to. Three months have brought nothing good. If anything, she is even more distraught than when she came.' Death filled her mind: she refused to eat or to take medication. She pleaded: 'I want to die. Please give me something so I can die.' She responded to Mrabet, now and again, who was able to persuade her to eat small amounts and to take her medicines, but only because, Bowles says, 'I think she thought it would have hurt him too much to refuse because he didn't understand. But she felt that I understood and that I was not helping her in the way she wanted to be helped.' What she wanted from Bowles was a quick death, and he was occasionally overcome with such pity for her that he had to harden his heart: 'I felt she didn't have a will to die. I always wondered if she were given something, whether she would do it. Would she have taken it? But I couldn't play around that way, of course. And I became an enemy more than ever because, although I sympathized with her desire to die and she knew I did, yet I couldn't admit it and I had to say, "But naturally, no one's going to give you anything, Jane." And yet if we'd been alone on a desert island, I probably would have given it to her.'

In all, Jane spent four months in Tangier with Bowles before returning to the Clínica de Los Angeles in Malaga. There, in the spring of 1970, she had a stroke after dancing 'too wildly' at a clinic party. She was regarded as having precipitated the stroke, having become wildly angry and excited after the nuns at the clinic had tried to restrain her. On 11 June, in a letter to Libby Holman, Bowles reported on her condition: 'I don't think there is any hope that she will ever talk again, or move at all. The doctor seems to have abandoned hope, and says we can only wait. She did recognize me, I'm sure, but it was something far away and fleeting, the recognition.' Mostly comatose, she nevertheless had occasional moments of lucidity and awareness during which she talked and could hear what was said to her. Her appetite improved a little. She conceived a wish to be converted to Catholicism, and was baptized into the Roman Catholic Church. By October she was blind.

In Tangier, between visits to the clinic in Malaga, Bowles was working on his autobiography, *Without Stopping*, commissioned by Putnam's. He had begun the book in the summer of 1969, and it was published in 1972. In the circumstances of its composition,

Bowles was naturally distracted. The book is so notably free of any personal feelings, that William Burroughs referred to it as 'Without Telling': it amounts to little more than a factual account of Bowles' life and travels, liberally studded with famous names which were mostly included at Putnam's insistence. Bowles was working at speed: 'I think the first half was personal enough, but the last half was hurried. Time was coming to an end and I had to meet the deadline.' The autobiography ends in the spring of 1969, with a passage reflecting on death. 'The Moroccans claim that full participation in life demands the regular contemplation of death. I agree without reserve. Unfortunately I am unable to conceive of my own death without setting it in the far more terrible *mise-en-scène* of old age. There I am without teeth, unable to move, wholly dependent upon someone whom I pay to take care of me and who at any moment may go out of the room and never return. Of course this is not at all what the Moroccans mean by the contemplation of death; they would consider my imaginings a particularly contemptible form of fear. One culture's therapy is another culture's torture.'

This less than elegaic paragraph was perhaps influenced by Jane's sufferings: which continued until 4 May 1973. Bowles was summoned from Tangier on 3 May. On 30 April she had had another stroke. Bowles spent the afternoon of 4 May, her last day, with her, watching over her in her coma. He left the hospital to have dinner. At nine he received a call telling him that she had just died. On 5 May, Jane Bowles was buried in the Catholic cemetery of San Miguel in Malaga. The grave is unmarked: Bowles, unconvinced that Jane's religious conversion was a true one, refused to commemorate her with a cross. Then, too, 'As far as I'm concerned she has no grave. I don't believe in cemeteries or graves. For what? For mourning? For getting over it? You never get over it. It's always with you. At least I don't, because it's disconnected me. I think I lived vicariously largely and didn't know it. And when I had no one to live through or for, I was disconnected from life.' To Virgil Thomson, Bowles wrote: 'my degree of interest in everything has been diminished almost to the point of nonexistence. That makes a great difference, since there is no compelling reason to do anything whatever.' In 1989, when asked about his marriage to Jane, Bowles prefaced a remark with the words 'when I was alive . . .' Asked why he writes, Bowles replied, 'because I'm still in the land of the living . . .'

Jane's death reinforced his sense of no longer being able to live vicariously. Jane had become remote from him in the last stages of her illness, and his autobiography ends with this passage: ' "Goodbye," says the dying man to the mirror they hold in front of him. "We won't be seeing each other any more." When I quoted Valéry's epigram in *The Sheltering Sky*, it seemed a poignant bit of fantasy. Now, because I no longer imagine myself as an onlooker at the scene, but instead as the principal protagonist, it strikes me as repugnant. To make it right, the dying man would have to add two words to his little farewell, and they are: "Thank God!" ' If he could no longer live vicariously, how was he to live at all?

To the *Paris Review*, which was attempting to describe Bowles as a 'kind of consummate expatriate', a paradigm of 'romantic images of the artist's life in exotic, far-away places', Bowles refused to see himself 'as a consummate anything. I don't see myself really, I have no ego.' He harboured no hostility to the United States or New York, though lamenting the changes in the country since his original departure. 'I don't think it will ever be put right; but then again, I never expect anything to be put right. Nothing ever is. Things go on and become other things . . . What does one mean when one says that things are getting worse? It's becoming more like the future, that's all. It's just moving ahead.'

Bowles' own life did not appear to 'move ahead' after Jane's death: but then it had never been merely a progression of events through which he moved determinedly as though on a forced march. Life, of course, continued: he maintained his apartment in the Immeuble Itesa near the American Consulate, he continued to see friends and visitors, he did not cease to work. The best thing about Tangier, he wrote to Virgil Thomson, echoing the impression the city had made on Truman Capote, 'is the feeling it gives one of being in a pocket of suspended time and animation. Nothing happens for such long periods of time that one dreads any change which might affect the stasis.'

That passivity, induced partly by the ethos of Tangier, contributed to Bowles' desire to remain in the city – or, rather, since he made nothing so conclusive as a decision, his surrender to circumstances: 'I did not choose to live in Tangier permanently; it happened ... I grew lazy and put off departure. Then a day came when I realized with a shock that not only did the world have many more people in it than it had had only a short time before, but also that the hotels were less good, travel less comfortable, and places in general much less beautiful. After that when I went somewhere else I immediately longed to be back in Tangier. Thus if I am here now, it is only because I was still here when I realized to what an extent the world had worsened, and that I no longer wanted to travel.'

Bowles regrets much that has happened in Tangier since his first arrival, but he defends the city:

I can say that so far it has been touched by fewer of the negative aspects of contemporary civilization than most cities of its size. More important than that, I relish the idea that in the night, all around me in my sleep, sorcery is burrowing its invisible tunnels in every direction, from thousands of senders to thousands of unsuspecting recipients. Spells are being cast, poison is running its course; souls are being dispossessed of parasitic pseudo-consciousness that lurks in the unguarded recesses of the mind. There is drumming out there most nights. It never awakens me; I hear the drums and incorporate them into my dream, like the nightly call of the muezzins. Even if in the dream I am in New York, the first *Allah akbar!* effaces the backdrop and carries whatever comes next to North Africa, and the dream goes on.

William Burroughs
and the Beats
in Tangier

Rome, in late December 1953, wasn't where William Burroughs wanted to be. His temper, never gladsome, turned surly. 'This Rome detour is costing me over $100, incalculable inconvenience and boredom.' He was waiting for Alan Ansen, with whom, that fall in New York, he had agreed to travel to Europe, to turn up with a list of addresses, useful information which could save a person a lot of trouble and valuable time. Without this resource, Burroughs was reduced to combing the local telephone directory for likely bath-houses, and following his nose to sniff out the interesting bars. But the baths had been closed, and the hottest bar he could locate was depressingly dull: 'a few dreary dykes in sweat shirts, a sprinkle of ugly queers, and some characters with beards playing chess'. The cutest thing in the bar was the waiter, Chi-Chi, but he was the son of the proprietor, so 'it looks like hands off'.

A typical Roman bar – 'a hole in the wall soda and ice cream joint, no toilet and no place to sit down, with the door propped open or missing altogether, where you can gulp a drink with a cold, blue hand' – was nothing like the San Remo, a New York joint where Burroughs used to hang out with Allen Ginsberg, Jack Kerouac and, at least on one occasion, Gore Vidal with whom, according to Ginsberg, Kerouac 'got drunk and boastfully queerlike – & went home with him & couldnt get a hardon & fell asleep in his bathtub'. Now the San Remo was something like a *bar*. Vidal was on Burroughs' mind: 'I am going to have something to say to Gore Vidal, and all these characters talking about how great Italy is and anything goes, and they got like a renaissance of culture. What a crock of shit! They can shove Italy all the way up.'

Ansen arrived late on 24 December and immediately Burroughs brightened: Ansen could speak the language and instantly 'negotiated several *affaires de coeur* in frigid doorways (average price $10 and pretty shoddy merchandise)'. Burroughs amended this in a PS to his letter to Ginsberg and showed signs of softening his attitude somewhat: 'No the price is only $3.20, but there may be extras if you suck in a buggy instead of a doorway. The fountains are wonderful (even old Cactus Boy melted at the sight of Trevi), and I feel that in spite of minor irritations Europe is just wonderful.' He had evidently got over his heavy cold and he had discovered, despite the fact that the 'heat is on junk, and the junkies of Rome are shivering sick in their traps,' a source for Paregoric. Cheap boys and an obliging druggist went some way to restore his equilibrium.

Alan Ansen, a classical scholar and former secretary to W. H. Auden, had been introduced to Burroughs by Ginsberg a few months earlier in New York. The trip they agreed to take together may have felt like a conclusion and a beginning to Burroughs who recognized that the erotic aspect of his relationship with Ginsberg had come to an end. Ginsberg, not sexually stimulated by Burroughs, had finally agreed to go to bed with him more as an act of friendship than from true desire. Burroughs appeared to need Ginsberg so much that Ginsberg decided to be generous with his body. But what Burroughs wanted was complete possession, and not just of his lover's body: 'am all hung up in a great psychic marriage with him for the month' wrote Ginsberg to Neal Cassady in September 1953. Ginsberg was, to Burroughs' annoyance, seeing girls as well – which struck Burroughs not only as improbable but disloyal. Ginsberg's less than wholehearted response, physically and psychically, was intolerable to Burroughs who continually pressed for a greater and more exclusive commitment. Ginsberg, goaded to the limit, finally turned on Burroughs: 'I don't want your ugly old cock.'

'I ever regret the wound I dealt his heart,' wrote Ginsberg in 1981, still appalled by his words. Burroughs had wanted to 'devour my soul parasitically'. Naively, perhaps, Ginsberg had merely gone along with Burroughs' wishes and desires because 'I respected him a great deal and so wanted to be as amenable as possible to anything practical. But at the same time I was going in my own direction.' The strength of their friendship survived Ginsberg's instinctive rejection and it was to Ginsberg that Burroughs was to write continuously from old habit and love: 'we stayed still faithful to the star on each other's forehead, still sacramental life-companions despite disturbance of erotic rapport,' remarked Ginsberg in 1981. 'I loved Bill and he loved me, as I still do decades later.'

Tangier had been in Burroughs' mind at least as early as September 1953, and by mid-November he had certainly fixed on it as his destination, the place he wanted to be. Presumably he had read Paul Bowles' novels, *The Sheltering Sky* and *Let It Come Down*, and he declared, 'I'm going to steep myself in vice.' Some elements in these novels may have given him fantastical notions of North Africa in general, and Tangier in particular, as a zone free of petty moral and official restrictions where drugs were routinely and habitually sold and consumed, where boys were – almost literally – two a penny, where women were granted little or no status beyond their domestic domains, and where credence was more readily, overtly given to the magical, metaphysical aspect of things. Bowles had given hints of such a world in his novels. Tangier was the last resort of the disinherited, the disillusioned, the degenerate and the depraved. Tangier was the end of the line, the journey towards it a lifetime's nightmare.

Burroughs proposed to make the twenty-four-hour ('forty-eight more like') trip from Rome to Gibraltar by rail, third class, and take the ferry across the Strait to Tangier – a prospect tailor-made to light his short fuse. Sure enough, on 20 January 1954 Burroughs was writing sourly to Ginsberg: 'The most loathsome types produced by the land of the free are represented in the American Colony of Tanger.' (He insisted on the French spelling.) 'There are like 2 American bars.' Presumably Dean's and the Parade. 'No.1 [Dean's] I hit dead cold sober at 1 o'clock on a Sunday afternoon. Horrible vista of loud-mouthed, red-faced drunks, falling off bar stools, puking in corners, a Céline nightmare. Bar No.2 [The Parade] is stocked with the dreariest breed of piss elegant, cagy queens . . . Nowadays I spend my time smoking weed with shoeshine boys in Arab cafés. Their manners are better and their conversation quite as interesting.'

If Burroughs had not been impressed by Italian culture, he was even less taken with Moroccan: 'What's all this old Muslim culture shit? One thing I have learned. I know what Arabs do all day and all night. They sit around smoking cut weed and playing some silly card game. And don't ever fall for this inscrutable oriental shit like

Bowles puts down. They are just a gabby, gossipy, simple minded lazy crew of citizens.' He never came to feel much more interest or sympathy for the indigenous culture, preferring for the most part to keep a cautious distance from Tanjawis, distrustful and uncomprehending in his self-contained exile and, more often than not, junk dreams, fantasies and reveries which, increasingly, intuitively, were informed by his immediate environment. The boys were not to dream about – they seemed to run a tight union, charging inflated prices up to five dollars and insisting on their masculinity: 'Ali is getting worried about his standing in the shoeshine set . . . He thumps his little scrawny chest and says "I am a man". Oh God! Such shit I could hear in Clayton Mo. . . . I never see such abject, repulsive, whining panhandling. A man might contract some loathsome venereal disease of the soul from these untouchables. Besides which it costs an additional $3 in Aureomycin for adequate pro coverage fore and aft.'

Frustrated in his attempts to take this low-life back to his hotel, Burroughs landed himself a room at Dutch Tony's at 1 calle de los Arcos, close by the Petit Socco, the hub of the Medina, in the Arab section of the city. Anthony Reithorst was frankly a pimp: he could be relied upon by visiting tourists to arrange assignations with compliant boys. Two of the rooms in his house were rented for income, and Burroughs' fellow lodger was a former Air Force officer from Indiana, David Woolman, who wrote a regular gossip column in the weekly *Moroccan Courier* under the pseudonym Barnaby Bliss. Neither Woolman nor Reithorst worried about the sex or the age of visitors to Burroughs' room, though Dutch Tony did urge some caution since his trade depended on discretion. Tangier was looking up: Burroughs was meeting the local expatriates: 'Junkies, queers, drunks . . . Most of them came from someplace else for obvious reasons.' He wasn't meeting the better class of expatriate residents, though junkies, queers and drunks could equally be counted among their number on the Mountain where, at least, they had more money and a little more privacy to conduct themselves with discretion and a veneer of propriety.

On 5 February 1954, Burroughs turned forty. A significant anniversary. Most men tend, at this point in their lives, to review and assess their progress and, more often than not, react with a certain sense of urgency and more or less controlled panic. A couple of days later, he wrote to Allen Ginsberg enclosing his 'latest attempt to write something saleable'. Burroughs had so far published one short book, *Junky*, which had been issued in 1953 by Ace Books. The first edition of a hundred thousand paperback copies had been printed back-to-back with another short book about drugs written by a former Narcotics Agent. Burroughs' take had been a net advance of $800. 'Certainly a shabby package', commented Ginsberg who had acted as Burroughs' agent. Ace Books was not a distinguished imprint, specializing mostly in paperback 'commercial schlupp with an occasional French Romance or hardboiled novel nervously slipped into the list' by Carl Solomon, Ace Books editor, who happened to be a friend of Ginsberg.

Burroughs had been diverting himself with his everyday displacement activities, 'reading magazines, making fudge, cleaning my shotgun, washing the dishes, going to bed with Kiki' (an eighteen year-old Spanish boy he had picked up and taken on as permanent companion), 'tying the garbage up in neat parcels and putting it out for the collector' (garbage containers were liable to be stolen), 'buying food for dinner, picking up a junk script'. But something had got to him and, two days into forty years of age, he finally decided: 'Now you must work.' He smoked some hashish, sat down, and 'out it comes all in one piece like a glob of spit.' What came out was 'almost like automatic writing produced by a hostile, independent entity who is saying in effect "I will write what I please". At same time when I try to pressure myself into organizing production, to impose some form on material, or even to follow a line (like continuation of novel) the effort capitulates me into a sort of madness where only the most extreme material is available to me.'

He was writing in longhand, having no typewriter and no money to buy one. His resources amounted to sixty dollars – which he reckoned out at two dollars a day for the rest of the month. But junk cost him at least that every day, on top of which he had to feed Kiki and give him fifty cents a day pocket money, most of which Kiki gave to his sick mother. Burroughs would then inevitably have to shell out another fifty cents so that Kiki could go to a movie or a football game. Strictly speaking, Burroughs was not poor, though he was often broke. He could rely on a regular monthly allowance of two hundred dollars from his parents back in Florida, but the cost of drugs bit savagely into these funds leaving little enough for rent, food, drinks and other necessities. His single possession of negotiable value, a camera, was regularly in and out of hock, and it was a convenient arrangement that he could apply to friends such as Ansen, Ginsberg, Kells Elvin, and others for small sums in travellers' cheques or certified cheques, just as Burroughs himself could be applied to by Ginsberg and other close friends. Occasionally, he would be reduced to eating bread and drinking tea for a few days or over a weekend, having nothing in his pocket but a few cents; but he could always, finally, get his hands on ten dollars to see him though a lean patch.

The letter of 7 February to Ginsberg is notable for one other matter that was evidently on his mind: he refers to reports of several persons who had tried to shoot glasses off people's heads, missing and killing their involuntary targets. Burroughs does not specifically refer to his own experience when, in Mexico in September 1951, he tried to shoot a highball glass off his wife's head, missed, and instead drilled a hole through her temple. This event, says Burroughs himself, was the principal motive that turned him into a writer: 'I am forced to the appalling conclusion that I would never have become a writer but for Joan's death, and to a realization of the extent to which this event has motivated and formulated my writing. I live with the constant threat of possession, and a constant need to escape from possession, from Control. So the death of Joan brought me into contact with the invader, the Ugly Spirit, and maneuvered me into a lifelong struggle, in which I have had no choice except to write my way out.'

Literary exorcism of his internal demons required that they be identified, described and recognized. Through naming them, Burroughs might atone and be free. Burroughs came to regard himself as much a victim as Joan, his wife, since he did not believe that anything was accidental. He did, profoundly, believe in personal demons, in the control exercised by inimical forces. The blame that attached to him was carelessness, failure to recognize the extent to which he had been possessed at that moment by an evil spirit. He had paid the full price for his neglect, for his failure to pay proper attention to the state of his soul. Possession by a malign spirit did not excuse the fact that he had killed his wife. The fact that he and Joan were equally victims did not mitigate the crime to any acceptable degree. The only appropriate atonement was rigorous attention, constant battle with the devil within, and writing was the means through which he could best deal with his constant, unremitting guilt.

There had been the immediate prospect of charges being brought against him by the Mexican authorities. A little judicious economy with the truth on the part of Burroughs and the witnesses to the shooting, some minor bribery of ballistics experts, a complaisant prosecutor, and a fair-minded judge resulted in the charge against Burroughs being reduced to 'criminal imprudence' which carried a maximum five-year sentence. Burroughs pleaded guilty, was released on bail, and in December 1952 he bolted from Mexico City at the cost of forfeiting the bail bond of two thousand dollars. Later, he heard that he had been sentenced, in his absence, to two years suspended.

Disillusioned with life and his relationship with Ginsberg in New York, Burroughs was also necessarily divorced from the middle-class life of his parents in Florida. As a homosexual, as a drug addict, as a petty criminal (he had a history of forged prescriptions, drunk driving, possession of narcotics, and now, euphemistically, 'criminal imprudence'), as a man who believed in a magical universe in which there was no such thing as coincidence or accident, Burroughs was ripe for Tangier, which appeared to him to be 'nightmarish' and perhaps, to that extent, satisfied his current condition of being. Bowles' novels had pictured North Africa, and Tangier particularly, as a place apart, for men apart, a cultural and psychic limbo, an appropriate place for experiencing and acting out the condition of despair, drugged crises, and existentialist self-discovery.

Though despairing, Burroughs possessed not only a taste and capacity for self-indulgence bordering on hedonism, but equally a strong will to survive. He had been a drug addict since 1944, when he was thirty. He was vitally interested in the symptoms, the pharmacology and the treatment of 'The Sickness', his term for drug addiction. In his introduction to the novel he had begun to write in Tangier, *The Naked Lunch*, he defines himself as an addict, a word he takes to 'mean an addict to junk (generic term for opium and/or derivatives including all synthetics from demerol to palfium). I have used junk in many forms: morphine, heroin, delaudid, eukodol, pantopon, diocodid, diosane, opium, demerol, dolophine, palfium. I have smoked junk, eaten it, sniffed it, injected it in vein-skin-muscle, inserted it in rectal suppositories. The needle is not important. Whether you sniff it smoke it eat it or shove it up your ass the result is the same: addiction.' In Tangier, he regularly smoked kif and ate hashish in the form of *majoun*. He is careful to draw a distinction between addictive junk and the hallucinogenic drugs. 'When I speak of drug addiction I do not refer to keif, marijuana or any preparation of hashish, mescaline, *Bannisteria Caapi*, LSD6, Sacred Mushrooms or any drug of the hallucinogen group ... There is no evidence that the use of any hallucinogen results in physical dependence. The action of these drugs is physiologically opposite to the action of junk.'

His addiction to drugs was less a means of escape from reality than a determined effort to confront the spiritual and magical reality of himself and the world. He did not evade the horrors, but confronted them with considerable personal courage. Burroughs was not a doomed victim – he was, indeed, a traveller and explorer of places, ideas, experiences, and terrors that would have driven a man with a less determined sense of personal mission utterly insane. He admitted frankly: 'Yes, I had and have an insatiable appetite for the extreme and the sensational, for the morbid, slimy, and unwholesome.' Burroughs lived in, and with, chaos as others live with reason and received opinions. He sought the structure in chaos, believing that it had its own metaphysical rationale that could, with attention and clear vision, be comprehended. Tangier's special attraction consisted 'in changing combinations' and appeared to Burroughs to resemble Mexico, for which he still occasionally longed, as being 'sinister and gloomy and chaotic, with the special chaos of a dream'.

His grasp of reality was perhaps somewhat stronger than those around him who were beached in Tangier without resources. An acquaintance was an English derelict, Eric Gifford, generally known as 'Calamity Kate', for whom nothing went according to plan. Rupert Croft-Cooke, in *The Caves of Hercules*, describes Gifford, before the war, cruising the purlieus of the Villa Harris, used as a billet for Spanish soldiers, and being discovered by a patrol 'offering himself with lowered garments to a long queue of infantrymen who, deprived of womenfolk, were impatient to find relief'. Arrested, he was charged as a spy – the Spanish, out of prurience, being unable to bring themselves to describe formally the actual nature of Gifford's offence. The charge of spying could not be proved, the true charge was unmentionable, and Gifford was released.

He headed for the West Indies where he set himself up as a bee farmer. He imported some swarms of very expensive and allegedly highly productive bees, only to discover that the island was the home of a violently aggressive breed of killer bees which instantly attacked and wiped out his blameless honey bees within a matter of weeks.

Returning to Tangier after the war, he naturally wished to inspect the condition of the villa he had left unoccupied. But first he called in at Dean's Bar to announce his return and intention. 'Just going up to see the villa.' The patrons of Dean's were unaccountably silent. 'An hour later he was back in the bar, suppressing tears. "There *was* no villa!" he said, and this was actually true. The simple neighbours had removed every scrap of it for more useful purposes of their own – tiles, stones, windows, latrines, even flooring and doorsteps. Calamity Kate found only a growth of nettles and some rusty tins on the site.' Gifford had the unfortunate knack of being, apparently, at the whim of inimical forces. His exit from a Casablanca café, for instance, was followed promptly by a bomb explosion. Such a character would naturally appeal to Burroughs who would scent not merely a misfortunate man but an interesting magnet for misfortune, a man at the mercy of malevolent forces.

Burroughs hired Gifford, in May 1954, to help him through a

difficult period. Gifford, more than usually broke, agreed for a fee
of fifty dollars to dole out a ration of drugs to Burroughs, feed him
regularly, and keep his clothes. Burroughs, desperate on the second
day of this regime, 'stole clothes from other boarder [David Wool-
man], sneaked out, and bought some Eukodol ampules and glutted
myself. Gifford found out about it, confiscated the remaining
ampules, and now the other boarder locks his door when he goes
out, and Gifford also took my money . . . Gifford, he's a hard man.
No use trying to coax an extra ampule out of him. "By God" he says
"I'm being paid to do it and I'm going to do it right." ' Burroughs,
however, had another ploy in reserve: 'I just thought of a scheme
to lure an Arab into my room (easy enough, they are always knocking on the window). And get his clothes on pretext I have to go
out and get money and all my clothes are in the laundry.'

At least since early April, Burroughs had been shooting up every
four hours with 'some semi-synthetic stuff called Eukodol'. This
was synthetic morphine which the German manufacturers had
withdrawn from the market; but there was still a stock in Tangier
which Burroughs cornered. One side effect of Eukodol was to promote a euphoria which was lacking in cocaine: 'When you shoot C
in main line . . . there is a rush of pure pleasure to the head. Before
you can clean the needle the pleasure dims. Ten minutes later you
take another shot. No visceral pleasure, no increase of enjoyment,
no sense of well-being, no alteration or widening of perspective.'
Eukodol was the stuff: from four hours, Burroughs reduced the gap
to two hours. This was a serious habit. He did nothing else. In *The
Naked Lunch*, Burroughs vividly described it:

Habit Notes. Shooting Eukodol every two hours. I have a place
where I can slip my needle right into a vein, it stays open like a
red, festering mouth, swollen and obscene, gathers a slow drop
of blood and pus after the shot . . . Picking up needle I reach
spontaneously for the tie-up cord with my left hand. This I take
as a sign that I can hit one useable vein in my left arm. (The
movements of tying up are such that you normally tie up the arm
with which you reach for the cord.) The needle slides in easily on
the edge of a callous. I feel around. Suddenly a thin column of
blood shoots up into the syringe, for a moment sharp and solid
as a red cord.

The body knows what veins you can hit and conveys this knowledge in the spontaneous movements you make preparing to take a shot ... Sometimes the needle points like a dowser's wand. Sometimes I must wait for the message. But when it comes I always hit blood.

A red orchid bloomed at the bottom of the dropper. He hesitated for a full second, then pressed the bulb, watching the liquid rush into the vein as if sucked by the silent thirst of his blood. There was an iridescent, thin coat of blood left in the dropper, and the white paper collar was soaked through with blood like a bandage. He reached over and filled the dropper with water. As he squirted the water out, the shot hit him in the stomach, a soft sweet blow.

Look down at my filthy trousers, haven't been changed in months ... The days glide by strung on a syringe with a long thread of blood ... I am forgetting sex and all sharp pleasures of the body – a grey, junk-bound ghost.

A German tourist had died in a ditch of a drug overdose, and the authorities were getting nervous. It was harder to score from the pharmacist, and even Dutch Tony began to sense trouble – the police were keeping a wary eye on his house, which was not good for Tony's business. Gifford did his best to regulate the dosage, and confiscated Burrough's clothing, and to add to the problem Kiki's mother had 'beefed to the fuzz' about her son's relationship with the degenerate American. By mid-April, he began to think about going away to lie low for a while. 'Everyone in Tanger bores me,' the weather was bad, the writing was not going well because Burroughs needed a responsive person to bounce the stuff off – Ginsberg, for preference, who intuitively understood Burroughs' 'routines' which, like a magic spell, were liable to recoil on the originator if they could not be received by a sympathetic receptor. The routine was liable to turn back on Burroughs, tearing him apart, the routine itself becoming 'more and more insane (literal growth like cancer) and impossible, and fragmentary like berserk pinball machine and I am screaming: "Stop it! Stop it!"'

But Ginsberg was in Mexico, and for a while, for the first two weeks of May, appeared to have disappeared completely. By the time contact by letter was restored, later in the month, Burroughs had been joined in Tangier by Kells Elvins, an old school friend who had encouraged Burroughs to write in the late 1930s. Elvins was distressed to find Burroughs looked sick and still, despite his attempted cure, 'taking six dollies a day'. He was trying to cut out drugs altogether, but he didn't reckon 'tea' as anything more than a light, recreational drug and so was high when he and Elvins visited 'an extraordinary Arab restaurant that looked like a remodeled bus station – bare, galvanized iron roof. A huge banana palm growing in this barn-like or hangar-like room with tables scattered here and there. Served by a snotty Arab queen who was barely courteous when we ordered two plates and one portion of Cous Cous.'

They had just come from Dean's Bar where they had been no better received. The atmosphere had been unaccountably hostile, and Dean had taken against Burroughs. 'Dean wanted not to serve me, rolling his eyes in disapproval, but there was Kells, a good customer. (Dean has heard that I am a dope fiend. More than that he instinctively feels me as a danger, far out, an ill omen.) So I sat there, loaded on tea, savoring their disapproval, rolling it on my tongue with glass of good dry sherry.' Whether or not this was paranoia, Burroughs felt ostracized by Tangier society: 'A number of people seem to have taken a violent, irrational dislike to me. Especially people who run bars. I am a bad sign and no mistake. When you see Willy Lee sitting at the bar, your trap has had it. This is *not* imagination, Allen.'

Elvins, checking out Tangier society a little further up the social scale, had dropped in at the Parade Bar 'where the elegant fags hang'. Sociably, he initiated a conversation with the guy next to him at the bar. Elvins had trouble drawing out more than monosyllables: 'You come here direct from the States?' asked Elvins. 'No, from Brazil.' 'So? And how did you come?' 'By yacht, *of course*.' Despite all Burroughs' hopes, Tangier was turning out to be a 'marrowbone conventional town'. Anyone, or anything, far out threatened 'this moneychanging town'. What nobody had told him, what Bowles' novels had neglected to inform him, was that Tangier was *provincial*, a small town with small town preoccupations and a small town system of organized gossip, snobbish and censorious. There were social climbers here like anywhere else – no equality of the damned and the degenerate. Even hell had its social strata, which Dante could have told him. Since everyone had his or her secrets to keep, the sheer force of projection was not merely a defence but wielded as a weapon. 'I have frequently encountered sheer black hate. It scares me. Not the hate itself but the condition that underlies it.'

The day Kells Elvins left for Madrid, 3 July 1954, Burroughs was laid up with what was later diagnosed as rheumatic fever. Tangier dragged him 'like a sea anchor'. He was feeling really ill, with 'pain and swelling in the joints', and he was flat broke. His illness had enabled him, by 8 July, to 'cut junk almost to vanishing point', and he had been solicitously cared for by Kiki even though there was no immediate financial reward in it for him. This apparent altruism, this seemingly selfless devotion, much impressed Burroughs who was more used to human leeches: 'find me an American kid like that'. His relationship with Kiki, though necessarily non-intellectual, involved at least 'real affection on both sides and some protoplasmic contact. In US such relations are always straining to be something more or different from what they are, with resulting unease for both parties. Actually US provides no counterpart to my relation with Kiki . . .' Burroughs was sleeping twenty hours a day, during which he endured constant nightmares. Kiki reported that Burroughs talked continually in his sleep and woke, starting, with a cry.

Most of Burroughs' trouble, physical hardships aside, was loneliness. Eric Gifford, David Woolman, the hostile Dean, and various other acquaintances were not exactly top-notch company, though they were adequate companions to harangue over a drink at the Café Central in the Petit Socco. But for all Burroughs' cynical congeniality he was not taken seriously in Tangier. Tangerinos knew he had written a book, *Junky*, but nobody who had read it understood it, liked it, or was impressed by it. He missed Neal Cassady, Jack Kerouac, Allen Ginsberg, Kells Elvins, Alan Ansen and all his old associates with whom, through regular letters to Ginsberg, he kept in touch. 'I have nobody to talk to except Kiki. Some artist and writer colony!' He had been introduced, by Woolman, to Bowles shortly after he arrived in Tangier, but Bowles was unaccountably cool when they happened to cross one another's paths. Burroughs put this down to Bowles' wish to dissociate himself from a known user of narcotics, 'fearing possible hassles with customs inspection and authorities in general if he is known to be on familiar terms with me – guilt by association. I don't know.' Initially, Burroughs had not struck Bowles very forcibly. He had met Burroughs during a period of convalescence after a bout of paratyphoid, and Burroughs had talked mainly about his contract for *Junky* which he was complaining about. 'If I remember correctly, he had good reason to be dissatisfied with its terms. His manner was subdued to the point of making his presence in the room seem tentative. I recalled having seen him before from time to time, walking in the street, not looking to right or left. We continued to cross each other's path, and now we nodded.' Burroughs was in a state where he required more than a nod of mere acknowledgement from an intellectual equal – the only person he had yet encountered who could be ranked as worth talking to seriously.

By mid-August, Burroughs was trying to book passage back to the States, thinking to try to join up with Allen Ginsberg, who he missed, in California. Meanwhile, he kept busy writing to Ginsberg and Kerouac, debating the pros and cons of Tangier and his relationship with Kiki to whom he had become firmly attached. He claimed to be tired of Tangier, that he had no friends there nor any prospect of making any. A permanent return to the States was no solution, but he had no firm ideas about where he might prefer to be. Tangier had its good points – sex was readily available, the cost of living was cheap, and the foreign community was not much bothered by the police who, in any case of trouble, could normally be relied upon to side with an American in any dispute with a Moroccan. 'I mean we are exempt from questioning, arrest on suspicion, any legal interference with our private lives.' This was a distinct plus. Tangier was very far from being the police state Burroughs suspected the United States to have become. 'Come to think of it the Tanger police are a model for just what police should be and do. They don't care at all about your sex life or whether you take junk (of course everybody smokes tea in the street like tobacco). All they do is maintain order (and do a pretty thorough job too).'

As for Kiki, there was no more trouble from his mother who was quite satisfied so long as he contributed regularly to her household expenses. Kiki, happy to be living apart from his own family, was a 'tranquil, healthy young male' who was happily prepared to spend hours on end dozing naked in bed with Burroughs, smoking a little, making desultory love and eating grapes. 'In fact', wrote Burroughs to Kerouac,

> I find myself getting jealous of Kiki – he is besieged by importuning queens. In fact I am downright involved, up to my neck in Maya. He is a sweet kid, and it is so pleasant to loll about in the afternoon smoking tea, sleeping and having sex with no hurry, running leisurely hands over his lean, hard body and finally we doze off, all wrapped around each other, into the delicious sleep of a hot afternoon in a cool, darkened room, a sleep that is different from any other sleep, a twilight in which I savour, with a voluptuous floating sensation, the state of sleep, feeling the nearness of Kiki's young body, the sweet, imperceptible drawing together in sleep, leg inching over leg, arm encompassing body, hips hitching closer, stiffening organs reaching out to touch warm flesh.

Burroughs was so delighted with this description of sex with Kiki, in the letter to Kerouac, that he recommended it to Ginsberg's attention. Kiki was healthy and simple. 'Example of his health and simplicity: he had some sort of infection or swelling in his rectum, and I gave him four shots of penicillin. The other day he was sitting on the bed naked and I asked him if his ass was all right. "Yes" he said with a boyish grin, and putting his hands on his knees rolled himself back showing me his ass. It was done without a trace of prissiness *or* exhibitionism, beyond a natural joy in his body that any young human male has. As you say', remarked Burroughs to Ginsberg, 'he is a dream for which I will have nostalgia. Hard to duplicate in the States.' His relationship with Kiki was also useful in a subtler manner. When Burroughs was high on tea, he snuggled next to Kiki and got 'ideas faster and better than at other times. It's like he is some sort of orgone battery that tunes me in. I have tested this many times. The difference is palpable. Trouble is I don't feel like, and it isn't appropriate, to get up and write them down. Though I have written some down and they are always good. I mean he is sort of a *medium* through which I get ideas . . .'

A reservation on the Italian Line, leaving from Gibraltar, was made for 7 September, and Burroughs determined to kick his junk habit rather than go through the risky business of trying to take any drugs into the US. Kiki, conscripted to help him, confiscated Burroughs' clothes. Not that there was much left in that line – a combat jacket, one pair of slacks and a cheap, flashy brown coat. He had given his last sports coat and spare pair of pants to Kiki as a bribe to prevent him from getting 'the beautiful copper-brown skin of his chest and shoulders and arms' tattooed. Burroughs, at first only half-listening to Kiki describing the terrific designs he had in mind, suddenly began to pay attention and became hysterical, wept and begged him not to do it. 'It's like you were going to put a plug in your lip, or a ring in your nose, or knocked out your front teeth to put in gold teeth – (some of the Arabs do this) – It's a desecration!' Burroughs' intensity impressed Kiki. It impressed Burroughs himself, who realized the extent to which he loved the boy. Instantly distancing himself, he commented to Ginsberg, 'Now I know I should not allow myself to be emotionally involved,' though love naturally made sex that much more enjoyable. What he feared was the loathing he always sought as the underside of love. Kiki could be sulky and abusive, though never for long and never bearing grudges, and such episodes invariably triggered Burroughs' 'fear with anyone I love that they really hate me and I will suddenly be confronted with their hate'.

Throughout the months he had been in Tangier, Burroughs had written constantly to Ginsberg and had perhaps created the semblance of closeness in a stream of intensely personal letters that, at some level, he may have hoped would result in physical intimacy when they met again in the States. Ginsberg was considerably alarmed by the prospect. He thought Burroughs had calmed down a little, but 'he still puts all his life in my hands . . . It's a real bitch, man.' He dissuaded Burroughs from joining him in California, so that Burroughs' only recourse was to visit his mother and father in Palm Beach, Florida, where he felt less than welcome.

He had no money to return to Tangier, and his parents were asking why in hell he'd come back to the US at all. 'Maybe I can blackmail them into sending me back to Tanger. They don't want me sitting around Palm Beach, that's for sure, and the hotel (they insist no room in the house, my bed having been removed to make way for a television set) is $5 per day.' Burroughs had come back less to see his family than to see Ginsberg: 'this is a beat setup'.

He was wrestling, too, with intense withdrawal symptoms – briefly hospitalized, he got to the stage of 'rolling around biting the bed and beating on the wall, and so wrung a shot of demerol out of the nurse . . . It was *literally* intolerable.' Towards the end of November he sailed for Tangier. Palm Beach had been 'a real horror. No slums, no dirt, no poverty. God what a fate to live there!'

Return to Tangier, Eukodol and daily fifteen- to twenty-hour sessions in bed with Kiki restored his spirits somewhat, though Eukodol evidenced an unfortunate side effect: it paralysed his bladder. Besides this, his vanity was offended by a ring of fat on his formerly flat stomach, accumulated in Florida as a result of the cure he had taken. He had relapsed in New York, suffered the eight-day voyage from the States to Tangier with no drugs, and was now hooked again. 'I never tried to kick a habit that hung on like this. And this fat is something new. The question is, can I make it without junk? I'd like to try without for a year or so. But I don't propose to be half-alive, and I don't intend to get fat either.' The drug store he patronized in Tangier had sold him his last ten boxes of Eukodol, and Kiki was doling them out to him on a strict schedule. He had moved, with Kiki, back to Dutch Tony's, cramped quarters with only one bed. Kiki was looking for a house to rent, and meanwhile Burroughs determined to set seriously to work 'to write a best seller'. What he succeeded in writing, however, read like 'notes for a novel, not the novel itself. The act of creation needed to unify material into a finished work seems beyond my power.'

By mid-December he had completed the first chapter of a novel 'in which I will incorporate all my routines and scattered notes. Scene is Tanger, which I call Interzone.' This was no time to be fooling around – the novel would be in his 'most extreme line' and, for that reason, probably unpublishable. Writing through Tangier, through junk, through sex, through his feelings for Ginsberg, through his whole life, might keep him sane and sober. The title of the novel, given to him later by Jack Kerouac, was to be *The Naked Lunch*. It would be a spontaneous act of creation: 'Routines are completely spontaneous and proceed from whatever fragmentary knowledge you have. In fact a routine is by nature fragmentary, inaccurate. There is no such thing as an exhaustive routine, nor does the scholarly-type mind run to routines.' This was a dig at the scholarly critic Kenneth Rexroth who had criticized a Burroughs routine about Roosevelt: 'you don't study Zen and then write a scholarly routine, for Christ's sake!' The material for the novel was regularly sent to Ginsberg for criticism and safe keeping. All Burroughs could do was 'include in the Ms. what I think is good. Judgement as to whether it is too much, too wild, I can't make – especially not as regards my own work. You [Ginsberg] do that, and I will accept your judgements.' In *The Naked Lunch*, Burroughs provides a

> Panorama of the City of Interzone . . . The Composite City where all human potentials are spread out in a vast silent market. Minarets, palms, mountains, jungle . . . A sluggish river jumping with vicious fish, vast weed-grown park where boys lie in the grass, play cryptic games. Not a locked door in the City. Anyone comes into your room at any time. The Chief of Police is a Chinese who picks his teeth and listens to denunciations presented by a lunatic . . . Hipsters with smooth copper-coloured faces lounge in doorways twisting shrunken heads on gold chains, their faces blank with an insect's unseeing calm.
>
> Behind them, through open doors, tables and booths and bars, and kitchens and baths, copulating couples on rows of brass beds, crisscross of a thousand hammocks, junkies typing up for a shot, opium smokers, hashish smokers, people eating talking bathing back into a haze of smoke and steam . . . Cooking smells of all countries hang over the City, a haze of opium, hashish, the resinous red smoke of Yage, smell of the jungle and salt water and the rotting river and dried excrement and sweat and genitals.
>
> High mountain flutes, jazz and bepop, one-stringed Mongol instruments, gypsy xylophones, African drums, Arab bagpipes . . .
>
> The City is visited by epidemics of violence, and the untended dead are eaten by vultures in the streets. Albinos blink in the sun. Boys sit in trees, languidly masturbate. People eaten by unknown diseases watch the passerby with evil, knowing eyes.

The Tangier of William Burroughs was not the city of Paul Bowles who coolly observed its behaviour and character and fastidiously, clinically plunged in his literary knife to expose its nerves and sinews. Burroughs thrust his hands deep into the reeking entrails of the city, pulling out its heart like an Aztec priest seeking inspiration for prophecy. Bowles anatomized Tangier like a police surgeon dissecting a corpse: Burroughs behaved with all the delicacy of a haruspex, divining from the living body which resembled a creation of Bosch. Bowles had largely cut himself off from his roots, preferring to inhabit another culture which he was at pains to understand. Burroughs, soul-sick, dragged around with him the global images of the Apocalypse which were intensified by Tangier, by its leprous landscape, by its gangrenous citizens.

Besides *The Naked Lunch*, Burroughs was enthusiastically urging a collaboration between himself and Ginsberg to compile the letters exchanged between them when Burroughs was in South America on his quest for the mystical drug Yage. 'I am planning to write, when I get the time, a short book on Yage like Huxley's peyote book.' This was intended to be a sober, serious book free of Burroughs' humorous fantasies, symbolic images, and colourful preoccupations: 'Positively no school-boy smut. No purple-assed baboons, no prolapsed ass holes, by God not even any piles, no gags like: "Gus," I said quietly, trying to keep my voice steady, "We're out of K.Y." What I mean is, Al, I'm going to keep it clean.'

On 12 January 1955, Burroughs was euphoric. The idea of the novel had seized him to the extent that he wrote humorously, with his cynical, deadpan wit, to Ginsberg:

Here is from the blurb jacket of the novel. Getting a bit previous, I admit. The theme just came to me in the form of this blurb:

'Suppose you knew the power to start an atomic war lay in the hands of a few scientists who were bent on destroying the world? That is the terrifying question posed by this searching novel.'

' "The book grabs you by the throat." Says L. Marland, distinguished critic. "It leaps in bed with you and performs unmentionable acts. Then it thrusts a long cold needle deep into your spine and gives you an injection of ice water. That is the only way I know to express the feeling of fear that reaches out of these pages. Behind the humor, the routines, the parody (some of it a bit heavy-handed to be sure), you glimpse a dead-end despair, a bleak landscape of rubble under the spreading black cloud of a final bomb.

'"The desperate struggle of a handful of men with the forces and emissaries of Destruction has the immediacy of a barroom fight, the kick to the groin, the broken beer bottle thrust at the eye."'

Three days later, on 21 January, Burroughs – ever liable to extremes – was labouring under 'a profound depression, the worst of my life'. Junk had taken him over, and the novel was stalled: he feared complete, final blockage of his talent for writing, and he was prone to sit for hours gazing at a blank page or his big toe. There was still no one to talk to, no receptor, no one to respond. The cod blurb now seemed ridiculous. He was depressed to be hung up on Eukodol, and depression caused him to take more of the stuff. A month later, on 19 February, he was writing to Ginsberg to report some progress: 'Something even more evil than atomic destruction is the theme – namely an anti-dream drug which destroys the symbolizing, myth-making, intuitive, empathizing, telepathic faculty in man, so that his behavior can be controlled and predicted by the scientific methods that have proved so useful in the physical sciences. In short, this drug eliminates the disturbing factor of spontaneous, unpredictable life from the human equation.' Alan Ansen arrived in Tangier in early March to Burroughs' delight. Ansen could always be relied upon to have a good time and spread good cheer. Energetically, Ansen enjoyed a boy almost every day and took Burroughs on a tour of Tangier's best restaurants. Kiki had been conscientiously doling out the Eukodol, and Burroughs had achieved some temporarily harmonious balance in his everyday life.

But by 20 April the Eukodol habit was again out of control. The drug had lost some of its charm: 'A shot of Eukodol is like a hot bath that isn't *quite* hot enough, if you dig me.' All his money was being spent on junk, leaving very little for proper food to nourish him. He was prone to wake up in the small hours of the morning 'with a character in mind who is writing "a great, gloomy, soul-searing homosexual novel. Six hundred pages of heartache and loneliness and frustration."' At the beginning of May he took a cure at a clinic on the Marshan where he was dosed with barbiturates and lost thirty pounds in weight. His disgust poured out in a letter to Ginsberg: 'Still sick and sensitized to the point of hallucination . . . I feel a great intensity building up, and at the same time a weakness like I can only keep myself *here*, back now in this doughy, dead flesh I have been away from since the habit started. (Feel like I was back from years in concentration camp.) Junk is death. I don't ever want to see it or touch it or commerce in it. Way I feel now I'd rather sell lottery tickets than touch The Business.'

The cure took two weeks, not long enough: by the beginning of July he was hooked again. He had suffered an excruciatingly painful neuralgia in his back and to deal with it he lapsed back again into demerol 'which is really evil shit'. His self-disgust was rooted deep this time – the sense of failure all-pervading. He noted his tricks and ploys – 'buying absolutely the last box of demerol ampules every day for the past 3 weeks', considered his old stratagem of having Kiki take away his clothes, resolved to switch to codeine to reduce his dependence quickly. But the neuralgia continued, and so did the junk habit. By now, he had re-encountered Paul Bowles with whom, says Bowles, he 'would discuss everything but writing'. Bowles introduced Burroughs to Brion Gysin, with whom he became friendly and, later in Paris, intimate in a way that was impossible with the austere Bowles who remained, despite some warmer overtures, 'very withdrawn and difficult to contact'. A moment of purest horror in September maybe renewed Burroughs' resolve to 'evict the Chinaman once and for all. Have tentatively arranged to take a cure here. I am going to a clinic and stay there until I am completely cured.' The determining event, related to Ginsberg in typical mordant manner, was thus:

Some nights ago I got hold of some ampules each containing 1/6 grain of dolophine and 1/100 gr. of hyoscine. Now 1/100 gr. of that awful shit is already a lot, but I thought the dolophine would offset it and shot 6 ampules in the main line.

The ex-captain [David Woolman] found me sitting stark naked in the hall on the toilet seat (which I had wrenched from its moorings), playing in a bucket of water and singing 'Deep in the Heart of Texas,' at the same time complaining, in clearly enunciated tones, of the high cost of living – 'It all goes into razor blades.' And I attempted to go out in the street naked at 2 A.M. – What a horrible nightmare if I had succeeded and came to

myself wandering around the Native Quarter naked. I tore up my
sheets and threw bottles all over the floor, looking for something, I
did not say what. Naturally Dave and the Old Dutch Auntie
who runs this whorehouse were alarmed, thinking my state was
permanent. They were vastly relieved to see me the following
morning fully dressed and in my right mind. I could only remember snatches of what had happened, but I do remember wondering why people were looking at me so strangely and talking in
such tiresome, soothing voices. I concluded that they were crazy
or drunk, and told Tony he was stinking drunk . . . I hope to
enter clinic in two days.

He regarded the time necessary for the cure to be a month at
least, probably two, during which time he would be isolated and
undistracted. For that period he could get to work on the novel.
The clinic was in the Jewish Benchimal Hospital, and the treatment
was dolophine every four hours. The cost was two dollars a day,
very cheap considering 'the dollar is going up like a beautiful bird'.
He had bought a new typewriter and had finally identified a circle
of pleasing acquaintances in Tangier: 'A good selection of people
in Tangier now: Dave Lamont, young Canadian painter who comes
to see me every day; Chris Wanklyn, Canadian writer; Paul and
Jane Bowles quite accessible these days; Charles Gallagher,
extremely intelligent and witty, writing history of Morocco on Ford
Foundation; Viscount des Iles, a brilliant linguist and student of
the occult; Peter Mayne, who wrote *The Alleys of Marrakesh*. In
short, plenty people around now.' Burroughs' fictional evocation
of the Jewish Hospital in *The Naked Lunch* describes fantastically,
manically, his cure and his immediate environment in terms of
nightmare:

> *Disintoxication Notes*. Paranoia of early withdrawal. . . . Everything
> looks blue. . . . Flesh dead, doughy, toneless.
> *Withdrawal Nightmares*. A mirror-lined café. Empty. . . . Waiting
> for something. . . . A man appears in a side door. . . . A slight,
> short Arab dressed in a brown jellaba with grey beard and grey
> face. . . . There is a pitcher of boiling acid in my hand. . . . Seized
> by a convulsion of urgency, I throw it in his face. . . .
> Everyone looks like a drug addict. . . .

Take a little walk in the hospital patio. . . . In my absence someone has used my scissors, they are stained with some sticky, red
brown gick. . . . No doubt that little bitch of a criada trimming
her rag.
Horrible-looking Europeans clutter up the stairs, intercept the
nurse when I need my medicine, empty piss into the basin when I am
washing, occupy the toilet for hours on end – probably fishing for a
finger stall of diamonds they have stashed up their asshole. . . .
. . .
The lavatory has been locked for three hours solid. . . . I think
they are using it for an operating room.

Burroughs left Benchimal Hospital feeling good: he had worked,
though the writing had been 'more painful than anything I ever
did. Parentheses pounce on me and tear me apart, I have no control
over what I write, which is as it should be. I feel like St. Anthony
of Hieronymous Bosch or however his name goes.' He had been reading Klee's writings and looking at pictures of his work. He had also
been reading Jean Genet's *Journal of a Thief* which he very much
admired for its prose and erotic content, though he found the translator's use of American slang outdated. He was feeling sexy, promiscuous, and in a mood to get shot of Kiki. He was bored with monogamy
and 'figure to start at one end of Interzone and screw my way through
to the other'. From the window in his hospital room he had been
able to watch the boys at the Italian school opposite through his field
glasses: 'They wear shorts, and I can see the goose pimples on their
legs in the chill of the morning, count the hairs.' He remembered, in
vivid detail, how he and an acquaintance had paid two Arab boys
sixty cents to watch them screw each other: 'Made me feel sorta like
a dirty old man.'
    The cure had certainly improved Burroughs' spirits: he rattled
off long, inventive letters to Ginsberg and started stepping out to
admire the countryside which suddenly inspired him: 'I used to
complain that I lacked material to write about. Mother of God!
Now I'm swamped with material . . . Beginning to dig Arab kicks.
It takes time. You must let them seep into you . . . I run across
one of your old letters, Al, and the following jumps out at me:
"Don't be depressed. There's too much to do." And that *is* a fact.
So much I am flipping. You're a fucking genius, Al . . . Actually I

am so independent, so fucking far out I am subject to float away like a balloon . . .' By the beginning of November, he was so fired up that Tangier had come to seem like 'the prognostic pulse of the world, like a dream extending from past into the future, a frontier between dream and reality –'

But Burroughs was not yet cured of dope addiction. By the beginning of the year, 1956, he had relapsed: 'it's like there was a vast Kafkian conspiracy to prevent me ever getting off junk'. He was hooked on dolophine, the substance that had been given to him in hospital to wean him off Eukodol. 'Not only do I have a habit, but a synthetic habit which is hardest to kick, most harmful to the health, and the least enjoyable . . . I have fallen into a state of chronic depression and hopelessness. All I can do is sit here day after day shivering and contracted over my stinking little kerosene stove waiting for money.' Money was being doled out to him, grudgingly and in small amounts, by his parents in Florida – never enough at any one time for him to cover the cost of a trip to London for another cure.

The symptoms of addiction were alarming: 'Last night I woke up with someone squeezing my hand. It was my own other hand.' He was expecting money any day, but his father preferred to make arrangements personally with a sanitorium in England, so Burroughs stayed on in Tangier meantime, deterred by the thought of 'being hung up in London *sans* junk and *sans* sanitarium'. Finally, he received five hundred dollars from his father in mid-April to take care of his minor debts in Tangier and to pay for his journey to London and incidental expenses. Reflecting on the significance of his sojourn in Tangier, Burroughs began to consider whether 'all the delay and the failures of the past two years were necessary to show me exactly how nowhere junk is, and I can't use it if I want to do anything else'.

The cure was as bad in London as it had been anywhere else. He was treated with a morphine derivative called apomorphine, originally an emetic used to treat cattle but found to be helpful in the treatment of alcoholics. By extension, it was discovered to be useful in the treatment of heroin addicts. One and a half grains of apomorphine produced almost immediate vomiting. The dose was then reduced to one twentieth of a grain, injected every two hours, for six days. Simultaneously, he was dosed with morphine, beginning with a quarter grain every six hours, reducing to an eighth of a grain. This was considerably less – about a tenth – of what he had been taking in Tangier. After six days, he was injected with apomorphine every four hours, and administered morphine every twelve hours. The treatment lasted fourteen days and was completely successful. Burroughs remained free of drug dependency for several years.

He wrote to announce his complete recovery to Ginsberg, but noted a distressing decrease in libido: 'I am physically able you dig, just not innarested. When I look at a boy nothing happens. Ratty lot of boys they got here anyhoo.' Burroughs hated London: it was a deadbeat town with ridiculous rules like pub opening and, more frustratingly, closing times: 'fucking blighted dump . . . I'd like to see the whole fucking city out in Hyde Park lined up on their hind legs for the chocolate I'd throw them . . . I have tried to like England but it's not possible. I'd sooner live in Hell.' He travelled to Venice ('like a Mohammedan heaven with boys') to meet Ansen, and returned to Tangier by way of Naples, Algiers and Tripoli, in September.

His interest in sex had revived, to judge by a letter of 13 September to Ginsberg: 'This writing finds me languid and sate, after a *divine* siesta *à deux*, *à trois* actually: Myself; the inevitable Arab boy, 18 and willowy, darling, with a skiiinnn like the inside of an oyster shell; and, of course, that ubiquitous old voyeur bitch Miss Green. By the lay, my fanny is back in combat, you might say if you were a type citizen to say a thing like that. How's this for an ad: You too can be screwed by a brace of Nubians and feel *nooooo* pain . . . Amazing new remedy will put your ass back in action . . . MA LEE'S PILE GOOK . . .' Miss Green was Burroughs' euphemism for tea which he continued to smoke on the principle that it was not addictive and was purely pleasurable, not to say a useful adjunct to eroticism. Miss Green, as Burroughs must have known, was a doyenne of the city, a feisty and formidable old lady well known to the citizens of Tangier.* They would have enjoyed one another.

Tangier, on his return, was 'subject to change at any time'. There had been isolated incidents of violence, random attacks on

* See pp. 250–4

Europeans, and Burroughs moved out of the Arab Quarter to a
room in the Hotel Muniria on the calle Magallanes. This room, on
the ground floor, had a private entrance and opened out on a
small garden. Tangier itself was relatively free of political agitation,
though there was a general strike in October and a march down the
boulevard Pasteur involving thousands of nationalists demanding
independence and the withdrawal of the French colonial regime.
On October 29, Burroughs wrote to Ginsberg to describe the events
in Tangier:

> This town really has the *jihad* jitters – *jihad* means the wholesale
> slaughter by every Muslim of every unbeliever. I am sitting in
> the Socco and suddenly people start running and all the shop
> keepers are slamming down the steel shutters of their shops – I
> plan to market an automatic shop closer whereby you press a
> button and your shutter falls like a guillotine – and everybody in
> the cafes drops their drinks and leaps inside and the waiters are
> closing the doors. So at this point about thirty little children
> carrying the Moroccan flag troop through the Socco . . . A few
> days ago we had a general strike. Everything closed, restaurants,
> drug stores, no cars allowed on the streets. About four P.M. I am
> out with my Spanish kid trying to score for a bottle of cognac,
> and everybody says 'No! Go away! Don't you know there's a
> strike on?' and slams the door. About this time such a racket
> breaks out like I never hear and I can see thousands of Arabs
> marching down the boulevard yelling. So I cut by police head-
> quarters, where about a hundred young Arabs are yelling at the
> cops, who have barricaded themselves inside. What had hap-
> pened, this idiot Frenchman climbed into a tree and harangued
> the crowd: 'How dare you say anything against La France.' For-
> tunately the police succeeded in rescuing him, and they had him
> locked in the station – On the boulevard I dig about 20,000
> Arabs, mostly teen-agers, yelling 'Fuera Français!' (Out with the
> French!) and jumping around and laughing . . . So nothing
> happened . . .

The Indendence Party made soothing noises, promising protection to the foreign community, and some rioters had been severely
punished in Meknes. Taking no chances, however, Burroughs

began to evolve and practice a technique of invisibility such as to make Bowles green with envy. He succeeded so well that he became known to all as 'El Hombre Invisible'. The trick was to notice people before they noticed you, and he succeeded to the extent of being avoided and remaining unpestered by the ubiquitous guides and little boys of the city. Burroughs so tenuously inhabited that edge between dream and reality that this mode of invisibility perhaps aroused more interest than his normal, substantial appearance. It certainly interested Isabelle Gérofi, when Burroughs happened to sidle off the boulevard into the Librairie des Colonnes. She has described how he used to loom in the little bookshop, wearing a filthy coat, peering round, saying nothing and buying nothing, looking like a ghost, thin and pale. This wraith-like appearance was undoubtedly rendered the more sinister by Burroughs' habitual CIA-grey suit, thin tie and shades.

He was working, exercising, and feeling horny. After a two-hour session with Nimón, his 'latest heart throb', he would consent to turn his mind to higher things such as physical exercise and work on the novel. In London, he had learned special abdominal exercises from a citizen named Hornibrook 'who learned them from the Fiji Islanders near as I can make out'. These were remarkably efficacious in keeping his stomach flat and lean, with the added advantage that they were liable to cause him to have spontaneous orgasms and, disturbingly, turn his erotic thoughts to women. 'You hear about these old characters find out they are queer at fifty, maybe I'm about to make with the old switcheroo. What are these strange feelings that come over me when I look at young cunts, little tits sticking out so cute? Could it be that?? No! No! He thrust the thought from him in horror . . . He stumbled out into the street with the girl's mocking laughter lingering in his ears, laughter that seemed to say "Who you think you're kidding with the queer act? I know you, baby." Well, it is as Allah wills . . .'

Tangier was, finally, where he wanted to be. The work was going well, he regularly rowed round the Bay of Tangier in a 'half-assed gondola' building up his strength and endurance, he got an 'average of ten very attractive propositions a day. My latest number is Spanish, 16, with a smile hit you right in the nuts. I mean that pure, uncut boy stuff, that young male innocence.' He was smoking tea, which he described as a 'swing on Miss Green's unnatural tit', but he didn't really need her any more. Lightly narcotized, he took pleasure in just walking around town or sitting in a café. 'I have no compulsion to write or do anything except when I am possessed by routines, which can happen any time.' He worked when he could sit still long enough or when he took 'time out from fucking'. The novel had taken complete shape, he was more and more friendly with Bowles – 'He is really a charming person'– and his room at the Muniria was perfect. 'I don't see how anyone could be happier than I am right now . . . I hope to God I don't have to leave Tanger . . . Tanger is my dream town. I did have a dream ten years ago of coming into a harbor and knowing that this was the place I desired to be . . . Just the other day, rowing around in the harbor I recognized it as my dream bay.' Tangier's beauty consisted in 'changing combinations', unlike Venice which never changed, which was 'a dream congealed in stone. And it is someone else's dream'. Burroughs lyrically evoked Tangier in a few, almost random, words: 'sky supersonic, orgone blue, warm wind, a stone stairway leading up to the Old Town . . . Coming down the stairs a very dark Arab boy with a light purple shirt . . .' The words, the revelation of a dream, appear very similar to Bowles' dream revelation which he experienced so vividly in New York City.

Kerouac and Ginsberg had finally agreed to visit Morocco, though they were worried about reports of political unrest in the country. Burroughs wrote on 20 December to reassure them, prefacing an address to their more serious concerns with a restated promise of Tangier's cheapness and the ready availability of boys. 'Morocco is really great and I know you will like it and the Arabs are not to compare with American counterparts for viciousness and it is sheer Provincialism to be afraid of them as if something special sinister and Eastern and unamerican.'

Burroughs was impatient with American timidity and xenophobia. He assured Ginsberg that the Sultan was respectful of the lives and property of foreign residents and that several capital sentences had been dished out to agitators in Meknes which, as a hotbed of unrest, was remote in distance and attitudes from Tangier, though Burroughs himself would not hesitate to go to Meknes or anywhere else in Morocco. Bowles, meantime, had gone to Ceylon, but was due back in June when Ginsberg would be able to meet him. He finished the letter with another exhortation, directly quoted from a declaration by the Istiqlal, the Independence Party: 'Order must be maintained. Cooperation with European colonists is matter of life and death for Morocco ... We promise protection to resident foreigners. Those who leave Morocco from fear are committing a grave error.'

A month later, on 23 January 1957, Burroughs repeated his message: 'I will say it again and say it slow: TANGER IS AS SAFE AS ANY TOWN I EVER LIVE IN.' Jack Kerouac was evidently feeling some anxiety, but Burroughs rubbished this by declaring his own fear and horror at the 'random drunken violence stalking the streets and bars and parks and subways of America. ARABS ARE NOT VIOLENT ... They *do not attack people for kicks or fight for kicks like Americans* ...' He blamed much of Moroccan resentment and nationalist feeling on the occupying French and credited the political temperature to the 'accumulated, just resentment of a people subjected to outrageous brutalities by the French cops used to strew blood and death over a city block in the Southern Zone.' In *The Naked Lunch*, Burroughs characterized the French as 'The Colonial bastards who is sucking your live corpuscles'. Kerouac and Ginsberg could expect to see progress on the novel by the time they arrived, in addition to the stuff being regularly mailed from Tangier to Ginsberg in New York.

It is more obscene than Genet hands down and cocks up and no holes barred ... Interzone is coming like dictation, I can't keep up with it ... The Ms. you have seen by now – I sent it in four separate envelopes – is just preliminaries. Golden Glove kid stuff ... Now my power's really coming and I am subject to write something downright dirty ... I am building an orgone accumulator to rest up in and recharge myself ... Also careful to row every day ... A man of my caliber has to watch himself ... I really love Tanger and never feel like this about any other place. Such beauty, but more than that it's like the dream, the other dimension, is always breaking through.

There was a real colony of Americans building up in Tangier, to whom Burroughs could relate, though some of them were naturally discreet about their pasts. To Ginsberg, Burroughs wrote asking for inside information: 'Ask around the Village if anyone knows this cat Rocky, a big spade is here in Tanger and it couldn't happen to a nicer guy. Interpol has him down as an international pusher of the white shit.' There was a 'hipster from Frisco', an ex-cop, an ex-schoolteacher who was having 'the affair of her life with a horrid Arab pimp disliked by everyone who know him. "Not a viler man in the Northern Zone than old Ali." ' Ansen was due to visit in March, Bowles would be back in May or June, and David Woolman, Tangier's star gossip columnist, on good terms with a confiding chief of security who could be relied on to know all the dirt on all these citizens, lived right next door. There was Australian George Greaves, a Sydney Greenstreet lookalike, an evil gossip, who had the goods on everyone, and Paul Lund, a Birmingham wide-boy who regularly shipped contraband in and out of the port.

Burroughs could be uninhibitedly himself: 'my disregard of social forms is approaching psychosis. Drinking with some very stuffy English people on their yacht and someone says something about somebody tied to a buoy, and I said "Tied to a boy? Lucky chap" and sit there doubled over with laughing, completely knocked out by my own wit . . . Now when they see me they get a *sauve qui peut* look and take off on the double, probably thinking "here comes that dangerous old fruit."' Friendship with Burroughs carried such risks, even for Paul Bowles. Burroughs was conscious of a certain lack of social polish: having become more and more friendly with Bowles, understanding that his reticence derived from his wish not to be intrusive rather than from stand-offishness or distaste, he appreciated Bowles' wit, charm and intelligence. In October 1956, Burroughs worried that he had blown their good relations: 'he is entertaining this rich American woman. So I was talking about Yage, and she says, "How long does it take to rot you?" and I said: "Lady, you should live so long" and she left the room. So I thought that finishes me with Bowles but nothing of the sort, and I have seen him twice since, and dig him like I never dig anyone that quick before. Our minds similar, telepathy flows like water. I mean there is something portentously familiar about him, like a revelation.' In *The Naked Lunch*, Burroughs characterizes Bowles as Andrew Keif, 'the brilliant, decadent young novelist who lives in a remodeled pissoir in the red light district of the Native Quarter', and credits him with possession of a chauffeur, Aracknid, 'The only native in Interzone who is neither queer nor available.' Keif employs this paragon as 'a useful pretext to break off relations with anyone he doesn't want to see: "You made a pass at Aracknid last night. I can't have you to the house again." People are always blacking out in the Zone, whether they drink or not and no one can say for sure he didn't make a pass at Aracknid's unappetizing person.'

Bowles had visited the Muniria and noticed 'the typed pages of a work in progress by Burroughs which had been lying on the floor of Bill's basement room these many months. Often I had looked down at the chaos of sheets of yellow paper being trampled underfoot, thinking that he must like to have them there, otherwise he would have picked them up.' Since it didn't matter to Burroughs in what order the pages and sections of his novel were read, the randomness of the scattered papers was not important. Bowles, meticulously neat and fastidious in his own person and character, was naturally struck by Burroughs' untidiness. He was also persuaded to step into Burroughs' orgone box, constructed on Reichian principles, in the garden. Burroughs swore by its energizing effect, though the theory sounded improbable and unscientific to Bowles' rigorously disciplined mind. Obligingly, Bowles consented to sit in the box for a while, to no apparent effect. It probably seemed like a quieter place to be for a while, a relief from chaos. The orgone box, in addition to other benefits, was supposed to build up the energy level of the libido, a matter of less importance to Bowles of course than to Burroughs.

Kerouac's visit to Tangier preceded Ginsberg's arrival. Kerouac set sail on a Yugoslavian freighter on 15 February 1957 and was met at the port, when the ship docked in Tangier, by Burroughs who conducted him to the Muniria hotel, thus avoiding the persistent, ubiquitous guides – 'Bastards!! Son of bitches!' – who hung around waiting to pounce on disoriented travellers. The room cost Kerouac twenty dollars a month, a couple of floors above Burroughs' own room. It had a wide balcony facing the sea and at first he planned to spend the rest of the winter and spring in Tangier. He was solvent, for a wonder: British rights to his novel, *On the Road*, had been sold to André Deutsch, a London publisher, who proposed to pay him £150. He had just signed the contract for the novel with Viking, in New York, in January. Publication was scheduled for October.

Tangier appeared peaceful enough to Kerouac, who began to relax. He read Genet and the New Testament in his room, strolled along the beach to watch the fishermen at work, and with Burroughs he explored the Medina and the Casbah, hiked for miles through the surrounding countryside, and consorted with three-dollar whores. On the debit side, the food wasn't terrific, and the sanitation was worse. He didn't like the opium he sampled, and the hashish made him violently ill with diarrhoea. Burroughs chivvied him along, taking him rowing in the bay, pounding the streets at a fast clip, satirically sniping at 'lard-assed hipsters' who couldn't keep up the pace. Looking around Burroughs' room, Kerouac offered to lick his typescript into shape, typing it up for him.

Burroughs had begun to alarm Kerouac somewhat – he was liable to take out a flick knife in the public street and discuss its deterrent effect on Arab thugs: 'Yessir, without it I'd be dead now. Bunch of Ay-rabs surrounded me in an alley one night. I just let this old thing click out and said, "Come on ya buncha bastards," and they cut out.' He moved through knots of citizens on the boulevard, scything at them with his elbows like rowing a boat in the bay, muttering 'just push 'em aside like little pricks'. The manuscript confirmed Kerouac's fears: it beat anything by Genet, whose novels were decorous compared with the scatological, homoerotic, violent, fantastical images conjured by Burroughs from God knows what private hell of raucous, terrifying, psychotic despair larded with black, mordant humour that intensified rather than moderated the horrors of the text. Kerouac had nightmares of pulling endless bologna sausage from his mouth.

Burroughs himself appeared to have multiple personalities, the worst of them bred from his writings. He was liable to go into routines, impersonating characters from the novel, all but taken over by them momentarily. It was entertaining when Burroughs snapped into one of his routines, rushing off at the mouth, but it was worrying. The manic monologues seemed to take him over, the characters to possess him, and Burroughs' explanation for his behaviour was liable to cause a person to edge away pretty smartish: 'I get these messages from other planets. I'm apparently some kind of agent from another planet but I haven't got my orders clearly decoded yet. I'm shitting out all my educated Middlewest background once and for all. It's a matter of catharsis, where I say the most horrible things I can think of. Realize that – the most horrible dirty slimy awful niggardliest posture possible . . .' Not unnaturally feeling distanced from Burroughs in this mode, Kerouac longed for the arrival of Ginsberg who did not hit Tangier until 4 April, just coinciding with Kerouac who – finally, having had enough – lit out on the 5th by ship for Marseille.

Ginsberg had travelled with his lover, the poet Peter Orlovsky. *Howl*, Ginsberg's long poem, had just been published in San Francisco and was shortly after denounced as obscene and confiscated, resulting in a much-publicized trial. Ginsberg had given readings in California and had achieved a certain notoriety. He was much taken by Tangier as a 'release from American constraints, and I don't mean sexual, I mean the constraints of anxiety and business, commerce, the civic constraints of the law on drugs, the constraints of the police state – the American style of the police state, as distinct from Moroccan-style police state.' Then, too, there was 'space, space, space – the light, and the vast open sky, the grandeur of the place – of the Mediterranean'.

Ginsberg and Orlovsky took over Kerouac's room at the Muniria. 'The view from Kerouac's room, which was three flights above Bill's, a red-tiled verandah, very extensive, with a nice little brick or stone parapet – the red-tiled room extending out to the red-tiled floor of the verandah, with a brilliant blast of sunlight coming through and shattering the blue sky, and the view of the Bay of Tangier – that for me was "the ancient parapets of Europe" – a phrase of Rimbaud – and my first glimpse of Europe. It was, for me, the open space, coming from New York.'

Ginsberg had brought with him the material Burroughs had been sending for three or four years. The entire text manuscript amounted to hundreds of pages which Ginsberg had carefully kept in chronological order in a springbound binder. Alan Ansen arrived from Venice, and the three of them sat down to assemble a final, authoritative manuscript. 'The big question', said Ginsberg, was how to order *Naked Lunch* – in what order to put it and edit it, because the routines developed sequentially and were repeated with greater developments. 'So how do you cohere them all, string them together, and what would be the cohering principle?' Ginsberg's own inclination was to run the stuff – the fantasies and routines – chronologically. But 'that posed a problem because each new version added more: which versions do you use? First, second, third, or all at once? And I never did understand how we could do it.'

The final edited arrangement of the material was done two years later, in Paris: it was not resolved that season in Tangier, despite the intense discussions, physical labour of typing, and earnest poring over the palimpsests. Though 'the main, main, main business was the literary', Ginsberg was also concerned to develop his relationship with Orlovsky. Aside from the plan to rendezvous with Kerouac and meet with Burroughs, Ginsberg and Orlovsky had decided 'what we would do was try and satisfy any fantasy we had. Between the two of us,' Ginsberg figured, 'we could do it. Like I really wasn't able to respond completely sexually at first in New York. And I felt that it was the first time with Peter that year that we'd had so completely a great rapport.'

The rapport between Ginsberg and his lover may have been terrific, but the rapport between the lover and Burroughs was fraught with tensions. Burroughs, perhaps feeling excluded from Ginsberg's affections, or at least sidelined, kept a jaundiced eye on Orlovsky who could do nothing right. He was extroverted and enthusiastic about Tangier, and was liable to rush up to citizens in the street, high on their hip appearance. Their perceived 'hipness' was, says Ginsberg, 'equated with "Fellaheen" by Kerouac twelve years before'. Burroughs became stony with disapproval. He ignored Orlovsky altogether for a while, cutting him out whenever possible. Burroughs claimed not to be jealous, merely unable to tolerate Orlovsky who got on his nerves. Ansen didn't much care for him either, referring to Orlovsky as 'a freeloading bitch posing as an assistant mahatma'.

Ginsberg, aside from the difficulties Orlovsky found in his relations with the others, in which Ginsberg was naturally involved, was relieved to be away from San Francisco and the trial that followed publication of *Howl*. He was pleased to be working with his friends on Burroughs' book, busy with a literary project rather than caught up in public activities in the States. He felt that his life in Tangier was 'kind of monastic': he was reading the Koran, and Tangier was a point of access to Africa and its mysticisms, particularly to 'a very active gnostic culture, in the sense of the Moroccan Gnaoui drummers and music and interior things – things that Paul Bowles knew about'. Ginsberg was keen to meet Bowles, who was then in Ceylon. He was 'mostly interested in Bowles' authority as a good judge of character and literature – I respected it, I'd read his books, and I'd heard lots about him from Bill through the letters. I was actually eager that Bowles appreciate Bill, because Bill didn't seem to me to be appreciated enough. I mean, to me he seemed like this great, colossal, genius teacher, and I very often measured people's literary capacity by the reaction of Burroughs. He was a sort of litmus test for me.'

In the absence of Bowles, Ginsberg encountered Jane Bowles to whom he introduced himself as 'Allen Ginsberg, the bop poet'. Jane, suffering the after-effects of her stroke, was baffled. The received version of the encounter between Ginsberg and Jane Bowles is contained in a letter Jane herself wrote to Bowles in mid-April 1957 to give her account of the meeting:

A boy has come here from New York called Allen Ginsberg. He was given a letter to us through Leo Lerman. I have his book of poems, called HOWL, *and Other Poems*, with an introduction by William Carlos W[illiams]. I suppose I must see him, but he is much more up your alley than mine. I will probably not be able to go on with my play if I do see him.

On the telephone he said: 'Do you know Philip Lamantia?' I said: 'No.' He said: 'He's this hep poet, been writing since he was thirteen, and he just had a vision in Mexico on *peyote* (Peyoti,

I gather.) I said: 'Oy weh.' Then he said: 'Honest, it was a real vision, and now he's a Catholic.' I said: '*Oy weh!*'

Then he named twenty-five men, none of whom I'd ever heard of, and I told him I'd been away a long time, and was too old anyway, and that I wasn't interested in peyote or visions. He said: 'Do you know Charles Ford?' and I said: 'yes, because he's old.' And he said: 'Well, don't you take majoun day and night?' and I said: 'I hate all that, and I'm sure you shouldn't see me.' And he said: 'Well what about Zen?'

Anyway, he's here and he is a friend of Bill Burroughs, who appears constantly in his poems, together with references to TANGIERS (sic), and he is part of a group. The Zen-Buddhist-Bepop-Jesus Christ-Peyote group ... Ginsberg asked me on the telephone whether or not I believed in God. I cannot decide whether or not he is up your alley ... With it all he sounds like a very sweet person. I imagine he shares Bill's habits.

Jane is said to have replied, in response to being asked whether or not she believed in God, 'Well, I'm certainly not going to discuss it on the telephone.' Ginsberg is somewhat vexed by this farcical account, and is at pains to give his own version:

I went out shopping, and walking along the Boulevard Pasteur, or to the Post Office with Jane. She has an account of that which is very inaccurate. I had always been involved with some kind of search, spiritual search, and was in some ambivalence about what I was looking for. I'd had some visionary experiences earlier, ten years earlier, I'd had some experience with peyote and mescalin, I think, and I was interested in whether she believed in God, and asked her, and she wasn't sure – didn't really answer – it's not an easy question, but it's a real question – and I assumed that she was literary, sophisticated enough to have considered it. Her version is a little like I was some kind of Beatnik kid, full of my own self-importance, offering her marijuana, and I thought we were pretty polite and respectful. And I think there was a basic friendliness, because she invited us to dinner. The version she gives wouldn't indicate that she would have us to her house for dinner, or that we would have an ongoing relationship over a number of years.

Ginsberg in retrospect, understands that his question about God might have startled Jane and given her a satirical peg on which to hang him for Bowles' benefit and amusement: but 'we'd been introduced, she knew who I was, and I really wanted to have a serious conversation with her, fast, you know, and also I realized she was an extraordinary person. But at the time I was maybe a little too bumptiously trustful that *tout comprendre, c'est tout pardonner*. Now [in 1989] I would resent such bumptiousness, somebody coming up to me – and yet, on the other hand, if it was somebody I thought had the literary élan, I would take it as a sort of come-on of a charming nature. You know, to be really serious. But I guess she had this picture of innocent Americans, unknowing Beatniks.'

He was entirely intrigued by her: 'she had an amazing reputation for being both enigmatic and grand, and extremely intelligent, and the height of chic in some funny way; and yet in person she was very retiring, shy and doubting, vulnerable.' She reminded Ginsberg very strongly of Joan Vollmer, Burroughs' wife: they looked, certainly, somewhat alike, and shared, in Ginsberg's view, 'intelligence and sharpness and shyness and vulnerability'. He couldn't quite figure the relationship between Bowles, when they finally met, and his wife:

it was confusing. I knew they were fond of each other, and that they were inter-dependent. As to whether or not they liked each other, I couldn't quite tell, though I think they did. I couldn't tell what was going on, because they lived in separate apartments. They were so private to begin with, and disliked intrusion, vulgarity. My own nature is a lot more gregarious and open, frank or candid. Jane made fun of that aspect of candour, openness, but on the other hand I don't know if it served her well to be so withdrawn. It was in a sense probably part of the complex situation that isolated her at the very end, and may have been a by-product of the illness she was going through. Plus natural reserve and natural sense of dignity and privacy. When Bowles came to visit America, I found him much more open.

Life in Tangier, all in all, was very pleasant for Ginsberg. Burroughs moderated his antagonism towards Orlovsky, the literary
chores were interesting, and food was cheap and plentiful. They
ate at a French restaurant on the boulevard Pasteur, and very often
at Dutch Tony's, though whenever Burroughs' mooch, Paul Lund,
came around to borrow a buck or cadge a meal he would be dra-
gooned into cooking a large dinner for them all. 'So generally every
day we'd go to the market and wind up in the Medina sitting in
the Petit Socco drinking mint tea and smoking on the *sebsi*, and
Peter and I wandered about in the neighbourhood, in the countryside, quite a bit.' By 24 April, when Ginsberg wrote chattily to
Neal Cassady, his money was running out and he pressed Cassady
hard to send $100 or $125 which, in any case, Cassady owed him.
'Bill in debt trying to support us (and beginning to rebel against
it) and we have been out of money for the last week and will be
out for another – camera and typewriter in hock.'

Ginsberg's description, in this letter, of the hashish-smoking culture at the Café Central in the Socco Chico is worth quoting at
length, the ritual apparently almost as elaborate and traditional as
any Japanese tea ceremony:

Haven't used much T. The way they do it here, everybody
smokes, all the arabs, all day, young kinds and old . . . bearded
grandpappys in white turbans and brown robes, is, they mix the
kif and tobacco, finely ground tobacco, and also with another
dash of what seems to be snuff, just snuff, and they carry around
a little pouchful in a small leather pouch about the size of a small
changepurse. The pipe is about a foot long, the bowl is a little
clay cheap bowl that fits on the bamboo pipestem – you can buy
the pipestem, plain for 30c a fancy painted one costs 50c – and
the clay bowls you buy anywhere, at tobacco stands or openair
pushcarts . . . 2c each, they break all the time and are replaceable.

So they sit down for a glass of mint tea and little music over
the radio in this cheesy one-table tearoom with a big brass urn
in niche in dirty concrete wall in some hole in the wall in the
casbah; and light up a pipe or two or three – or else just setting
down in their robes under a tree or by a fence downtown to rest
– squatting – but they don't get high, they just get a buzz off this
mixture, and they smoke maybe 25 to 50 pipes a day, a continual

buzz – sort of like smoking straight tobacco cut with a little tea, they use it for tobacco smoking not for tea purposes. They don't dig getting a real high, just makes them sleepy or dizzy like drunk, bugs them.

Ginsberg also sampled *majoun*, which Burroughs made in his own characteristic manner: 'Other way of taking it is to make it into Majoun – cake-candy type. Mix finely chopped Kif, heat it till its sticky & should harden a little like fudge (tho Bill's drunken-made rapid wild chopping tea spilling all over the floor, clouds of cinnamon in the air, boiled fast – winds up consistency of sticky shit). Get high on that lasts all night, off a tablespoonful, takes a few hours to work but feels like peyote a little, except no nausea – just slow strong fine tea high.' Burroughs gave his own recipe and description of *majoun* in *Naked Lunch*: 'Cannabis dried and finely powered to consistency of green powdered sugar and mixed with some confection or other usually tasting like gritty plum pudding . . .' Burroughs, in an article submitted to The British Journal of Addiction in 1956, emphasized his belief that 'marijuana is not habit forming. I have never seen evidence of any ill effect from moderate use. Drug psychosis may result from prolonged and excessive use.' He attributed American horror of cannabis to the fact that the national American drug, in his opinion, was alcohol and anything else was therefore regarded with hysterical terror. He admitted that marijuana, taken during a depression, 'makes a bad situation worse', just as it rendered a happy frame of mind euphoric. But the use of marijuana 'varies greatly with the individual. Some smoke it constantly, some occasionally, not a few dislike it intensely. It seems to be especially unpopular with confirmed morphine addicts, many of whom take a puritanical view of marijuana smoking' – though not Burroughs, who didn't give a shit one way or the other. Let everyone go to hell in his own way.

Generally enchanted by Tangier – which he described in 'Man's Glory', written in August 1960, as 'There in Tangier in Soco Chico there God's Grammar Arabic jabbers shoeshine poverty beneath the ultra silent mosque' – Ginsberg left with Orlovsky, sooner than intended, in early June. They set off for Spain, leaving Burroughs alone again – characterized by Ginsberg in 'Fragment: The Names II' in 1960–1 as 'Bill Burroughs in Tangiers slowly transfiguring into Sanctity season after season no God save impersonal solitude.'

In July, Burroughs himself set off to visit Kells Elvins in Copenhagen, returning in September to work long hours on his novel, transcribing the messages that came to his brain in great chunks. He hoped to finish by Christmas. The novel had exhausted him – mined, as it was, from his own contradictions of character, his deepest fears and obsessions, his dilemmas and the conflicts of his life. The novel was a contemporaneous account of his present situation, transcribed as it happened – and if the novel did not appear to make conventional sense, did not accord strictly with logic and reason, then neither did Burroughs' own life and responses to that life. He was attempting to construct a pattern from chaos, and to make it coherent, accessible, so that he could achieve some totality, integration of his apparently multiple personalities. Tangier had seemed to be the ideal, the dream place, but now he was not so sure: a place that could inspire his recurrent routines, make them palpable, surely had its dangers. He had been in Interzone since January 1954 – four years in a pretty approximation to Hell. It was time to get out. In mid-January he left for Paris to join Allen Ginsberg.

He returned briefly, in April 1959, looking to take a break from Paris. Six months earlier, he had written facetiously to Paul Lund to suggest a scheme for importing Moroccan kif, concealed in camel saddles made for sale to tourists, into France. It happened that a friend of Lund's, a sailor named Stevens, was arrested in Tangier for possession of half a kilo of opium. In his statement to the police, Stevens implicated Lund and 'an American with glasses' in order to minimize blame to himself. Lund's premises and possessions were searched, and Burroughs' letter was discovered. Threatened with deportation to England, a fate Lund emphatically wished to avoid since there were still some outstanding charges against him there, he fingered Burroughs as the bespectacled American mastermind behind a plan to smuggle opium. The police were willing to credit Burroughs as being the French connection, and it was Burroughs' bad luck to turn up in Tangier at this point when Lund was feeling the heat.

Burroughs indeed happened to drop in on Lund while he was being questioned by the police who, perhaps over-excited by Lund's

WILLIAM BURROUGHS AND THE BEATS

imaginative and frantic efforts to preserve his own skin, omitted to ask for his visitor's passport or to pay much attention to him. Alone with Burroughs, Lund admitted that he had given the police the letter and set Burroughs up to take the rap as the Moriarty of dope-dealing. Burroughs was understandably enraged, but Lund succeeded in mollifying him by admitting freely his failure to resist police pressure. 'You know, Bill, there comes a time when you're broken ... They broke me.' Burroughs squinted sourly at the broken man and, if he did not quite regard Lund's contrition with total sympathy, at least he could believe him. Still, not much chance of a relaxing vacation in old Tangier this time around, and Burroughs returned to Paris where, in July, Maurice Girodias, proprietor of the Olympia Press, published *The Naked Lunch* in an English-language edition of ten thousand copies. Grove Press bought the American rights, and there were a number of small deals for German, Italian and French rights.

With the advance of eight hundred dollars from Girodias, about a couple of thousand dollars from Grove Press (after Girodias' cut of one third), and some cash in hand from the European deals, Burroughs was back on drugs, though he quickly tried to kick by going back on the apomorphine prescribed for him in London during his last cure. There was some fall-out from the Lund letter: the Moroccan police had passed information to the French police and in October, after a preliminary brush the month before with a *juge d'instruction*, Burroughs was tried before three judges who, impressed by his standing as a man of letters, handed down a suspended sentence and fined him eighty dollars. He did not return to Tangier until 1961, intending to spend the late spring and summer at the Hotel Muniria.

Coinciding with Burroughs in Tangier in that year was the American composer Ned Rorem, who resumed a long-standing friendship with Paul and Jane Bowles. Gossip had it that Rorem, understandably vain of his extraordinary good looks, was the original of the amoral, adolescent Racky in Bowles' story *Pages from Cold Point* – having encountered Bowles many years before in Mexico while on holiday with his parents. Rorem noticed 'the comforting depths of *entente*' between Jane Bowles and Cherifa who appeared to have little conversation for one another and 'nothing in common but surface, that is, the depths of getting through the day'. For

Jane, getting through the day was probably enough to deal with in her precarious state of health, whereas futurity for Cherifa – like many Moroccans – was not something that could or should be rigorously planned for in advance. To attempt to secure the future, the day after next, was close to being sacrilegious.

Conversation naturally turned now and again to the subject of homosexuality, Jane declaring, 'homosexual, I wouldn't be anything else'. Rorem 'was relieved (she was like me) but felt, all the same, she was quite serious'. Jane had evidently tossed off the remark as a flippant aside, but it was something in 1961 – even in Tangier – for anyone to come out briskly and uncompromisingly with a matter-of-fact declaration in favour of homosexuality as a preferred condition. In New York, the first overt expression of an organized movement for Gay Liberation was eight years in the future. Meantime, most homosexuals kept their heads down and did not seek to make an issue of their sexual preference. It was a matter for insider gossip, levity among the *cognoscenti*, and mostly regarded as a condition to be bravely and – if possible – lightly borne.

Homosexuality in Tangier was taken more or less for granted: the city was a bolt hole, in some cases, for expatriates who felt threatened by censure and the possibility of criminal prosecution at home. There were occasional alarms in Tangier, but generally nothing so far to worry about. Rorem was already familiar with Tangier: he had visited Morocco some years before, pursuing a long and serious love affair with a French doctor, Guy Ferrand. But now, alone, he wondered 'what could this city do to me (a middle-class Wasp forever) if I remained: the strangeness is risky, lethargic, heady, sentimental, distant, odiferous, sensual, dangerous, and how would it alter the music? But mine's just a passing tourist's life of sun, liquor, cruising. What is a real man? The answer is here.'

Without the anchor of work, a lover, a permanent touchstone of reality, Rorem was disturbed by Tangier: his own roots in the stable, prudish, puritanical traditions of the middle-class America of the Eastern seaboard, like those of Bowles, were liable to be undermined and subverted. Bowles, by and large, kept a cool head, but Rorem had fewer defences. He was liable to be seduced, perhaps, by the sensual effects of Tangier which induced a soporific lethargy in its victims. A real man was at risk here, like Hercules offered the choice between Virtue and Pleasure. Immortality, the reward of productive toil in preference to dissipated pleasure, was scarcely possible for the creative artist in Tangier which promised every distracting delight of carnality. Virtue, the Wasp burden of consistent effort, offered a more enduring reward. Bowles managed to transcend Tangier – Rorem was not so sure that he could be so self-sufficient.

Even in the negative, 'the answer is here,' remarked Rorem. And, as an afterthought, 'So, by the way, is Allen Ginsberg . . . who breakfasts on éclairs in the Socco Chico, who inhabits a shack-penthouse with William Burroughs . . . in short, the original obstreperous Beatnik, tells me middle-classedly to "hush" when I ask Paul, in the Mahruba restaurant too loudly before the other diners, if the dancing boy is queer.' Not only Ginsberg – Alan Ansen and Gregory Corso had arrived to see what was cooking. They felt right at home in a Tangier that had become transformed into Hip City by a mob of long-haired, sandal-footed Beatniks, precursors of the later Hippie invasion, who mooched around looking for God and drugs and an easy lay.

The boulevard Pasteur began to look like high summer on Bleecker Street. Burroughs, in his fastidious mode, was disgusted – this was the tribe he had helped to create. They had all read – or, more likely, merely heard gossipy reports of – his books and had taken up his attitudes towards non-conformity as their own without thinking them through, without full understanding of the processes by which he had arrived at them and without thought for their implications. They were an idle, self-indulgent crew, citizens in search of a city, constituents high on his manifesto but reckless of the consequences. Burroughs, like Ginsberg, had become their guru. Devouring his kiss-my-ass style, they had come to kiss the hem of his robe. Burroughs didn't need them: they had changed Tangier, and not for the better. They made it untidy.

There had been a subtle shift in Burroughs' status among the Beat writers: publication of *The Naked Lunch* had had the effect of stabilizing, solidifying Burroughs who – as distinct from his first time in Tangier when his life had appeared random to the point of chaos – now presented himself as orderly and buttoned together, a fastidious and assertive man of achievement to whom others might apply for instruction and wisdom. He was no longer a supplicant, sexually dependent on Ginsberg or doubtful about his creative powers and his ability to use them constructively. Confidently, he could – and did – now associate with other writers not merely on a basis of equality but as father of the Beat tribe who was due a little respect. Partly, this attitude was defensive, but partly it was also a realistic self-assessment of his own worth to his contemporaries who regarded him with cautious veneration. He sometimes adopted a hauteur that suited his incisive, cold wit which cut through their moral perplexities and uncertainties with a withering certainty.

The Beats, in the summer of 1961, were about to be conscripted into the nascent psychedelic movement. In August, Dr Timothy Leary arrived in Tangier. Leary was a visionary who happened to be Director of the Center for Research in Personality, at the Harvard University Department of Social Relations. Folded in this cloak of academic respectability, he was engaged in studies into the effects of consciousness-expanding drugs such as mescaline and psilocybin, syntheses of age-old fungi and flora used by mystics in Mexico and South America to heighten and expand consciousness. In January 1961, he had written excitedly to Burroughs, urging him to try his magic mushrooms which, he claimed, 'give not only a memorable high but leave the vision and mind uncluttered – in an enduring way'. This come-on was liable to be irresistible to Burroughs, who agreed to sample the wares of Doctor Feelgood. 'Yes, I would be very much interested in trying the mushrooms and writing up the trip . . .' In the event, the psilocybin did not agree with Burroughs when he finally got round to trying it in Paris in March – the drug rubbed him up the wrong way, promoting nausea, irritability and unpleasant visions. Still, Leary's research – which promised to become a social and political crusade – was interesting in principle.

Ginsberg had recommended Burroughs to Leary, whose counter-cultural credentials were impeccable – he had gained support and counsel from philosophers such as Alan Watts and Aldous Huxley, both respected commentators on transcendental religious matters, and the California-based expatriate British intellectual guru Gerald Heard. Leary was lyrical about the possibilities of hallucinatory drugs: 'Medicine has already preempted LSD, marijuana is the football for two other powerful groups – Bohemia and the narcotics agents. Mescaline and psilocybin are still up for grabs and it is our hope to keep them ungrabbed, uncontrolled, available. We are working along these two lines: We are turning on as many well-known opinion-making people as we can. When the issue comes up for legislation we hope to have a strong team to fight the noncontrol game.' Burroughs rather carelessly gave his moral support to Leary: 'I think the wider use of these drugs would lead to better conditions at all levels. Perhaps whole areas of neurosis could be mapped and eradicated in mass therapy.'

Dr. Leary agreed: indeed, he had already begun to dose volunteer inmates at a state prison in Massachusetts with magic mushrooms. This was combined with a social programme and Leary's own personal vision of turning on the screws as well, turning the Concord prison into a paradise of regenerate citizens, their minds blown and purified, their behaviour miraculously modified. Given that the gates of perception could be opened by psilocybin, it was only a matter of time before the gates of Concord could be opened too. So far, Leary was legitimate, licensed in effect by Harvard to explore his drug philosophy and, in practice, accountable only to himself in his personal crusade for the psychedelic revolution. Naturally, his magic quest interested the Beats who had advocated in their writings consciousness-expansion counter-cultural principles and distrust of authority, as would their Hippie successors.

Tangier, as a resort for renegades, had played its part in the Beat movement. Burroughs and Bowles had been adopted, like it or not, as hip tour-guides to an alternative culture dependent, initially, on soft drugs such as kif rather than on the later laboratory-manufactured hallucinogenics. Tangier was weird without being strange – it blended an Eastern culture with recognizable Western attitudes; it appeared laid-back without being laid-out. It was cheap, it was accessible, it was hallowed ground – the city was a portal, a gateway to revelation, a point of entry to an entire Moroccan culture founded, if the buzz could be believed, on the mellow effects of hashish. Leary checked into Tangier in August and immediately linked up with Burroughs and Ginsberg who introduced him to Alan Ansen, Gregory Corso and two English boys who had attached themselves to Burroughs. In a room at the

Muniria, they all prepared to dip into Dr Leary's little bag of mind-bending mushrooms.

Ansen immediately hit a high, the psilocybin zapping through his neurones. Pure ecstasy, effortless euphoria. Ginsberg plunged into a depression, recognizing the essential coldness of Burroughs and his own earthbound nature, his feet rooted to the ground while his spirit struggled hopelessly for release. Burroughs was wiped out: he looked more than ordinarily spectral, sagging and dispirited. According to Ted Morgan, Leary remembered Burroughs sounding 'a word of warning. I'm not feeling too well. I was struck by juxta position of purple fire mushroomed from the pain banks. Urgent warning. I think I'll stay here in shrivelling envelopes of larval flesh. I'm going to take some apomorphine. One of the nastiest cases ever processed by this department. You fellows go down to the fair and see film and brain waves turning in on soulless insect people.' Pregnant with this apocalyptic warning, Burroughs brought his own experiments with psilocybin to an end – once had been bad enough, twice was just plain disagreeable.

Nevertheless, he recognized the power of the drug and did not discount its potential to initiate a world-bending alteration of global consciousness if it could be made widely available. Leary promised him a 'better experience with peyote. But later encounters with Leary disillusioned Burroughs who, intellectually and scientifically interested in the research programme, was less impressed by Leary's messianic world vision, his self-adopted mission to turn on the world to love and cosmic unity. The scientific content of the research programme was low, the philosophic extremes of Leary's mission were suspect, and Burroughs concluded that his primary attraction for Leary was his influence with the principals of the Beat movement whose support Leary needed to achieve his egocentric, almost megalomaniacal ends. Burroughs didn't like the Doctor's mushrooms, and suddenly he didn't like Leary who, he began to feel, had ruthlessly manipulated him and unimaginatively tried to use him.

His return to Tangier had not, by and large, been successful or helpful: the city was no longer as useful as it had been, now that it had lost its mystery, now that it felt like a cut-price Green-wich Village. Before Leary's descent into Tangier like some sort of spaced-out dark angel, Burroughs had experimented with dimethyltryptamine, a hallucinogenic powder called Prestonin. Ether-based, it gave a short but intense buzz – not always pleasant. He shared it with Bowles who consented, warily, to sniff the powder that almost blew his head off, melted it like toffee and sent it spinning into cosmic space. Burroughs, for his part, made what felt like a fast trip through an incinerator. Neither of them thought that Prestonin was much fun. Perhaps dazed by it, the next day Burroughs sorted out some photographs which he laid on a grey silk dressing gown on his bed. He added a few *objets trouvés* and photographed what appeared to be a random assortment, associated only in his subconscious mind. Alan Ansen, when he arrived and inspected his friend's photo-montages, remarked: 'when you smash a mirror because you don't like what it reflects, the fragments continue to wink the old message.'

Disorderly order is a sort of order, after all – Burroughs was creating an elaborate oxymoron. Burroughs needed to make stories, to shape the random into meanings which revealed the sub-structure, the real beneath the flux. He began, now, to be interested in the patterns of chaos, the myriad coincidences thrown up by chance multiplied by eternity. His need to find meaning and order made chaos more interesting. Thus it was that he felt sidelined and misused by Leary that summer when he was not permitted to explore scientifically the implications of Leary's research which was interesting to Leary only as a means of developing 'a religious do-good cult': an amorphous concept.

Disgusted with Leary and disappointed with Tangier, Burroughs left for New York to begin work on a new novel, *Nova Express*, and continue to experiment with cut-up writings, assemblages of photographs and newspaper clippings, recorded sounds and apparently random objects. He then abandoned New York for Paris and, in the summer of 1963, returned again to Tangier which, unfortunately, was more than usually infested with deadbeat American and European dropouts straggling along the streets on the first leg of the enlightenment trail. He took a house at 4 calle Larache, on the Marshan, and settled to deal with the arrival of his sixteen-year-old son Billy who had been looked after by his paternal grandparents in Palm Beach since the death of his mother. Billy's academic achievements at school had not been brilliant, he had a cynical, sardonic humour that owed something to his father's style, and the latest expression of his reckless and self-destructive attitude had been an accident featuring a .22 rifle with which he had almost killed a friend. Billy was turning out to be a pretty wild kid, though the incident with the rifle had sobered and depressed him, reminding him of the death of his mother at his father's hands. He suggested to his grandparents that he might like to go to Tangier to see Burroughs.

Billy stayed six months, until January 1964, when he and his father finally gave up on their guarded and defensive attempts to come to terms with one another. Billy's loutishness and don't-give-a-shit attitude stemmed largely from inarticulate resentment which met the wall of Burroughs' inexpressible long-standing guilt about the death of his wife and his long-term neglect of his son. There was mutual incomprehension. Billy began to miss his familiar life and the security of his home with his devoted grandparents in Palm Beach, took no interest in the romantic, alternative reality of Tangier and had nothing to give to his father. Burroughs, for his part, continued to live the life to which he had been long accustomed, unable to compromise his habitual routine except by token attempts at parental discipline which he soon abandoned. His principles of personal freedom, his temperamental distrust of the conventional, hardly fitted him to be a disciplinarian.

Billy found himself left largely to his own devices in a house inhabited by his father, who disappeared for long periods to work or to sit inaccessibly in an orgone box, and by the two gay English boys who had attached themselves to Burroughs. The younger boy, Mikey Portman, little older than Billy himself, was jealous, constantly chipping at Billy in an attempt to be one up on him. The older boy, Ian Somerville, almost instantly made an abortive pass at Billy, but became protective of him and took time to tutor him in mathematics. Drugs were always available, and straight away a special expedition was made to buy Billy his own *sebsi* so that he could smoke pot with the rest of them like a proper adult. Burroughs made random attempts to create a home for his son, but Billy's resistance and apathy wore him down. They had nothing to say to one another, nothing in common but the accident of blood, separated by emotions that could be expressed only lamely when they were not avoided altogether. There was much to say, but no means of communication.

Billy, off his own bat, decided to return to get his high school diploma in Palm Beach, and put a good face on things at the airport where he and Burroughs said goodbye: they had resolved nothing, but at least had made a crude contact. Returning to calle Larache, Burroughs found that his son had left a legacy: perhaps unwittingly, he had been hanging out on the roof of the house, disturbing the neighbouring Moroccan women who were horrified at being seen unveiled by a Nazarene male. Burroughs and his boys were the only foreigners in the street, and the hostility of the neighbours was exacerbated by Ian Somerville's homosexual promiscuity with local young Moroccans and the fact that Burroughs did not employ any Moroccans as domestic servants who would have afforded him some protection. First, mud was flung at the door, then children threw stones at the house. Whenever Burroughs stepped outside, he was insulted in the street. People regularly pounded on his door at six in the morning, and women gathered to chant curses.

Being short of money, Burroughs was obliged to stay put. He was owed five thousand dollars by Maurice Girodias, but there was no hope of collecting, though he did make a special trip to Paris in January to try to dun the old rascal. He applied to Bowles for advice, but there was nothing to be got out of that sphinx whose attitude, as ever, was non-involvement and an oyster-like disinclination to open up with the pearls of wisdom he had accreted slowly and painstakingly as an old Morocco hand. Burroughs would have to learn for himself that he could not pretend Moroccans scarcely existed in his world, that he could not ignore them or pay less than due deference to their traditions. Since adaptation to Moroccan mores, even simple friendliness with the natives, was not Burroughs' long suit, there was not much Bowles could do to help, so – reasonably – not much was what he did.

Burroughs' purgatory came to a merciful end with a substantial payment from his American publishers, Grove Press, in May 1964. He stowed away a couple of thousand dollars in a Gibraltar bank and moved from calle Larache to the blessed isolation of a penthouse in the Lotería building at 16 rue Delacroix. High in his eyrie, furnished like the cabin of a sea captain, he had space and shelving to lay out his collection of cut-up materials, classified and collated and pasted into large folios. He was willing to explain these arcane, esoteric assemblages to anyone who appeared interested, though he was careful to stress that the cut-up method was not for the uninitiated, the dabbler – it worked only 'in the hand of a master'.

The cut-up method of literary composition was an attempt to map psychic areas – Burroughs being the cosmonaut, the latter-day Columbus of inner space. His new methodology was a form of self-analysis, therapeutic and aesthetic, though not in the traditional manner of psychological word-association techniques. This was magical, emancipating, liberating, poetical and political – the equivalent in literary history of the rupture of form and technique in art initiated by Cézanne's consciousness-altering paintings, or by the mind-expanding methods of Surrealism and Dada. Cut-ups, potentially, were the means to total knowledge, personal ubiquity, omniscience and – perhaps – control.

His penthouse was a sky-high refuge, but Burroughs was still liable to be brought down to earth with a bump by shoeshine boys in the street. Earthly harassment brought him unavoidably back to solid, physical reality: street kids, if not nippy on their feet, were liable to be cracked round the head or get Burroughs' good right elbow in their faces. He, in turn, could count on being socked by a rock on his knee. The Moroccans were bad enough, but maybe the tide of grubby hippies was worse. Nationalist feeling in Tangier, never kindly even towards regular tourists in the 1960s, was intensified in its distaste for these degenerates who tarred the resident colony of foreigners with a brush that threatened to sweep away the last of their long-standing privileges.

Writing to Brion Gysin in Paris, Burroughs indicated that enough was enough: the city disgusted him like a venereal disease. 'I must get out before I open up with laser guns on the wretched idiot inhabitants.' Jane Bowles also felt despair – the hippies were a threat to her way of life, to the traditional standing of the resident foreign community which, by and large, had respected the Moroccan way of life and had been tolerated by the native inhabitants who now, no longer under international government, made little or no distinction between the behaviour of the expatriates and the insensitive, egocentric eccentricities of the hippies who did not understand, and made no effort to accommodate themselves to, the morality of the Moroccans who were horrified by their casual improprieties. Above all, the nationalists were not only ill-disposed to foreigners as a whole, they disapproved of homosexuality. There was some feeling that homosexuals, and particularly pederasts, had had their day in Tangier. 'No guts left in this miserable town,' thought Burroughs, and left Tangier at the end of 1964 arriving in New York on 8 December.

He did not return until Christmas 1965, and then only for a short visit because his three-month visa for a trip to London had expired. That Christmas Day, Jay Haselwood – the proprietor of the Parade Bar – dropped down dead. At the funeral on 30 December, Burroughs – formally dressed in his habitual bank clerk mode – was interested to see *le tout Tanger* turn up at the English church, St Andrew's, to pay their last respects; 'all the cooks and waiters who had worked for him over the years,' remarks Ted Morgan in his biography of Burroughs, 'and the old biddies that Jay used to have lunch with, and the patrons of the Parade, from the *beau monde* to the naughty boys, and the shameless moochers who were always cadging drinks.' Burroughs, writes Morgan, 'reflected that it was the end of an era. Gone with Jay Haselwood was the old Tangier, with its colourful characters and live-and-let-live attitude. Now it was like every other place – the government had both feet in your business.'

Or, perhaps, Burroughs had made what use he could of Tangier by 1965. He was fully established as a writer – his trilogy, his 'mythology for the space age' – *The Soft Machine*, *The Ticket That Exploded*, and *Nova Express* had been published, the first two in 1961 and 1962 by Girodias at Olympia Press, the third by Grove Press in 1964. *Junky* and *The Naked Lunch* were modern cult classics, particularly the latter, from which his subsequent trilogy flowed, incorporating material that had been pruned from it and mixed with cut-up matter. His Tangier periods had been time in limbo, periods of rich feeding on its concentrated pabulum – what Oliver Harris describes as 'a transitional condition he termed "larval" ' Tangier had been an edge, a frontier, a place described by Bowles in *Let It Come Down* as 'counterfeit, a waiting room between connections, a transition from one way of being to another, which for the moment was neither way, no way'. Like Nelson Dyar, the hero of Bowles' novel, Burroughs had been 'coreless, he was no one, and he was standing here in the middle of no country'. The novel that emerged from this condition – *The Naked Lunch* – was described by Mary McCarthy as 'based on statelessness', deriving from his years of exile in a city not yet usurped by state bureaucracy.

In Tangier, it had once been possible to live outside the law, like the original American frontiersman who made his own deal with politics and morality, remote from control. Like his characters, Burroughs had been picaresque – himself a character in philosophic pursuit of ultimate questions that led him inevitably to the limits of his world, to Tangier as a border country inhabited by refugees from control who sought some ineffable salvation in complete *laissez-faire*, beyond any familiar social context. Tangier had been, for a while, 'the place in the world where the dream breaks through'. For Bowles, that dream continued – increasingly like a nightmare after the death of his wife in 1973. It seemed to have trapped him. But for Burroughs, the dream shifted, the patterns of his life moving like the infinite, myriad, random patterns of a kaleidoscope – the difference being that he was more centred in himself rather than in any one place. Tangier had given him identity, a core that remained constant in the surrounding flux, had liberated him.

David Herbert
and
the Beau Monde
in Tangier

Cecil Beaton's first diary entries describing Tangier are character-istically ornate and predominantly floral. His eyes, accustomed to the dark, grey tones of the London winter he had left behind, by means of a train from Charing Cross and a P. & O. steamer bound for Morocco, were dazzled by colour. 'After we had waited much too long in the Customs Room at the Docks, my first impression on shore of the Tangier that had sloped in glittering cubes up from the sea was of a boy walking down the steep slopes against a curdled wall, carrying on his head an enormous basket of flowers – the boy looked as if he were wearing a most elaborate Edwardian hat of blue iris, mauve tulips, dark red and pale yellow roses – a pudding of flowers too numerous to mention.' A place where even the chil-dren looked to Beaton as though they wore hats in the style of Lady Desborough, was bound to be satisfactory. It was March 1939, and he had come to the city with a close friend, the Hon. David Herbert, second son of the Earl and Countess of Pembroke.

They were able to rent a small house in the Casbah, for three pounds a week, from the painter Jim Wyllie. It was, reported Beaton, 'a lovely little Moorish house of white walls in the most beautiful spot in Tangier'. There were rambling steps, roof gardens, a courtyard shaded by a tremendous fig tree (under which, Wyllie claimed, Samuel Pepys had sat to write his diary) and, as a bonus, there was a view looking into part of the Sultan's Palace, 'a white scene of columns with Corinthian capitals,' breathed Beaton ecstatically, 'flaked white walls and an incredible serenity. Both in the changing lights of the sun and at night by the light of the moon and lanterns, it is breathtaking in its atmosphere of mystery and Romanticism.' Immediately, Beaton and Herbert itched to decor-ate their house. They rushed to the market where they snatched up bunches of 'profuse and incredibly cheap flowers', ransacked the souks for gaudy materials with which to make curtains and cushion covers, and commanded enormous pots of azaleas – white and pink and cerise – to enliven the garden.

The flower pots were, for Beaton, 'a sop to time'. At any minute they would very likely 'have to clear out leaving behind our pots and the bottles of drink we had ordered', since the news about Hitler and Czechoslovakia had just reached them and daily reports from Herbert, who rang home each day to Wilton, were no more encouraging. War seemed inevitable; but in the meantime, in mid-April, Beaton had been spared 'one month of bliss and contentment in the setting of which it is impossible to tire'. Every minute should be made to count in terms of pleasure since at any moment 'world war would put an end to all our interest and enjoyment'. Beaton set to work: he was determined to finish the drawings for his spoof biography, *My Royal Past*, purporting to be the frank memoirs of a middle-European Baroness, lady-in-waiting to a fanciful Grand Duchess. 'In no other atmosphere could I have worked so solidly without getting completely exhausted. For three weeks on end I remained in the house doing the drawings for my Baroness book – never imagining they could take so long.' David Herbert helped 'in many ways with his enthusiasm, often by drawing for me some of the intricate and boring bits in my illustrations' or, more often than not, 'by returning from the town with really first rate imitations of the people he had seen and giving me all the news, political and trivial local gossip'.

He had busied himself socially to considerable purpose. Within a very short time, Herbert knew more about Tangier than most of the residents who had lived there for years: 'after three weeks David has become a complete Tangerino, knows all the local gossip of this oriental Cheltenham, and knows every inch of the town.' The time generally passed blamelessly and pleasantly, industriously and domestically. 'We came to love the house the more we knew it under different circumstances – in the windy weather our fig tree and courtyard sheltered us – when the rains came down in such tropical profusion it was funny to see how flooded everything became – the garden became even prettier as we bought more potted plants, and the sitting room was a haven of peace, charm and flowers. The first week passed eventfully and slowly – and as always, the others passed with increasing momentum. The Cranbornes were here for several days and slightly alleviated our anxiety over the general situation with their charm and intelligence . . .'

This apparently innocent reference in Beaton's diary to Lord Cranborne, Under-Secretary of State for Foreign Affairs, is disingenuous. Cranborne, who had been visiting Marrakesh with his wife, had been specifically invited by Herbert to visit Tangier to investigate a subject of local British social and political concern. On his social, gossipy excursions into Tangier society, David Herbert had been apprised of the strained relations existing between Mr and Mrs Keeling, the British Consul-General (known as the Minister) and his wife, and Mr and Mrs Hoyland, the British Consul and his wife. Magda Keeling was Italian, known to all as a Fascist sympathizer, and the Hoylands had been plainly snubbed by the Keelings who had never invited them to the British Legation. Whether out of mischief or a sincere desire to establish *détente* – though probably the former – Beaton had suggested inviting both couples to a cocktail party. The thing was done: 'we asked everyone we could think of', wrote Herbert in *Second Son*. 'When people arrived, they were surprised to see that the Hoylands were the guests of honour, but when Mr and Mrs Keeling arrived and we formally introduced them, everyone got the point, including the Keelings, who stood self-consciously aware of the barely suppressed amusement at their expense.'

Hardly satisfied with this minor stroke, Herbert prepared his coup. He summoned the Cranbornes and vividly outlined the situation to them over lunch, after which Cranborne departed to interview the Minister. Readily recognized as a bad egg, Keeling was promptly replaced shortly after Cranborne's return to the Foreign Office in London. The long arm of Herbert's connection with London and international European and American society was very quickly perceived as a powerful and useful tool by Tangier society which, already impressed by his charm, sociability, the interest – amounting to addiction – he showed in the affairs and gossip of the colony and his energetic pursuit of pleasure, adopted him wholesale as a leader of the expatriate pack. He was immediately a vital force, galvanizing a torpid town with his incisive wit and decisive activity. Beaton greatly admired Herbert's vivacity, though occasionally he found it trying. 'The high spirits that David possesses have succeeded in warding off mass depression and hysteria about the

general situation' but he tended too much to insist on glossing
over bad news in favour of any good signs, however unimportant.
'His incessant good spirits too make me feel guilty that I am so
often bored, tired and disinterested – I am a critic, he has no critical
faculties ... I am decidedly too difficult and flee to be by myself
as soon as possible. When however I am in a good mood I find
David incredibly amusing and he has a great knack and strength
for breaking through my bad moods and getting a real laugh out
of one.'

When he wanted to be alone, Beaton would retire to one of the
roof terraces to write or sketch. Up there, he could look down
into the square of the Casbah where gaggles of tourists could be
regularly seen and heard 'screaming with hysterical horror at the
snake charmer who does his stunt much too long and they get
bored after they have taken their Kodak snaps'. On Fridays, the
Governor (the Mendoub) would come to a nearby mosque to
pray, accompanied by guards who played the national anthem.
Thursdays were interesting on account of crowds of 'sorrowful
women in white with baskets of food to take as presents to their
children in the small boys' prison opposite.'

Beaton had at first been struck by the interesting position of
Wyllie's house, and regularly commented on it in postcards home:
'the house is Romantically situated between the prison and the
madhouse.' But, on longer and closer acquaintance with the reality
of this intriguing situation, there appeared to be some noisy draw-
backs. By degrees, Beaton 'realized that some of the cries I had
imagined to be from some bread or flower sellers were those of the
lunatics next door ... only after three weeks did I learn of these
four lunatics shut in their cell so small that one with a wooden leg
had had a hole bored for him to stretch it into – throughout the
night one hears tormented wails – I now have the habit of waking
to hear one madman who sings with great force a song of such
infinite sadness as the prelude to dawn.' Besides these distressing
noises, the ordinary sounds of the Casbah included the blaring,
long notes, three times a day, of the garbage collector's trumpet,
continual neighing of donkeys, the regular calls to prayer ('a ghastly
moan'), children singing their begging prayers in 'rasping nasal
voices', the crowing of cocks and a constant, day-long noise of hens.

Beaton's fastidious nature was beguiled by the charm of the

faux-naif, captivated by the artificiality of beauty, amused by the self-parody of the picturesque. He liked effects, rather than an intrusive reality from which he preferred to keep his distance – the distance of the critic's taste. When Tangier had delighted him sufficiently, when its discomforts began to intrude, when its limited horizons began to close in, he was anxious to get back to work in England. Tangier had been a pleasant interlude, but there was little in the city to detain him. 'I am pleased to go, for I now do not wish to become too embroiled with personalities here, and I feel that the essence has been fully savoured.' Herbert, on the contrary, had sampled Tangier in its every aspect and found it – like a drug – very much to his taste. After war service as a wireless operator in the Merchant Navy, he returned with Beaton – who had distinguished himself as a war photographer – in 1949 to a Tangier which, according to Beaton, was now full of 'black-market gangsters, Spanish crooks, French expatriates, the different Legations and the old eccentric English, the old ladies who have lived here all their lives and the decadent ones who come here merely for louche reasons'. The city was still 'an oriental Cheltenham', stuffily provincial.

The summer of 1949 was more lively than most, according to Jane Bowles who wrote animatedly to Katharine Hamill: 'I've become very British, by the way these last weeks. Our English summer crowd is here (2 people), one of them Cecil Beaton, and the locals are all going to a masquerade very soon given by C[ecil] dressed as *events*. Isn't it awful? For me, I mean, because as usual I don't remember what's happened.' To add to the universal gaiety, Truman Capote had also arrived, 'Tangier was not really to Truman's taste,' commented Paul Bowles, 'but he stuck it out all summer at the Farhar with Jane and me because of Cecil's presence. There were some good parties that summer, including one given by the Comtesse de la Faille, in which she cleared out the ballroom, leaving only the Aubussons on the walls, and covered the floor with straw for the snake charmers and acrobats. The Moroccans built a fire in the middle of the room and made themselves completely at home.' Bowles is discreet about the Comte and Comtesse de la Faille, and gives little detail about this extraordinary party. David Herbert, in *Second Son*, the first volume of his

autobiography, is less reticent. He records the event, its complete
jaw-dropping dreadfulness, with satisfactory gusto:

> The night of their fancy-dress party, everything went wrong. The
> refrigerator had broken down and the ice Phyllis had ordered did
> not arrive. She forgot to send for the food, which had been pre-
> pared by a shop in town: by the time she remembered, the shop
> was closed. The taxi bringing the Moorish musicians and dancers
> broke down on the way from Tetuan.
>
> By this time both the de la Failles were drunk. The food eventu-
> ally arrived, so did the orchestra, but it was too late to save the
> party. By then the atmosphere was electric and fights had broken
> out in every corner. Ada Green, who always retained her dignity
> even during revolutions, moved slowly round the room eyeing
> people through her lorgnette. She stopped by Truman Capote,
> who never looked young, and said: 'And what are you supposed
> to represent?'
>
> 'Spring!' lisped Truman.
>
> 'Well, you don't look it,' said Ada and, picking up a snake from
> the hand of the snake-charmer who was vainly trying to entertain
> some guests, proceeded to charm it herself.
>
> Two guests were severely bitten by the dogs chained under the
> tables and a young man had the top of a finger removed by an
> infuriated macaw. The party was a complete fiasco, but neither
> Charles nor Phyllis noticed, as they had both long before passed
> out.

The fights at the party were instructive to an attentive ear and
eye:

> People had been asked indiscriminately; many of them had not
> spoken to each other for years. A flirtatious Spanish woman
> noticed a handsome dusky young man in an exquisite uniform: she
> thought he was a potentate from a Black African state and made
> flagrant advances to him – to which he naturally responded –
> only to discover later that he was one of the servants dressed up
> in the ambassadorial full-dress uniform which had belonged to
> Charles's Belgian diplomat father.
>
> The Spanish woman was furious at having been made to look

foolish and screamed abuse at the young man. She summoned her husband for support, and he threw a glass of champagne at the servant, who ducked. The glass struck a harmless English visitor, Mrs Malcolm, who received a gash in the face and never came to Tangier again. Pandemonium broke loose, sides were taken, someone called the Spanish woman a whore and her husband a crook; the husband retorted that all the men present were pederasts. 'What about your own son,' someone shouted, 'he's not only a pederast but a cissie as well!' Cecil quietly said: 'Who sold fuel-oil to German submarines that torpedoed our ships in the Straits of Gibraltar?'

The Spanish couple fled to their car, only to find that the other Moorish servants had let the air out of their tyres; but having made their ignominious exit they didn't dare return and bumped off down the drive on the hubs of their wheels.

The Comte de la Faille, Charles, was Belgian. His wife, Phyllis, was half-Scottish, half-American. She, according to David Herbert, was 'noisy, loud and domineering'. He was 'quiet, weak and gentle'. They lived in a state of some grand squalor, taken over by a menagerie of animals to which Phyllis was apparently devoted, though her notions of animal welfare were often eccentrically at odds with recommended standards of hygiene and common respect for animal dignity. Dogs were chained on short leashes to any available piece of furniture or locked into cramped kennels. Birdcages littered the house, rarely cleaned out and randomly stocked with rotting raw meat for the owls, or putrescent fruit, crawling with ants, for the parrots. 'All was gloom and frustrated animal misery,' commented David Herbert, 'even the bathrooms were filled with different living creatures – goldfish in the bath, newts and frogs in the wash-basin. I once found a snake in the lavatory. The house stank.' Etienne de Beaumont, delivering his verdict on this ménage after a visit, described the house as 'the first concentration camp for animals I have seen in my life'. Phyllis had her own rationale, which she stated to David Herbert: 'The sooner you realize that the animals are here for my pleasure and not for theirs, the better.'

Cecil Beaton's own extravaganza took place outside Tangier, on the beach and in the cave known as The Grotto of Hercules. The guests were conducted into the tremendous cavern which had been

decorated by Beaton for the occasion and served champagne cooled
in the sea and hashish. Bowles thought it noteworthy that 'Truman,
who claimed to be afraid of scorpions, had to be carried by a group
of Moroccans down the face of the cliff in order to get there. An
Andaluz orchestra was partially visible, surrounded by rocks and
lanterns; the guests lay in the moonlight among cushions on the
sand, went swimming, and sat around a big fire.' Beaton's own
diary description of the party is, unfortunately, embargoed by his
executors for some' years and one can only guess at his personal
comments in his diary for 1949. He would certainly have been
delighted by Truman Capote's presence, just as Capote himself was
delighted by Beaton: 'wouldn't you know that we two iron-winged
butterflies would find ourselves in the same hollyhock? If not for
him, I'd move on.'

Capote stayed on, beguiled by Beaton, but his impression of
Tangier, recorded many years later in *Answered Prayers*, testified to
his distaste for the hybrid hokum of the city as

> a white piece of cubist sculpture displayed against a mountainside
> facing the Bay of Gibraltar. One descends from the top of the
> mountain, through a middle-class suburb sprinkled with ugly
> Mediterranean villas, to the 'modern' town, a broiling miasma of
> overly wide boulevards, cement-colored high-rises, to the sleazy
> maze of the sea-coasted Casbah. Except for those present for
> presumably legitimate business purposes, virtually every foreign
> Tangerine is ensconced there for at least one, if not all, of four
> reasons: the easy availability of drugs, lustful adolescent prosti-
> tutes, tax loopholes, or because he is so undesirable, no place
> north of Port Said would let him out of the airport or off a ship.
> It is a dull town where all the essential risks have been removed.

Beaton, concurring with Capote's estimate, left in September. To
help share the expenses of the Villa Mektoub, which had been
loaned to him by Loel Guinness, David Herbert asked Paul and
Jane Bowles to move in with him until arrangements could be made
for Jane to go to Paris and Bowles to Ceylon.* They took kindly to
Herbert, who in turn became devoted particularly to Jane: 'the one

* See p. 128

ABOVE: Brion Gysin

RIGHT: Tennessee Williams

BELOW: (left to right) Paul
Bowles, Allen Ginsberg,
William Burroughs, Gregory
Corso and Michael Portman

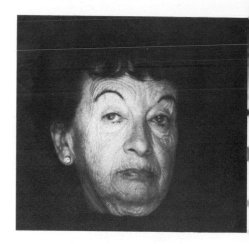

this page
ABOVE: Lily Wickman
LEFT: George Greaves
BELOW: Joe Orton, Greaves and hashcake
opposite
ABOVE: Orton and friend on the beach
ABOVE RIGHT: Arab women at market in
traditional dress
BELOW: Bowles and Mohammed Mrabet

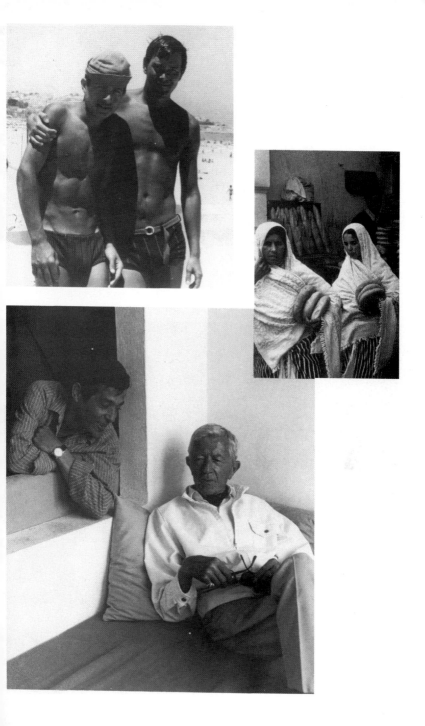

Malcolm Forbes' 70th birthday

RIGHT: Malcolm Forbes with Elizabeth Taylor and Robert Maxwell

BELOW: The procession of maids into onion-domed tents

person I have met who may be said to have been "touched by the finger of Genius" '. He regarded her writings as superior even to those of Bowles – but both were 'brilliant' and to be with them was 'an unending pleasure'. During his years in Tangier, Herbert remained close to Jane and was greatly distressed by her condition during her last years. Beaton, with a career to pursue, had sensibly left Tangier, and the Bowleses were soon to leave on their various occasions. But Herbert was not at a loss: there remained apparently limitless resources for amusement, particularly 'the old eccentric English, the old ladies' who formed the backbone of expatriate society in Tangier.

Beaton had ambitions beyond this banal repertory company, these players in summer stock. In the country of the ornate, or the fantastical, only the plain man is unusual. Barbara Hutton and David Herbert had cast themselves more or less happily – happily, because they gave no thought to acting beyond type – in parts perfectly suited to one of the few places on earth where they would not be heckled off the stage as hams. They acted up a storm, delighting visitors to their private threatre, who were fascinated and seduced by their character acting for a few performances, but prepared to leave when the play had begun to bore them with its tedious repetitions. Beaton was unusual in that he had arrived in Tangier unhampered by any fantasy that it might complete his life. Like Capote, Beaton had not come to a full stop or a dead end in his career – Tangier was a *cul-de-sac*, an ante-room to limbo, a shadow play. For Beaton and Capote, Tangier was a city where time stood still, a breathing space. For David Herbert it was the breath of life itself, a kingdom to be won and ruled.

David Herbert has been characterized by Ted Morgan, in *Rowing Towards Eden* as 'Randolph Norman', a rather grand remittance man provided with an income perfectly sufficient to allow him

to live on a scale that would have been prohibitive in England, in a house that was Moorish on the outside and Victorian on the inside. He entertained constantly, and had a cook, a butler, two maids, and two gardeners ... In Tangier, Randolph came into his own as the social arbiter of the expatriate community. He was no longer the younger son, but a minor potentate who decided who was acceptable. His rule was just but sometimes severe, and those who fell out of favor had no way of knowing that one wrong word could be enough. The English consul's Italian wife told him shortly after their arrival, 'You're lucky to have us, we're embassy, not consulate.' Randolph, who considered himself the permanent ambassador to Tangier, and the consuls transients of small significance, said, 'She's a *donna de niente*,' and refused to see them.

Morgan's little vignette is a clever piece of work, centred around a dinner party given by Randolph Norman who conducts himself with the mannered, aristocratic facility of a man born to privilege, thwarted in his ambitions by the law of inheritance and succession that all – money, estate, title – went to the elder brother, leaving precious little for the second son, and by the fact that, 'trained for nothing', he was fit for little. But there was a little more to Herbert than the social butterfly, the family dependant, the disinherited. In *Second Son*, Herbert presents himself as a lightweight, a hedonist, and a realist prepared to make a good life better. 'In England the younger sons of great families often receive very little, but they have one great advantage: they can lead their lives with complete freedom. I began to realize very early on that I would not have been temperamentally suited for the role of eldest son . . . I have always been too much of a rebel by nature, too adventurous and unconventional in my ways to fit into the required traditional pattern.' As for ambition, 'I do not envy ambitious people because so often they seem restless and discontented. I have seen ambition devour the characters of some of my contemporaries. It has made them lead lives quite different from those they have fundamentally wanted and which would, perhaps, have made them happier people.'

Ambition, it seemed to Herbert, had not made his great friend, Cecil Beaton, happy. Beaton's desire to be noticed 'was part of his plan and all-important to his future'. His 'flamboyant appearance and special way of talking' occasionally embarrassed Herbert, who nevertheless admired his 'immense courage and great energy'. However, he believed that Beaton may have sacrificed more to ambition than he gained: 'He fell in love like everyone else, but never enough to curb his ambition. For example, if he was having an affair with someone in London and he was offered a job in

America, he would up stakes and be off without a moment's hesitation. This sounds callous, but to be a success was just that much more important to Cecil than being in love. A character like Cecil's does not make for happiness.'

Herbert could be strong-minded about happiness, and found self-pity intolerable. Towards the end of his life, Beaton visited David Herbert in Tangier for the last time in 1978. Pushed into the house in a wheelchair by his secretary, Eileen Hose, Beaton's first reaction on seeing Herbert was to

> burst into tears and he did so off and on for the first week. I decided that too many people in England had said 'Poor Cecil' and treated him as a hopeless invalid.

Herbert goes on to claim that he knocked Beaton back into shape by brisk words and driving him out into the garden to start drawing again. This *soi-disant* role as Beaton's therapist was hotly disputed by Herbert's sister, who stated firmly that long before his visit to Tangier, nine months after his stroke, Beaton had been busily painting with his left hand and, far from Herbert needing to send Miss Hose imperiously off into town to buy painting materials, Beaton had brought his paints with him. He was already under the care of physiotherapists. Weepy Beaton may have been, but he was no basket case to be rallied, Lazarus-like, from his depression by Herbert.

Beaton could hardly begin to comprehend his old friend's life in Tangier. He wrote in his diary, 'David has voluntarily cut himself off from the fatherland – where he has so many friends – position and tradition – in order to be a big frog in a little pond . . . He has completely identified himself with the place of his choice, so that his friends here are his only real friends. He cares and minds for these people because they are part of his real life. When he comes to England and goes to parties he considers them small and pointless. However small a local entertainment may be, David will give it his backing. It is his kingdom, which is well up to a point.' Herbert's creation of himself, in collusion with the expatriate community, as uncrowned king of Tangier might be all well and good in its way, but at what cost to the fantasist? Beaton considered it too high: 'even if there one has no tax to pay, and life is cheap with masses of badly trained servants at one's command, there is a terrible penalty that all expatriates must pay. In all cases they feel they have to justify their choice, they are forever making excuses. They know they have turned their back on a certain fundamental truth . . . They do not know it is a lie, yet no moral code exists.'

The truth of actuality, one supposes, did not figure largely in the minds of Herbert and the other expatriates, whose excuses for loitering in limbo Beaton considered spurious – if not apologetic. Even Bowles' rationale that the rest of the world was going to hell, and that Tangier was a sort of temporary lifeboat, would have cut little ice with Beaton. Herbert and the rest did not even offer that as an excuse – they were vitally interested in the greater world, albeit filtered through the eyes and attitudes of their important, socially prominent, rich and glamorous friends who came to visit. It was noticeable to Beaton that Herbert, when observed in action beyond the familiar ground of Tangier, took little interest in the actuality of the beau monde when he could not control and supervise their activities in the greater world. The restricted manner of life in Tangier dismayed the free-wheeling Beaton who, accustomed to wider horizons and a global village of artists, socialites, international aristocracy and plutocrats, rather piously supposed that 'there is more malice and venom in small communities.' In Tangier, 'the broadcasting, the repetition of gossip is quite appalling to a stranger . . . I know my own life is only saved from complete pettiness of this sort by my attention to work. But it does seem that a sense of proportion about social values is lost here quicker than need be.'

The social values of Tangier were anachronistic, perhaps, still traditionally based on the diplomatic niceties of the consular corps that had ruled Tangier for many years. The artificiality of social conventions had not been significantly relaxed: Herbert himself admits that the system was ludicrous in a society that, before and immediately after World War II, 'consisted of a collection of petty officials of all nationalities augmented by respectable gangsters, smugglers and a few crooked bankers. They lived cheek by jowl with the Committee of Control, the Administrator and the numerous representatives of the twenty-odd Legations. It was a completely false atmosphere but hilariously funny if you did not take it seriously. Most of these people were immensely grand, battling for the best seats at functions, offended and insulted if wrongly placed at luncheons and dinners.' In *Second Son*, he pokes disingenuous fun at those women to whom placement at meals seemed to be of overriding social significance: 'they minded very much if they were not seated in what they considered was their rightful place. It was once at my house that, for the first and only time, I saw a French woman, married to an American diplomat, turn her plate upside down and refuse to eat or speak during the entire dinner.'

If 'social life was ridiculously pompous and grand' in Tangier in the 1940s, no doubt the unassailable conventions derived at least in part from the precariousness of Tangier's political situation and the fact that standards are more scrupulously observed in a backwater concerned to preserve its privileges than in centres more firmly established and more confident of their power. 'Sad to see these English and Americans speeding over the mountain sides to keep up with one another,' remarked Beaton, 'and not being able to frequent certain spots for fear of going too far and letting the side down.' Beaton suggested that Herbert, as 'self appointed Ambassador' to these expatriates, was largely responsible for setting the tone and enforcing the rules. He could not be absolved from responsibilities he had arrogated to himself, however much he might deride them privately. He 'will not allow anyone to see a perfectly ghastly English couple. He will not go to certain Hotels or bars . . . In his chosen freedom there is little freedom, for "one must keep up a standard."'

In his terrific snit about Tangier, Beaton concluded his diary reflections with a final dismissal of the doomed efforts of the expatriates: 'What are the benefits? The gardens are all disappointing. Yet the owners toil with their mountains of manure to try to grow things that do not suit this climate – at no time of the year does one see the gardens full – often there are only large patches of cocoa-coloured earth to be admired. For the stranger and for a visitor spending a week here there is a certain easy satisfaction, but for anyone to keep his sense of proportion and to have to live here all the year round, that is just about the "jumping-off fence".' Beaton regarded Tangier, after independence, as having lost its prosperity and character:

> it is depressing to live in a town that once flourished and is doing so no more . . . There remain a few expatriates who try to turn their backs on the truth. 'Don't tell me we're in a *cul-de-sac*!'. . .

But it's an ugly little backwater now – with the new buildings going up like Manchester. By degrees the Moroccans are themselves destroying so much that was delightful. Social life now centres less around the Petit Socco, with its oriental buzz, the coffee drinking callers, the half hidden figures behind the balconies of the hotels, than around the Place de France – this is surely one of the ugliest parts of the city, has no Arab quality and is certainly anti-aesthetic with its ghastly pyramid of cardboard advertising the local fair or late arrival of the King.

It is perhaps a mark of the moralist to declare that only a stern and unflinching recognition of reality can firm one's character, provide one with the advantage of a full and fulfilling life, and permit one to breathe one's last with confidence that the battle has been wholeheartedly engaged. Avoidance of reality, like tax avoidance, is perfectly legitimate. Evasion, of real life or tax, is the true sin and crime. By any standards, David Herbert's has been a charmed life: its morality is open to dispute. Like any monarch, he has made an effort to keep up a certain style which some may judge a pose, others an affectation, and friendlier critics a sustained achievement in a world that might be duller without his gallant perseverance in preserving a certain mode that surely must occasionally have been onerous. How burdensome, perhaps, the isolation of one's *façon de vivre*, how it must have rendered, occasionally, one's *état d'âme* so terribly *noirci, n'est-ce pas?*

A regular dinner guest at Herbert's Tangier table in the 1930s and in 1949 had been Miss Jessie Green who, on extensive acquaintance, 'never disappointed us'. Witty and well brought-up, she could, commented Beaton, never be anything but a lady and in full possession of her dignity even when the single cocktail she allowed herself to drink had somewhat gone to her head. Other visitors might wear badly, but Jessie Green was always good value. She was like a public monument in Tangier, having first arrived during the reign of Sir William Kirby Green, appointed British Minister to Tangier in the 1880s, 'on loan' to her aunt, Lady Kirby Green, as companion to their only daughter Feridah. 'They both talked Arabic as if it were their native language,' said David Herbert of Jessie and Feridah, 'and were liked and respected by everybody.' This is a kindly, doting remark by a partisan whose further comment on the characters of the Misses Green persuades one to take any such universal indulgence towards them with a grain of salt. 'They were intelligent, with a caustic wit, and I know of no occasion when anyone has got the better of either of the Misses Green.' The Greens fascinated Herbert, who describes them, and Feridah's sister-in-law, Mrs Ada Kirby Green, as 'rulers of Tangier's social scene.'

Truman Capote, who made their acquaintance, agreed that

between them they manage more often than not to have the last say here. All three are past seventy: Mrs Ada Green is famous for her chic, Miss Jessie for her wit, and Miss Feridah, the oldest, for her wisdom. She has not visited her native England in over fifty years; even so, observing the straw skimmer skewered to her hair and the black ribbon trailing from her pince-nez, one knows she goes out in the noonday sun and has never given up tea at five. Every Friday in her life there is a ritual known as Flour Morning. Seated at a table at the foot of her garden, and judging each case as it is presented, she rations flour to Arab applicants, usually old women who otherwise would starve: from the flour they make a paste which must last them until the next Friday. There is much joking and laughter, for the Arabs adore Miss Ferida, and for her, all these old women, such anonymous bundles of laundry to the rest of us, are friends whose personalities she comments on in a large ledger. 'Fatima has a bad temper but is not bad,' she writes of one, and of another: 'Halima is a good girl. One can take her at face value.' and that, I suppose, is what you would have to say about Miss Ferida.

Feridah didn't greatly care about her appearance: 'lame, shape-less, she screwed her hair up in a knot, wore pince-nez spectacles attached to a black ribbon, and dressed like a rag-and-bone-picker,' reported David Herbert. She never married, devoted herself to charitable works and 'became more and more Muslim in her out-look as time went by'. In addition to her regular Flour Fund Fri-days, Feridah also ran the Infant Welfare Centre for Moorish Children. More than ten thousand children a year passed through the clinic. When Feridah herself finally fell on hard times, being forced to rent out her own house for income, she elected to live in a 'lean-to', consisting of two rooms, kitchen and bath, which she added to the house and christened 'the Wart'. 'She would receive one in the morning at about eleven o'clock,' wrote David Herbert, 'sitting in a wire cage like a meat-safe, which she had had con-structed and which was large enough to hold a table and two chairs. This was placed on the veranda; one entered it by a low door which was firmly shut behind one by Minah, her Moorish maid. "Sit down, my dear," said Feridah. "We've got the better of those flies: they won't molest us here." And for an hour or so one listened fascinated to her anecdotes while drinking tepid tea and eating stale rock cakes.'

Feridah perhaps did not inspire the terror of her more aggressive cousin and sister-in-law, but was no less formidable. Though she had not visited Britain for half a century, she was a devoted patriot who, for her charity work, was awarded the OBE during World War II. Equipped with this impressive token of her sovereign's goodwill, she immediately proceeded to the Grand Socco where, mounted on a wooden box, she harangued the crowd which gath-ered at her skirts. Displaying the medal, and speaking fluently in Moroccan Arabic, she expounded the virtues of the British and their King who, under pressure from his enemies and in his darkest hour, still took care to honour his subjects: 'You see what wonderful people the British are! Even my Sultan, who is being eaten up by his foul enemies, still has time to remember old Feridah Green! We will never be beaten!' There was a great deal more in this chauvinist vein, addressed not only to the Moroccans but also – and probably more pointedly – to the Spanish, Germans and Italians in the crowd.

In direct contrast to Feridah's carelessness about appearance, her sister-in-law Ada, Mrs Kirby Green, was a sight to behold. David Herbert describes her as

tall, thin and elegantly dressed. She was dark-skinned, used heavy eye make-up and wore deep red lipstick. She invariably wore different coloured turbans, the ends of which were wound round her neck until eventually they fell over her shoulders forming a cape. Many rings sparkled on her fingers and she smoked Russian cigarettes incessantly, through a long ivory holder. Ada received one lying on a chaise-longue in her drawing room with Coco, the green parrot, on her shoulder and Omar, her peacock, reclining beside her, his tail spread out to form a brilliant coloured coverlet. Putti, her minute black servant ... was dressed in an ankle-length white linen gown, with a white turban and a long dagger on a belt strapped round his waist. He wore such heavy gold earrings that the lobes of his ears were nearly two inches long. Putti hovered around his mistress carrying an African leather switch with which he swatted any fly or mosquito that came near her. Later, when Ada broke her hip, he became her lady's-maid; he bathed her, dressed her, brushed her hair, manicured her nails, sat by her night and day and carried her around like a baby in his skinny but powerful arms.

Of the three Kirby Green women, Herbert considers Jessie to have been

the strongest personality of the three, and the most worldly. For many years she ruled Tangier with a rod of iron. Socialites stood in awe of her, and also officials of all nations, including the Moroccans. Her energy and her humour were boundless, and with her short curly hair, her fearless eyes, her straight back, caustic wit and quick brain, she was someone to be reckoned with ... At eighty-nine she was as soignée as ever. Her make-up was impeccable and her nails manicured and painted a deep rose. Her colour sense was unsurpassed; she usually wore soft shades of lavender pink and blue. When dressed for a party she was magnificent and at the end of her life her entrance into a room was still a performance well worth watching.

Her legendary quickness of wit was no respecter of persons. 'People she disapproved of, especially those in official positions, got short shrift. One of the British Consul-Generals had long wavy hair and wore his Homburg hat at a rakish angle on the side of his head. Jessie detested him. 'Common, dear,' was her summing-up. 'He trains his hair over the brim of his hat like ivy!'

The summer of 1949 had been amusing. The company had been as agreeable as the weather. A fellow could make a comfortable life here. Tangier offered more interesting diversions and a cheaper, more luxurious standard of living than any town of comparable size in England. The place seemed ready-made for a bachelor gentleman just approaching his fortieth birthday, possessed of taste, time to dig himself a comfortable social niche, and a certain fixed income. Jessie Green, much taken with Herbert, had stated her intention of leaving him her house in her will, but now she pressed him to make a decision: she had lost much of her money during the War and, unless he could arrange to rent her house and build her a smaller one in its grounds, she would be obliged to sell it. Herbert weighed the pros and cons carefully. As the second son, he could not hope to inherit Wilton and his father's title; he did not view with any relish the prospect of living in the social shadows with a dominating mother in England; and there was, perhaps, the residual question of his homosexuality which would not be well regarded by the British authorities.

> On the side of Tangier there was a house that I had loved for many years and which I had known would one day be mine . . . The life of Tangier I knew well and enjoyed, and financially I should be a great deal better off if I did not have to pay British income tax. I realised that I could be equally happy anywhere provided I could transport my own surroundings – my pictures, furniture and books . . . My incurable desire to try something new made me decide on Jessie's house . . . the prospect of getting to work replanning the rose-pink bougainvillea-covered dilapidated Moorish house with its marvellous view and completely undeveloped land was irresistible.

Herbert may have been decided in his own mind about the virtues of a permanent move to Tangier; it was another matter to convince his then lover to accompany him. Jamie Caffery, a nephew of the American ambassador to Paris, lived in London and worked as a researcher for the American magazines *Fortune*, *Time*, and *Life*. He was a regular visitor to David Herbert's house, the Park School, in the grounds of Wilton, where they gardened and entertained at weekends. He was very much opposed to Herbert's intention to settle in Tangier, but his arguments in favour of London and England, and his personal disinclination to pick up sticks and change countries yet again, were useless in the face of Herbert's determination.

In August 1950, they left England. The export of currency was strictly regulated, and Herbert was allowed to take only five thousand pounds and his household effects out of the country. 'In those days it was three years before one was allowed to return to the United Kingdom. If I broke this rule, I paid full British tax.' Five thousand pounds, in the circumstances, was a small enough sum to last him three years, but he would survive by occasionally selling pieces of furniture and other things. With Caffery, he toured France and Italy for a few months, finally arriving in Morocco towards the end of October. Since alterations to Jessie Green's house were not yet finished, though the little house he had arranged to be built for her had been completed, they rented a house nearby on the Mountain and settled to deal, first of all, with Jessie's intemperate demand for a wall around the garden. Herbert's finances were already stretched, and a wall seemed an impossibly expensive luxury: 'but she was adamant. I wondered, after my mother's dominating character, whether I had been wise in choosing to live in such close proximity to so formidable a person.' Caffery attempted to mediate a compromise: 'Jessie, do drop the idea of the wall; you are making things very difficult for David. I know he'll build it as soon as he can.' Jessie would not be mollified: 'Mind your own business and to hell with you!' Matters were resolved eventually, and until March 1970, when Jessie Green finally died at the age of ninety, she and Herbert remained steady friends, living close to one another 'in comparative harmony'.

As to regrets about leaving England, Herbert was confident that friends would come regularly to see him. He had enjoyed to the full a lively social life before the war in which too many friends had been killed on active service. Others had now moved abroad, like himself, or were settling quietly into middle life. In any event, after he had established residence in Tangier, he could come to England for three months in every year if he cared to do so: but his immediate concern was to make a life in Tangier, rather than consider England as 'home'. The expatriate colony, already aware of his potential as a social leader and ability to dramatize the dull, diurnal routine of Tangier, was at least as interested in him as he was in their local affairs. Herbert took up the challenge with enthusiasm: there was a job to be done, licking the colony into a suitable social shape.

Herbert's brio extended beyond the expatriate colony to include Moroccans with whom he happily and naturally associated. Caffery, contrarily, regarded them distrustfully and unsympathetically, preferring the Spanish even to the extent of insisting on Spanish rather than Moroccan servants. He and Herbert parted, Caffery opting to live with a young Spaniard with whom he opened a shop selling wicker and wrought iron furniture. Herbert attributes the final break in their friendship to a pantomime organized by the expatriate community to raise money for Anglo-American charities. Herbert, who had temporarily in his youth been an actor and nightclub singer in Berlin, was drafted to play the part of a pantomime dame first in *Cinderella* and, the following year, dragged up again as an aged dame in *Beauty and the Beast*.

> Neither of these roles are particularly becoming and I made myself as hideous as possible. The Spaniard, though admitting my performances were good, lost no opportunity of saying how monstrously ugly I was. Jamie's affection for me seemed to wane from that moment. It was sad that our friendship was broken up after twelve years, but sadder still that the break was caused by my playing the part of a female impersonator in aid of charity.

Caffery and the Spanish boy finally left together for Spain where they opened an antique shop. They were not together long, since the Spaniard was flighty and improbably, in the end, married a middle-aged Englishwoman who lived in Torremolinos. Caffery himself became a landscape gardener and took seriously to drink.

Herbert continued to take pleasure in Tangier society which centred mostly around entertainments supplied by the various Legations. These were formal occasions, each Legation determined to maintain a high level of diplomatic grandeur. There were parties given by the diplomatic functionaries, personally, in their own houses, and it was unusual for an evening to pass for *le tout Tanger* without cocktails, a dinner, an official reception, or a ball. Before Independence in 1956,

> it seemed that Tangier never slept: hours were late; cocktail parties started at 7.30 or 8 and were followed by dinners, dances and receptions. Still later the night life started; there were expensive, smart clubs such as the Emsallah Gardens where you danced in the open air to the smell of orange blossom from the surrounding trees; hot dark bars where a piano tinkled drearily away till dawn; cabarets of every description, some showing belly dancers, some of the latest French, English or American torch-singers, some Spanish dancers, and others female impersonators.

Among the favourite diversions of Tangier society was a nightcap at the Bar Safari, described by David Woolman as

> a late place made tops both by the easy personalities of its Danish managers, Mogens Andersen and Guy Muller, and by the polished quality of their dance combo. 'Andy' played a rippling piano, Guy added guitar accompaniment and sang such romantic oldies as 'Je suis seul ce soir', 'Anime e Cuore', and 'You're the One Rose That's Left in my Heart', in a husky voice, while Hugh Levy of London played a sweet clarinet and Juice Wilson, a sad-eyed black from the American Midwest, chipped in with a honeyed saxophone almost as big as he was. The Safari was the coolest night club that Tangier, or for that matter, Morocco, ever had.

Before going to bed at about 4 a.m., says David Herbert, 'we would go the Mar Chica, a little Spanish bar near the port, with sawdust on the floor and wobbly wooden tables and chairs. Here you found *flamenco* dancers and singers performing to an upright piano, a violin, a guitar and the clicking of castanets. Apart from the professionals employed there, individuals would get up impromptu and perform. Some were remarkable and truly inspired, others embarrassingly bad.'

David Herbert's habit of descending on the Mar Chica Bar with visitors from the *beau monde* did not entirely please some of the bar's *habitués*, including the expatriate writer Rupert Croft-Cooke who, in *The Caves of Hercules*, declared that Herbert had grossly idealized the place, investing it with a louche glamour that it never possessed. Herbert, in *Second Son*, had described some of the bar's denizens in romantic terms, focusing on Carmella, a 'middle-aged Spanish gipsy with a flat, slavic face' who 'possessed a certain charm, and, on occasions, when she had not drunk too much brandy, sang beautifully. She had been a star in her day but was now reduced to singing in this sordid bar, or anywhere she could find employment. Most of the time she was a cheap whore.' Lustrous amid this shoddy glamour was Louis, the gypsy dancer.

Slim and elegant, with a finely drawn face and smouldering amber eyes, he danced superbly and could have gone much further and become a star if he had not been such a feckless creature. Gipsy-like, he married when he was seventeen and produced a horde of children – eight by the time he was twenty-seven. His bedraggled skeleton of a wife was pathetic and wrung one's heart so that whenever she appeared at the Mar Chica, which was rarely, pesetas, francs, pounds and dollar notes piled up on the plate which Louis handed round to the customers.

Carmella, too, who smelt so badly, was regularly said to be dying and without funds for a funeral. The plate was passed round the customers again.

Croft-Crooke snorts disgustedly as he pulls aside this spangled literary veil: the Mar Chica was 'a dockside pothouse chiefly frequented by young Spaniards, became for a time a hang-out for Moorish dockworkers and such, till the death of the dumpy little Malagueña who stank and danced and begged there on evenings when she was not too drunk to mount the stage'. It closed in the 1960s, 'a loss not to tourists, who rarely found it, but to residents who enjoyed its squalid atmosphere and dreggy dimness, its thumping handclaps and strummed guitars and its young Spaniards hoping to be treated to beer or cheap brandy or given a few pesetas to provide a night's entertainment'. Croft-Cooke regarded it as his personal haunt which he visited nightly. He claimed not to resent

David Herbert's 'using it as a picturesque piece of local colour to which to take visitors slumming, though I remember Diana Cooper acutely embarrassed when he brought her there'; but he did thoroughly resent the intrusion of 'Paul Bowles importing such characters as Allen Ginsberg, Gregory Corso and Tennessee Williams to try to pretend there was something of Greenwich Village about it'. Croft-Cooke preferred to keep it a slum rather than aggrandize it by social or literary associations: he disputed Herbert's kindly assertion that Carmella sang beautifully and had been a star in her day: 'neither of which statements even remotely resembles the truth' and Louis (whom cut down to size, he prefers to call Luis) had an 'insignificant waist and broad shoulders'. But he could 'forgive David Herbert because of one remark he made in my hearing in the Bar la Mar Chica. "Tell me," said a young woman who was learning about the sexual complications of Tangier. "Which is this one who has just come in? Jack or Jill?" "That, Oh *that's* just the pail of water," said David and I forgot his calling clumsy Spanish peasants by the proud name of gypsies.'

The Bar la Mar Chica was a low-class dive, but others had more pretensions to class and style. Dean's Bar became a legend far beyond Tangier. Dean, the owner, is a figure more of myth than known, established fact. He may have told one story to one customer, another to another, who went away convinced that they alone knew the truth. Croft-Cooke states, with a show of authority, that 'his mother had been a Ramsgate lodging-house-keeper and his father a West Indian passing through Kent'. David Herbert gives his origin at some length in *Second Son*, claiming that Dean's mother was the French wife of a Hastings businessman who, on a trip with her husband to Egypt, quickly discovered that that country 'could offer more subtle distractions than repeated visits to the Pyramids'. She gave birth in England to a very dark-skinned little boy, adopted by Mr Dean who forgave his wife and brought up the little bastard as his own with his three legitimate sons. Romantically, Herbert goes on to state that after Mr Dean's death 'Mrs Dean returned to France taking her beloved black child with her. She set up house with her old friend, Cléo de Mérode, the last of the great courtesans, which must have afforded quite a contrast to Hastings.'

Dean, according to this story, had been educated at Westminster School, 'but his outlook on life seemed to owe more to the later days in France'. His career after Westminster School (where he was said to have acquired 'a wonderful English voice') was a matter of some interest to the likes of Gerald Hamilton who delightedly declared him to be 'the wickedest man I ever met' and to Robin Maugham who was perfectly certain that Dean's surname was Kimfull and that he had been a gigolo in London before the First World War. William Burroughs believed Dean's first name to be Joseph. None of this mattered much, since Dean was not the only resident of Tangier who preferred, or even encouraged, speculation about his past perhaps in order to obfuscate, beyond any hope of the truth being discovered, the banal reality.

Dean, in the 1930s, was head barman at the El Minzah Hotel. 'There wasn't a celebrity in the world whom he didn't know or to whom he hadn't served a drink during his wandering career as a barman: Paris, New York, Monte Carlo, Berlin and Cairo were a few of the places where he had held sway,' remarked David Herbert. 'His manners were perfect and, behind the bar, Dean was King, so you treated him accordingly.' When Dean established his own small bar opposite the British Legation, just down the street from the El Minzah Hotel, he became one of the tourist attractions of the city. The journalist Michael Davidson, in his autobiography, remarked that in the years following the Second World War 'the name of Tangier has come to denote merely the environs of Dean's Bar; and a silent blackball from Dean – indicated from behind his well-bred bar by a subtle movement of those haughty brows, perhaps a flutter of the dark, unfathomable eyes – can seem socially far more damaging than being turned down for the Royal Enclosure.'

'Dean's', wrote David Woolman, 'became a refuge, a consolation and a gossip shop for Tangier's socially weary and their visiting friends.' Robin Maugham described the bar as a focal point for 'the highly coloured collection of the fake and the genuine, the cruel and the kind, which forms the international society of Tangier'. The American journalist Robert Ruark took one look round the premises and wrote, for the benefit of his readers, that the denizens of Dean's were 'smugglers, fugitives from justice and people who were being paid by other people to stay out of England'. His view of Tangier, from the bar of Dean's, was that Sodom, by comparison, 'was a church picnic, and Gomorrah a convention of Girl Scouts'. Out there in the streets and soccos of Tangier were more 'thieves, black marketeers, spies, thugs, phonies, beach combers, expatriates, degenerates, characters, operators, bandits, bums, tramps, politicians and charlatans' than he'd ever had the pleasure to shake a stick at in any other misbegotten part of the world. 'In his bar,' wrote Rupert Croft-Cooke, 'I met almost as many persons of repute (though rather less attractive ones) than I did in the Bar la Mar Chica, from the Dame of Sark to Cecil Beaton, from Helena Rubinstein to Ian Fleming.' He cites also Cyril Connolly, John Gielgud ('who hated Tangier and apart from this brief call scarcely left the Minzah Hotel during his stay'), and T.S. Eliot as having visited the place. Dean himself, who took an instant dislike to William Burroughs when he appeared at the bar, was 'a mean and grasping man', according to Rupert Croft-Cooke who was, in any case, ornery about most people. Dean's conversation, said Croft-Cooke,

> was repetitive and impressed only the newest arrivals among tourists, while it is almost safe to make the assertion that he never did a kind act for anyone. Few who frequented his bar during their holidays in Tangier failed to receive a letter from Dean on their return to Europe explaining that he had to go into hospital immediately and had no one else to turn to for the few pounds he needed in order to save his life.

Yet such is the reputation, however earned, that Dean of Dean's Bar, the mystery man, the reputed wit with his twenty jokes learned by heart, the dark-skinned elderly host who never lost his Home Counties lower-class voice, was known throughout the Mediterranean, and his funeral was attended by nearly a hundred people. I think it was that believers in Tangier as an exotic city felt there ought to be an exotic bar-owner in it, and picked on this coloured chatterer of dubious origins to fill the role.

Nevertheless, despite his misanthropy, Croft-Cooke

liked Dean. I listened to his malicious chatter and name-dropping and went into his little dive with pleasure to hear his corniest jokes . . . Dean's Bar stood, as it were, midway from the Mountain with its cliques and genteel tribalism, to the Bar la Mar Chica with its dockside slumming and picturesque 'low life'. Between them came the more bourgeois resorts, the Parade Bar, Madame Porte's café, and the various little upstart bars which Englishmen, chiefly in pairs, opened up to earn a living by bringing together their fellow countrymen and the young Moors who had replaced the Spaniards as entertainers for tourists.

Madame Porte's Salon de Thé was a comfortable, convenient resort in the modern town for the prosperous bourgeoisie, the Tangier equivalent of Fuller's or Gunther's for afternoon tea and pastries or a post-prandial ice-cream. It was a popular centre of gossip for middle-class ladies of the city, although it was pretty well known that Madame Porte and her husband were Fascist sympathizers and, indeed, were to be blacklisted as such by the British authorities in Tangier. This may have discomposed some British expatriates who boycotted the place on patriotic principle, but there were enough Italians, Spanish, some French, several Germans, and even a few British who favoured appeasement, to maintain Madame Porte's profits. That she cared about profit was indisputable – she was never known to move from the cash desk near the entrance to her establishment. Porte's was an enduring social landmark.

The expatriate community also greatly favoured the Parade Bar, which was run by two Americans, Jay Haselwood and Bill Chase, and a White Russian woman, Ira Belline, whose family had fled the Russian Revolution and settled in Paris. A reputed niece of Stravinsky, Ira Belline had worked to help support her father, mother and semi-invalid brother in Paris from the age of eleven and in the 1930s she had succeeded, initially through the Diaghilev Ballet, in becoming a leading theatre costume designer. During the war, the family – possessing no passports, only identity cards issued by the deposed French government – went into hiding at a property owned by the Countess Pastré near Marseille where, after the Allied invasion of Europe, Ira joined the American Red Cross, working in a canteen where she met Haselwood and Chase. Together, they decided to open a small business in North Africa and happened to land in Casablanca.

It is at this point that their story enters the realms of apparent fantasy. According to David Herbert, who became a close friend of Ira Belline, the trio moved from Casablanca to Rabat without much idea what to do with themselves. Their small capital was running short, Morocco was more expensive than they had bargained for, and they were depressed. It was a little while before they noticed a large, expensive chauffeur-driven car cruising backwards and forwards past the café where they were sitting reviewing their desperate situation. The car stopped, and from the back seat emerged a remarkable figure – a woman of a certain age, fair-haired, wearing a pair of large dark glasses, with a white and yellow cockatoo perched on her shoulder. Around her feet, tumbling and yapping, was a pack of a dozen or more dogs, some large but mostly small and distressingly hairless. The woman approached them directly. She said: 'I hope you will excuse me, but I have come to tell you that I consider you the three most beautiful human beings I have ever seen. Will you come to dinner? It is now twelve noon. I will give you until seven o'clock to reflect. If you decide to accept my invitation, meet me at the bar of the Tour Hassan Hotel.' Thereupon she returned to her car, piled herself high with her dogs, and departed as abruptly as she had arrived.

The adventure was too good to miss. After some debate – was she mad? was she drunk? was she an hallucination? – they decided to put in an appearance at the hotel, the grandest and most expensive in Rabat. From the entrance hall they could hear the frenzied yapping of the Chinese hairless dogs. In the bar, flanked by two Afghan hounds and with the cockatoo still on her shoulder, sat their woman of mystery. She was evidently a few drinks ahead of them already, since they had chosen to arrive half an hour later than the appointed time. David Herbert recounts the conversation as it was related to him by Ira Belline: 'So you've come. I thought you would. Have a drink, have two drinks – I've had four. Now tell me your names – Ira, Jay and Bill – that's fine. What are you doing here? Nothing – I see. No money, from the looks of you. That's a pity if you want to stay in Morocco. You want to start a restaurant in Tangier, do you? Plenty of room for another restaurant there. Incidentally, I have a large house just outside the town. You can stay there if you like while looking for suitable premises.' And so it was fixed.

Their benefactor, their improbable fairy godmother, was Phyllis, Comtesse de la Faille, who, true to her decisive adoption of these three adventurers, financed the rental of a suitable property in Tangier, its conversion as a bar and restaurant, its decoration and complete furnishing. The Parade, says David Woolman, 'immediately challenged Dean's as the paramount bar and social centre in Tangier, due entirely to the popularity of its three founders.' He describes Haselwood, a Kentucky man, as 'tall, handsome and wittily glib'. Chase, a New Yorker, 'was more suave and his management of the kitchen made the Parade one of the best places to dine in all northern Morocco. Belline's White Russian background and her claim to be Igor Stravinsky's favourite niece gave her a guaranteed cachet. For a time, the Parade and its owners became, like Dean's, internationally famous.'

In *Answered Prayers*, Truman Capote conjured up the Parade under Haselwood's management as 'a swanky little joint operated by a kind and gangling Georgia [sic] guy who had made a moderate fortune from dispensing proper martinis and jumbo burgers to homesick Americans: he also, for the favoured of his foreign clientele, served up the asses of Arab lads and lassies – without charge of course, just a courtesy of the house.' Three such strong characters were not likely to survive together for long. The bar flourished during the immediate post-war years until the partners had a falling-out. First Ira Belline left, in dispute with Chase about the running of the business. Shortly after Chase left, edged out because, says Herbert, 'Phyllis, who was the virtual owner, fell in love with Jay. She ignored Bill and in any argument sided against him.' The restaurant closed and Haselwood 'became gigolo to the Countess. As Jay had a marked preference for boys, Charles de la Faille was not unduly disturbed. He considered his wife in perfectly good hands.' The Parade Bar transferred to new premises in the Rue des Vignes, run by Haselwood until he died in 1965 at the age of forty-eight, probably of drink. In his day, says Herbert, 'Jay was a great showman and, thanks to his magnetic personality, the Parade Bar in Tangier was as well known a name as the Ritz Bar is in Paris.' After Haselwood's death, it was taken over by a French woman, Lily Wickman, who ran it until she died in 1980, after which it closed.

Ira Belline, after quitting the Parade, opened a flower shop which was not successful. 'For some reason, probably climatic,' wrote David Herbert in his autobiography, 'the flowers died almost immediately, so that her show-window was filled with drooping roses, tulips, daffodils, delphiniums, lupins and canterbury bells.' These flowers, to satisfy the European tastes of diplomatic wives who ardently desired Constance Spry-type arrangements, had been flown in specially from Holland and Belgium. Besides the native Moroccan blooms, they looked dispirited and tired. 'Ira was in despair and one day Cecil and I, trying to help her, made a splendid display of locally-grown flowers. The result was exquisite but the passers-by thought otherwise. "The impertinence of that woman," they said, "selling wild flowers in a shop!" ' Even the delicate genius of Beaton was defeated on this occasion. Ira Belline resorted to selling antiques in a shop owned by Jacques Robert, a Swiss, who also sold Moroccan jewellery, caftans, leather goods and glass designed to appeal to the Arab taste.

Things went well for a while, and Ira was able to afford to bring her father and brother from France to Tangier. The strain of coping with a semi-invalid and an autocratic father wore down even Ira's considerable strength and force of character. 'Father was a tall handsome man with a flowing white beard. A retired Admiral from Czarist days, he was autocratic and never satisfied with what was done for him. He treated Ira like a child. I remember,' remarks David Herbert, 'bringing her home after dinner – at about 10.30 – and as we opened the door a deep voice bawled at us down the stairs in furious Russian. "What is he saying, Ira?" "Whore, where have you been?" she replied.'

When Robert decided to sell the shop, Ira was again out of work until Herbert had an inspiration: she should become companion-housekeeper to Barbara Hutton who needed help to run her house in the Casbah. Her employment there lasted several years before chronic asthma obliged Ira to retire to Marrakesh to a house bought for her by Barbara Hutton where she settled with her brother to run the property as a commercial farm selling olives, oranges and vegetables. Here, in the Palmeraie at Marrakesh, Ira Belline began again to paint and exhibit her pictures.

David Herbert had met Barbara Huttton, the Woolworth heiress, several times in the years before she acquired a palace in Tangier. 'I have known Barbara Hutton', he wrote in his autobiography, 'since she was a plump, pretty, fresh New York debutante . . . Generous, kind and spoilt, she is the epitome of a "poor little rich girl". As a rule she is unhappy, searching desperately for what seems unobtainable. On the rare occasions when she is happy, no one can be more delightful.' In the summer of 1946, at the age of thirty-eight, she had just given her London mansion, Winfield House, as a gift to the United States government for use as the official residence of the American ambassador to the Court of St James. Having disposed of this substantial property, she thereupon heard that Maxwell Blake, the US Minister to Tangier, wished to sell his residence in the city. Within a few weeks she had installed herself at the El Minzah Hotel, took a fast and almost perfunctory tour of Blake's property, and offered one hundred thousand dollars for its purchase. This was double the fifty thousand dollars that Blake had been offered by Generalissimo Franco who had taken considerable trouble to have the property surveyed and appraised by experts. Blake instantly and gratefully closed with Hutton, the necessary paperwork was rapidly completed, and she was confirmed as mistress of the palace of Sidi Hosni.

Blake had spent a decade beautifying the palace, importing the finest craftsmen in stone and wood from Fez to decorate the rambling house in traditional Moorish style, filling the rooms with rare and exquisite furniture, materials and *objets d'art* from the Orient, lavishing a devoted love, refined taste and considerable amounts of money on aggrandizing the property which originally had consisted of seven houses surrounding a large central structure of seven rooms. The history of the palace had been varied: at first it had served as a prison for Moroccan debtors, then became a café before it was acquired in 1870 by a local Muslim holy man, Sidi Hosni, whose tomb stood nearby. In 1925, the family of Sidi Hosni had sold the house to Walter B. Harris, the celebrated correspondent for *The Times*, who began its transformation by connecting the seven houses one to the other and incorporating them with the central, inner, seven-roomed core of the property. Harris died before completing his grand design which Blake took over and, after much labour, triumphantly finished. The result was an architectural and decorative work of art, sensitively attuned to the highest traditions of Moroccan architecture and decorative taste.

The blank whitewashed walls of the building rose high above the steep and narrow rue Ben Raisul in the Casbah, shutting out much of the noise from the street. Inside, the house was a bewildering maze of corridors, courtyards, rooms and terraces on any number of levels, here and there lit by the sun falling through fretted stone, precisely cut in arabesques and geometric Islamic designs. Blake and his artisans had worked a miracle of architectural fantasy, which Hutton bedecked with furniture flown in from store in Britain and America, with new acquisitions from all over the world, with authentic Moroccan antiques acquired principally from Jacques Robert's shop, and special commissions that are described in detail by her biographer, C. David Heymann:

For the main sitting room, Murano Glassware near Venice was commissioned to design a chandelier that came down massively in a cascade of milky white and pastel swans' necks. The same firm designed Barbara's Moroccan table setting. The set contained twenty blue-and-silver pieces per setting, and there were a hundred settings. James R.W. Thompson, the American-born founder of the Thai Silk Company in Bangkok, produced rolls of shimmering silk for the palace, complementing and enhancing the effect of the ornamental stone carving, the lattice-work tiles, the painted and carved panels of hard and soft woods. In every room and bath Barbara installed a signed gold mantel clock from Van Cleef & Arpels. There were thirty such clocks at Sidi Hosni, priced at $10,000 apiece. And there was an art collection that included works by Fragonard, Braque, Manet, Kandinsky, Klee, Dali, El Greco, Grandma Moses and Hassan el Glaoui, the son of the Pasha of Marrakesh.

The *pièce de résistance* was the 'Millon Dollar Tapestry' she acquired from the Maharajah of Tripura – a fifteenth-century Indian wall-hanging tied with gold threads and encrusted with jewels. It was complemented by a collection of matching floor cushions, dozens of them, embroidered with diamonds, pearls, emeralds and rubies.

It was in this setting, a Thousand and One Nights fantasy, that Barbara held court as a princess of the city. Truman Capote has described her as 'a dime-store maharani . . . the Ma Barker [sic] of Bab's bunch, to quote Jay Haselwood. Miss Hutton, with an entourage of temporary husbands, momentary lovers and others of unspecified (if any) occupation, usually reigned in her Moroccan mansion a month or so each year.' According to C. David Heymann, her most powerful ally in Tangier was the local delegate of the Moroccan Ministry of Tourism, Mohammed Omar Hajoui, who recognized her crucial importance to the economy of Tangier. Barbara Hutton was his most glittering, most powerful, most mag-netic propaganda tool in his campaign to attract tourists to the city. He introduced her to Morocco's leading families, to the country's aristocrats and political leaders, and smoothed her progress to the least detail. No impediment was put in the way of her full enjoy-ment of the city. The arches of the Medina and Casbah were too narrow to permit passage of the Rolls-Royces she had imported from England? No matter. The problem was of the simplest – a city ordinance was promulgated requiring all new arches in Tangier to be of a width sufficient to permit the passage of cars as wide as a Rolls. Those arches that did not conform to this specification were of course torn down and reconstructed in the approved width. Discreetly, Barbara Hutton paid for such notable services: Hajoui provided her, on her request, with a list of charities in Tangier and, annually, she distributed cheques to these philanthropic organiza-tions in varying amounts from a thousand to fifty thousand dollars apiece.

Perhaps her most obvious gesture towards improving the lives of the many poverty-stricken Tanjawis and Riffians who had flocked to Tangier in 1945 to seek relief from the famine that had struck the surrounding mountains was the establishment of a soup kitchen which fed large numbers of tribesmen every day. Many of them lived in the most appalling, squalid conditions in the section of Tangier called Beni Makada which was transformed into a *bidonville*, a sprawling camp where the inhabitants foraged desperately at the lowest level of living. Barbara Hutton described, in letters to friends, 'whole families that cook, eat and sleep in wooden packing crates strewn by the sides of roads' and how others lived 'in tiny hovels without plumbing or cooking facilities, the ceilings so perilously low they have to crawl to get from room to room'. The Medina itself was no less disturbing to her. 'So much heat, so many piled-up colours, such congestion'. As well as food, she regularly distributed gifts of clothing and toys to the poorest children.

Hajoui ardently desired and required that his most prestigious client should shine bright as an ornament of the city. He eagerly assisted her to compile guest lists for her parties, suggesting invitations to prominent Moroccans and encouraging lavish display by arranging her catering and employing suitable entertainers. 'Her personal favourites were the belly dancers, many of whom worked in the local night clubs' (one hesitates to think that Carmella or Louis from the Bar la Mar Chica were regularly summoned to Sidi Hosni for the delight of Hutton's guests) 'and the picturesque "Blue People", descendants of the nomadic Berbers who, wearing their distinctive blue robes, put on exuberant singing and dancing exhibitions.' Hajoui, interviewed, joyously declared: 'Every tourist to Tangier wanted an invitation to one of her parties. There was a whole black-market operation, lots of invitation scalpers. If people couldn't get an invitation, they wanted at least to see her palace. It was one of the main tourist attractions – the house with the sentry box in front and the American flag flying overhead. The local guides included it on their itinerary: "And this is Sidi Hosni, the palace of her Serene Highness Barbara Hutton, the Queen of the Medina!" '

Hajoui expanded happily on this theme to C. David Heymann:

Her parties attracted the biggest names: Charlie and Oona, Greta and Cecil, Ari and Maria. Since she was always marrying and divorcing, the engraved invitations read: 'Mrs Barbara Woolworth Hutton requests the pleasure of your company . . .' When the parties were to be held on the roof, there was always a notation in the bottom right-hand corner of the invitation: 'In Case of Wind, Your Hostess Requests You To Indulge Her By Coming Another Night.' Two hundred guests on the average would be invited to the larger parties, and a thousand would come. People brought their friends, which is customary in Morocco. Others came to watch. They would crowd the streets and climb the neighbouring rooftops for a better view. It reached the point where the descendants of Ali Baba were gouging precious stones out of the tapestries and harem cushions. She had to hire discreetly armed plainclothesmen to patrol the rooms during her parties. And when that became too much of a bother she began holding them outside Sidi Hosni – behind the walled gardens of Guitta's Restaurant and at the Parade Café or in large tents at the Caves of Hercules, the limestone quarries several miles outside Tangier.

Truman Capote's description of a Hutton party was published in *Answered Prayers*:

A seven-foot Senegalese in a crimson turban and a white jellaba opened iron gates; one entered a garden where Judas trees blossomed in lantern light and the mesmeric scent of tuberoses embroidered the air. We passed into a room palely alive with light filtered through ivory filigree screens. Brocaded banquettes, piled with brocaded pillows of a silken lemon and silver and scarlet luxury, lined the walls. And there were beautiful brass tables shiny with candles and sweating champagne buckets; the floors, thick with overlapping layers of rugs from the weavers of Fez and Marrakesh, were like strange lakes of ancient, intricate colour.

The guests were few and all subdued, as though waiting for the hostess to retire before tossing themselves into an exuberant freedom – the repression attendant upon courtiers waiting for the royals to recede.

The hostess, wearing a green sari and a chain of dark emeralds, reclined among the cushions. Her eyes had the vacancy often observed in persons long imprisoned and, like her emeralds, a mineralized remoteness . . . And yet, in a touching, shrunken way she was rather pretty – a prettiness marred by her seeming to be precariously balanced on the edge of pain. I remembered reading in some Sunday supplement that as a young woman she had been plump, a wallflower butterball, and that, at the suggestion of a diet faddist, she had swallowed a tapeworm or two; and now one wondered, because of the starved starkness, her feathery flimsiness, if those worms were not still gross tenants who accounted for half her present weight.

The heiress sighed into the banquette's goose-stuffed brocades . . . and tapped curving, slavishly lacquered apricot nails against a champagne glass, a signal for the Senegalese servant to lift her, lift her away up blue-tiled stairs to firelit chambers where Morpheus, always a mischief-maker to the frantic, the insulted, but especially to the rich and powerful, joyfully awaited a game of hide and seek.

In the midst of this fantasy which Hutton played out as a Princess of Tangier, it is pleasing to relate a little domestic anecdote concerning her nocturnal habits. As Capote colourfully suggests, Hutton was an insomniac and, city gossip has it, hypothermic, a condition that was not relieved to her satisfaction by hot-water bottles. She is said to have discovered that a local doctor's wife, Helen Little, happened to be hyperthermic – more than usually warm to the touch. Mrs Little was regularly summoned to Sidi Hosni to warm Hutton's bed. Helen, the human hot-water bottle, hopped in and radiated warmth between the sheets when Hutton, shivering, hopped out. One imagines they could have kept up this performance all night. For her trouble, Mrs Little was apparently showered with mink coats (surely an unlikely gift for a human radiator) and jewels.

One of Barbara Hutton's most spectacular parties was held in 1961, attended by David Herbert and Cecil Beaton. By this time, David Herbert had become Hutton's social arbiter, deeply in collusion with her about the style of her parties and – crucially – about who should be invited. In his diary, shortly after arrival in Tangier, Beaton noted: 'At once, we're immersed in local scandals and gossip . . . I hear about the rival social factions among the expatriates who are carrying war to the stiletto heel – the leading social figure is being merciless that any members of the opposite camp shall be present at the big Ball.' This is a discreet reference to the long-standing, ever-simmering dispute between David Herbert ('the leading social figure') and David Edge, a constantly waged feud that was a source of endless discussion among all those Tangerinos who were either peripherally caught up in the long campaign or wisely steered clear of it altogether. It was not possible to be friends with both Herbert and Edge – one had to make a clear choice between them, since no one who accepted an invitation to Edge's house would ever be invited to Herbert's. In the second volume of his autobiography, *Engaging Eccentrics*, David Herbert at last comes clean about his long standing disrespect for David Edge who, for a start, is described as 'flamboyant, witty, crooked and entertaining'. Possessed of 'great flair', he was 'a compulsive liar. Hardly a word of truth passed his lips. Everything was in his imagination. His palace in Luxor, his pavilion near Beirut, and several other castles in Spain were non-existent. As he got older, he became more exotic wearing only caftans day and night, and always bedecking himself with second-rate jewellery.'

Edge had been a shadowy ('shady' says Herbert) figure in the art world of Europe and the United States, and had pretensions to being a member of international 'café society' – ambitions which, according to Herbert, were more protested than real: 'he never quite made the grade . . . The nearest approach to it came whilst he lived in a palazzo in Venice.' Herbert adds, sniffily, that café society will go anywhere for a party 'and David Edge gave parties. Eventually, he left Venice under something of a cloud and returned to London.' Edge and Herbert had never met until the former turned up in Tangier 'and bought a tumbledown palace in the Casbah. The house was refurbished and filled to overflowing with *objects d'art* – some good, some bad, some fake, but flamboyant like himself.' The palace's central patio had been roofed over, the only illumination coming from a small skylight in the roof. Through the gloom, one could discern 'objects of every description – tables, chairs, pictures, carpets on the walls, Chinese pots, plates, gongs and potted palms. In an alcove stood his canopied bed with hangings of tarnished gold and a jewel-encrusted bedspread. Most of these objects were covered with a layer of dust. The effect was theatrical, the atmosphere sinister.'

Edge's origins, in Herbert's short account, were dim though not without surprising incident and improbable, to the point of fantasy, figures: 'I believe he started life studying to be a singer and eventually sang small parts in opera. He is supposed to have been "picked up" by the Bishop of Hungary [sic], who tried to get him a job at La Scala, Milan. On account of this, so the story goes, the Bishop was defrocked and settled down with David Edge in the English countryside. After the death of the Bishop, David inherited some money, and as the years passed he became a well-known figure in certain quarters of the art world.' This sounds about par for the course so far as an investigation into the past of a mysterious Tangier resident is concerned.

In Edge's favour, Herbert admits that 'he was a good raconteur and could hold your attention for hours.' But, like most of his stories, he was exaggerated – his speech and gestures were fanciful, and at any moment he was quite liable to become 'an impossible vulgarian, losing his temper and using the filthiest language'. Superficially, he pretended to 'great opulence and unending resources. In fact, he never knew where the next penny was coming from, and the last year of his life he was kept by a young Spaniard, Adolfo de Velasco, whom he had befriended and started in the antiques business.' In the end, compassion got the better of contempt and David Herbert, though he had resolved never to let Edge across his doorstep, relented and acceded to Edge's longing to see his house. 'He was lonely and sad . . . so I swallowed my pride and invited him to dinner. I asked the few friends he had left and one or two new acquaintances. The dinner turned out to be a success as he was on his best behaviour, and the evening passed pleasantly.' Three weeks later, Edge was dead.

In 1961, however, Edge and his partisans were definitely on Herbert's black list. 'Nobody that has ever been present at Mr. David Edge's house', confided Beaton to his diary, 'will be invited [to Barbara Hutton's Ball] – this is seen to by his rival David Herbert.' Even Helena Rubinstein, who had incautiously visited Edge, was blackballed for her audacity. David Herbert 'had heard she had been to Edge's – and in fact saw her riding past the Café de Paris in his Rolls-Royce'. Left to herself, Hutton would have welcomed the multitudes: 'If only my house were as big as my heart I would ask the whole world,' she had been heard to declare. But Lloyd's of London refused to insure the safety of her roof if more than one hundred and seventy guests were invited. People had travelled long distances in the hope of gatecrashing the spectacular event, but a rigorous admissions policy, a ruthless checking of invitation cards, was to be strictly enforced.

There were some little difficulties beforehand: Beaton, in his diary, records that the build-up to the Ball excited the greatest interest – 'jealousy and the worst possible human instincts were aroused.' Then, too, Barbara Hutton's 'condition' was occasioning some concern among her friends. 'That poor girl has a great problem. It seems she has been fighting for years to stop drinking but she seems to think it is hereditary . . . Barbara had said to David "if I knew what it was that made me take that first drink then I'd know" . . . Would she appear at the Ball at all? Or if so, would she be drunk and disorderly? She had been drinking for a week now without stopping, without more than a few hours sleep, with nothing but a plate of mushroom soup for weeks. She had not emerged from her house until a few days ago when she had rushed off to the Polo field where she had kissed everyone indiscriminately in an excess of zeal. Mrs Nairne, the British Consul's wife, had taken her for a walk and told her quite straight that she was a disgrace, that she must pull herself together. Barbara cried hysterically and kept saying "Christ died for me." '

The Ball was a disappointment to Beaton who picked critically at the guests, the décor, the band and the general atmosphere that weighed upon him oppressively, heavy and listless. The guests had been asked for 10.30.

By eleven thirty a hundred missorted people of all ages wandered aimlessly from room to room wondering when the hostess would appear to greet them. The house is almost too oriental in its excess of lace work, tiles, painted and carved booths, filled with velvet cushions. David had arranged a great number of flowers but somehow there was nothing to surprise or delight and quite a lot of the more distinguished older guests sat around drinking and making veiled comments of disapproval. Trapped by consuls' wives or ex-ambassadors I revolted – this was not what I'd come to Tangier for. I sought out Ira Belline . . . [who] conducted me to the roof terraces and these were splendidly transformed for the night. In brilliantly arranged shafts of light there were scarlet and orange tents piled with cushions from which Barbara would receive. The floors lined with orange and magenta semi-circular cushions. Arabic designs in brilliant coloured stuffs everywhere and obelisks, balls and architectural figures of flowers were really very exotic in magnolias, zinnias and sunflowers. The effect was made more remarkable by the night scene of Tangier's inhabitants peering from the neighbouring white houses – and in the distance the silhouette of the old town.

Suddenly the hostess was on view. She sat brilliantly illuminated in a scarlet-flame (gladioli-coloured) tent strongly lit with apricot and a greenish light. The first sight was enough to give one a little frisson for the glitter was so unexpected. The scene represented a little Turkish fatima entertaining a succession of admirers. The glittering actress was smiling in the most direct and simple terms to convey to the admirers her pleasure at receiving these dignitaries. But the scene was real, the performance given only for tonight. The theatre was real. The real emeralds as big as prunes were embedded in a great fillet of real diamonds. The exquisite pearls at her neck had an unholy brilliance . . . her dress was heavily embroidered in diamonds. It was a little Byzantine empress-doll. But she was no mere doll, for the glittering came from an act which was part of the performance of her life that she was playing in the role of gracious hostess.

Her gestures of greeting and affection, her smiles, her graceful weaving of the head, the look of surprise or delight, these were all played in the grand manner, an arm extended for the hand to be kissed, a graceful turn of the head to welcome a Moroccan big wig, a wide open-armed welcome to an old friend. Head thrown back with lowered lids and a moue of the mouth. Every sort of smile and coquetry. David was amazed. 'Oh, isn't she superb! I do give her full marks. Her courage! When you know what an effort she has made. She's really great. Look what marvellous manners.'

I stood by, as did quite a number of spectators, as if she was in reality playing a scene on the stage. She seemed quite oblivious of the stares – or of the flashlights that registered her every mood. In her gladioli tent with the brass tray at hand for the champagne glass, she received the most important Tangerinos until suddenly she decided to leave her igloo to go to a higher roof to watch some local dancing. Her progress across the floor, supported by boy friends, was precarious and painful . . . I would have liked the opportunity to talk to her during the evening and to find out if she made any sense whatsoever, but she was too far gone in euphoria to be able to articulate except by pantomime, and to do spasmodic little dances à la Bali with neck shaking from side to side and a wiggle of her shoulders . . . As the evening progressed she overplayed her role. She was in need of a director to tell her that she was forcing her effects too much.

Nonetheless I was fascinated and beguiled by her beauty. The eyes are lustrous, large and sad, the thick furry eyebrows save the face from mere prettiness, the nostrils are exquisitely chiselled. The contour of the neck and chin is a perfect oval – and even in profile the double chin has been corrected. This perfect oval face was seen at its best with the Helen of Troy hair do . . . yet she looked like someone who had been dead and who was now artificially brought to life to give some frenzied final performance. Any minute the curtain might come down for ever. Meanwhile the delicate little child's hand applauded, the exquisite little feet shod in the most exquisite of Cinderella's sandals were beating time ineffectually with the toes turned in.

Beaton had seen enough: 'Although intrigued by the house and beauty I came away much too early for those who were making a night of it, but an hour and a half too late for myself.' He had seen the mechanical Queen of the Medina, crowned with the fabulous emerald and diamond tiara that had once belonged to the Empress Catherine of Russia, and – to his puzzled discomfiture – had been disappointed. What he had seen was a performance, a perfectly rehearsed actress who displayed the most refined manners with a simulacrum of animation.

The unreality of Barbara Hutton's setting and appearance struck not only Beaton but also Paul Bowles who, when it was reported to him that she refused to have his novel, *The Sheltering Sky*, in her house on the ground that it was 'objectionable', commented:

This seemed an odd reaction from a woman who had been five times married . . . When I met her I understood. She liked everything around her to show an element of the unreal in it, and she took great pains to transform reality into a continuous fantasy which seemed to her sufficiently *féerique* to be taken seriously. One summer, when she gave a ball, she brought thirty Reguibat camel drivers with their racing camels from the Sahara, a good thousand miles distant, merely to form a *garde d'honneur* through which the guests would pass at the entrance to the house. The animals and men stayed encamped in the Palace Sidi Hosni for many days after the party, apparently in no hurry to get back to the desert.

David Herbert admits that Barbara Hutton's parties were variable:

> if she was in a good and happy mood, Barbara was a perfect hostess. If she was tired or sad or had had too much to drink beforehand, her parties could be a disaster. On these occasions she would sometimes not appear the whole evening. Naturally this made people nervous. If she had sent a message saying, 'I am not well, but do enjoy yourselves and have a lovely time', all would have been fine, but she didn't, so we waited around, talking to each other, looking every other minute at the door through which she would appear. The orchestra played on in a dreary fashion, and there was a little desultory dancing, but when finally we realized that Barbara would not join us, the party died and, little by little, people drifted home.

By nature, says Herbert, Barbara Hutton was

> clean, tidy, immaculately turned out and slightly disapproving. She also had perfect manners and great dignity. All these charming attributes disappeared when she drank. She slurred her words, the mascara ran in rivulets down her cheeks, the lower part of her face became smeared with lipstick, and she staggered about the room holding on to anybody or anything for support. During these alcoholic bouts, which sometimes lasted two weeks, she never slept, and her friends – or more aptly hangers on – were expected to remain with her round the clock. It was during these periods that she gave away so much of her jewellery to the surrounding vultures. Another of her habits was to telephone people all through the night, sometimes three or four calls to the same person. She made very little sense, but it was no good hanging

up because she would ring again, unaware that she had just talked to you. Sometimes these conversations would end in maudlin, loving words, at other times in furious abuse, but most frequently in floods of self-pitying tears. Poor Barbara.

Ben Dixon, like Herbert, was the recipient of late-night telephone calls: she would phone at three in the morning and again at nine. Dixon's successor, Hal Eastman, spoke to C. David Heymann about a series of calls he received from Barbara at all hours of the night. Her fixation was Coca-Cola:

> She didn't care for the taste of Moroccan Coca-Cola, and she wondered if I, as American Consul-General, couldn't import the stuff from the United States. I told her that we drank Moroccan Coke in the embassy, but that answer didn't suffice. Couldn't I at least get some Coca-Cola for her in Gibraltar? Well, I said, I wasn't aware that the Coke on Gibraltar was any tastier than Moroccan Coke. The sweetness of the beverage must have been a drug-related necessity, because she knew the exact proportions of syrup to liquid in every country's supply. Each bottling plant used its own formula and she wanted the company to produce a uniform product. None of this, however, made a great deal of sense at three or four in the morning.

But little enough made sense in Hutton's life in the early-to-mid-Sixties, though Tangier was a better place than most in which she could simultaneously indulge her fantasies to the limit and also live a relatively normal and quiet life. Barbara Hutton's life in Tangier was, largely, a retreat from a more pedestrian world: says C. David Heymann, 'Sidi Hosni was her magic palace, a refuge, a hideaway in which to evade the curiosity, the envy, the judgements of the outside world.' According to David Herbert, she had it easier in Tangier than elsewhere. In Tangier, 'the poor Moroccans had no feeling of resentment against her or her wealth.' On the contrary, ordinary Moroccans were accustomed to lavish display and expected it of those who had the means and position to put up a good show. She could walk anywhere, mingling with the crowds, sitting in cafés, like anyone else. She learned some Arabic, enough to be able to follow simple stories told by the professional storytellers in the Socco. She drank mint tea at Madame Porte's, sat on the beach listening to the sea, sometimes swimming. In 1960, she fell in love – again – this time with a young Englishman called Lloyd Franklin to whom she was introduced by David Herbert. Franklin, a former trumpeter in the Life Guards, had arrived in Tangier with an introduction to Herbert who found him 'tall, handsome, musical and charming. Before settling down he had decided to see something of the world and had worked his way through France and Spain to Morocco, playing his guitar and singing like a medieval troubadour.' Herbert fixed him up with a job singing at Dean's Bar and invited him often to dinner. Later in the evening he would be asked to sing, which he did 'in a pleasant voice, nothing special. But there was something so winning about him that he became very popular. People used to go to Dean's not to hear him play but to see him.'

In August 1960, Barbara arrived at Sidi Hosni and accepted an invitation to dine with David Herbert who also invited the American Ambassador, some local expatriates from the English and American community, and Franklin. Instantly, Barbara 'had eyes for no one else'. After dinner, Herbert asked Barbara to give Franklin a lift back to his hotel. 'She took him back to Sidi Hosni instead, and early the next morning the phone rang. It was Lloyd to thank me for inviting him, and also for introducing him to Barbara. Then Barbara got on the line. "Isn't Lloyd wonderful?" she said.' Herbert has nothing but good to say about Franklin, whose friendship with Barbara Hutton lasted three years. 'Lloyd loved her deeply, though he was many years younger than she, [there were twenty years between them] and, in spite of being plunged for the first time in his life into a world of great riches and luxury and self-indulgence, never became spoiled or greedy or blasé. He never forgot his old friends and Barbara, appreciating this, would always entertain them.' She naturally plied him with gifts – the list given by C. David Heymann includes 'guitars, trumpets, flamenco and voice lessons, a Rolls-Royce embossed with the insignia of the Life Guards, an MG, a dozen polo ponies, a stable to house the ponies on fifteen acres of real estate adjacent to the Royal Golf and Country Club, a complete wardrobe and a pair of Patek Philippe watches.'

In a lightly fictionalized book about life in Tangier, *Rowing*

Towards Eden, Ted Morgan (actually an anagram of Sanche de Gramont), who lived for a while in Tangier, tells a third-hand story about Barbara Hutton and Lloyd Franklin in which Barbara Hutton is 'Betty Blue . . . the detergent heiress'; Franklin is

> Alec Somerset, the impecunious horse guard with the beautiful manners. I heard the story from a taxi driver who was working for her as a chauffeur, bit of a crook but not a bad fellow. He went down every morning to get her mail and brought it back to her bedroom. Well, this one morning he heard these sounds, oh and ah and mmmm. The door was slightly ajar, and out of curiosity he looked in and saw Betty lying on her back with Alec Somerset down on her, platin' her with his tongue up her puss. She looked up and saw him and jumped up and covered herself and asked, 'What do you want?' 'I came to deliver the mail,' he said. 'Leave it there,' she said, and he went out. That same day she called him in and said, 'Did you see what was going on?' 'Oh yes, Princess,' he said. 'Did you know what it was?' 'Oh yes,' he said. 'Do you like it?' she asked. 'Yes, I like it,' he said. 'Well, try it sometime,' she said.

In August 1962, Barbara and Lloyd, together with David Herbert and Ira Belline, set out in two cars on a tour of Morocco. 'Barbara was at her best,' recalls Herbert, 'drinking only Coca-Cola.' She seemed perfectly happy, driving with Franklin in a Peugeot while Herbert and Ira Belline trailed them in a Renault. They travelled from Tangier to Meknes, Fez, Midelt, Tinerhir, and Ouarzazate where the local Pasha laid on a two-day feast in their honour. Thence they drove to Taroudant where they stayed at La Gazelle d'Or, one of Morocco's most renowned, comfortable and expensive hotels. Herbert was puzzled to discover that they were the only guests – until it dawned that Barbara had reserved the entire hotel at a cost of forty thousand dollars a week. They stayed three weeks before moving on to Marrakesh.

In Marrakesh, Ira Belline decided to visit Raymond Doan, a Vietnamese chemist she knew, who worked for a French oil company but who considered himself in reality an artist. He painted scenes of Moroccan street life in pastel oils, and Barbara was looking for some paintings of Morocco and Moroccans to decorate a house at Boubana, outside Tangier, that she had given to Franklin. 'Ira took us to a semi-detached villa in the European part of the town,' writes Herbert. 'We were shown into the sitting room where we sat on an upright settee in a line, like birds on a perch. The room was hideous beyond belief. While his French wife gave us coffee, Raymond proceeded to display one picture after another. Barbara disliked them all and kept whispering, "Let's get out of here." At last Raymond produced a painting of what he imagined one of Barbara's parties in her house in Tangier to be like. Barbara was touched and, though she disliked the picture, bought it. We left thinking we would never see him again.'

Shortly after this visit, Barbara started to receive anonymous poetry through the post. The poetry was execrable: 'in French and full of romantic imagery, the sort of garble a love-sick schoolboy might send his girlfriend. Reading it,' says Herbert, 'I had to stifle a laugh.' Barbara, looking at the postmarks on the envelopes, was sure she knew who the poems were from: 'Raymond Doan, of course. Who else do I know in Marrakesh?' Herbert warned Barbara to be careful, insisting that they were in fact from Raymond Doan's elder brother Maurice, an opium addict and homosexual. 'She was angry with me for shattering her dream. Always easily flattered, she became more and more intoxicated by the exquisite references to herself. A normal reaction of any woman, but particularly for Barbara, who had had a long series of unhappy marriages but always believed that the current husband was deeply in love with her, when he was more interested in her money.' Barbara Hutton's rage with David Herbert, who urged caution, resulted in a deep rift between them which was not healed for many years during which they ceased to see one another.

Barbara and Lloyd had never married, though he had certainly very much wanted them to do so. She felt that the age difference between them was too great, and that he should have his own younger wife and children, his own family. David Herbert felt that she could have had many happy years with Franklin, the best of the many men in her life, but he was inevitably ousted by the appearance of Raymond Doan who, by the testimony of Mrs Bryce Nairne who had coincidentally heard Maurice Doan conspiring with his brother in a Marrakesh café, had been urged to co-operate in staging an exhibition of his paintings at the Tangier Casino in the summer of 1963. Among the paintings was a study of Sidi Hosni. Barbara bought up the entire show, bought Maurice Doan an apartment in Paris, gave Ira Belline a villa just outside Marrakesh, and moved Lloyd Franklin out of Sidi Hosni. Franklin was very deeply injured by his abrupt dismissal. In time, however, he married a young Englishwoman, Penny Ansley. Barbara Hutton gave them a house on the Mountain as a wedding present, and Franklin – through his in-laws – became a successful stockbroker. The Franklins had one son, Julian, to whom David Herbert became godfather. Tragically, on 1 January 1968, Lloyd and Penny were killed in a car accident, driving back to Tangier from Marrakesh where they had celebrated the New Year with friends. A child had darted out into the road in front of their car. Turning the wheel sharply to the right, Franklin missed the child but lost control of the car which smacked into a tree. Franklin, aged thirty-one, died first. His wife, pregnant with their second child, died the next day.

On 7 April 1964, in the Jiutepec City Hall in Mexico, Raymond Doan and Barbara Hutton were married. The groom stated his age as forty-eight, and Barbara registered her own as fifty-one. She had been born on 14 November, 1912. By marriage, she became a Princess for the third time. Her first and fourth husbands had been Princes, but she had bought Doan's title for him in Rabat at the Laotian embassy where, for a price of fifty thousand dollars, an elderly clerk had surrendered his own perfectly good title of Prince Champacak and transferred it to Doan. Barbara and her retinue had arrived in Rabat two months after Doan's Tangier exhibition. With Jean Mendiboure, her hairdresser, Vera Medina, her dressmaker, Tony Gonzales, her personal maid, Ira Belline, her housekeeper, Colin Frazer, her bodyguard, and Bill Robertson, her major-domo, she had set off from Sidi Hosni on 30 October 1963 for the Tour Hassan Hotel.

From Rabat, they moved to the Mamounia Hotel in Marrakesh. Doan had given up his job, and also his wife whom he was divorcing and had packed off, with the children, to the Canary Islands. As they travelled further south, they acquired more passengers and continued on to La Gazelle d'Or in Taroudant where, says Jean Mendiboure,

Raymond Doan gave Barbara a huge amethyst ring and matching bracelet as an engagement present. She put the ring on and commented on how attractive it looked, then slipped it off suddenly and hurled it against the wall. 'Give this junk to your wife!' she screamed. The ancient Greeks believed that the amethyst prevented intoxication and that was how she took it – as a commentary on her drinking. But even more amazing than her action was Doan's reaction. He stooped to pick up the ring, fumbled it and stooped again. Thereafter Barbara humiliated him whenever she felt like it. One of her favourite pastimes was to tempt people with money. And Doan was perfect for that mode of entertainment.

Doan's resilience in the face of insult was no doubt fortified by generous gifts – he is said to have received a cheque for one and a half million dollars on the occasion of his marriage, a sum to match the cheque also given to his brother Maurice. Besides new clothes, a substantial monthly allowance, and the usual hardware, Doan was given a house, the Villa Barbarina, built by local architect Robert Gérofi, on the site that had once been occupied by Lloyd Franklin's stables. In the autumn of 1965, Barbara was again in residence at Sidi Hosni. She began meddling in the affairs of the American School in Tangier, for which she had established a scholarship fund. She made a tour of inspection and ordered the dormitories repainted in brighter colours. She entertained the scholarship students to tea and discovered that they spoke little Arabic in comparison to their comparative fluency in French and English. To remedy this scandalous state of affairs, she transported them a little way down the coast to the village of Asilah where she installed them in a rented villa with an Arabic tutor. Her domestic routine was also liable to eccentric whims. She regularly despatched her nurses – local women chosen according to some intuition Hutton had conceived about their character rather than for their medical skills – to the beach to bring back buckets of sea-water for her bath.

In the later manner of Jane Bowles at the Parade Bar, Barbara Hutton became glad-handed with her money and possessions. She had always been impulsively generous, but she began disbursing jewels and other valuable objects to anyone who approached her with a hard luck story or who had rendered her some small service.

Her lawyer, Graham Mattison, had already become seriously alarmed about her level of expenditure, and had taken control of her chequebook. As a legal resident of Tangier, Barbara had effortlessly reduced her tax liability. During the late 1940s and throughout the 1950s, her annual tax-free income was estimated at about three million dollars. But even this level of income was hardly sufficient to cover her expenses and gifts. To one woman in Tangier who regularly spent long hours in her company, Barbara gave a gold and pearl necklace which she claimed had once belonged to the Empress of Japan. It was worth some two hundred thousand dollars. To Jane Bowles, an acquaintance merely, who had visited her one evening, she gave a magnificent diamond ring which Jane, realizing that Barbara was hardly responsible for her actions, returned the next day. Others were not so scrupulous. The ring was no sooner back in Barbara's possession than it was given away again.

Paul Bowles, commenting to C. David Heymann on Barbara Hutton's appearance and whims in 1965, remarked:

She was drinking Coke laced with crème de cacao and was receiving callers in her throne room, where she lay upon mountains of gold cushions, a tiara on her head. Her complexion was powdery. and her arms were thin as broomsticks. She had difficulty remembering the names of all her husbands. When someone asked her why she refused to walk, she said: 'Because I can afford to pay others to do my walking for me.' Her eyes were weak and she had a stream of readers come in to read to her. I was told by one of her servants that on certain days she insisted everyone on her staff sing to her. Anything they would normally say they had to sing.

The Queen of the Medina did, in fact, take to receiving visitors from various types of throne – from hillocks of golden pillows, from a jewelled divan, from a high-backed gold chair mounted on a high dais strewn with oriental rugs. 'The purpose of all this was', says her biographer, 'to discourage any kind of familiarity that her guests might be inclined to assume towards her.' Apparently far gone in her insecurity and extravagant manias, Barbara Hutton nevertheless appeared to the American Consul in Tangier, Ben

Dixon, to possess immense staying power. 'She was extremely self-destructive, but she also had tremendous inner strength and stamina. She perpetually seemed to be on the edge of extinction, but at the last possible moment she would save herself . . . When it would seem physically impossible for her to face up to her sad life she called on some inner reserve and somehow managed to handle whatever life threw at her.'

In addition to her taste for alcohol, Barbara Hutton was somewhat addicted to barbiturates. In August 1969, she received news that one of her former husbands, Count Haugwitz-Reventlow, the father of her only child, Lance Reventlow, had died in New York at the age of seventy-three after heart surgery. The death made little impression on her – she had her own health to consider, and that depended, she decided, on larger doses of barbiturates than were prescribed for her by her physicians. Alarmed by symptoms she herself diagnosed as heart palpitations, she telephoned the American Consul-General, whom she apparently regarded as her Pooh-Bah in Tangier, to make an emergency appeal to her doctor in Hollywood who was, apparently, deaf to her own distressed calls. She required that an official message be sent to her physician demanding his instant presence at her bedside. In the event, her doctor was due to make a house call, flying seven thousand miles to do so, within the next few days. When he put in an appearance at Sidi Hosni his advice was not at all to the satisfaction of his patient – he recommended a reduction in Hutton's current levels of medication. Her response was to set light to a feather fan she kept by her bed and throw it at the hapless doctor. Complaining bitterly to the Consul-General, Howard D. Jones, she claimed that the fees charged by her doctors and lawyers would beggar her. This, since Jones had heard that her Hollywood doctor had been offered a million dollars to abandon his practice and take on Hutton as his sole patient, seemed the oddest of her complaints. The doctor had turned down her offer.

That summer in Tangier, Barbara Hutton had become reconciled with David Herbert and they buried their differences about the Doan brothers. They resumed their friendship, meeting regularly. He was ready to overlook her state of mind which he found 'edgy and morose' and to rediscover 'the same sweet person I had always known and loved'. She was also reconciled with her husband who had mostly retired a safe distance from Tangier to live in an ashram in southern Spain where he had grown his hair, devoted himself to a spiritual search beyond the material comforts that his wife could afford him and was busy writing poetry – perhaps attempting to improve on the first efforts that had brought him such rewards. He returned to Tangier to find Barbara immersed in a rose-coloured contemplation of her past, younger days when, as she wrote to an aunt, she remembered how, in Florida, they had spent an entire December by the sea, 'broiling ourselves in the sun and how we walked up the beach in search of seashells and other gifts from the ocean. At five o'clock we would lie on the still warm sand and listen to the sound of music from the club as the notes drifted out to sea.' She made a trip out of the city to the Caves of Hercules, at Robinson's Beach, where she made a dash for the edge of the cliffs. Doan, who had accompanied her, snatched at her in time to prevent her going over the edge.

She returned to Tangier, for the last time, in 1975. By then, at the age of sixty-two, she had become very seriously depressed. 'The most minute function became an overbearing task. She would no longer eat or sleep or bathe or change her clothes.' She could not tolerate bright light, appeared to subsist on Coca-Cola and Valium, and lived with the constant intention of committing suicide. A new doctor weaned her off Valium, substituting chloral hydrate with which it was impossible for her to attempt an overdose. But she added a variety of drugs to those prescribed for her, and passed her days pretty much in a permanent daze. She abandoned her idea of a huge ball that year in Tangier, and instead invited eight guests to a dinner which she did not trouble to attend. She did, however, make an effort to dine with David Herbert who had invited some old friends to meet her. Her appearance was shocking: 'she looked like one of those theatrical madwomen with layers of rouge and white power all over her face, mascara smudges around her eyes, lipstick slashed across her mouth and chin.'

In *Engaging Eccentrics*, Herbert describes the last gift he received from his old and well-beloved friend: 'The last time she was in Tangier, a few years before she died, I received a large parcel. I untied the ribbon and continued to untie ribbon after ribbon as the package got smaller and smaller. Finally there lay a small round object wrapped in cotton wool, a golden egg. On the card was written: "For darling David, from the goose that has laid so many golden eggs." ' On 11 May 1979, after intensive care at the Cedars-Sinai Medical Center, where she had been treated for severe congestive cardiomyopathy, a condition marked by distension and impairment of the heart muscle, its function affected by alcohol excess, Barbara Hutton died in her suite at the Beverly Wilshire Hotel in Los Angeles. Her bank account showed a balance of less than three and a half thousand dollars.

Paul Bowles' judgement that Barbara Hutton's animating desire and constant effort was to 'transform reality into a continuous fantasy which seemed to her sufficiently *féerique* to be taken seriously', to array her impossible aspirations with a sufficient glamour that would give them solid weight, render them credible enough to replace – if not eliminate – the discomfort of actuality, recalls his own first impression of Tangier as 'a dream city', its surrealistic topography resembling 'ballet sets designed in false perspective' designed to stimulate and delude the imagination. It takes a rigorous denial of actuality to accommodate oneself to unreality, a constant suspension of disbelief to pick one's way confidently through a landscape tilted at a slight angle to the world, to accept the ever-present risk of stumbling or banging up against the scenery and props. Cecil Beaton, who knew as much about stage sets, *trompe l'oeil* and theatrical effects as anybody, was finally disappointed in Hutton, in Herbert and in Tangier – of course, since there was nothing for him to do but observe the posturings, the empty drama of actors, lost in their roles, going through the same performance day after day, night after night. His was a bit part, a few lines spoken from the chorus, a matter of giving simple cues to keep the principals in motion.

But the master orchestrator is Herbert. As the Cecil B. de Mille of Tangier, another of the social roles he has assumed over the years, Herbert has directed and deployed a constantly changing cast of major players and a multitude of starry extras. 'Over the years, the city has been visited by a continuous stream of the most varied, outstanding, eccentric, engaging people imaginable – artists, writers, actors, political and social figures. I entertained all of them, and have brought many kindred souls together.' For forty years he has been the social arbiter, the Petronius, the Beau Nash of the international expatriate community which he has ruled with a whip of knotted floss silk. That life has suited David Herbert very well – better, perhaps, than any other for which he might have opted: 'from the moment I decided to leave England and live here, where else but Tangier could have developed my tastes, my hopes and indeed the very concept of my life?' Significantly, he adds that as a young man he aspired to be an actor. 'However, in the life which I chose to lead in Tangier, I believe that I have played the part of an actor as well as that of director and puppet manager. No other town could have fulfilled my purpose to that extent.'

Most of the British royal family, at one time or another, have dined in Tangier *chez* David Herbert, not to say most of the old aristocracy of Europe and its new aristocracy of money and power. He has introduced Prince William of Gloucester to Barbara Hutton, entertained Princess Alexandra and Angus Ogilvy to lunch on their honeymoon, has provided an emergency reception for Winston and Clementine Churchill when their plane, diverted from Gibraltar in bad weather, made an unexpected landing at Tangier airport. The Churchills had been on their way to meet the Onassis yacht which sailed to Tangier to pick them up the next day when Herbert was invited to dine on the yacht which he described as 'very much one's idea of what the very rich would want'. He preferred the Niarchos yacht as 'less spectacular, less garish and done with good taste'. Few yachts now call at Tangier: its dizzy, dazzling days as a hub of international intrigue, immorality and indecorous display have all but disappeared. They have been lean years for Tangier since Independence. The city 'remained static . . . and did not progress. It did not collapse,' but only a faded scent remained of its formerly heady perfume.

Still, '*toujours gai*', as Mehitabel the cat might say, scratching for fish heads in the alleys of old Tangier, and David Herbert would perhaps not quibble with her optimistic philosophy that there's always a little piece of sardine left in the can, always the prospect of a dish of cream round the corner. Tangier 'still has an international flavour and has never quite lost its happy-go-lucky atmosphere'. There still remains a handful of survivors from the wave of expatriates who settled in Tangier after the War, sophisticated mastodons, relics of a giddy, privileged social class who could for a while carry on in their villas on the Mountain as though the world had not changed. There was no shortage of servants prepared to work for cheap wages, the erosion of class differences could largely be ignored, and there were no tiresome socialist governments to threaten their standards and attitudes. Then, as now, any attempt to talk politics had the same effect as dropping ice cubes down the necks of the expatriates.

Their formal and antiquated manners have moderated, though they still persist to a limited extent among Tangier's astonishing and lively octogenarians and nonagenarians who, braced by the climate, the air, the wind, or God alone knows what private practices and expedients, continue tripping out to regular luncheons, teas, cocktails, dinners, bridge parties and other polite entertainments. The Mountain is – no two ways about it – Tilling. Its residents are the Miss Mapps, Lucias, Georgies and Major Benjys described by the novelist E.F. Benson who took his inspiration from the quaint, cobbled purlieus of Church Square in Rye. Variously regarded as a *de facto* ambassador, Beau Nash, Cecil B. de Mille and King of the Mountain, David Herbert can finally, quintessentially, be identified as the Lucia of Tangier. It takes no great effort of the imagination to clothe others of his circle in the garb of Miss Mapp, Diva, Quaint Irene and the rest. Olga Braceleys – visiting divas – are adopted and fêted with a mixture of graciousness and gall. A fresh face, if amusing, beautiful, well-connected or famous – intelligence is not essential (indeed, rather counts against one) though wit is desirable – is at once a welcome diversion and something of a threat to the delicate balance of the status quo. The pecking order is precise, and beaks are kept sharpened.

The combination of serious money, substantial social status, charismatic character and, preferably, a title, will certainly and effortlessly transcend all barriers to social acceptance. There is constant speculation that the palace of Sidi Hosni, once the focus of legendary *luxe*, will be acquired by some dazzling notable –

preferably European, female and royal – who will make a dramatic entrance into the salons of Tangier. This will be an intoxication liable to go directly to the heads of Tangerinos who have long lived in hopes and dreams of the reanimation of a moribund city by the resurrection of the great days of the international glitterati. Fantasy races ahead and apace – there will be once more be delicious dinners and luxurious luncheons, glamorous soirées and gleaming yachts in the bay. From the New Mountain to the Old, from the Marshan to the Charf to the Casbah, Tangier will echo with the gay gibble-gabble and sophisticated laughter of latter-day equivalents of Barbara Hutton, Cecil Beaton, Truman Capote and Lady Diana Cooper. All will be bliss and beatitude. The thin blood will race through narrowing arteries and rheumy old eyes will glisten with gratitude.

Tangier's richest visitor in recent years had been the American publisher Malcolm Forbes who, in August 1989, threw a party, the most spectacular seen in the city since the Hutton heyday, at his palace in Tangier. In the event, it was to turn out to be Forbes' swan-song, a lavish coda to his life which came peacefully to an end at his home in New Jersey in February 1990. The occasion for the party had been Forbes' seventieth birthday. The summer had been a season rich in parties, given by residents and visitors, but by any standards the Forbes extravaganza was exceptional. 'To be honest,' commented David Herbert, an honoured guest, 'it was difficult to understand what it was all about, as three-quarters of the guests had never met Malcolm. It was more a giant publicity stunt than a birthday party,' though this motive did not detract from, very likely magnified, the character of the party as 'a glorious spectacle'. The cost to Forbes was minimal in terms of his personal pocket: the three million dollars spent on the event was mostly tax-deductible, a fact that occasioned some comment back in the United States where taxpayers grudgingly felt that they had subsidized the festivities which, nevertheless, in terms of the vicarious thrill enjoyed by taxpayers in terms of media coverage, was probably worth the public subsidy.

In addition to the usefulness of the party as a piece of positive self-promotion for the self-styled 'prophet of capitalism', it was an opportunity for Forbes to entertain high-ranking employees, bankers, high-spending advertisers in his publications, media moguls, politicians, company presidents and royalty. Among the guests, more or less distinguished, were Henry and Nancy Kissinger, Donald and Ivana Trump, Rupert Murdoch, Robert Maxwell, former King Constantine of Greece and his sons, Angus Ogilvy, Lee Iacocca, Walter Kronkite, Barbara Walters, Sir James Goldsmith, Julio Iglesias, several scions of Morocco's royal family and a scattering of billionaires somewhat richer or poorer than Forbes himself who was reputedly worth some five hundred million dollars.

The guests had arrived by chartered Concorde and Boeing 747, by yacht or by private jet. They were mostly installed at the beachfront Solazur Hotel which Forbes, after commanding its complete redecoration, had hired for the weekend. Tangier as a whole was in a ferment: streets were cleared of traffic, police were stationed at every corner, troops personally provided by King Hassan guarded Forbes' palace, the Solazur and the airport to ensure the safety of the guests who, it was estimated, were collectively worth some forty billion dollars. The slaughter of lambs to feed the guests rivalled the carnage of the annual feast of Aid el Khebir; six hundred chickens had their necks wrung, fifteen hundred eggs were rounded up; and two thousand bottles of wine were uncorked for the six to seven hundred guests who, like David Herbert, presented themselves at the entrance to the Mendoubia, which now belonged to Forbes.

The large open square of the Marshan, close to the palace, was spread with Oriental rugs to a total of a thousand square metres or more. A guard of honour of two hundred and seventy-four of the King's horses with riders splendidly arrayed in traditional Moorish costume was drawn up to greet the party-goers. Six hundred dancers and musicians had been brought from all over Morocco to the city to perform outside the Mendoubia – a diversion very welcome to those who were obliged to stand in line for some considerable period of time outside the narrow entrance to the palace. Inside, there were six enormous Moroccan marquees, topped by domes and lined with satin, painted in the colours favoured by Forbes – 'gold and dollar green' – lavishly decorated and cleverly lit, festooned with flowers. Seating for dinner was by lottery – guests pulled tickets, directing them to a particular tent and table, from a drum. Says David Herbert, who found himself separated from his friends, seated in the Gold Tent at a table with fifteen Americans, none of his dinner companions had 'ever seen, let alone met our host. They were all in some measure associated in a business way with the "Forbes Empire".'

The occasion naturally put some noses out of joint in Tangier – but as a mutually satisfactory public relations exercise for the benefit of Forbes and Tangier, the party perfectly achieved its objective in terms of massive, international media attention which naturally focused with interest on reports that the guest of honour, Elizabeth Taylor, might soon consent to become Mrs Malcolm Forbes. Tangier, giving the matter some thought, was sceptical of anything but a marriage of convenience. In view of the revelation, after his death, of Forbes' homosexuality, his attachment to Tangier became more readily apparent to those who had not paid close enough attention to the gossip of the city which had already painted him in gay colours. There were, to a practised eye, one or two paintings in the Mendoubia, hung in private corridors and rooms, which indicated a certain taste. Wilder rumours circulated which spoke colourfully of a Leather 'n' Levis' room secreted in the basement which was not unfamiliar to certain Moroccan youths – and so the Arab telephone rang hot with business as usual – improbable and audacious speculation.

Forbes' last fantastical party prompted some disrespectful rumblings from disaffected journalists who regarded the whole affair as ineffably vulgar, but Tangier – and Forbes – had never been particularly subtle. They suited one another precisely. It was surely a satisfactory burst of magnificence with which to end a dull decade that, despite Tangier's constant hopes for revival, had seen the city decline still further into anonymity and the effects of mass tourism, become less and less a stimulating resort for larger than life characters who had found the regular world too cramped and censorious. Sitting one evening with David Herbert and Gavin Young in the empty, echoing, somewhat dilapidated dining room of Guitta's restaurant, I complained bitterly that I was bored by the apparent respectability of the city which, to frustate most carnal intents and purposes, closes up early what little it now, at least on the surface, has to offer the casual visitor. I expressed nostalgic regret that I had missed the louche heyday of Tangier. Herbert, in his early eighties, spry and lean, uncompromisingly bewigged and with the knowing eyes of an ancient saurian, was immediately on guard, alert as a corporate public relations executive. As Tangier's most loyal apologist, he disputed the word 'louche'. 'My dear, it was never louche. Quite the wrong word. No, no, you're quite wrong. I've been here forty years and more, and *I know*.' At this point Gavin Young chipped in – having polished off his plate of Gibraltar bacon and Tangier eggs – to support the allegation of loucheness. He was in a difficult position, like a senior Parliamentary back-bencher obliged by principle and conscience to contradict the confident assertion of his Prime Minister. The result was, regretfully, rather a spat and a short period of sulks.

If louche won't do, try raffish – which implies a certain nonchalant charm and ease of manner that excuses certain shortcomings in behaviour. The characteristic expatriates of Tangier, and its regular visitors, have collectively created an enduring image of the city which, interpreted by writers and artists, journalists and photographers, has scandalized and excited – out of all proportion to the reality – a prurient public which has believed Tangier to be a last refuge for those who, finding the conventional and moralistic world unsympathetic, have established an enclave for the eccentric, a bolt hole for the irregular, a happy hunting ground for promiscuous homosexuals, and a haven for those with less than impeccable *bona fides*. This view has a certain improbable charm for anyone who seriously believes that there is a terrestrial paradise to which to flee for safety, or an earthly hell where the degenerate may safely be confined. Tangier, for all its supposed laxity, can be difficult – more difficult than usually for those in personal moral, financial or other crisis who hope to lose themselves, bury their reputations, or escape the intolerable demands of their lives. Tangier is not, by and large, a sympathetic city. It amplifies rather than ameliorates flaws in character, encourages rather than mends personal failings.

The character of Tangier as a city of illusory vanities persists. Like a mirror, it merely reflects what one wishes to see: there is truth in Tangier only in one's perception, in one's response to the image it gives back. It is easy to be caught, trapped, by the reflection of one's desires. Tangier is less obviously ensnaring than Marrakesh or Fez – the city is less beautiful, in conventional terms of esoteric charm, than either of them. But it is more insidious, more dangerous, because it lies in wait for the passive man, draining energy and giving little back. Tangier is a vampire city which suited Burroughs sunk in a junk dream, which satisfies Bowles who no longer wants to know or to participate in the world outside, who inhabits 'the land of the living' as a man who has chosen deliberately to detach himself from its mendacity and pursuit of 'progress'. David Herbert, for all his energetic conviviality, inhabits his own time-warp in Tangier, living out a mode of life and respecting manners that ceased to exist forty years ago in Europe. It is difficult to resist the image of the city as *Maja Desnuda* gazing dreamily into her looking glass. Tangier, in its soul, may just be the last resort of the living dead, alive but not madly kicking.

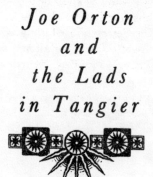

Joe Orton
and
the Lads
in Tangier

On 25 May 1967, the thirty-four-year-old London playwright Joe Orton was sitting outside the Café de Paris in Tangier with some friends. Beside them sat 'a rather stuffy American tourist and his disapproving wife' eavesdropping on Orton's conversation which, colourful to begin with, he deliberately began to exaggerate. '"He took me right up the arse," I said, "and afterwards he thanked me for giving him such a good fucking. They're most polite people.' The American and his wife hardly moved a muscle. '"We've got a leopard-skin rug in the flat and he wanted me to fuck him on that," I said in an undertone which was perfectly audible to the next table. "Only I'm afraid of the spunk, you see, it might adversely affect the spots of the leopard."'

One of Orton's group, identified in Orton's diaries as Nigel, a forty-five-year-old retired teacher, 'very middle-class but it doesn't show too much', became mildly alarmed. 'Those tourists can hear what you're saying.' Orton, working up his rhetoric, was dismissive of propriety. 'They have no right to be occupying chairs reserved for decent sex perverts.' He continued to dilate excitedly on the danger to the leopard-skin: 'He might bite a hole in the rug. It's the writhing he does, you see, when my prick is up him that might grievously damage the rug, and I can't ask him to control his excitement. It wouldn't be natural when you're six inches up the bum, would it?' Nigel, feeling the chill as the frozen American couple settled their bill and fled, remarked that Orton 'shouldn't drive people like that away. The town needs tourists.' Orton was implacable. 'Not that kind, it doesn't. This is *our* country, *our* town, *our* civilization. I want nothing to do with the civilization they made. Fuck them! They'll sit and listen to buggers' talk from me and drink their coffee and piss off . . . It isn't a joke, there's no such thing as a joke.'

In *Second Son*, published in 1972, David Herbert piously lamented
the reputation Tangier had acquired as a buggers' playground.
'Without wishing to sound pompous, there is one aspect of Tangier
life that many of us who live here do find disagreeable, and
occasionally embarrassing. No doubt attracted by Tangier's old
reputation as a city of sin, the summer months bring a swarm of
European "queens" who seem to imagine that every Moroccan
they see is for sale. Great offence is caused by their lack of discrimi-
nation and if someone gets knocked on the head it is usually their
own fault.' Old Tangerino hands, evidently, knew the form and
exactly how to minimize risk, unlike tyro tourists who had been
misled by unfortunate literature and other propaganda. At the
beginning of the 1970s, Herbert could reasonably complain that
'Morocco has been given a bad name lately by some English
authors who have chosen it as the background for some most mis-
leading and on the whole disagreeable novels.' No doubt he principally had in mind *The Wrong People* by Robin Maugham, published
in two versions in 1967 and 1970, and *Exiles* by Rupert Croft-
Cooke. There have been other sensational novels since then, William Bayer's *Tangier* being of particular note in that the author, a
former resident of the city, took very little trouble to disguise the
relations its principal characters bore to real-life Tangier counterparts. Such novels, says Herbert, have painted a picture of a town
peopled by undesirables and a society composed principally of
those who have been driven to or chosen a life of exile for thoroughly
nefarious reasons.

It is, of course, the bad penny that attracts attention among the
otherwise blameless small change, and Herbert admits that 'under
the international régime you were probably right in presuming that
the people you met might be fleeing from the law or the disapproval
of those at home.' Such was certainly the presumption held by the
minor British journalist, indefatigable autobiographer and novelist
Rupert Croft-Cooke when he arrived in Tangier in 1954 'fresh' –
as he claimed David Herbert had unkindly remarked – 'from gaol'.
The 'wary and crablike' reception initially accorded to him by the
Tangerinos of the Mountain was astonishing to Croft-Cooke who
considered he had paid his dues to good society. It was hard that
he should be pilloried again by the inhabitants of a Moroccan
Cranford. He had come to Tangier to settle himself comfortably

among like-minded companions who, surely, could be counted upon to be sympathetic and consolatory, tolerant at worst and welcoming at best, of a man ill-used in his own native country 'by the malice of a few dirty-minded police and law men' whose distaste for Croft-Cooke's homosexual activities had landed him for a stretch in Wormwood Scrubs.

From his miserable experiences, Croft-Cooke had fabricated a book, *The Verdict Of You All*, which dwelt in detail on the facts of his 'crime' – a homosexual misdemeanour that would nowadays be regarded more tolerantly – his trial, his prison experiences and his outrage at a 'monstrous and absurd injustice'. Croft-Cooke was no Oscar Wilde, and his book was no *Ballad of Reading Gaol*, but it had sold pretty well and Somerset Maugham had sent him a cheque for five hundred pounds that enabled Croft-Cooke to quit England altogether with the good wishes of sympathizers such as John Gielgud, Beverly Nichols, Lords Kinross and Faringdon, novelists Sheila Kaye-Smith and Olivia Manning and 'fellow sufferers' like Edward Montagu and Michael Pitt-Rivers. In Tangier, 'of all places', it was insufferable to have his adventures regarded as 'misfortunes', his character as having fallen into 'disrepute'. Yet here, 'in this refuge for undesirables, or at the best heterogeneous people,' he 'encountered – not hostility, but a certain diffidence, a determination to show that they had not had the same experience that I had.' Croft-Cooke installed himself in a house on the Mountain, where he stayed for eight years before moving into an apartment in the city itself. He bided his time, waiting until 1974 to take his revenge, cold as a *crème de menthe frappé*, in *The Caves of Hercules*, his principal memoir of Tangier.

The Mountain set had, in its time, no doubt tolerated worse than Croft-Cooke and, within a short while, somewhat relented. The question of his status was a matter of some nicety: he considered himself to be more a writer than a social figure, claiming to rank with Paul Bowles in literary consequence. From this point of view, he could safely condescend to those with mere titles or superior family connections living in a miasma of faded glory. On the other hand, he was distinctly a cut above the rackety riff-raff, 'not quite bohemian enough to be dismissed as one of the town-living fellowship . . . but not quite clearly categorized as exclusively a friend of the peerage like David Herbert. I was in fact a bit of an anomaly, asked on most occasions when I particularly wished to be, but not considered by any means a *sine qua non*.' In this *soi-disant* role of privileged outsider, the objective writer and cool observer to whom no doors, whether of palace or hovel, were closed, Croft-Cooke cultivated not only creditable acquaintance, in the manner of Swift, but also the company of those snubbed by the Mountain social lions as irretrievably low-life. He consorted amicably with the likes of Calamity Kate, characterized by Croft-Cooke as a bum; American pederasts who took a shine to 'the youngest of the bootblacks'; shabby beachcombers who hung out in the Petit Socco; drunks who 'made a pathetic and much too numerous collection'; writers and artists who 'were scarcely more reputable or industrious'.

Croft-Cooke's lofty self-sufficiency and limitless self-regard may have warped his critical judgement which, firmly based on a high opinion of his own facile literary industry and ability – he aimed to write at least two thousand words a day, every day, to keep up a reasonable income – inclined him to snub Kerouac, Corso, and Allen Ginsberg in particular, who was singled out as 'a rather smudgy tittering individual'. For William Burroughs, Croft-Cooke reserved a particular incomprehension and mild distaste. 'One did not, one does not yet, perceive in William Burroughs genius of any kind, though he was a pleasant enough fellow when I knew him before he started being taken seriously.' Croft-Cooke had not taken *Junky* at all seriously. He recalled Burroughs as 'unnaturally gaunt, hollow-cheeked, meagre in body' mooching round the Petit Socco 'in suits which, he told me, he bought from supplies of used clothing sent from American charities for the poor Moroccans and sold by them to anyone who could pay for them'. Burroughs, says Croft-Cooke, 'was anxious to write another book and was always asking to borrow my typewriter'. He admired Burroughs' courage in taking a cure for drug addiction, though 'it did not make him any more of a writer.'

Croft-Cooke's mild but persistent misanthropy, his disdain for diplomatic niceties, whether with Tangerinos or Tanjawis, caused some local ill-feeling. He was not universally popular, but his stoicism was wonderful to behold. 'On one bizarre occasion in the Socco Chico,' wrote David Woolman, 'he won a degree of admiration by continuing to sit at the Café Central smoking his inevitable cigar albeit he had just been hit over the head so hard by an irate

Tanjawi newspaper boy that the heavy glass ash tray used as the weapon had broken, and blood coursed down Croft-Cooke's face and on to his suit.' If he was not at the Café Central, Croft-Cooke was at Dean's Bar. Dean, he wrote, 'may have been what my father would have called a "scoundrel" whom I myself in more fastidious days would have avoided, but in the atmosphere of that city in that time I was quite fond of him'. Scoundrels were pretty thick on the ground in Tangier in the 1950s, and Croft-Cooke became rather a connoisseur.

There were degrees of infamy. 'The heir of a wealthy town councillor from the Midlands', for one, was mild enough in his excesses. He arrived in the city with a friend 'who had a vicious blond-haired charm' and who obtained a loan from a local shopkeeper by handing over his passport as a guarantee of good faith. Immediately he 'went down to the Embassy and Consulate in Rabat and obtained a new passport on the plea that he had lost his own. He then returned cheerfully to England, some hundred pounds in pocket. The councillor's son stayed fatally in Tangier, said he was a provincial nobleman, whatever that meant, became enormously bloated in body and face ("Glands", said Dean) and "took to drink" as the Victorians called it.'

Other misfortunates and remittance men were 'victims of drugs and depression', but some adopted a more lively character. Among the fantastics were 'the absurdly pretentious, the near-transvestites, the Münchausens, such as a man who dressed up in cloaks and fur capes to receive his guests in a villa in the *medina* which was like a conservatory, while there were plenty of ingeniously invented titles being exchanged, few to be found in the Almanac de Gotha.' One can be sure that Croft-Cooke officiously checked the credentials of pretenders. 'There were the "fallen stars" of politics like Ian Horobin and others, and some outright lunatics like one [John Scott, the son of a titled laird] who held conversations with a plastic parrot which he carried on his shoulder, or another who only came out at night so was rarely seen, except by George Greaves who cultivated such curiosities.'

Michael Davidson, in *The World, The Flesh and Myself*, identified George Greaves as 'one of the great characters of Tangier. His Australian truculence, his power of verbal venom, the Hogarthian vigour of his satire, and his infinite knowledge of the private lives of anybody who mattered, from the British Minister down, made him a personage to be respected. For his friends he possessed an unfailing fund of kindliness; for those whom he chose to make his enemies, his ruthlessness was waspish.' Such was Greaves' reputation in Tangier in 1944, and it had not moderated or become gentler with age in 1967 when he met Joe Orton whose bawdy and lack of reserve matched his own ebullience. 'He told me', wrote Orton, 'of a woman he'd helped by forging someone's name on a legal document. "And I thought of myself as I did it, well you've been a sodomite, and every other shitty thing you can think of and now you're committing forgery."'

Orton was enchanted by Greaves' frank and uninhibited scurrility. At his most vigorous and venomous, at his funniest and most foul-mouthed, Greaves amounted – in Michael Davidson's estimation – to a social pontiff on a level, in his time and in his prime, with Dean, characterized by Davidson as a 'gracious and lovable dignitary who, with the *hauteur* of a Versailles duchess, the *cortesia* of a Papal chamberlain, a heart made of honey and, often, a tongue like a scorpion's sting, rules over Dean's Bar.' Greaves may have lacked Dean's suavity, but he was just as acute in ferreting out salacious gossip and astute in converting it into personal power. Greaves had a valuable edge on Dean: he was a stringer for the *Daily Express* and, as an occasional gossip journalist who retailed the badly kept secrets of the city, helped to invent Tangier for the pleasurable disgust of the shockable, prurient British public. 'To sit with George Greaves outside the Café de Paris or on a pavement of the Zoco Chico', wrote Davidson,

was to become a privileged peeper into the souls of the passers by. His great bulk hunched forward in the cane-chair, chins resting on one hand with an erect forefinger ranged along the imperial nose, trilby hat tilted over the pale eyes, he would watch the passing notables derisively. Suddenly he would explode in an expectorant noise of disgust, like the beginning of a full-blown Neapolitan gob. 'See him,' jerking his head in the direction of a trim supernumerary in the British Legation who was also a local commercial magnate. 'Don't touch 'im – don't *touch* 'im. Poison, that's 'im. *And* he murdered 'is first wife – puts flowers on her grave every anniversary of the day he murdered 'er. I *know*, fuck me if I don't.' His destructive eye would fall on a prosperous-looking Arab. 'That one – used to be the kept boy of a former French Minister: *now* look at 'im – wouldn't tell you the time if he 'ad two watches . . . Hah! There's P.' – mentioning a famous name. 'In the Foreign Office, he was. Foreign Office my arse! Only diplomacy 'e does now, 'e does on small girls!'

And so, appallingly, on – a long litany of crime, perversion, opportunism and defamation. Davidson indulgently recalled Greaves as a 'delightful companion: amusing, informative, generally shrewd, mouthing sardonic imprecation in his fruitily uninhibited Australian vowels; and a wonderful friend – as long as you *were* a friend'.

Orton and Greaves met pretty frequently, whether by arrangement or by chance. The Orton *Diaries* provide ample, salty examples of Greaves' wit and the vividness of his conversational bombshells:

> I went to dinner at a restaurant called Grillon. An American woman runs it. She looks as if she's Eve Arden's stand-in's stand-in. She makes witty wise-cracks throughout the meal. She's not a bad type and her food is good. We saw George Greaves again on the boulevard as we strolled along. George was with a rather stuffy man with gingery hair, nearly bald, who he introduced as Somebody St. John. The man chatted – when he finally got up I said, 'Who is he?' 'Oh,' George said, 'she's a silly queen who's lived out here for years. She's doing some typing for me.' 'He looks rather tight-arsed,' I said. 'Don't you believe it, laddie, she's had camels up her ring-piece. I don't mean their pricks,' he said, as an afterthought, 'I mean their heads.'

On a trip by car to the Diplomatic Forest, a nearby resort, Greaves informed Orton: 'This is where to come if you want to get raped.' He then 'began singing in a loud bass voice, "Make way for the buggery bus. Here comes the buggery bus."' Continuing on to Asilah, further down the Atlantic coast, the car stopped 'several times on the way to chat to boys and give them cigarettes. Very shy boys. "I like the ones who blush," George said. "I remember I used to fuck the blushes off their faces and when they said

'Madre mio. Oh! Oh! Please don't,' that's when I used to shove it up." He cackled and then looked sad at the memory he had conjured up.'

Some days later, Orton was interested to see Greaves 'with two respectable looking Americans, a man and his wife. George was being respectable. Quite benign. Does he have a special selection of stories for respectable occasions, I wonder.' Greaves had originally settled in Tangier in the late 1930s, just before the War. Though he liked to present himself as a cynic, declaring that 'every damned thing in this crazy world is shoddy, crooked or fake,' he was at least fondly remembered by Michael Davidson and Joe Orton who dressed him up – perhaps trussed him – with his own words and afforded him some minor measure of literary immortality. Greaves died in poverty in Tangier in 1983, at the age of eighty-four. In his last illness, his friends rallied round to take up a collection, first to pay the overdue rent on his rue Goya flat, and then his large telephone bill. Another collection was started to raise funds to repatriate him to his native Australia. He was cared for to his last moments, it is said, by a young Moroccan who had been his long-time companion. Tangier can occasionally take care of its own, capriciously indulgent and charitably disposed towards its monsters.

The Mountain set nervously kept its distance from the likes of Greaves, and how they must have shuddered when Croft-Cooke gossiped freely about his latest catch in the deep waters of the city. By comparison with this major shark, the small fry of Tangier's robust community of *contrebandiers* and common criminals were mere piranhas: Billy Hill, a substantial London gangster, virtual Godfather to the menacing Kray twins, had taken up residence in the city. Croft-Cooke considered himself, when it suited his purpose, an informed and thoughtful connoisseur of criminals, largely thanks to his enforced association with such a variety in Wormwood Scrubs prison. Rather grandly and graciously, as a literary man who had tasted life in all its flavours, sour and sweet, he regretted – rather disingenuously – that his interesting underworld acquaintance should not have been entertained more widely in Tangier. 'I realize that not everyone could be expected to feel the interest which I as a writer felt in the arrivals and departures of villains, or the small talk they indulged in, yet I sometimes felt how much

the ladies and gentlemen on the Mountain missed by their exclus-
iveness. I suppose it depends on which you would find more interesting, Ronnie Kray or David Herbert, Jessie Green or Gypsy Hill.'

According to Croft-Cooke, Hill was an interesting fellow, more
interesting at any rate than policemen whose reminiscences made
him yawn with boredom. Criminals were rarely boring, though his
picture of Hill, 'an intelligent and unusual man', tends to render
him as a spent force, probably uncomfortable and disoriented in
Tangier if one is to judge by the fact that 'the flat he furnished in
Tangier might have been in Maida Vale if its windows had not
looked out on a sunlit mosque,' and his preference was for English
food, which he brought with him, 'never forgetting several pounds
of beef sausages'. Hill maintained an interest in several matters,
mainly gambling, in London. He had retired, but had recruited the
Kray brothers, Ronnie and Reginald, to supervise his remaining
business interests. Ronnie Kray accompanied Hill to Tangier, and
immediately found a sympathetic friend in Croft-Cooke who
regarded his sojourn in Tangier as in the nature of a little holiday
for the lad, an opportunity for rest and recuperation after some
trying circumstances:

> why should Billy not have sympathized with the young man who
> had recently been confined in both a prison and an asylum and
> who without his twin was embarking on some dangerous courses
> in London? Why should he not have seen that a break in sur-
> roundings as strange and interesting as Tangier might help the
> scarred mind and violent nature of Ronnie? There would be no
> temptation to crime since no English criminal would attempt any
> away from his associates and familiar surroundings. In Tangier
> he would find a people who spoke a foreign language, were
> altogether incomprehensible and belonged to films rather than
> reality. He would feel 'lost' as only a Londoner abroad can feel.

Still, no doubt Hill's beef sausages and cosy flat, furnished in best
suburban style, would be an anchor if Ronnie Kray were to find
himself wholly at a loss. Croft-Cooke was moved by Kray, 'not then
considered a schizophrenic or more of a bully than was necessary to
make himself a powerful figure in the cruel and savage world of
London crime . . . There was something sympathetic and touching

about this powerful little-educated man, so anxious to know, so modestly ready to ask questions.' Kray learned quickly. He was twenty-seven years old and apparently amiable. He 'smiled and made himself pleasant to everyone about him, picked up good-looking Moroccan boys and bought too many drinks for himself and others in the bar at night, much as other young Cockneys on holiday liked to do'. Kray developed a devoted interest in a Moroccan boy called Hassan, buying him a second-hand car as a present and laying plans to take him back to England. He confided details of this infatuation to Croft-Cooke with whom he stayed on several occasions, behaving 'like any other Cockney gentleman, of whom I have known a number'. To Croft-Cooke, it was plain that Kray 'considered women to be of a lower order of beings and wanted no truck with them'.

All in all, Croft-Cooke presents a comfortable picture of Ronnie Kray as a simple, smiling villain, sentimentally attached to young men and spontaneously generous with money. The only evidence of ill temper Kray was liable to show was when others insisted on paying for drinks. He considered Kray – properly or indulgently – to have been perhaps emotionally stunted and crippled by the circumstances of his youth, by heredity, by conditioning in 'the jungle of the East End' and by 'the notoriously cruel treatment in military prisons like Shepton Mallet'. He regarded the Krays as Davids rather than Goliaths, with 'a facility for taking ruthless and unfair advantages'; but 'there are as many aspects to crime, to me engrossing, as there are to virtue, which leave me unconcerned. In Tangier,' remarks Croft-Cooke, 'I saw and learned a great deal of both.' Croft-Cooke was vitally interested, like most Tangerinos and Tanjawis, in the gossip of the city. As a writer, as a name at least familiar to visiting journalists, he was regarded as a source of minor news and trivial information which could be aggrandized in print for the British public who were generally led to credit Tangier as a pit of iniquity.

Girl tourists were regularly said to have been wilfully seduced by Moroccan fantasists who claimed to be powerful and aristocratic Caids possessed of wide estates and teeming harems; teenage Spanish boys were inevitably described as professional bullfighters; tumbledown shacks were glamourized as war-damaged, the circumstances of war remaining carefully undefined – but surely there was always a war somewhere in Morocco? The silliest stories about expatriates were given wide publicity, passed on without a moment's reflection by anyone harbouring a grudge. Tangier's reputation in the 1950s and 1960s was at least romantic, at best glamorous, at worst depraved. The actuality was minor eccentricity, bathetic pathos and little sense of the ridiculous among the exiles. Croft-Cooke, in *The Caves of Hercules*, reels off a score of names, once famous but now dim and scarcely remembered. These period pieces and their activities in their time relieved the boredom of Tangier, were puffed up to provide cocktail-party gossip, circulated with more or less malice according to the scores they conveniently settled and finally passed into dusty legend to be resurrected occasionally as evidence that life as an expatriate in Tangier had been rich in character, incident and eccentricity of style. There had been farce, there had been tragedy; there had been pleasures, there had been sorrows. The trivial scandal was magnified to the degree necessary to validate it as a topic of vital cocktail-party concern; the truly epic tragedy was condensed to proportions that fitted it for dinner-table conversation.

The scandal that arose suddenly in the autumn of 1958 was serious enough to alarm a substantial number of expatriates who, contrary to normal police practice, found themselves severely harassed and, in some cases, briefly imprisoned. William Burroughs, on arrival in Tangier in 1954 – coincidentally, in the same month and year as Croft-Cooke – had been appreciative of the fact that the local police interfered very little with the foreign community and tended, when intervention became necessary, to take the part of a foreigner over the interests of a Tanjawi. But in this instance, on this occasion, the priorities were disturbingly reversed.

There is some dispute as to the circumstances and actual events of the great purge of 1958, but Croft-Cooke and David Woolman more or less coincide in their published accounts of the incident which has been dubbed by Croft-Cooke as 'The Great Scandal'. A new and officious Chief of Police, an Algerian, had been appointed to Tangier's international force. 'Selected', says Woolman, 'because Tanjawis lacked experience as police administrators, the Algerian meant to sparkle by ridding Tangier of her worst people.' Croft-Cooke attributes the spark that lit the powder trail to the disappearance, after a visit to two Englishmen, of a young Spanish boy whose parents reported his absence to the police. The boy had 'only run away for a lark', but the police took the parents' report seriously. 'One of the two Englishmen disappeared on the Gibraltar ferry and for the other and his associates the hunt was up,' reports Croft-Cooke.

Another contributory circumstance was the case, says Woolman, of Ahmed Yacoubi, arrested and charged with the sexual molestation of a teenage German boy. 'Tanjawi authorities were supposed to have reasoned that if they could act against their own people in these matters, why not rid themselves of resented foreigners in the same category while they were at it?' A blacklist was drawn up, and to general shock it was discovered that several prominent British residents figured on it. The surprise was all the greater because 'the British', says Croft-Cooke, 'were not numerically or in any other way chief among the European colonies, but their connections with Tangier were traditionally respected up to the time of Moroccan Independence.' These names, among others, were said to have been provided by an informer who, by his action, successfully prevented his own name from appearing on the blacklist. It is tempting to identify the informer as Woolman himself, since Croft-Cooke, without naming him specifically, clearly identifies him as 'an American cashiered from his country's Air Force and now surrounded by twelve-year-olds'. Burroughs attributes to Woolman the remark that he lost interest in boys as soon as they had learned to walk. 'Tangerinos', wrote Woolman himself, 'found it exceedingly odd that one of their number, a long-time and very prominent resident whose exact occupation was as mysterious as his proclivities were not, should be the only man known to have the mimeographed police list, and that he should be blithe about it because he, of all people, was not on it.' This 'form of defence', says Croft-Cooke, 'only led to his arrest and appearance before a *juge d'instruction*'. However, not only homosexuals and pederasts were on the infamous list: there was a move also against, according to Woolman, 'Those known to be jobless or without funds (many of the Socco Legion fell into this category), those known to pass bad checks or to avoid paying new Moroccan taxes'. Croft-Cooke maintains that 'the authorities, both police and judiciary, concentrated on the pederasts, the perverters of young children and left the more mature "offenders" to their own devices. But this meant a surprisingly large number of those who had chosen Tangier as a refuge.'

The blacklist, says Woolman, 'included some of the most socially important names on the Mountain, some of the most disgusting riffraff, and a good many Tangerinos in between. Travel agencies did a sudden spurt of business as listed individuals left Tangier by every conceivable means. Detectives rounded up and questioned most of them at the Socco Grande police station, but put only sixteen of them in the Malabata prison.' According to Croft-Cooke, 'the cells behind the town's police station were full. The most exalted luncheon parties of the Mountain set were interrupted by plain-clothes men asking questions and demanding to see passports, though they had examined them a dozen times . . . There was trembling in the fastnesses of the Mountain and an unprecedented exodus to Spain where Franco was reported to have said that he was not worried as in Spain these things did not exist.' Scandalously, Woolman identifies one of the grandest of those on the blacklist as getting 'off the hook by inviting the Winston Churchills, who were luckily in Tangier Bay aboard Aristotle Onassis' yacht at the time, to dinner. The police were so impressed with the local gentleman's powerful friends that, rightly or wrongly, they left him alone after that.' The grandee, since the Churchills only called once at Tangier, may reasonably be identified as David Herbert. Some, more charitable than Woolman, might take it that Herbert was never implicated at all and that there was no need to parade his notable acquaintance with the rich and powerful to make an unnecessary point to the authorities.

Among those imprisoned, according to Croft-Cooke, was a 'very tall man from Denmark, who had associated with youngsters less than half his size'. He spent a year in prison, 'while an old German photographer, in spite of an effort to prove that his tastes were comparatively innocent by removing all his false teeth to show the police his peculiar faculties, followed him, and an English wireless mechanic was soon sent to join them. Thereafter came a Welsh Non-conformist Minister with a short sentence who afterwards took his caravan to Gibraltar whence he was promptly expelled.' This colourful Welshman may be identified as Dowell Jones, described by David Woolman as a robust old man of seventy who 'admired very young Spanish and Moroccan boys, entertained them

constantly in wholesale lots, and enjoyed himself immensely ...
He lived well in a series of Tangier apartments, using the Socco
Chico as his command post.'

The scandal caused a great deal of talk and frank alarm. 'It was
called a witch-hunt,' says Croft-Cooke, 'though it was nothing of
the sort. Considering the age and size of the witnesses who were to
be called, it was no more than a rather unskilled police force doing
its job in putting down the corruption of minors, even though it
was hard to consider bribing Moroccan street-boys of any age as
corruption.' Manolo's, the most famous male brothel, closed on
account of its owner's incarceration, and Dutch Tony (Anthony
Reithorst) discreetly moved across the Straits for a time. 'While
many of the accused fled Tangier,' reported Woolman, 'most
stayed. They were right. The purge ended as abruptly as it began,
with no reason given.' Croft-Cooke agrees: 'It subsided as suddenly
as it had come ... But it had caused a shaking like the Agadir
earthquake a few years later. It is part of the charm of living
in Mohammedan countries that a short while after it, nobody
could believe it had happened. Manolo's opened, the Dutchman
returned, and for the boys growing rapidly to manhood it was
business as usual, on the beaches, in the hotels by permission of a
cognizant hall-porter, in the rented holiday apartments and in the
homes of the Tangerinos.'

Woolman attributes the end of the crisis to the intervention of
the King who, it was said, did not want his regime to appear
anti-foreign.

Some said that Rabat removed the too ambitious Algerian police
chief, and with him his policies, because it was afraid that the
better connected people on the blacklist would give Tangier a
bad press by divulging facts about the morals of the Moroccans
themselves. They told the story of the American [Woolman himself, one does not long hesitate to surmise] who demanded to
know why the law didn't apply to everybody equally, and why
the police didn't arrest their own Tanjawi layabouts and homosexuals, since they so vastly outnumbered the Europeans in these
categories. He reported later that the police told him with straight
faces that what Tanjawis did was one thing, but what Tangerinos
did was something else. Even if they did the same things, and

even though the law applied to everybody, only the Europeans were wrong and punishable. This typically Tanjawi line of reasoning notwithstanding, the crisis was over.

David Herbert, in *Second Son*, claims that most expatriates who have come to live in Tangier in the twenty years since the early 1970s have settled for entirely humdrum reasons: 'taxation or retirement'. Nevertheless, despite this disclaimer, by a loyal apologist for Tangier, of any motives for residence beyond a perfectly respectable desire to minimize tax liability and domestic stress, it is not difficult to move even now – if that is one's inclination – in circles in the city that are almost exclusively composed of homosexual men. The official attitude, according to David Woolman writing on the subject in 1977, 'has appeared to be that so long as homosexual relationships are restricted to the privacy of the participant's domiciles, the law will not interfere'. The police, he says, take a tolerant view of homosexuality, though the Moroccan Penal Code, on a strict interpretation, 'makes any sexual activity outside marriage punishable by large fines and extended imprisonment'.

It is certainly a fact that sexual relationships between expatriate and visiting foreigners and Moroccan youths are commonplace, though Moroccans are no longer quite so complaisant as in the past. There is a distinct feeling, perhaps more in Casablanca and Rabat than in Tangier or Marrakesh, that the days of colonial and sexual exploitation of Moroccans are long gone, that increased consciousness of national identity and pride in the Islamic religion have given Moroccans a stronger feeling of independence and that Western mores, or lack of them in the context of the behaviour of foreigners towards Moroccans, can no longer be tolerated. The traditional 'corruption' of Moroccan youth by foreigners is considered now more shameful. Nevertheless, even despite AIDS, there is still a great deal of sex – homosexual and heterosexual – in Tangier.

Conventionally, in Muslim cultures, a woman is expected to be a virgin on the occasion of her marriage, and heterosexual promiscuity in Morocco is less common than in Western, 'Christian' cultures. There are a lot of horny boys walking the streets, many of whom are unemployed and have no aversion to taking a job as a houseboy with a foreign homosexual man. 'Tanjawi males', says

David Woolman, are in any case 'overwhelmingly bisexual'. He quotes, in support, the eminent anthropologist Edward Westermarck, who made a special study of Moroccan beliefs and customs and who says in *Ritual and Belief in Morocco* 'that homosexuality is regarded with indifference except in the case of boys who prostitute themselves, or grown men who practise passive pederasty. In the case of the latter, Tanjawis believe that such men will, in the next world, be condemned to wash their faces forever with the urine of Jews. Masturbation is considered more reprehensible than pederasty or even bestiality.'

Woolman further attributes Tangier's popularity with homosexuals to the fact that it is the closest Moroccan city to Europe, easily accessible for holidays. But he dismisses out of hand 'the idea that Europeans introduced homosexuality to Tanjawis' and takes issue with 'the hypocrisy of Tanjawis in pretending that they themselves are guiltless when their partners are merely Christians, or that it is the foreigners in Tangier who have perverted their innocent lads. The Tanjawis believe that anything they do with a non-Muslim is perfectly all right so long as they are paid for it.' Woolman regards Tangier's reputation among homosexuals as a sexual paradise to be a distinct bonus to the city's economy:

> The gain to Tanjawis for selling a commodity upon which they place so little moral value is considerable, doubtless a genuine economic factor in a city the size and character of Tangier. Crime drops where basic desires can be satisfied simply, and Tanjawi youths can easily earn money for such simple pleasures as movies, food or candy or renting a bicycle or motorcycle through prostitution. But much more is possible and even usual – money for school clothes, trips both in Morocco and abroad, and most sensible, precious jobs either in Morocco or abroad. A few Tanjawis have received cars, houses and meaningful inheritances from Western friends.

The examples of benefit to Kiki from his relationship with Burroughs, or Ahmed Yacoubi's association with Paul Bowles, are two that tend to bear out Woolman's case which, perhaps, he somewhat overstates so far as the generality of relationships of this nature are concerned. The fatal mistake, often enough, for foreigners is their sentimental and romantic tendency to fall in love with their boys, most of whom are at best bisexual, at worst truly heterosexual in character. Woolman very definitely discourages such deep attachments: 'For Westerners, a Tanjawi homosexual affair is often tragic, for they tend to invest affection and security in a situation that is counterfeit to begin with, demanding at best and one-sided at all times.' While he was not referring particularly to this area of interest, Paul Bowles claimed that it is almost impossible to have a genuine friendship with a Moroccan. 'Unless a Westerner is wise enough to admit that instant, purchased sex is no basis upon which to build a lasting, full-fledged relationship, made vastly more difficult by the extreme divergences in language, culture and education, he quickly comes to grief in Tangier.'

At the end of the summer of 1968, Rupert Croft-Cooke decided to leave Tangier. The city had changed during his fourteen years of residence and not, he thought, for the better. British influence was on the wane: the British Post Office had long since closed its doors; there was no longer a British bank; the local branch of Saccone and Speed had ceased trading; and the little European bars had suffered substantial losses since the general city-wide clampdown on the sale of liquor. Old friends had been distressingly cut down, like the great trees in the Zoco Grande which had been turned into a parking lot at the expense of the colourful market where country Berbers had sold their fruit and vegetables and, in winter, offered cakes and hot chestnuts in the gaudy light of flares. Gone, with the trees and the market, were the likes of Eric Gifford – 'Calamity Kate' of absurd memory – Carmella, many of the Mountain set and the distinguished Scottish artist James McBey who had treated Croft-Cooke kindly. Both Dean and Jay Haselwood had died, and their bars were no longer the famous institutions that Tangerinos and tourists had known as regular and inevitable ports of call. The Bar la Mar Chica was but a pungent memory.

The Petit Socco was less characterful now: the time 'when its cafés had become mint-tea shops, and its days as a mart for male and female prostitutes of all nations seemed a memory'. Restaurants, in Croft-Cooke's gastronomic view, had degenerated in quality and quantity, and 'the *feeling* of cosmopolitanism had departed with the smuggling ships under many flags, and nearly all the shops in the town were owned by Soussi Moroccans [the traditional master merchants] or local Jews.' Moroccans were becoming more Westernized, wearing European clothes and driving 'so many motor cars that the streets for the first time knew traffic blocks and parking meters were introduced'. Morals, too, were changing, but only to the extent of supplanting one vice with another: 'Blackmail had begun to be levied and two rich Dutchmen lost not only large sums of money but their private aeroplane to a notorious crook who had made a room available to them for the purpose of pederasty, then called in a policeman working with him.' Worst of all, perhaps, tourism had markedly increased. The beaches were teeming and overcrowded with 'white-skinned northerners'. Tangier 'would soon become as impossible as those coast towns across the water on the Costa del Sol'.

Tangier, Croft-Cooke felt, was in decline. It was fated to linger on as nothing more than 'a drab Moroccan port and city with none of the gaiety, the mixed European and Moorish characteristics, the absurdity, the wayward freedom and festivity that it had shown the world when I had first arrived'. By the mid-1960s, Tangier's reputation as a resort without sexual restrictions for homosexual visitors had firmly re-established itself. 1958 was a long-forgotten and aberrant hiccup. Joe Orton, who first visited Tangier in the early summer of 1965, and had returned every year thereafter, took a moment out from his busy bugger's schedule on Sunday, 11 June 1967, to consider the pleasurable privileges the city afforded the lover of adolescent boys: 'not for the first time I reflected that having had a boy of his age in England I'd spent the rest of my time in terror of his parents or the police. At one moment, with my cock in his arse, the image was, and as I write, still is, overpoweringly erotic.'

Orton, accompanied by his lover, Kenneth Halliwell, encountered Rupert Croft-Cooke who described him in his usual patronizing manner as 'so much the local boy who made good, so surprised at his own success, so much the peeling-nosed Londoner at the seaside as he paddled and bathed on the town beach, that he *had* to have talent to have written a play at all, let alone a brilliant one.' This accords pretty well with the description of Orton, by Ronald Bryden in 1966 in the *Observer*, as 'the Oscar Wilde of Welfare State gentility'. Halliwell, Croft-Cooke was interested to observe, sported 'a huge wig from behind which he peered out like a Cairn terrier'. Their conversation was vivid: Halliwell and Orton 'used to relate hair raising tales of the effect on them of *majoun*, cannabis in the form of jam, with which they were experimenting at the time'. Orton struck Croft-Cooke as being 'a mixture of naivety and knowingness, good humour with touches of spite, pride in himself and his work, and deference to Kenneth, to whom, he once said, he owed it all'.

Orton had, often and loyally, credited Halliwell as important to his work, as having introduced him to ideas and literature that he might not have so easily or quickly found for himself. Halliwell, early in their relationship, was supposed to be the one with literary ability and the prospect of a career as a writer, but his literary voice, in comparison to Orton who quickly found himself in full command of an astonishingly articulate style as a writer, was derivative and arch, somewhat sub-Firbankian and dated. Orton, by contrast, was entirely modern, following in a theatrical tradition from the Elizabethan work of Ben Jonson, the eighteenth-century comedies of Sheridan and Congreve, the fast wit of Wilde, the political comedy of Shaw, the drawing-room theatrics of Coward and Rattigan, the laconic absurdities of Pinter. His work included broad farce, political satire, elements of Surrealism and Dada, and a wholly up to date 1960s anti-establishment, amoral irreverence that expressed itself largely in episodes of fast-moving farce rooted in sexual bewilderment. His anarchic humour found its best expression in matters of sex: revising his play *What the Butler Saw*, he recognized that what he needed to give the audience was 'much more fucking, and they'll be screaming hysterics in next to no time'. He regarded himself as a tough little case, bred in the gutter, and scornful of artistic sensitivity which he regarded as flabby and self-indulgent. To counteract weakness of character, to overcome any residual feelings of inadequacy, Orton relied on the power of the penis in real life, as much as in his written and performed work, to maintain control over situations in which he felt threatened. Sex was not only pleasurable relief, it was an expression of potency, of complete mastery and strength.

As Orton's star soared, so Halliwell's importance in the relationship waned. Halliwell's self-esteem was dangerously low, and still ebbing fast, when Orton, in December 1966, began to keep a detailed diary. By May 1967, when he and Halliwell visited Tangier for the last time, he was richer than he had ever been in his life, and famous as the author of *Entertaining Mr Sloane* and *Loot*. By December 1966 he had written and rewritten *The Erpingham Camp*, *Funeral Games*, and simultaneously with the *Diaries* he began to write *What the Butler Saw*. His visit to Tangier was purely a holiday during which he did no work. With Halliwell, he arrived on 7 May 1967 and drove straight from the airport into town where they had rented an apartment at 2 rue Pizzaro in which, coincidentally, Tennessee Williams had written *Suddenly Last Summer*. The flat, decorated with antique furniture and mirrors and gilded chandeliers, wasn't to Orton's taste – 'awful shit, but comfortable. The kind of taste I abhor, but as I am staying in Tangier for two months I want privacy, comfort and quiet.'

Immediately they made for the beach, establishing themselves at a familiar beach café, The Windmill, run by an Englishman and an Irishman and staffed by obliging Moroccan boys. Orton and Halliwell were precisely the sort of 'European "queens"' so despised by David Herbert. Orton's bawdy, uninhibited account of his adventures with Halliwell in Tangier was not written to protect delicate sensibilities or, indeed, to protect Halliwell's fragile sense of security. It was as uninhibitedly funny as his plays, all the more offensive to Halliwell for its direct, sometimes brutal, always precise adherence to telling detail. Orton's promiscuity depressed, disgusted and enraged Halliwell who was no contender in the sexual contest that vitally engaged Orton's energies and did such damage to Halliwell's illusion that he and Orton still operated inseparably as a team. John Lahr, Orton's biographer and editor of his diaries, quotes the critic and novelist Penelope Gilliatt who, as a friend of Orton's, reckoned that 'the household they had was a fake household and Joe knew this, Joe knew the fakery well enough to kick it about and endanger it as much as possible by staying out late, by promiscuity, by every means he could. To see how far he could drive Halliwell. I think Joe hated himself for accepting domesticity and carrying on with it.'

Orton was having fun in Tangier while Halliwell was forever flouncing about in a permanent pet, deeply depressed by Orton's cockmanship. He inevitably contrasted it with his own sexual competence which was largely limited to masturbation with the boys

he took up with in Tangier. He was romantically attached to Orton
who had mostly lost sexual interest in Halliwell and, having become
the more successful, the more powerful partner in what was left of
their relationship, felt only a residual loyalty to the man he had
regarded as his mentor but whom he had now far outstripped in
terms of material, social and literary distinction. Orton was, to a
large extent, Halliwell's creation and in the summer of 1967 Halliwell was about to lose him.

Desperately, he made an effort at the beginning of their holiday
to cater to Orton's mood, to appear to condone and actively encour-
age his sexual promiscuity, to attempt to control the situation by
acting the pimp. He could at least be Leporello to Don Juan, act
the role of a collaborator, but Orton would have none of it: on the
beach, says Orton, 'We were hailed with "Hallo" from a very
beautiful sixteen-year-old boy whom I knew (but had never had)
from last year. Kenneth wanted him. We talked for about five
minutes and finally I said, "Come to our apartment for tea this
afternoon." He was very eager. We arranged that he should meet
us at The Windmill beach place. As we left the boy, Kenneth said,
"Wasn't I good at arranging the thing?" This astounded me. "I
arranged it," I said. "You would have been standing there talking
about the weather for ever." K. didn't reply.' The next day, Halliwell made a further effort: he had picked up a boy called Larbi
with whom he had sex in the apartment. '"I've arranged for you
to have him tomorrow," Kenneth said in a confidential tone when
the boy was out of the room. "But I've already arranged to have
Mohammed tomorrow," I said. "I really wish you wouldn't play
the procuress so much. I'm quite capable of managing my own
sex!"' At some level of thinking or feeling, Halliwell perhaps hoped
to unite himself with Orton through the medium of shared boys.

Orton's view of life on 3 June, a day of wind and cloud, was that
'provided one spent the time drugged or drunk, the world was a
fine place.' He experienced a moment of purest aesthetic pleasure
when, in the afternoon, one of his boys arrived for tea and sex:

> How incredible it is, I thought later as I watched him take a
> shower, to really see a nude fifteen-year-old. That small waist,
> sudden jutting of the bum; it wasn't just sex, it was an aesthetic
> experience. Sitting in the bath, he looked as if he were on canvas

by a French impressionist – some painter of the stature of Renoir.
There was a faint flush of hair in the small of his back, spreading
out to the top of the buttocks. He stood quite naturally and
unselfconsciously towelling himself, and I thought that nothing
ages one more than the sight of one's juniors, if they're beautiful
in the nude. I glanced into the mirror recognising at once that I
was old enough to be the boy's father.

Orton was not much impressed with the social pretensions of the
expatriate set bowered in their Mountain villas. 'The English
colony have succeeded in turning a fair-sized hill near Tangier into
a replica of a Surrey backwater. Twisty lanes, foxgloves, large pink
rambling roses, tennis courts and gardens watered by sprinklers.
Only here and there does the presence of a palm show that Africa
is waiting.' The view from the Mountain, however, was spectacular:
'The town lay spread beneath us, and the bay and the mountains
in the distance, a soft almost purple light covered the whole scene.'
The purple haze may be attributed less to atmospheric conditions
than to the fact that Orton was high on hashish. The Mountain
was dull – down in the city things were more lively, and Orton
was feeling happy. A parade of naked post-pubertal boys regularly
trooped through the apartment, all perfectly willing to be laid for
a few dirham; he was regularly popping Halliwell's Librium and
Valium pills on top of hashish; and he felt 'as though the whole of
creation was conspiring to make me happy'.

To his diary he confided: 'To be young, good-looking, healthy,
famous, comparatively rich *and* happy is surely going against
nature, and when to the above list one adds that daily I have the
company of beautiful fifteen-year-olds who find (for a small fee)
fucking with me a delightful sensation, no man can want for more.'
On the question of 'going against nature', he responded abruptly
to an acquaintance who remarked, 'I really think, Joe, that you
shouldn't bring nature into your conversation quite so regularly,
you who have done more than anyone I know to outrage her.' 'I've
never outraged nature,' said Orton. 'I've always listened to her
advice and followed it to wherever it went.' Halliwell, suffering
from a plague of boils on his inner thigh, was inclined to urge some
caution. Orton and he 'sat talking of how happy we both felt and
of how it couldn't, surely, last. We'd have to pay for it. Or we'd be

struck down from afar by disaster because we were, perhaps, too happy.' Something had to be sacrificed, asserted Halliwell, some scapegoat had to be offered in propitiation 'in order that we may be spared disaster more intolerable'.

On 4 June, Orton flew back to London for three days to attend the première of his play, *The Ruffian on the Stair*, which was being staged at the Royal Court Theatre in tandem with *The Erpingham Camp* under the omnibus title of *Crimes of Passion*. The reviews on 7 June were lukewarm, and he was mildly depressed when he flew back to Tangier by way of Gibraltar. Back at the apartment, he was enraged to discover that Halliwell had taken Mohammed, one of his boys, to bed. Even 'on a purely wanking basis' this was intolerable. Orton fell into a sulk: perhaps 'because of the nervous excitement of the last few days and the plane journey,' he supposed himself to be 'very depressed. Tired. Behaved rudely to Kenneth who is getting on my nerves.' Sex with the regular repertory company of beach boys relieved some of his superficial anxieties, and from the heights of orgasmic ecstasy he viewed the London newspaper reviews with a longer perspective. The holiday continued until late June, a mixture of incessant sex with various Mohammeds and regular sniper fire between Orton and Halliwell.

But 'even sex with a teenage boy becomes monotonous,' admitted Orton on Sunday, 25 June. 'Ecstasy is as liable to bore as boredom.' He was beginning to feel lethargic, to need some stimulus: the holiday had generally been enjoyable and, on the whole, a success, but 'neither Kenneth nor I will be sorry to leave on Friday. I feel the need to do something fresh. Not work – though undoubtedly I shall finish *What the Butler Saw* – just a change of scene.' The insidious *mollesse* of Tangier had evidently begun to seep into Orton's bones, though he was acute enough to realize the effect and realize that he needed London as a counteragent to ennui. On 27 June, Orton and Halliwell were invited to the home of one of their boys in a suburb of Tangier. Their tour of the half-ruined, half-built house was nothing special, until the boy, Larbi, whipped out a gun and pointed it at Orton who held up his hands. 'I kill you,' Larbi shouted wildly. We all laughed as he pulled the trigger. I had the feeling that no writer with an eye for the ironic could resist having the gun loaded and the playwright of promise falling dead beside the telephone extension. "An Evelyn Waugh touch," Kenneth said, as I told him after the gun had clicked harmlessly.'

Beneath the smiling and apparently eager complaisance of Tanjawi boys there lurked an unpredictable violence. Even expressed in terms that could be taken as joking, it should have alarmed rather than amused Orton who was to experience, later in the day, another scene that was ominous in character and implication. Orton noticed that Halliwell had given Larbi a pink shirt. He had originally bought it for Orton, and when Orton casually let Larbi know that it had been his, Halliwell took offence at what he supposed to be Orton's tactlessness. Nigel, an uncomfortable spectator of the spat, intervened with light conversation and expressed interest in one of the boys. Orton records that 'Kenneth, anxious to sell his share of the boy, said, "Yes, he's very good in bed, and he'll do anything."' Orton, bored, interrupted: 'How do you know? You've only asked him to do so little.'

Orton's taunts of sexual inadequacy or lack of imagination had a startling effect on Halliwell who 'became violently angry after this' and attacked Orton, hitting him about the head and knocking a pen from his hand. Both left the apartment in a rage. When Orton returned, he found Halliwell

lying in his bed in a towel dressing gown, looking tight-lipped. I realised that it was no good talking to him, the 'sore' would come sooner or later. I'd just settled down for the night when the door opened and Kenneth entered. I was selfish, I couldn't bear not to be the centre of attention. I was continually sneering at him for only wishing to be masturbated while I was 'virile' in fucking boys. 'I saw you in Nigel's car,' he said, 'and I've never seen you at a distance before. I thought, what a long-nosed ponce.' The holiday had been too perfect. I was determined to spoil it somehow. 'And when we get back to London,' he said, 'we're finished. This is the end!' I had heard this so often. 'I wonder you didn't add "I'm going back to Mother",' I said wearily. 'That's the kind of line which makes your plays ultimately worthless,' he said. It went on and on until I put out the light. He slammed the door and went to bed.

Halliwell had another fit of sulks the next day, first about getting a new strap for Orton's suitcase. He had looked for one in the Boulevard shops without success. Orton went out and bought a new strap with no difficulty. 'Life is difficult,' he said to Halliwell, 'but not intolerable.' Then Halliwell's rage at their woman servant – which had been simmering for weeks – came to a head. He turfed her clothes out of the apartment, and seemed satisfied by this stroke of minor revenge. 'Joe wanted to ignore her,' he said to Nigel on the beach, 'but she's got to be made to realise.' They fell to discussing some nearby boys. Referring to one in particular, Halliwell remarked, 'Well, all I'd like to do to the creature is whip him.' 'You're simply substituting violence for sex,' said Orton. 'Your psychological slip is showing. A whip is a phallic symbol. You're doing on a symbolic level exactly what I do in reality.'

On 30 June they flew from Tangier to London where, on 9 August, in their tiny shared apartment in Islington, Kenneth Halliwell beat Joe Orton to death in the early hours of the morning before taking his own life with an overdose of sleeping pills. Halliwell had taken a hammer to Orton's head, stoving in his cranium with nine blows. He then swallowed twenty-two Nembutals, washing them down with grapefruit juice. On the desk in their room was found a note from Halliwell: 'If you read his diary all will be explained. K.H. P.S. Especially the last part.' On arrival in London from Tangier, Orton had said to Halliwell: 'The party's over.' Halliwell, looking around the London streets, had said, 'How dead everyone looks.' The homecoming was more than an anti-climax: it was a deadly depression. Morocco, says John Lahr, 'slaked the tension that was always erupting in Orton's life between his emotional needs and the society's social and sexual taboos'. On a visit to Brighton on 27 July, Orton had cruised Brighton Pier, inspecting the 'nearly naked young boys' sunbathing on the beach. 'After passing a fifteen-year-old youth lying face-downward wearing red bathing drawers, I said in a rage, 'England is intolerable. I'd be able to fuck that in an Arab country. I could take him home and stick my cock up him!'

Orton, frankly and without compunction, had used Tangier as a bordel to appease his Dionysiac mood. Whether or not his, and Halliwell's, experiences in Tangier had anything but a marginal effect on the ultimate violence of their lives must be speculation, but perhaps it helped to provoke the tensions that already existed between them. Orton's rage at least derived partly from the frustration that even in Tangier sexual ecstasy could, ultimately, become boring and mundane. The problem was not just the 'tight-assed civilization of England' that denied him sex with under-age boys – he could get those any time in Tangier – but a wider need for personal and creative freedom which was inhibited, for the time being, by Halliwell. Halliwell in turn felt constrained by sexual inadequacy and jealousy of Orton. Tangier had brought them into bruising contact with reality by subverting and exposing them to the fictions they had constructed to mimimize their deeper dissatisfactions.

Orton, in his ruthless philandering in Tangier, was at least clear-eyed and sensibly unsentimental about his beach boys. He did not, at heart, expect them to make him happy for more than a moment of erotic or aesthetic pleasure. They served their purpose like professionals, and earned their small fees. He had no thought, like many more moonstruck tourists, of taking any of them home with him. Rupert Croft-Cooke could, in any case, have warned Orton against any such notion. In *The Caves of Hercules,* he took a gratuitous swipe at the likes of Bowles who, he suggested, 'dressed up young Moors and attempted to introduce them into the drawing rooms of European capitals'. Croft-Cooke disapproved of attempts by well-meaning but, in his view, misguided enthusiasts who attempted to broaden the experience of young Moroccans beyond the confines of their own customs and country.

Not that Croft-Cooke was vitally interested in the welfare of Moroccan boys in any case. On the contrary, he frankly disclaimed any interest in them whatsoever, a failing he did not much regret, claiming to have come to Tangier 'too late in the long quest for "experience" that my life has been'. He spoke English, some French and some Spanish, but never troubled to learn the Maghrebi dialect. In view of the cultural importance he attached to language, this was a substantial impediment to his insight into the Moroccan character. As it was, conversations with young Moroccan lads picked up by Croft-Cooke naturally tended to monotony and banality. He found the boys dull, and hastily concluded that 'the Moroccan has a natural distaste for small talk ... Perhaps he is inarticulate even in his own language.' This view was not uncommon, but those among the Moroccans who achieved literacy and articulacy had a story to tell that piercingly contrasts the lives of the expatriates and tourists of Tangier with the conditions of the native city. They are two faces of the same coin, the one side polished bright, the obverse tarnished and worn. The negotiable value of the coin, from whatever side it is presented, is limited. The shining streets of the new town and the shadowed alleys of the Medina are the Janus faces of the city.

The Moroccan City

The view from the alleys of the Medina, looking up to the modern town hovering in the middle-distance, was a doubtful prospect for Mohammed Choukri. The short-range view of his immediate environment, for that matter, was none too encouraging. The squalor and sudden violence of the dirt-poor life of a street urchin in the last years of the international administration of Tangier is harrowingly told in the autobiography Paul Bowles was helped by Choukri to translate. *For Bread Alone*, published in Britain in 1973, is a chronicle of suffering and destitution that sharply punctures the bubble reputation of Tangier for frivolous luxury, easy money and easier sex that lured so many light-hearted and light-minded visitors to the city. Choukri's narrative is not, more's the pity, an account of a unique experience, though Choukri is unusual in his ability and determination to transcend it.

In 1942, driven out of their homes by drought, starved out of their rural way of life by famine, many Riffians descended on Tangier. There was bread, they knew, in the city. In *Tanger le Paradis* they would be less likely to die of starvation. The Choukri family, like the rest of their neighbours, walked from the mountains to the city: 'All along the road there were dead donkeys and cows and horses. The dogs and crows were pulling them apart. The entrails were soaked in blood and pus, and worms crawled out of them. At night when we were tired we set up our tent. Then we listened to the jackals baying. When someone died along the road, his family buried the body there in the place where he had died.' Tangier was only marginally better: 'I did not see as much bread in Tangier as my mother had promised me I should. There was hunger even in Eden, but at least it was not a hunger that killed.' The quality of garbage was good – bones and ends of dry bread could be salvaged. Nazarene garbage, seven-year-old Choukri learned, was best of all.

Choukri's father looked for work, every afternoon coming home
disappointed and taking out his inarticulate rage and impotent
despair on his captive victims – his wife and children.

Not a movement, not a word, save at his command, just as nothing
can happen unless it is decreed by Allah. He hits my mother.
Several times I have heard him tell her: I'm getting out. You
can take care of those two whelps by yourself.

He pours some snuff onto the back of his hand and sniffs it, all
the while talking to himself. Bitch. Rotten whore. He abuses
everyone with his words, sometimes even Allah.

My little brother cries as he squirms on the bed. He sobs and
calls for bread.

I see my father walking toward the bed, a wild light in his eyes.
No one can run away from the craziness in his eyes or get out of
the way of his octopus hands. He twists the small head furiously.
Blood pours out of the mouth. I run outdoors and hear him
stopping my mother's screams with kicks in the face. I hid and
waited for the end of the battle.

In the morning, the family buried little Abdelqader and wept over
the grave. Soon after, Choukri's father, who bartered tobacco and
bread with Spanish soldiers in exchange for uniforms which he sold
to Tanjawis in the Medina, was denounced as a deserter from the
Spanish army by a Moroccan soldier to whom he had refused to
sell a blanket at too low a price. The authorities had been looking
for him for quite a while, and took their opportunity to commit
him to prison. Choukri's mother was fatalistic.

She goes to the city in search of work. She comes back disappointed, just as my father used to do when we first arrived in
Tangier. She sits biting her nails distractedly. She sobs. Sorcerers
make her talismans to wear around her neck; perhaps my father
will get out of prison and she will find work. She says her prayers
and lights candles at the tombs of the saints. She looks for luck
at the fortune teller's. There is no way out of prison, there is no
work, no luck, save by order of Allah and Mohammed his prophet; this is what she says. I begin to think: Why doesn't Allah
give us our good luck the way he gives it to other people?

To survive, Choukri salvages garbage, cabbage leaves and orange peel picked up in the street, to fill his stomach. Occasionally his mother buys a large quantity of dry bread from the beggars with the little money she has left, and takes it home to boil it up in water, sometimes with a little oil and pepper, to make a very basic soup. To make ends meet, she begins to buy and sell vegetables in the market, leaving Choukri at home.

Choukri's father was released after two years and the family moved to 'a house by an orchard in the quarter of Ain Khabbès'. Choukri's father was perfectly content to send his wife and son out to work to scrape a living for the family. While his mother continued to sell vegetables in the street, Choukri had by this time acquired some streetwise skills. He ran errands for neighbours and worked from six in the morning until after midnight in a nearby café, earning a wage of thirty pesetas a month which was smartly appropriated by his father. In the café Choukri learned, as a boy, to smoke kif by day, eat *majoun* by night, and drink wine. By the age of twelve, he learned that the most important thing that preoccupied the thoughts of the café customers was making money. Feeling used, if not actually abused, by others, Choukri began to consider what he might do for himself. The decision was not difficult. 'I can steal. I can steal from anybody who uses me. I began to think of stealing as a way of regaining that which had been taken from me.'

Choukri's mother gave birth, in the course of her life, to thirteen children, all but four of whom died. The cause of death in most cases was diagnosed as tuberculosis but, comments Choukri, 'they died of misery – total misery.' Like Choukri himself, they had been 'born into a class shunted off to the margins, impoverished, miserable – it's almost impossible to describe'. Tangier, for the first few years, was indecipherable to Choukri. Like most boys of his age and class, he was wholly illiterate.

I didn't know much. At the age of seven, you don't analyse human relations. I thought of nothing but how to find things to eat or things that gave me pleasure as a child. But in reality I didn't have a childhood – my childhood was stolen from me. All I knew of Tangier was the old city, the Petit Socco – the cafés and the places round about it – at that time I couldn't go up to the boulevard [Pasteur]. The Medina was open to everyone in Tangier – first of all the Moroccans, then the Spanish, and then foreigners in general, the French, the Americans, everyone. But the boulevard was different. It was different because the Europeans, the middle-classes if you like, didn't care to have anything to do with Moroccans except middle-class Moroccans, a class of Moroccans who were accepted if they were well dressed and also if they had a socially acceptable job in the governing Tangerois society or if they were children of petty officials.

Down in the Medina, marginalized by poverty and class, the easiest way for Choukri – in stiff competition with other street urchins – to scrape acquaintance with foreigners was to pester them to the point of distraction until they agreed to hire him for a few pesetas as an unofficial guide through the bewildering maze of streets. It was less expensive to hire Choukri than to risk him running off with their wallets or purses – purses, mostly, which were more accessible than wallets, women also being less likely to give chase. Choukri was aware of the city's power either to seduce foreigners or appal them with equal facility, depending on their experience of their visit. 'It was a pretty town – in everyone's imagination, it was a town of myth and magic, the myth being that it was built by Antaeus, and the folk-memory of Moroccans has it that Noah descended on Tangier in a cloud. For a stranger arriving in Tangier, he either adapted to live, or left the city.' Choukri trots out an anecdote of Mark Twain who,

when he visited Tangier in 1867, wrote letters to his friends saying he'd discovered a paradise. The next day, he wrote letters to the same friends saying he thought of nothing but leaving this hell. What happened to him? Who knows – perhaps he was robbed, threatened, drugged. But that's Tangier – you stay or you leave.

*　　*　　*

Tangier was a very liberal town, very open – you were free to do what you liked. There was everything – traffic in drugs, money, every sort of goods, and there were a lot of thieves and criminals who sought refuge in Tangier. It was a sanctuary for them – for the whole world of criminals, thieves and traffickers.

Choukri himself was not above, could not afford to be above, some minor trafficking on his own account:

> a little contraband, yes. I sold, for instance, smuggled cigarettes, I sold a little kif to Americans, but I never was involved in any major league trade, though I knew some big-time smugglers and knew, without participating in it, about some heavy trafficking. You could live your life in Tangier as you liked, with or without money. If you didn't have money, you only had to steal to get it or get involved in a smuggling operation. For me, Tangier was a town where I could live by one means or another: I could do no matter what to live and there were a lot of things to do in Tangier. Such things were not just tolerated – they were innately characteristic of the environment, the prevailing tone of Tangier. The libertine character of the city had been created, and the authorities tolerated this sort of liberty in Tangier to differentiate the city from other cities of Morocco or beyond.

Choukri's view that Tangier was innately corrupt, and that its reputation was condoned by the city authorities is perfectly reasonable. Undoubtedly, some control existed, but it was principally and superficially directed at keeping the peace rather than cleaning up any perceived immorality or enthusiastic free enterprise. 'It wasn't so dangerous to live in Tangier: there were security forces that controlled everyone, and there were always petty larcenies, minor thefts, nothing out of the ordinary.' A boy could make a living one way or another, in ways that might have been considered shockingly criminal beyond Tangier, but which were pretty much taken for granted as a way of life in the Medina that did not, to any alarming extent, percolate upwards to infect the life of the boulevard Pasteur. The tourist took a reasonable risk if he or she left the modern town to cruise the Petit Socco, of course, but such tourists were, very likely, looking for more than the cool formalities of tea at Porte's or a drink at the Parade. Choukri, like any of the other teenage touts of the Soccos, had no qualms about leading the tyro tourists to whatever their beating hearts most desired.

I took the tourists into the little bars, the little *cabarets*, and the brothels. There were three brothels – the Spanish bordel, the French bordel and the Moroccan bordel. The Moroccan bordel was a little too private to have much contact with strangers, with Americans or Europeans. They no longer exist, but in those days a guide knew all the houses. Mme. Simone's was the most famous of the period, best known among Europeans because it recruited its girls internationally from all over the world – Italians, French, Spanish, Jewish girls, girls from all over. The bordels were not only for tourists: they were popular with the people of Tangier – the Moroccans, and then the Spanish and foreigners in general – French and American, everyone. Tangier has changed, though: places and people. Tangier is always on the move. A city haunted by shadows. It's finished as the great cosmopolitan meeting place, the wild nights.

Choukri has very little nostalgia for the city of '*les grandes rencontres cosmopolites, les nuits folles*'. Nor does he much sympathize with Bowles' yearning after the old life of Tangier, the city of yesteryear. 'I was miserable all that time. After Independence, quite the contrary, my life changed for the better.' At the age of twenty, Choukri was seized by the desire to learn to read and write. He bought an Arabic primer and a friend gave him an introduction to the head of a school in Larache where he was accepted as a student. After four years' study, Choukri became a primary school teacher of Arabic. He is now a Professor of Arabic at the Collège Ibn Batuta in Tangier. 'I began by learning to read and write: I was self-taught, if you like.' A chance encounter with a friend who introduced him to a teacher led Choukri to literacy. A chance encounter with a writer led him to Bowles and a career for himself, too, as a writer.

I decided to write at the time I was going every night to a café. I was spending all my money listening to the juke box – Aznavour and *Ma vie* by Alain Barrière. I noticed a man who came in every night and who seemed to be highly regarded by everyone. I asked the waiter what he did for a living. He said, 'he's a writer.' He was well dressed. So I began by getting myself a jacket and a tie. Then I read his four books, and one night I said to myself that I had a head full of stories as good as his. I wrote fifteen pages

which I showed him the next day. He encouraged me to carry
on. I carried on . . .

The writer was Edouard Roditi, who introduced Choukri to Paul
Bowles and suggested that Bowles translate some of Choukri's
work. 'I'd published stories and poems in Lebanese magazines and
Arab papers. I wrote in classical Arabic. Paul was used to translating from Moroccan dialect – he had translated two books already,
Driss Charhadi's A Life Full of Holes and Mohammed Mrabet's Love
With a Few Hairs.' Working together, Bowles and Choukri set to
reduce the classical Arabic text of For Bread Alone first into Moroccan Arabic that Bowles could understand and then, says Bowles in
his introduction to Choukri's autobiography, 'we used Spanish and
French for ascertaining shades of meaning.'

Literacy and authorship in the years following Independence
enabled Choukri to participate in the cultural life of Tangier, a life
that had hitherto been closed to him. Besides Bowles, he met Jean
Genet in 1968 and Tennessee Williams in 1973. These brief encounters resulted in Choukri publishing short memoirs of his meetings with both writers. Choukri's reputation is more familiar to
Lebanese, Iraqi, American, French and British readers than it is to
Moroccans. He has published six books, four of them in Arabic in
Morocco. Two have been banned in his native country, including For
Bread Alone, 'on account of its immorality. They have condemned my
writings as pornography.' Choukri argues that, far from sen-
sationalizing or commercializing sex, his books speak eloquently of
the misery of sexuality. For Bread Alone describes conditions of poverty that, says Bowles, were 'excessive even for Morocco. Eight of
his brothers and sisters died of malnutrition and neglect. Another
brother was killed outright by Choukri's father in an access of hunger
and desperation. Mohamed and one or two others managed to survive, even under these worst possible circumstances.'

Encounters with whores, with homosexuals, with girls whom
Choukri describes as acting with less than Islamic decorum, are
narrated flatly and without sentimentality in the autobiography. As
a portrait of Tangier, it is shocking rather than moving. Choukri's
experiences have hardened and honed his heart as much as his art.
No doubt it shocked the Moroccan authorities which were reluctant
to permit such trenchant criticism, such clear-eyed first-hand

evidence of neglect and corruption, clothed in the dignity and authority of a book, to be widely circulated among the author's own people. There is, in Choukri's work as in the work of any other, no case for censorship, though censorship of national and foreign literature, claimed by officialdom to be in the Moroccan national interest, is still an instrument of government. Even to evade censorship, Choukri does not believe that he could have written about any place other than Tangier.

> I've always lived in Tangier. I was away only for four years in Larache. Even then, during the holidays, I came back to Tangier to earn some money working at the port. I was not in the habit of travelling. I thought that in Tangier one could see everything; everyone came to Tangier. Later, to promote the translations of *For Bread Alone*, I travelled – but I like Tangier. I like it all the more when I go away and compare it with other cities, and I find that my destiny is to live in Tangier, like Paul Bowles. He told me once that he found his destiny in Tangier and that he cannot leave it. I'm married to Tangier, and even when I'm divorced, it's a Catholic divorce – separated but always attached.

For Mohammed Mrabet, Tangier – says Paul Bowles – 'is a magic world, cut off from the real world. He is so convinced that there is nothing beyond Islamic culture that he has no desire for European values. For people like him, the French might just as well have been Yugoslavians. Only the Spanish had any effect on them in Tangier, because of the language but also, according to Mrabet, because during their time in Morocco they brought to light Muslim graves, which the French never did.' The Spanish, perhaps owing something to the tradition of Islam in the culture of southern Spain, were perceived as more respectful of Islamic values than the

French. This was a matter of some importance to Mrabet, who derived from a Riffian family which, like Choukri's, came from the mountains to Tangier during times of rural hardship.

Born in the Spanish-occupied Rif in 1940, and coming to a Spanish-occupied Tangier, Mrabet's early life was, like Choukri's and Layachi's, difficult. In an interview with the French magazine *Actuel*, he declared:

> I have suffered all my life. The whole time. Always. I began running away from home at five years old. Tangier then was still international. If I wanted something, it was impossible. With a father, his two wives and his twenty-four children, it wasn't possible to go to school. For a man who works for twenty-three, twenty-four – no, twenty-eight, twenty-nine people – the money he earns soon goes. At that time, when I saw that, it offended me and I left home . . . I'm still alive and, thanks be to God, I've done many things I never thought to do.

Choukri's father beat up his family; Layachi preferred the cold comfort of an orphanage to his own home; and Mrabet started running away more or less as soon as he could walk. The three principal native novelists of the city, all born under an international administration, all thoroughly disadvantaged by their early circumstances, can reasonably be taken as representative of a large underclass of the city which was at least overlooked, if not positively repressed, by the French and international authorities. An old, residual bitterness, amounting to a smouldering hatred particularly for the French, still haunts the attitudes of many middle-aged and elderly Tanjawis who remember former harassments and humiliations at the hands of the Nazarenes.

Bowles, the confidant to whom, as amanuensis and translator, Choukri, Layachi and Mrabet have all trusted their autobiographies, is inclined to take them all with a pinch of salt. 'I've given up,' he remarked to *Actuel*. 'I no longer expect the truth. For Moroccans, as soon as one tells the truth, when one has revealed all, one falls under the power of the person to whom one has opened oneself up. That's why they will never volunteer their full names. I don't attribute that to the Islamic code. Illiterates, as much as others, are still very superstitious. They have to protect themselves against the fortunes of life, remain anonymous so that the person one is talking to doesn't know more than you think he does, certainly not what you keep in your heart or your head.' If this reserve makes life difficult to the point of incomprehensibility, if nobody can fathom what is a lie and what is the truth, Bowles likens Moroccan caution to a piece of twine. 'One never lies completely. One must mix the true and the false, thread by thread, as one would weave a cord, and when no one can disentangle it, one feels safe with others. Of course, one ends up contradicting oneself. But even when one is unmasked, there is nothing shameful about it. Yesterday was yesterday. Today, things have changed. *Inch Allah*.'

Nevertheless, bearing in mind the innate Moroccan preference for an economy with the truth that could give lessons to politicians and diplomats, the testimony provided by Tangier novelists about the conditions endured by the native underclass is remarkably consistent. They also speak of opportunities that, for a bright and obliging boy, must have been difficult to resist. The boys on the beach who hardly hesitated to succumb to the blandishments of Orton and Halliwell, and indeed would have been outraged not to have been propositioned, were not too sophisticated. The sixteen-year-old Mohamed Choukri, picked up in the street by an elderly man who took him to his car and gave him his first blow job, was astonished:

> They suck it for five minutes and they give you fifty pesetas. Do they all suck, the ones who are like that old man? Are all the *maricones* as nice as he was? Do all the ones who suck have cars, and do they all give fifty pesetas? A new profession, to add to begging and stealing. I must pick one of the three until a further choice appears. One of the three or all of them, depending on circumstances. And why not? . . . What I had done was no different from what any whore does in the brothel. My upright sex was worth fifty pesetas, looked at in that light.

There was some element of self-disgust, but no moral crisis over the transaction, and no sense that a homoerotic encounter had compromised Choukri's sexual interest in women. It had been undignified, largely incomprehensible to Choukri who had been obliged to fantasize about women to keep himself tumescent, and the next day he fearfully ran away from the advances of a drunken

Moroccan who had more serious business in mind than the old man in the car. For Choukri at least, it was unlikely to be his profession of choice.

Fifty pesetas for being fellated was good going in 1951, but better-looking kids could hold out for substantially more. Mohammed Mrabet, in his late teens and early twenties, looked enough like a young Marlon Brando to devastate the café society of Tangier. His tough, muscular beauty, spectacular even by the high standard of his peers, young Arabs of the Petit Socco, was complemented by a slick line of chat. By the age of sixteen he had made himself financially independent by wangling a job as a caddy at the Boubana golf course, and had arranged with a friend to share the rent of 150 pesetas a month for a two-roomed house just outside the city. Hanging out one night at the Café Central in the Petit Socco, Mrabet fell into conversation with two Americans he calls, in his autobiography *Look and Move On*, Reeves and Maria. They had been in the city only two days, living in an apartment which they invited Mrabet to visit. After dinner, during which Mrabet demolished a whole chicken, several mounds of bread and jam, salad, fruit and an entire bottle of mayonnaise, he nonchalantly took off his shirt, complaining about the heat. Reeves and Maria very much admired his well-developed chest, commenting particularly on his nipples which reminded Maria of a girl's. 'In the first place,' said the sixteen-year-old Mrabet casually, 'I haven't made love very often yet, and in the second place I come from a very healthy race.'

The second point was not lost on Reeves and Maria; the first point they evidently could do something about. First Mrabet buggered Reeves, and then moved into Maria's bedroom for the rest of the night. The next few days were eventful: Mrabet fell ill, attributing his acute nausea to the rich and unfamiliar food he had eaten at dinner. Returning home, he fell into a fight with his co-tenant who stabbed him in the belly, resulting in his hospitalization while the wound healed. Later, when he had recovered, he went with a friend, Stito, to the Bar la Mar Chica where, he remarks, 'all the Europeans stared at us.' Carmella was there, dancing and pounding her feet, singing to the guitar accompaniment of Manolo, her husband. They sat down at an empty table, grandly ordered a vodka and a Fundador brandy, and inevitably were picked up by

an Englishman who gave his name as Albert, and Albert's companion, a large black who was apparently in charge of a flock of four
good-looking young Spanish boys.

Albert and his black friend invited Mrabet and Stito to 'a little
party' at Albert's house. Consulting with his friend, Mrabet
decided that he was not too drunk, and Stito declared, 'I can fight
three at once.' Confidently they consented to check out the party,
privately agreeing to tear it apart if it didn't look right. The party,
involving the four Spanish boys, the black, several more Englishmen and an impressively large and strong black from the south of
Morocco, quickly degenerated into a sadomasochistic homosexual
orgy. Mrabet decided he was offended. Interrupting the southern
Moroccan in full coitus with a vocal young Spaniard, Mrabet spoke
words of burning reproof. The southern Moroccan declared that
he was happy in his work, and perfectly prepared to carry on
humping the Spanish boys, one after the other, as a sort of floor
show for general entertainment. 'Happy', said Mrabet, 'with any
American or Jew or Englishman, or any filthy Frenchman, yes?
They come here and you show them your backside and everything
else you've got. And they take pictures of you doing your work,
and sell them later in Europe. And you like that.'

The Moroccan, rolling off the boy he'd been busy with, said, 'if
you've got a better job to offer me, I'll take it.' Mrabet suggested
he could make a living carrying sacks of wheat on his back at the
port, a notion which did not appeal to the Moroccan who offered,
instead, to take Mrabet on next after he'd finished with the boy in
hand. Albert, meanwhile, not understanding a word of Mrabet's
Arabic, stood uneasily to one side, nervously fingering the whip
he'd been using to beat the Spanish boys. Mrabet's temper, always
on a short fuse, expressed itself violently. He ground his vodka
glass against the Moroccan's chest, drawing blood, and slashed the
jagged edges of the glass against the man's face. Then he did a
thorough job of beating him up while the other guests looked on
aghast. The fight sprawled out into the garden, where Albert –
incautiously attempting to tackle Mrabet – was pushed back into
a row of flower pots, one of which Mrabet crashed down on his
head. The rest of the party, appalled, ran for their cars, reluctantly
taking Mrabet back with them to the city and dropping him off
with his friend on the boulevard, whence they proceeded to the

Café Central for a restorative beer and some ham sandwiches.

Maria happened to pass by, and urged Mrabet – by this time somewhat the worse for wear – to go with her to her apartment. As a coda to an eventful night, their meeting resulted in an argument about the direction of Mrabet's life: Mrabet declaring that he'd stop racketing around when he was twenty-five, old enough to take on adult responsibilities; Maria evangelically expressing her own, and Reeves', wish to save Mrabet from his vicious life. Mrabet, asserting his independence, at first refused the offer: he'd never gone hungry, he had family to help him if necessary, he was living the life he'd chosen for himself, and – in any case – there was no offer of help without strings. Maria's suggestion that she and Reeves would treat Mrabet as though he were their own son struck Mrabet as ludicrous. He laughed, and had the decency to point out the facts of life, as they appeared to a sixteen-year-old Tangier boy who had seen life in all its aspects, who understood himself perfectly well and knew, like all Moroccans, that life was a deal that required skill and hard, ruthless negotiation. There were things about Tangier that Maria should understand; most kids would not take the trouble to describe the reality of the situation so frankly:

> Don't tell me you think of me as your son. That's not what you mean. You mean you both like to have me with you in bed, that's all. And I like to play games in bed. But it's not very important to me. I like to drink and smoke kif, but I don't think much about love. Love ruins you faster than anything else. Half the Europeans who live here in Tangier like to live with young Moroccans. When the old English ladies go back to London they leave their boy-friends behind, and you see the boys wandering around the streets looking like ghosts. They have money in their pockets, but their health is gone. And it doesn't come back . . . The old women take everything out of them.

In the event, Mrabet came to a compromise with Maria and Reeves who, in a private agreement between themselves, colluded to share Mrabet's sexual favours. Mrabet's advantage was principally financial – by the end of the relationship he had wheedled enough out of his patrons to buy a house for half a million francs, in addition to other benefits – and he accompanied Maria and

Reeves first on a trip to Marrakesh, then to New York. Mrabet had thought through the deal for himself, and it seemed advantageous. Sex was amusing, love was out of the question, and whatever problem Maria and Reeves might have with their marriage was up to Maria and Reeves to deal with. Nothing to do with him, Mrabet thought to himself:

> I was young, but soon I was going to see the world. After that I would understand everything much better than I did now. I could not read or write and I had no trade. I had nothing. In a few years I would be twenty. I wanted to see that, and I wanted to see the twenty years that would come after that. The cities grew, and the world grew, the way a person does. The day would soon come when the only people who would be able to get work would be those who could read and write. It seemed to me that if I wanted to have anything when that time came, I would have to use my head now. Otherwise I could end up very badly. I began to imagine myself living in poverty and poor health, and it made me feel worse.

Even though Mrabet's autobiography was published in 1976, twenty years after this process of thought, there seems no reason to doubt that he made these sensible calculations at the time, however more lucidly and economically expressed in retrospect. Chances were, for all his strength of character and the limits he set on his personal morality, that he might succumb to a vicious life – a miserable drunk, peddling his arse on the boulevard or in the Socco, penniless and without hope. There were worse people than Maria and Reeves. The true scandal would be to reach the point at which he had no choice but to serve the pleasure of types like Albert, like the abused and demoralized Spanish kids, being whipped and sodomized like a performer in some perverted circus show for the entertainment of corrupt Nazarenes. The prospect was not unlikely if he did not look out for himself. If he was to be a gigolo at all, best to get it over with, in some style and to some advantage. Consorting with Reeves and Maria didn't touch his heart or his head: it was a game Mrabet knew how to play, a deal he could live with.

The novel experience of feeling like a foreigner in New York somewhat discomposed Mrabet who, when he flew back alone to Tangier, felt immediately reassured by the familiarity of his own house, his own possessions, his own family, and his own city. There was nobody to bother him any more – no one to fuss about where he was going, where he had been, whether he liked or disliked the food, or worry about him getting drunk in bars. He had stoutly maintained his independence with Maria and Reeves, but it was a relief not to have to worry about either of them. Mrabet now had a house, enough clothes to fill five suitcases, a satisfying wad of American dollars in his pocket, and an attitude that almost immediately got him into trouble. He beat up a young Italian who was trying to hustle a Moroccan girl. The boy's father happened to be a police inspector in Tangier, and Mrabet was forced into hiding for about three weeks until the Italians returned to Europe.

Occasionally, Mrabet regretted leaving America: Tangier, after the initial euphoria of being back home had evaporated, seemed the same dead-and-alive town it had always been. He now had a bit of property, a little money in hand, but still no prospects. He didn't blame anybody else: his problem was his own. 'I began to understand that my life was never going to change by itself, and that if I wanted something different I would have to find it. Even getting drunk was no help.' He gave up drink, continued to smoke a little kif, and went to the beach. He still, like most Moroccans, had a lurking respect for luck that would transform his life. On the beach at Merkala, two things happened; he met a girl he calls Zohra el Allali who lived on the Marshan and worked in a place that manufactured women's lingerie. Mrabet resisted the impulse to make love seriously to her, and began to court the girl whose family, however, had other ideas for their daughter: she was affianced to a suitor from Casablanca, after a suitable bride price had been agreed between the families, and for a while she disappeared from Tangier.

Mrabet's second significant encounter on the beach at Merkala was with Paul and Jane Bowles in the spring of 1964. His own account fills in some detail. They were all sitting on the terrace of a café that overlooked the beach, Mrabet puffing away on his *sebsi*, so raptly that Jane called across to him to comment on his unusual intake of kif. They struck up a conversation in the course of which Mrabet reminded Jane that they had met before, twice, at parties in Tangier, and remarked to Bowles that he had seen him now and again in the street and out at the fishing rocks, sometimes with Yacoubi and sometimes with 'El Hombre Invisible'. Mrabet walked with his new friends from the beach to the town, up through the suburb of Dradeb, and was invited in to see their apartment. Over tea with lemon, and a pipe of kif which Bowles, after looking first at his wife, shared with Mrabet, they settled to exchange information. Mrabet, it appeared, was presently unemployed. Bowles said he wrote books. 'How's he going to write with a head full of kif?' Jane demanded to know, as Mrabet packed a filter cigarette with kif and gave it to Bowles who in return passed the *sebsi* back to Mrabet. 'I hate kif,' said Jane. 'I hate the way it makes me feel, and I hate to see my husband smoking it.'

Mrabet returned to Bowles' apartment a few days later. Bowles picked up a book to show him – a book with a photograph of Larbi Layachi, an acquaintance of Mrabet's, who worked as a watchman at the Merkala beach café, on the cover. Since Mrabet knew for a fact that Layachi was as illiterate as himself, Bowles explained the process of dictation into a tape recorder and played an extract from Layachi's tapes. Mrabet was not much impressed. 'Larbi was talking about taking care of sheep. It was not very interesting, and it was probably all lies anyway.' He was more deeply struck by the fact that Layachi had made some money – enough to get married – from these recordings. Giving the matter some thought, in his usual careful way, Mrabet came back to see Bowles after two or three days, and asked whether he himself might make some tapes. Bowles agreed, and so began a series of regular sessions, several times a week, during which Mrabet recounted some 'tales I had heard in the cafés, some were dreams, some were inventions I made as I was recording, and some were about things that had actually happened to me. Paul did not translate all of them, and a lot of the ones he did translate he put away so that no one ever saw them. But he said he liked them, and wanted me to do more.'

Mrabet was a natural storyteller: in the days before radio and cinemas, he might have made a living as a storyteller in the Socco. Bowles was at least intrigued: this was first-hand material, the pure uncut stuff as Burroughs might say. Mrabet decided that this was the piece of luck for which he'd been waiting so long. He set about making himself indispensable. He began a long campaign to persuade Bowles to buy a car, a Volkswagen station wagon. Since Bowles complained that he no longer cared to drive in Tangier, Mrabet volunteered his services as chauffeur. The process of hustling Bowles to the point of finally buying the car took Mrabet several months of unrelenting pressure until Bowles finally gave in. Jane, who had been ill since the spring of 1957, watched the developing relationship without intervening. She claimed to like Mrabet, but Mrabet nevertheless was aware of some resentment. She would occasionally sit listening as Mrabet dictated, 'but I could see that she did not like to have Paul spend so much time working on my tapes and typing them out in English. She wanted him to write his own books.' As he gained in confidence and experience, Mrabet began a long story that took three months to complete. By the end, Bowles judged that he had achieved a novel, which he set about translating. The result was *Love With a Few Hairs* which Bowles placed with his London publisher, Peter Owen, who accepted it and paid a small advance. The novel was published in London in 1967.

Love With a Few Hairs, which was later adapted as a television play in Britain, draws its principal theme from the relationship between Mr David, a European who runs a small hotel in Tangier, and a somewhat sulky seventeen-year-old Moroccan named Mohammed. They are lovers, content with one another, until Mohammed becomes infatuated with a young Moroccan girl named Minah who, unaccountably, does not return his feelings. Mohammed resorts to a local witch who makes him a love charm, a *tseuheur*, which is efficacious. Minah marries Mohammed, and they live blissfully together for a little while until Minah's suspicious mother breaks the spell and Minah falls out of love with Mohammed who finally leaves her and returns to the doting Mr David. If any one story deftly sums up the collusion between Moroccan and European Tangier, it is *Love With a Few Hairs*. The character of the sentimental, glad-handed homosexual expatriate Mr David, romantically in love with his young Muslim, is typical of the European settler being willingly taken for a ride by a young Moroccan who skilfully plays him for personal advantage. Mohammed's Muslim family, while disapproving of the boy's relationship with a Nazarene, is nevertheless respectful enough of the material benefits it brings them to condone, tacitly, such a friendship.

Which said, Mohammed is nevertheless a sympathetic character, genuinely fond of his long-suffering, patient and loving patron who truly attempts to respect Mohammed's autonomy, to reinforce his self-respect and firm up the boy's innate capacity for loving and being loved. Until *Love With a Few Hairs*, most such stories had been written from a European point of view by foreign novelists. Mrabet's narrative was the first to be recorded in the true Tangier vernacular, from the standpoint of a dyed-in-the-wool native of the city whose emphases, subtly different from those of European or American writers, gave freshness and directness to a well-worn theme. Mrabet's collaboration with Bowles was regarded with some suspicion by purists accustomed to texts composed in classical Arabic, and there was some dismay that Mrabet, by colluding with a Nazarene, would give the game away – tell too much, too clearly. Mrabet, a natural artist with an innate, economical feeling for literary form, has continued to tell his stories and Bowles has continued to translate them – more than a dozen published novels and short story collections, mostly set in Tangier and giving glimpses, no more than that, of a culture inevitably affected but not profoundly altered by Western ideals of 'progress'. Mrabet's Tangier is a secret city to which non-Moroccans still have very limited access: the secret city is mental as much as material.

Trips abroad with Bowles, in the days when Bowles still travelled, only served to reinforce Mrabet's Islamic chauvinism and partiality for Tangier as his mother city. In America, particularly, he met with racial prejudice not only from native white Americans but, curiously to Mrabet, from Hispanics desperately attempting to subordinate their native origins and traditions – in order to render themselves more acceptable as Americans – to what they considered to be the American social norms. Mrabet, strolling around Los Angeles in flowing white Moroccan clothes, perhaps deliberately attracted attention to which he responded with ill humour. His lack of freedom, outside Tangier, struck him as being a form of imprisonment: only in Tangier, in Morocco, could Mrabet feel wholly at liberty, taking the life of the city for granted. 'Without the aid of custom and usage,' remarked the French aphorist le Duc de La Rochefoucauld, 'I would not know how to cross the room.' In Tangier, Mrabet had the advantage of foreigners, fast on his feet while they hesitated and stumbled, stubbing their toes on the furniture of the city.

Before accompanying Bowles to California in September 1967, Mrabet had succeeded in marrying the girl he had met and fallen in love with on Merkala Beach. There had been some dramatic difficulties before, as much as after, the marriage. Mrabet provides some lurid details in his autobiography and an ostensible piece of fiction entitled *Marriage With Papers*. To précis the course of events: Mrabet, discovering the girl was about to be married, doped the prospective bridegroom the night before the wedding and deflowered the bride-to-be. Afterwards, he cut his hand with a pocket-knife, sprinkled some drops of blood on the bed, and between them the girl and Mrabet undressed the unconscious man and deposited him in the bed. When, three days after the marriage, the newly-wed husband discovered the deception and tackled Mrabet, Mrabet beat him up. The next day bride and groom were divorced and soon afterwards Mrabet married the girl who was pregnant with his child. The marriage got off to a troublesome start: feeling misused and kept short of new clothes, Zohra – as Mrabet calls her in his autobiography and his short novel – set about poisoning Mrabet's food. His mother-in-law began leaving pieces of paper inscribed with cryptic writing under and behind the furniture. Money was running short. Zohra frivolously spent what little they had. The baby died. There was only one solution to the mass of intransigent problems besetting Mrabet – the house, and his wife, had to be purified, exorcised of the *djinn* that had been allowed to take up residence in the house.

Advised by a local *fqih*, Mrabet learned that Zohra had inadvertently thrown water on a brazier burning in the patio. 'At that moment,' said the *fqih* authoritatively, 'there was a small *djinn* in the fire, and the water surprised him, and he threw the ashes that were in the brazier against her leg.' The remedy was to cut the throat of a black rooster in the patio, and at the same time burn two papers provided by the *fqih* who would also provide bottled water to rub on Zorah's legs. The house could be purified by white-washing and a little milk sprinkled in each corner. Bowles, remarking on this saga to journalists from *Actuel*, smiled as he told them that Mrabet's story was just about par for the course as an account of a Moroccan marriage. The journalists themselves looked

forward to the day when Mrabet's stories were adapted for television as a sort of Arab version of *Dallas*. By any account, and
Mrabet gives several, his marriage can perhaps be broadly interpreted in terms of his wife's hysteria, his own resentment at any
restriction on his personal freedom of action and thought, and the
undoubted distress of both of them at the familiar Tangier tragedy
of infant mortality which robbed them of all but four of their sixteen
(the figure given by Mrabet to *Actuel*) children. Nowadays, still
married to his wife and proud of his two surviving daughters and
two sons, the eldest of whom was born in 1962, Mrabet presents
himself as a successful farmer and landowner, an author of international repute, a citizen of Tangier.

More than any other Tangier author, Mrabet is censored in his
own country. Choukri, himself once or twice a victim of censorship,
has little sympathy. What Mrabet has to tell, he says, is already
well known to Moroccans. Old hat. What's the use of publishing
something from which one can learn nothing? Mrabet's stories he
considers are fit only for Westerners who, unlike Moroccans, have
everything to learn from them. In this view, Choukri reflects a fairly
common opinion which, however unjustly, holds Mrabet to be a
neo-colonialist collaborator with Bowles. The perceived sensa-
tionalism of Mrabet's stories is not well-regarded: he lets down,
perhaps, the high moral tone that Islam is concerned to adopt as
characteristic of all good Muslims. He does not take care to put an
appropriate gloss on scandals, major and minor, that reflect badly
on Tangier, incients that will cause the ungodly to laugh. Mrabet,
say some, lacks proper respect.

Envoi

It is difficult, in all conscience, to be respectful of a city that has known so many crises of identity, been beset by so many disparate influences, that its character, constantly reassembled to pander to every contingency, to satisfy every demand, can only be described as conditional. A larger city would have had less trouble integrating its conflicts and establishing a firm personality. Tangier was perhaps too small, too weak, too vulnerable. It has been likened to a ripe fig impaled on the point of an Arab scimitar. As a figment, a fiction of the fevered imagination, the sticky fruit has attracted a swarm of adventurers and mythographers dreaming all, like Pistol, of Africa and golden joys.

Since Tangier has always been perceived as a territory at least on the edge of, if not beyond, the mundane world, it has been the victim of the myths, the fantasies, the dreams and ardent desires imposed upon it by its colonists. The result, of course, has been an irreparable fragmentation of the city's character. Required to satisfy – satiate – the infantile, polymorphous perversities of so many, Tangier has remained formless, eternally embryonic, never fully able to mature. Like a brain perplexed by too many conflicting demands, or like a computer fed with a mass of conflicting data, it has often been rendered inert, passive at best, at worst seized by intermittent fevers in its struggles to distinguish priorities. For the likes of Mrabet, Choukri and many other natives of the city, the world comes inevitably to Tangier: what need is there to travel elsewhere? For most, like the Tangier-born but now Paris-based novelist Tahar ben Jelloun, the end result of travel is simply a comparison of the mother city with cities elsewhere, rarely to the detriment of Tangier. For native exiles, forced out of the city by the necessity to work in Spain or France, the summer vacation is an annual opportunity to travel back, at great personal expense and difficulty, to suckle at the pap they never cease to desire.

For outsiders like Bowles, who sixty years ago perceived the city as the 'magic place', a 'dream city', the superstitious, serendipitous character of Tangier still exerts a subterranean, secret fascination. If Bowles was inevitably fated to live most of his adult life and find the inspiration for his most accomplished work in Tangier, he thereby gave a cue to others. William Burroughs, on his own admission, was inspired to settle in Tangier by the image of the city as presented in a Bowles novel – *Let It Come Down*. In the end, his personal experience of Tangier contributed to his development of the literary 'cut-up' technique, an apparently random but unconsciously related juxtaposition of literary and pictorial images. Bowles, having made attempts to perceive the city as an insider, so far as that was possible, seemed to suggest that magic was the principal underlying cohesive force of Tangier, superstition the binding element. Burroughs, the resolute outsider, open to magic and responsive to metaphysical forces, contrarily ended his association with Tangier by perceiving magic as the chaotic factor, the rogue element, a metamorphic explosive that he used to shatter modern literature.

The magic of Tangier, for David Herbert and Barbara Hutton, was more in the nature of a fantasy to be woven into an ideal life. Tangier was a social vacuum, a society of expatriates without a natural ruler. The crown of society was there for the taking by any suitably energetic and appropriately qualified aspirant. Herbert had old class and a little money; Hutton had new money and a little class. Together, and separately, they formed a morganatic alliance of convenience that dominated the upper reaches of the city's society. There, they were able to transcend the tedious social difficulties of the post-War world in which Tangier preserved itself, a city crystallized by international consent as a neutral zone unaffected, for the time being, by external forces. Its circumstances were, perhaps, anachronistic, but there were more urgent matters for foreign governments to deal with elsewhere. Tangier could meantime be safely left to its own devices. It was, almost literally, a place out of time, a galantine of ingredients layered one on top of another, set in the aspic of an international administration that coolly continued to observe diplomatic fictions and tolerate the polite manners, the class and racial distinctions and the social axioms of pre-War society that elsewhere in Europe were breaking up in post-War conditions of material shortages and social uncertainty. Compared to the capitals of Europe – Berlin, Paris, London – Tangier was Shangri-La.

Tangier afforded personal freedoms that elsewhere were increasingly under threat: Rupert Croft-Cooke, like many other homosexuals, came to Tangier with every expectation that there he would be free of pettifogging and Puritanical restrictions on his sexuality, the mundane morality of the British bourgeoisie. To find the British class system alive and flourishing in Tangier, in the villas and gardens of the suburban Sultans of the Mountain, was a little dispiriting. Orton and Halliwell, too, in search of a gay ghetto in Tangier, were disappointed to find themselves cheek by jowl with lumpen heterosexuals who dragged down the tone of *their* city, *their* very own and golden city given over, as ideally it should be, to hedonistic homosexual indulgence, pederastic pleasures, sodomitic sensuality. Orton's particular desire that Tangier should be off-limits to tourists who took exception to homosexual activity, who imported with them their tight-lipped civilization and turned frigid when Orton entertained his friends with 'buggers' talk' at café tables, who did not understand that 'This is *our* country, *our* town, *our* civilization,' was somewhat at odds with Tangier's ancient tradition of being all things to all men. Tangier had never been narrow in its capacity to please. It had always been a complaisant city, turning a blind eye not only to the excesses of Europeans but equally, when a new wave of Gulf Arabs, enriched by oil, turned up in search of pleasures forbidden in their own countries. In Tangier, such potentates could enjoy all the pleasures that money had been able to buy the English, particularly in a city which still retained an Islamic ethos somewhat softened by its reputation for concupiscence.

Money, of course, is as powerful an aphrodisiac as any, and for centuries Tangier had excited the lust of financiers and entrepreneurs who regarded it as a sugar plum, an unfettered free-market economy unrestricted by inconvenient rules of morality. The opportunities to satisfy greed were, in theory, limitless – piracy, gun running, drug smuggling, currency and property speculation, loan sharking, and whatever else appeared profitable just as circumstances and opportunity arose. Money talked as the lingua franca of the cosmopolitan colonists of the city. Money, imbued with its own magic, was a major cohesive and motivating force in Tangier. Money moved ships and cargoes in and out of the port; money lit the discreetly muffled lanterns of the smugglers' boats plying the Strait; money once moved the constant slow, plodding enfilades of camel trains, laden with goods, merchants rocking high in their saddles, on the long trek from the sands of the south to the Socco Grande; money reduced autocratic, spendthrift Sultans to bankrupt exile in the city; money bought an American five and dime store heiress a palace and a jewelled fantasy life in the Casbah; money procured discretion, privacy and prestige in Tangier for those whose indiscretions, public image and reputations in the world at large were questionable. Money secured a multiple entry visa to a land of Cockaigne.

The orrery that was Tangier, this little universe of spinning worlds held interdependently together in orbit, occasionally made perfect sense. A notable instance of a personality who lives a life of complete integration with the city is Mohammed Tazzi, the son of the last Mendoub of Tangier and grandson of the first.

Tazzi, as a schoolboy in Tangier, had been ferried from the Mendoubia to the Lycée Regnault in a chauffeured car with a bodyguard. The grounds of the palace were guarded, and the women of the Mendoub's harem did not have the right to go out. Apart from the formal reception rooms of the Mendoubia, the palace was largely a closed world. Tazzi's grandfather particularly maintained a state that would not have disgraced 'a pasha of former times'. As the Sultan's representative in the International Zone, he was regarded in effect as 'the king of Tangier'. But he did not scorn modern innovations – to the young Tazzi's delight, there were regular film shows at the Mendoubia, particularly 35mm Walt Disney movies. Tazzi, when permitted to go out to the movies, went to 'the Mauretanian Cinema where they had American films. The whole of Tangier knew James Cagney. And there were Egyptian films. Few French movies came to Tangier. We went out to visit friends, of course, and this was the time of the Tango and the Cha-Cha-Cha.' A life of privilege insulated the young Tazzi from all but the most superficial contact with the less salubrious aspects of the city.

He was sent, in due course, to continue his studies in Paris where

– like other Moroccan students at the Maison du Maroc – he discovered the work of Paul Bowles: 'a book called *Une Vie, Pleine de Trous* [*A Life Full of Holes*] by Charhadi'. This was Bowles' translation from the Maghrebi dialect of an oral autobiography told to him by a young working-class Tangier youth, Driss ben Hamed Charhadi, better known as a writer under his *nom de plume* Larbi Layachi. 'This book affected us profoundly because it told of someone from the working class who for once had achieved the dignity of a book and this was absolutely absorbing – simultaneously, the old books were stripped of their sanctity, debunked, for us, and one could hear Charhadi's experience.' Meeting later with Bowles himself, in Tangier, Tazzi was impressed that 'men like him understand the soul of Tangier much more than others.'

Tazzi is impatient with the idea that, as a stranger, Bowles – and other foreigners – cannot truly comprehend Moroccan thought. Bowles himself, rather mordantly, has said that 'thought is not a word one can use in connection with Morocco,' implying not only that rational thought and Morocco are a contradiction in terms but also expressing his own bewilderment when confronted with its paradoxes and seeming illogicalities. Bowles is fond of quoting a Moroccan adage which takes some thinking through before its pertinence as typical of the Moroccan, and Tangier, instinct for evasion becomes apparent:

> You tell me you are going to Fez.
> But if you say you're going to Fez,
> That means you're not going.
> But I happen to know you are going to Fez.
> So why do you lie to me, your friend?

Nevertheless, Tazzi believes that an outsider who loves Tangier may see and understand more of the game than others less sympathetic and, indeed, will know the soul of the city better, even, than certain of its natives.

What Bowles has done is wonderful work. To talk of strangers being unable to understand is completely stupid. To talk of strangers in Tangier is to talk of a town that for two thousand years has been a mixture of all kinds of people, even different

sorts of Moroccans, people from the Rif, Soussis, Fassis, as well
as all sorts of Europeans. At the Lycée there were two thousand
students, all kinds of nationalities among my own friends who
included Moroccans, Jews, French, a Russian, an Algerian, a
Spaniard, a Dane.

The internationalism of Tangier inevitably affected the native
population. While some resented the occupation and, on that score
alone, supported the aims of nationalism, others, who had broader
reasons for supporting their country's independence and the liberation of Tangier from an international adminstration, benefited from
the wider experience that contact with other peoples provided. Like
many young people in Tangier, born during or after the Second
World War, Mohammed Tazzi was constantly aware of Europe,
conscious that only a narrow strait of water separated the city, in
terms of distance at least, from the coast of Spain. Just as his eyes
were opened, at first by a book, to working-class conditions in
Tangier, so his eyes were often focused on Spain: he could almost
see the sand on its beaches. Spain, and by extension Europe,
became part of his life. 'I don't know what that says to strangers.
Now I live partly in Paris, partly in Tangier. Tangier, for me, is
my birthplace, the place where I've lived a life that has opened me
up to the outside world and which has made me understand that
it is, above all, these intense interchanges which constitute life.'
For Tazzi, a profound sense of the past characterizes Tangier as
an open city, ever receptive to external influences. In Tangier, he
senses a continuity that, inevitably, has left its mark on the people –

these people, like the Riffians and the Djiblis, have always been
open to the rest of Morocco, to all the regions of Europe, down
the centuries, for two thousand years. When we speak of the
Roumis [a local name for foreigners], that means we speak of the
Romans. It's still as if we continue what happened before. The
Europeans are a continuation of the Romans whose Empire
extended at one time to cover Morocco. And even when we speak
of the Nazarenes, that is to say the Christians, it is a continuation
of that epoch when, if one spoke of Jesus, it was of the man of
Nazareth. Here, the whole history is always living.

Tazzi's insistence on the continuing influences of history, ancient as much as modern, on the long connections that Tangier and North Africa have maintained with Europe and the rest of the Arab world, perhaps somewhat moderates the idea that Morocco, and Tangier, is ineffably mysterious and impenetrable to visitors, a closed society to strangers. For him at least, the stranger in Tangier is no problem. Quite what the stranger may think, what problem the visitor may have, is another matter. From the inside, looking out, the view from Tangier is as clear as the beaches of Spain on a good day.

Moroccan for thirty years, Tangier retains a faint air of nostalgic glamour. The seductive courtesan of yesteryear is now a game old girl, her lipstick uncertainly applied, her cheeks a trifle too heavily powdered, her cocktail hat slightly askew on her hair bright with henna, her eyes black with kohl. She puts on a good show, tottering along the boulevard with a glance for every likely prospect. She puts her old feet up at the Café de Paris and orders a glass of mint tea: bound to be someone along soon to whom she can open the picture albums she always totes around with her. The clouds, at mid-morning on a winter's day, roll around her head like grey fog. The wind whistles through the palms in the garden of the French Consulate, ruffling their leaves like the crest feathers of cockatoos. From the Medina comes the scent of mint and motor oil, the whiff of fish, blood and lemons from the foetid alleys of the covered market. And here, blue-kneed in shorts, swathed in three layers of T-shirts, complaining of the cold, comes a miserable band of tourists whose travel agent had recklessly spoken of the comfortable climate of North Africa in January. She herself, like any sensible Moroccan, is bundled up in a thick burnous that smells strongly, after the recent shower, of wet wool.

Like the Ancient Mariner, she fixes her victims with a piercing eye and pulls out her albums. Here are Wenceslaus Holler engravings of old Tangier in the time of Charles II of England, reproductions of paintings by Delacroix – who needed 'twenty arms and forty-eight hours in the day' to give the least idea of everything he saw. In the darkling light of dusk in 1832, walking in the streets, he was struck by the noble aspect of men in the street repairing their worn-out shoes, consular figures with an air of disdain, worthy of a Cato or a Brutus, as though they were masters of the world. These were men possessed of nothing but the robes they stood up in, slept in, and would be buried in, yet who wore the satisfied air of a Cicero before his senatorial chair. Look here, especially – M. Delacroix's famous *Noce Juive*, tableau of a Jewish wedding in Tangier. And do not neglect the celebrated canvases – of course these are merely reproductions – *cartes postales* – of Monsieur Henri Regnault – the French Lycée here bears his illustrious name – *Le Cavalier marocain partant pour la fantasia* and *La Sentinelle marocaine* dating from the 1870s. A shower of paintings falls from her album – works by Benjamin Constant, Fortuny, Monticelli, Sir John Lavery – portraits particularly, one fine full length study of Caid Maclean – a Kokoschka from 1965, sketches by Beaton, a costume design by St Laurent, etchings by McBey, and a sheaf of Matisse, bright with the light of Tangier – *Le Rifain debout*, *Fatmah la mulâtresse*, *Zorah sur la terrasse*, *la Porte de la Casbah*, *le Café arabe*, *Arums*, *Iris et mimosas* . . .

Shifting slightly in their chairs, exchanging glances with one another, as if she is another tout trying to sell them something, the tourists appear slightly perplexed. Perplexity turns to dismay as she pulls out another dusty volume – photographs, posed in high style, of Walter Harris, Lawrence Harris, Cunninghame Graham, Caid Maclean, looking disturbingly like music-hall comedians in moustaches and baggy Moroccan pantaloons. And here, serious and resplendent in official dress, are the ambassadors, the ministers, the legates, the consuls, the administrators in their cocked hats, waving plumes, gold braid, morning suits, top hats, gloves, ceremonial swords, stiff collars and medals of honour. Here, too, Kaiser Wilhelm, the Sultan el Brouze, on his horse, poking the low clouds with the spike of his helmet. Most distinguished, you will agree. From her pockets, the old lady produces long documents with a flourish worthy of a stage magician – at the feet of the tourists unroll pacts and protocols, acts and instruments, concords and communiqués. Sheafs of official Minutes of the proceedings of the Committee of Control flutter in the wind and fly around like confetti. Urgently, in several languages – French, Spanish, English, German, Arabic – she expounds the most important points and orders another round of mint tea to refresh her bemused audience. There is more.

Everybody loves holiday snaps – here are some choice examples: Beaton photographs of old Feridah Green, Truman Capote,

Barbara Hutton, David Herbert. And, too amusing – snapshots of Paul Bowles by Allen Ginsberg, and snapshots of Ginsberg by Bowles. Pictures of Burroughs, Ansen, Corso, Orlovsky, Leary, the cream of literature and society, you understand. Do look – pictures of Orton eating *majoun*, pictures of Orton posing with beach boys, pictures of Orton in full Moroccan dress, and this one of Kenneth Halliwell astride a rather phallic cannon. Others of Orton with Mohammed and – Mohammed. And with Larbi. And who's this? Ah, Mohammed – they are well known to everyone in Tangier. Look – there are more. Many, many more. Monsieur Genet with Monsieur Choukri, Mr Tennessee Williams with – ah – Monsieur Choukri. Would you care to see? You have all the time in the world – all the time in Tangier, which is to say all the time that God made. Nobody has to rush. Everything will wait. We will have another mint tea, and I will show you all my souvenirs . . .

But the clouds have passed, the sun is shining through the windows of the Café de Paris and the tourists have, one by one, sneaked out through the doors leading to the boulevard. She mumbles to herself, the lady of Tangier, as she scoops up her pictures, her souvenirs, her mementoes, like so many fallen leaves – Miss Hutton – Mme la Princesse – ah! such jewels! – Mme la Comtesse de la Faille – so many animals – pretty little Mrs Bowles – her trees are gone from the Socco – Truman Capote – afraid of scorpions – Monsieur Beaton, *le beau* – Fleming – Beckett – Morand – Nazarenes – Romans – Arabs – Phoenicians – Hercules – Antaeus, son of Poseidon . . . ghosts crowd around her, swirling her pictures and papers, rustling her robes like a sudden gust of the *cherqi*. These shades, these phantoms of the white city and sepulchre will do, one day, perhaps, to make a book, a memorial, for those tourists and travellers who come to Tangier, who sigh that Morocco is not Africa, that Tangier is not Morocco, that Tangier is not what it was, regretting the passing of the Parade, Porte's, Dean's Bar, the final stamp of Carmella's foot in the saw-dust of the Bar la Mar Chica . . .

SELECT
BIBLIOGRAPHY

The edition cited is the issue used as a source, and does not necessarily indicate the date or place of first publication. All quotation in the text is derived from the relevant source cited below.

ASSAYAG, Isaac J.: *Tanger . . . un siècle d'histoire* (Tangier, 1981)

BARBOUR, Nevill: *Morocco* (Thames & Hudson, London, 1965)

BARTHES, Roland: *Incidents* (Editions du Seuil, Paris, 1987)

BORROW, George: *The Bible in Spain* (John Murray, London, 1842 edn. reprinted)

BOWLES, Jane: *Out in the World: Selected Letters 1935–1970* (Millicent Dillon [ed.], Black Sparrow Press, Santa Barbara, Ca. 1985)

BOWLES, Paul: *Without Stopping* (Ecco Press, New York, 1972)

BOWLES, Paul: *Let it Come Down* (Arena, London, 1985)

BOWLES, Paul: *Their Heads Are Green* (Peter Owen, London, 1985)

BOWLES, Paul: *A Hundred Camels in the Courtyard* (City Lights Books, San Francisco, 1986)

BRADSHAW, Jon: *Dreams That Money Can Buy* (Morrow, New York, 1985)

BRYANT, Arthur: *Samuel Pepys, Saviour of the Navy* (Collins, London, 1938)

BURROUGHS, William: *Letters to Allen Ginsberg* (Full Court Press, New York, 1982)

BURROUGHS, William: *The Naked Lunch* (Paladin, London, 1986)

BURROUGHS, William: *Junky* (Penguin, London, 1977)

CAPOTE, Truman: *A Capote Reader* (Hamish Hamilton, London, 1987)

CAPOTE, Truman: *Answered Prayers* (Plume, New York, 1988)

CANETTI, Elias: *The Voices of Marrakesh* (Marion Boyars, London, 1978)

CHOUKRI, Mohamed: *For Bread Alone* (Peter Owen, London, 1973)

CROFT-COOKE, Rupert: *Smiling Damned Villain* (Secker & Warburg, London, 1959)

CROFT-COOKE, Rupert: *The Caves of Hercules* (W. H. Allen, London, 1974)

DAVIDSON, Michael: *The World, the Flesh and Myself* (Quartet, London, 1977)

DILLON, Millicent: *A Little Original Sin: The Life and Work of Jane Bowles* (Virago Press, London, 1988)

GINSBERG, Allen, and CASSADY, Carolyn: *As Ever: The Collected Correspondence of Allen Ginsberg and Neal Cassady* (Creative Arts Book Company, Berkeley, Ca., 1977

GINSBERG, Allen: *Collected Poems 1947–1980* (Viking, London, 1985)

GRAHAM, R. B. Cunninghame: *Rodeo* (A.F. Tschiffely [ed.], Heinemann, London, 1936)

GROVE, Lady Agnes: *Seventy-one Days Camping in Morocco* (Longmans, Green & Co., 1902)

HARRIS, Lawrence: *With Moulay Hafid at Fez* (Smith, Elder & Co., London, 1909)

HARRIS, Oliver C. G.: *The Last Words of William Burroughs* (Unpublished thesis)

HARRIS, Walter: *Morocco That Was* (Eland Books, London, 1983)

HERBERT, David: *Second Son* (Peter Owen, London, 1972)

HERBERT, David: *Engaging Eccentrics* (Peter Owen, London, 1990)

HEYMANN, C. David: *Poor Little Rich Girl: The Life and Legend of Barbara Hutton* (Lyle Stuart, Inc., Secaucus, N.J., 1984)

HUGHES, Richard: *In the Lap of Atlas: Stories of Morocco* (Chatto & Windus, London, 1979)

LANDAU, Rom: *Invitation to Morocco* (Faber & Faber, London, 1950)

LANDAU, Rom: *Portrait of Tangier* (Robert Hale, London, 1952)

LANDAU, Rom: *Morocco Independent* (Allen & Unwin, London, 1961)

LAYACHI, Larbi: *Yesterday and Today* (Black Sparrow Press, Santa Barbara, Ca., 1985)

LAYACHI, Larbi: *The Jealous Lover* (Tombouctou Books, Bolinas, Ca., 1986)

LUKE, John: *Tangier at High Tide: The Journal of John Luke 1670–1673* (Helen Andrews Kaufman [ed.], Librairie E. Droz, Geneva; Librairie Minard, Paris, 1958)

MAUGHAM, Robin: *The Wrong People* (Heinemann, London, 1970)

MAXWELL, Gavin: *Lords of the Atlas* (Century, London, 1983)

MCBEY, Marguerite: *Memoir of James McBey* (manuscript, Aberdeen City Arts Dept.)

MORGAN, Ted: *Rowing Towards Eden* (Houghton, Mifflin, New York, 1981)

MORGAN, Ted: *Literary Outlaw: The Life and Times of William S. Burroughs* (Henry Holt & Co., New York, 1988)

MRABET, Mohammed: *The Beach Café & The Voice* (Black Sparrow Press, Santa Barbara, Ca., 1980)

MRABET, Mohammed: *The Chest* (Tombouctou Books, Bolinas, Ca., 1983)

MRABET, Mohammed: *Love With a Few Hairs* (Arena, London, 1986)

MRABET, Mohammed: *Marriage With Papers* (Tombouctou Books, Bolinas, Ca., 1988)

MRABET, Mohammed: *M'Hashish* (Peter Owen, London, 1988)

MRABET, Mohammed: *Look and Move On* (Peter Owen, London, 1989)

NICOSIA, Gerald: *Memory Babe: A Critical Biography of Jack Kerouac* (Penguin, London, 1986)

ORTON, Joe: *The Orton Diaries* (John Lahr [ed.], Methuen, London, 1986)

PORCH, Douglas: *The Conquest of Morocco* (Papermac, London, 1987)

RIGO DE'RIGHI, Eleanor: *Holiday in Morocco* (G. T. Foulis, London, 1935)

RONDEAU, Daniel: *Tanger* (Quai Voltaire, Paris, 1987)

ROREM, Ned: *The Later Diaries of Ned Rorem 1961–1972* (North Point Press, San Francisco, 1983)

SAWYER-LAUÇANNO, Christopher: *An Invisible Spectator* (Bloomsbury, London, 1989)

STUART, Graham H.: *The International City of Tangier* (Stanford University Press, Stanford, Ca., 1955)

VAIDON, Lawdom [David Woolman]: *Tangier: A Different Way* (Scarecrow Press, Metuchen, N.J., 1977)

VICKERS, Hugo: *Cecil Beaton* (Weidenfeld & Nicholson, London, 1985)

WHARTON, Edith: *In Morocco* (Century, London, 1984)

WINTER, G. & KOCHMANN, W.: *The Rogue's Guide to Tangier* (Tangier, 1986)

Writers at Work. 3rd Series. (George Plimpton [ed.], Penguin, London, 1977)

Periodicals

ACTUEL

THE DAILY MAIL

THE DAILY TELEGRAPH

LONDON MAGAZINE

THE NATION

THE OBSERVER

PARIS REVIEW

SUNDAY DISPATCH

THE SUNDAY TELEGRAPH

THE TIMES

INDEX